The Failure of I
Mental Health Care

ALSO BY JOHN WEAVER

Evangelicals and the Arts in Fiction: Portrayals of Tension in Non-Evangelical Works Since 1895 (McFarland, 2013)

The Failure of Evangelical Mental Health Care

*Treatments That Harm Women,
LGBT Persons and the Mentally Ill*

JOHN WEAVER

McFarland & Company, Inc., Publishers
Jefferson, North Carolina

Portions of Chapters 4 and 5 originally appeared in "Unpardonable Sins: The Mentally Ill and Evangelicalism in America," *Journal of Religion and Popular Culture* 23, no. 1 (2011): 65–81. Reprinted with permission from the University of Toronto Press (www.utpjournals.com), © University of Toronto.

LIBRARY OF CONGRESS CATALOGUING-IN-PUBLICATION DATA

Weaver, John, 1980–
    The failure of evangelical mental health care : treatments that harm women, LGBT persons and the mentally ill / John Weaver.
        p.   cm.
    Includes bibliographical references and index.

    ISBN 978-0-7864-9594-8 (softcover : acid free paper) ∞
    ISBN 978-1-4766-1742-8 (ebook)

    1. Mental illness—Religious aspects—Christianity.
    2. Mental illness—Alternative treatment.
    3. Psychotherapy—Religious aspects—Christianity.
    4. Evangelicalism. I. Title.
BT732.4.W43 2014
261.8'322—dc23   2014039635

BRITISH LIBRARY CATALOGUING DATA ARE AVAILABLE

Front cover image of hands with cross © 2015 Ossi Lehtonen/ Hemera/Thinkstock

Printed in the United States of America

McFarland & Company, Inc., Publishers
  Box 611, Jefferson, North Carolina 28640
  www.mcfarlandpub.com

To the Mercy Survivors Network,
for their support, and
to Ruth Johnston—may peace be with you
and your family always.

Table of Contents

Acknowledgments

My work on this book has a list of people to thank that is almost too large to mention. First, I should mention professional colleagues who helped in this process. Gayle Whittier, my dissertation director and close friend, provided me with many critical insights into the history of medicine from her work in the "medical humanities," without which this work would have been much poorer. A similar role was played by my friend Mikhail Gofman, whose training in computer science led him to point out problems in biblical counseling's theory of the mind that I myself might have missed. As always, I could count on my friend Josh Lewis for welcome relief from the stress of writing a book. Ramona Mazzeo has over the years provided me with valuable insights into how professional psychiatrists think. And I also continued to benefit from the advice given me by Nick Nace for my previous work, *Evangelicals and the Arts in Fiction* (2013).

Independent researchers Rachel Tabachnick and Bruce Wilson were vitally important in the writing of this book. Rachel in particular provided extremely valuable feedback, and also patiently worked with me as I explored the ins and outs of the New Apostolic Reformation (NAR), a movement that would have been indecipherable to me without her input and the scholarship of Rene Holvast. Bruce provided extremely valuable input on the NAR. In addition, Rachel's and Bruce's extensively documented posts at the blog "Talk to Action" provided me with valuable Web links to NAR and other Charismatic and Pentecostal primary source material.

My friends and family obviously played important parts in this work, and in many ways it was written for them. My father provided me with valuable evangelical books free of charge through his work as a used-book dealer. In addition, his nearly encyclopedic knowledge of evangelical denominational allegiances, which is greater than my own, allowed me to navigate a few areas of interpretation where I felt unsure. My brother and sister, David and Rachel, provided moral support. My grandparents allowed me to live at their home over the summer of 2013 while I was finishing up this work; my aunt and uncle, Mildred and Chester Jezierski, allowed me free access to their computer, even at ungodly hours of the night. My cousin Danny Phillips served as a valuable sounding board for early ideas, and I doubt it would have been possible without the encouragement of either cousin Danny or my aunt Martha and uncle Dan. I'd also like to thank Brittany Morgan for her encouragement.

A more specialized area of thanks belongs to the numerous "discernment bloggers" and "survivor" advocates with whom I dialogued over the last two years. Cindy Kunsman's insights into Quiverfull ideology and her promotion of my work on her blog were particularly welcome. Several Independent Fundamentalist Baptist (IFB) survivors proved willing to help me out with valuable information on the IFB, unfortunately not all of which made it to print. Especially welcome to me was the Wartburg Watch Web site of Dee Parsons and Wanda (Deb) Martin. Their site provided links to primary source articles on virtually every piece of information on modern Calvinism I ever wanted to hear about, and their research and commentary skills would put almost any mainstream academic to shame. This book would have been a much poorer work without these two women's obsessive devotion to pursuing the truth. Similarly, the Sovereign Grace Ministries (SGM) Survivors Web site provided me with links to some badly needed material as well (the SGM survivors work on YouTube was also of some use to me).

Some of this work was based on a previous book I had sought to do on Mercy Ministries. Critical to that work was the input of Lisa Kerr and many of the women and men involved with Mercy Survivors. Sean, Chelsea, Kate, Russ and Sarah were especially helpful in this regard. (I owe a special debt of gratitude to Sean for getting me more actively involved in advocating for mentally ill evangelicals.) While that work was never completed, much of the research undertaken for it found its way into Chapter 4.

Finally I would like to thank some of my local evangelical friends and students for providing me with a chance to dialogue with them over the last two years. Phil Chapman is a young man of great courtesy and insight who showed me Calvinism at its very best, challenged me to look at my own faulty presuppositions and even introduced me to the surprise evangelical rap hit "Precious Puritans." Rachel Mott and Michael Martinez exposed me to elements of Pentecostal and Charismatic theology that I had not been previously aware of (Mike's insights into emerging evangelical views of demonology proved especially interesting to me).

I offer my thanks to Katrina Bates for pointing out to me how important Bill Johnson is to modern Charismatic belief and for our frequent friendly disagreements over Charismatic theology and healing practices. I doubt this book was what she would have wanted me to write, but I felt her, and all my other evangelical students, looking over my shoulder as I wrote it. I hope I portrayed their culture—my former culture—as honestly as I could. What true insights are in this book are largely the result of the people I have listed here. The faults, unfortunately, are my own.

Preface

Vincent: You want to know how I did it? This is how I did it, Anton: I never saved anything for the swim back—*Gattaca.*

Ecclesiastes 7:13: Consider what God has done: Who can straighten what he has made crooked?—*NIV*

I write this book on the edge of a knife, and I fear the knife is my own. This work is the byproduct of more than five years of activism on behalf of mentally ill evangelicals. I initiated that activism, not out of altruism but because the evangelical church's stance towards the mentally ill had profoundly affected two generations of my family. I have seen family members attempt suicide, engage in self-harm, deal with severe body image issues, and refuse to take vital psychiatric medication, all based on teachings evangelicalism promoted.

That mental illness is becoming an increasing issue of concern for evangelicals is hard to deny. A recent study found that nearly half of evangelicals, fundamentalists, and born again Christians believe that prayer and Bible study alone can allow mentally ill people with issues like schizophrenia, bipolar, and depression to overcome their mental health issues. This compares with the beliefs of only 35 percent of the United States population as a whole. The issue of the evangelical church's relationship to the mentally ill has become increasingly prominent in the wake of the suicide of megachurch pastor Rick Warren's son Matthew Warren. What is lacking in almost all discussion of this issue is a substantive "naming of names" of which figures in evangelicalism have promoted this kind of stigmatization of those diagnosed with mental illness. Indeed, so pervasive is the misinformation coming out of the evangelical community that the very *Huffington Post* article I refer to in this section uses Timothy Clinton, president of the American Association of Christian Counselors, as a benchmark of respectable Christian counseling. As we will see in Chapter 8, that is a seriously questionable use of sourcing ("Prayer Alone Heals").

1

Writing about evangelicalism's alternate therapeutic system leaves the potential author in a vexing position. Ideally, such an author should be a psychologist or a psychiatrist. However, this presents an immediate problem for several reasons. First, the evangelical audience for such a book would often immediately discount the work because of skepticism (sometimes warranted) of psychiatric and psychological professionals' view of religion, as well as psychiatry and psychology in general. Secondly, psychologists and psychiatrists within evangelicalism have traditionally been reluctant to point out the real failures of the evangelical community as related to the mentally ill (not to mention women and the Lesbian, Gay, Bisexual and Transgender [LGBT] community), mainly because powerful members of the evangelical community have either expressed skepticism about mental illness or aligned themselves with anti-psychiatric organizations. Thirdly, to truly understand the history of evangelicalism's relationship towards psychotherapy, one must understand multiple, often very dissimilar, theological systems that fall under the banner of evangelicalism. For instance, the biblical counseling model is pretty much the only model in use among many Reformed evangelicals, and it also tends to predominate among most, though not all, fundamentalists. Biblical counselors almost always oppose the deliverance model of mental health care (a.k.a. exorcising the mentally ill person of demons) as "unbiblical," though their own model is not necessarily an improvement. The deliverance model, in contrast to the biblical counseling model, has mainly a Charismatic following, but it also attracts some fundamentalists and even mainline Protestants. It has become the most widespread Charismatic treatment model for mental—and indeed, physical—illness. Thus, a psychological or psychiatric background is not necessarily the best vantage point from which to view the history of mental health treatment within the evangelical community.

In any case, my own field of study is not psychology or psychiatry, but evangelical studies broadly defined (my PhD and master's degrees being in English, and my BA in English and history). Though this might seem at first to be a major hurdle in examining this topic, in reality it is not. The movements that are dealt with here are almost all explicitly anti-psychiatric in orientation[1] and, with the exception of some of the biblical counselors aligned with the Christian Counseling and Educational Foundation (CCEF), often anti-intellectual in orientation as well. There is almost no discussion of scientific matters within biblical counseling materials (and none at all within deliverance and exorcism manuals) that is not easily accessible to even the average layman, let alone someone with a college education. In addition, I have the benefit of access to the advice of my friend and former colleague Mikhail Gofman, a computer science professor at California State University, Fullerton, whose knowledge of the basic contours of neurological debate within the biblical counseling community (the only area where any scientific input might be useful) is extensive. Indeed, a number of the arguments that this book makes concerning mental health diagnoses have their origins in my interaction with Mikhail.

The current work is the first secular book-length study of its kind. Indeed, the secular community seems to be largely unaware of evangelicals' views of mental illness, and the awareness of how these views affect LGBT and female evangelicals has often been piecemeal at best. This is quite unfortunate, as the mistreatment of mentally ill evangelicals has extremely wide-ranging implications, from the exorcism murders of autistic children ("Autistic Boy Dies") to the butchery of "witch children" in Africa (through the encouragement of deliverance) (Houreld) to the sexual abuse of women at the hands of biblical counseling believers in fundamentalist churches. In short, the effects of biblical counseling, deliverance ministries, and other forms of alternative mental health treatment among evangelicals have such far-ranging, even global, implications, that they both deserve and demand closer scholarly analysis. This book is meant to be an introduction to this topic, but the reader should be forewarned this history is so multifaceted that not every important deliverance ministry, major player in biblical counseling, or other evangelical anti-psychiatric advocate is covered here. Reparative therapy, a form of supposed psychiatric treatment for LGBT individuals, for instance, does not get as extensive a treatment as it deserves and I wish I had several more chapters to devote to how this phenomenon relates to and reacts to deliverance ministries and biblical counseling.

I do not wish to leave the impression, however, that there are no works of interest in relationship to this field, just that there are none directly on point. For those interested in deliverance ministries, the best works to peruse are James Collins's *Exorcism and Deliverance Ministry in the 20th Century: An Analysis of the Practice and Theology of Exorcism in Modern Western Christianity* (2009) and Michael Cuneo's *American Exorcism: Expelling Demons in a Land of Plenty* (2001). Theophostic Prayer Ministry (TPM), which is briefly treated in this book, has no significant academic works on point, though two scholarly articles by David N. Entwistle were of particular use to me in critiquing that form of prayer ministry and counseling. In addition, readers should look at Jan Fletcher's self-published *Lying Spirits: A Christian Journalist's Report on Theophostic Ministry* (2005), which to date is probably the best piece of journalism on theophostic ministry currently available. Those interested in a different view of biblical counseling than that presented in this current work should consult David Powlison's *The Biblical Counseling Movement: History and Context* (2010), the definitive pro-biblical counseling history of that movement, written by one of the movement's foremost proponents. Though Powlison's work is obviously (and, to his credit, admittedly) biased, it is still the main work outside of this one that deals with the history of the biblical counseling movement in depth. Susan E. Myers-Shirk's *Helping the Good Shepherd* (2010) also provides an overview of the pastoral counseling movement, though the attention it pays to biblical counseling, or to conservative counseling in general, is relatively brief. Finally, three other works are of general interest. Steve and Robyn Bloem's *Broken Minds: Hope for Healing When You Feel Like Losing* (2005) challenges the dominance of psychophobic rhetoric within the evangelical community. It is not a scholarly study, but it is important in that it critiques the dominant psychophobic views within evangelicalism. Matthew Stanford's *Grace for the Afflicted* (2008) and Dwight L. Carlson's *Why Do Christians Shoot Their Wounded* (1994) are books by evangelical psychiatrists for the evangelical community that try to dispel some of the myths evangelicals have about mental health treatment. Both works are clearly well intentioned, but neither provides a historical context for seeing how such negative viewpoints of the mentally ill developed in the first place, and thus are of little use for secular scholars or laypersons in understanding how evangelicals view mental illness. For those interested in the history of reparative therapy, there is a copious amount of excellent material available. Since space is brief, I would merely point the reader to Tanya Erzen's *Straight to Jesus: Sexual and Christian Conversion in the Ex-Gay Movement* (2006), a groundbreaking study of the ex-gay movement. I can only hope that my study can serve a similar role, in more primitive form, for those evangelicals dealing with mental health concerns.

Introduction

Overview and Definitional Issues

The preface and introduction provide a brief synopsis of the mental health beliefs of evangelical Christians, and also deal with definitional issues concerning the terms "mental illness" and "evangelicalism." As we will see throughout this work, neither of these terms is entirely unproblematic. Broadly speaking, the book argues that there are two major problematic non-psychotherapy-based mental health practices within evangelicalism (one explicitly based on anti-psychiatry), in addition to a number of faulty pop psychology and even clinical psychology practices. The first of these two practices is the deliverance and inner healing movement, which practices exorcism as a form of mental health treatment. This practice is widespread throughout Charismatic Christianity and has some followers within mainstream evangelicalism and fundamentalism. The second practice, alternatively described as biblical counseling or nouthetics, was an explicitly anti-psychiatric form of pastoral care and counseling founded by Reformed thinker Jay Adams. Adams's counseling theory is founded on a combination of Szaszian critiques of the mental health system and Mowrerian notions of achieving successful therapeutic results through inducing guilt rather than questioning it. Adams's theory of counseling would treat almost all people diagnosed with mental illness (a term Adams saw as a misnomer) as having personality flaws and moral short-comings that were engendered by sin rather than by biological and environmental deficiencies as in the medical model of mental illness. Adams's practice would become the dominant one through much of Reformed and fundamentalist circles.[1]

Chapter 1, traces the origins of the modern deliverance movement within Charismatic, Pentecostal and evangelical circles, which, though hearkening back to the teachings of Christ himself, finds its modern expressions primarily deriving, from the twin related influences of William Branham and the Charismatic renewal. Chapter 1 highlights how many of these ideas would engender phobia of the mentally ill, particularly the variations on deliverance theology promoted by the immensely powerful theocratic group known as the New Apostolic Reformation (NAR). Significantly, and somewhat in contradiction to previous researchers into deliverance, I argue that understanding the practice of strategic level spiritual warfare (SLSW), as envisioned by the NAR, is crucial to understanding how deliverance practice became so prominent among evangelicals (particularly Charismatics). Two of the major deliverance models covered in subsequent chapters, the sozo model and the RTF model, have their bases within NAR thinking. Also critical to Chapter 1's discussion will be understanding how Pentecostals and Charismatics in particular create demonic taxonomies, and how these taxonomies problematically differentiate—or fail to differentiate—between mental illnesses and demonic oppression or demonization.

Chapter 2 explores how modern deliverance practice has evolved over the last forty years taking advantage of Freudian ideas while maintaining its essentially nonprofessional healing practice. In line with scholarship from evangelicals like David N. Entwistle and Linda Hunter, I point out the blurring of the lines between faith healing and psychological practice that occurs in many of the modern purveyors of deliverance and inner healing, particularly Ed Smith's Theophostic counseling model and the immensely influential sozo model now being promoted by Bill Johnson's wildly popular Bethel Church. The particularly troubling effect of deliverance and inner healing on women, as well as on individuals falsely accused of abuse and specific subgroups of the mentally ill who are targeted with these therapies, are specifically noted.

Chapter 3 explores a particularly egregious deliverance provider, Mercy Ministries, whose widespread abuses led the ministry's Australian branch to be closed down. Here the influence of Alcorn's life history and view of deliverance on Mercy Ministries' treatment of its anorexic, bulimic, mentally ill, and sexually traumatized clientele is examined. Alcorn's close links to extremist elements within the NAR, particularly Bill Hamon, is closely investigated.

Chapter 4 begins with a short description of my own experience with biblical counseling to give insight into biblical counseling methods and then gives a biographical sketch of Jay Adams. The chapter then explores the specifics of Adams's counseling ideology. Adams's anti-psychiatric beliefs became the basis for a specifically anti-psychiatric form of evangelical pastoral counseling—biblical counseling, also known as nouthetics—which, ironically, rather consistently used behaviorist ideas inherited from O.H. Mowrer and William Glasser for the purpose of pathologizing populations deemed culturally deviant by the biblical counseling movement, namely the mentally ill, LGBT individuals, and trauma victims.

Chapter 5 explores the second and third generations of biblical counseling, showing how the movement tried to impose its counseling program on the entire American military in a farcically abortive plan; how a suicide by a biblical counseling recipient led to one of the most unusual lawsuits in American history; and how the modern generation of biblical counselors are deeply embedded in one of the biggest sexual abuse scandals in evangelical history. The chapter also traces the evolution of biblical counseling doctrine in its second and third generation as it slowly reacted to changing cultural forces and expectations on the part of the movement's adherents.

Chapter 6 looks at the patriarchal counseling movement, which is primarily, though not exclusively, committed to a biblical counseling model. Of particular concern is how major biblical counseling proponents Elyse Fitzpatrick and Martha Peace interacted with the Quiverfull movement. Similarly, this chapter highlights the potentially problematic consequences of the "Calvinizing" reforms to counseling within the Southern Baptist Convention (SBC). The chapter concludes with a brief exploration of crisis pregnancy counseling (CPC) theory.

Chapter 7 deals with reparative therapy and gay conversion therapy. Though relying extensively on secondary resources, this chapter also tries to distinguish between various forms of conversion therapy, pointing out that deliverance and biblical counseling models differ radically from reparative practice, and are even more dangerous than the pseudoscience promoted by mainstream professional psychologists within the reparative therapy movement.

Chapter 8 explores professional evangelical psychology, as well as its pop psychology variations. While appreciative of some of the more nuanced views expressed by some of these psychologists and their allies, I argue that, ultimately, mainstream Christian psychology has failed to protect its mentally ill clients (let alone female and LGBT clients) and at times has endorsed practices that *secular lay people,* let alone psychiatrists, would clearly see as nonscientific. Though no single chapter on professional evangelical psychology could be comprehensive, this chapter highlights many of the most famous and prominent theorists within the world of professional evangelical psychology. It also looks at the major ideological divisions within that world.

Last is the conclusion to the book. It recommends that mentally ill, female and LGBT evangelicals put aside whatever ideological differences they may have and work to the mutual benefit of all three communities. Crucially, the conclusion argues that the continuing pathologization of LGBT individuals by mentally ill evangelicals represents an act of cultural suicide, as it is fundamentally predicated on the exact same ideological ideas that allow the evangelical movement to denigrate the mentally ill as a subclass of sinners. In the conclusion I strive to make clear what is implicit in the rest of this text: That the mentally ill are, in evangelicalism, the other "queer" community. The book includes two appendices, one on the need for a new Christology for the mentally ill, the other on Mercy Ministries' view of eating disorders.

There are three areas of definitional clarification, however, to which I must turn before we begin the study proper. The first is the whole vexed usage of the term "mental illness" itself.

The Diagnostic and Statistical Manual of Mental Disorders (DSM) *and the Definition of Mental Illness*

When most people think of mental illness or mental disorder, they think of the terms as easy-to-define concrete elements of the physical body, typically linked to brain dysfunction. An overview of the history of the *DSM*, though not necessarily discounting this picture, points to a need for more complex reasoning when dealing with the subject of mental illness.

The modern *Diagnostic and Statistical Manual of Mental Disorders* plays a crucial role in how mental health conditions are approached by a variety of powerful institutions within our country. Because the *DSM* "standardizes symptom criteria ... and codifies psychiatric disorders," its diagnoses play a crucial role in determining disability claims and insurance coverage. Similarly, the *DSM* is often important in resolving custody disputes and legal cases grounded in defenses predicated on mental illness. The *DSM*'s influence also extends considerably beyond diagnosis. It plays a crucial role, for instance, in getting approval for new drugs, as well as in the regulation of medications that have already received approval (Cosgrove and Wheeler 644–645). The U.S. Food and Drug Administration (FDA) requires that there be a determination of an "identifiable psychiatric condition" before it grants any approval for new psychotropic medications, which has established what some critics have charged is a disturbing alliance between "authors of diagnostic and treatment guidelines, drug regulators, and drug manufacturers." Such criticisms have continued into the recent controversy over the creation of the *DSM*-5 task force and its eventual adoption (Cosgrove and Wheeler 645).

Much of the controversy surrounding the *DSM* and the classification of mental illnesses in general is rooted in the creation of the *DSM*-III and the events immediately preceding it. The first official manual of the American Psychiatric Association (APA), the *DSM*-I, was predicated on the views of the so-called dynamic psychiatrists, particularly Adolf Meyer, America's most influential psychiatrist during the first half of the twentieth century. The *DSM*-I saw symptoms as reflecting "underlying dynamic conditions or as reactions to difficult life problems" (Mayes and Horowitz 249). This led to a radically different approach to psychiatric conditions than exists today. Karl Menninger, a leading psychiatrist during this period, contended that differentiating individual mental disorders into discrete categories based on a unique set of symptoms—the traditional method of scientific medicine—was a mistake. Menninger instead viewed all mental disorders as being rooted in a basic inability of suffering persons to adapt to their environments. He contended that psychiatrists should concentrate on this failure of adaptation rather than focusing on symptomology (Mayes and Horowitz 250). From the turn of the 20th century to roughly 1970, the focus of dynamic psychiatry shifted from the treatment of neuroses to more generalized problems of behavior, character, and personal issues. Psychiatry gradually became "transformed from a discipline that was concerned with insanity to one concerned with normality" (Mayes and Horowitz 250).

At a single stroke, the *DSM*-III changed all this. A diagnostically based system, the *DSM*-III completely altered how mental illness was conceptualized. It used a diagnostic model imported from medicine in which diagnosis was seen as the basis on which one was to conduct medical practice and clinical research (250). Psychiatry moved diagnosis from the margins of its treatment system to a place where it became the center of the specialty. As Mayes and Horowitz point out, the *DSM*-III "emphasized categories of illness rather than blurry boundaries between normal and abnormal behavior, dichotomies rather than dimensions, and overt symptoms rather than underlying etiological mechanisms" (250). The *DSM*-III categories benefited a number of communities. Research-oriented psychiatrists were now able to measure mental illness in what they felt was a "reliable and reproducible" way. The new system also helped alleviate some of the pressure brought on psychiatry by critics of the previous system who had charged that mental illness could not be objectively defined. Perhaps most important, the new diagnostic system legitimized claims by physicians that what they were treating were real diseases, allowing the physicians to receive reimbursement from third party insurers (Mayes and Horowitz 251–252). With concerns about the purported rise of mental illness in Western culture, as well as the aftereffects of the movement towards deinstitutionalization of the severely mentally ill, the *DSM*-III moved psychiatry back to a re-embracing of the positivistic principles of nineteenth-century psychiatry (Shorter 302), basing itself on a modern formulation of the thought of German psychiatrist Emil Kraepelin (Mayes and Horowitz 260). Kraepelin's approach to psychiatric classification predicated itself on the assumption that mental disorders were best conceptualized as analogous to physical diseases. He also assumed that classifying mental disorders was dependent on the use of careful observation of visible symptoms instead of "on inferences based on unproven causal theories." Most important, Krapelin believed that empirically based research would eventually find a biochemical and organic reason for the existence of mental disorders (260).

The result of all this tinkering with the *DSM*, as we enter into the era of the *DSM*-5, is that, though the diagnostic accuracy for individual disorders has improved significantly since the pre–*DSM*-III era, there is still a lack of a reliable definition of mental disorder, and the validity of most *DSM* syndromes remains unestablished (Pierre 853) (which is not to say they do not necessarily reflect real emotional or even physical distress, just that the presumed syndrome-based reason for those factors cannot be scientifically established at this time). This, in turn, has led anti-psychiatric critics, such as Thomas Szasz, to argue that psychiatric illnesses are not real illnesses at all, as Szasz made a sharp bifurcation between physical and mental disorders (Pilgrim 539; Porter 274; Szasz, Location 75). Although many of Szasz's critiques of psychiatry, particularly its institutional practices, were penetrating, his belief that the "legitimacy of physical disorders," as opposed to mental disorders, was unproblematic was actually itself problematic. As David Pilgrim points out, the grounds for "querying the scientific merits of the diagnosis of mental disorder can be applied reasonably some of the time in physical medicine. Many diagnoses of 'true' physical pathology are vulnerable to similar criticisms, such as a lack of aetiological and treatment specificity" (Pilgrim 539). Therefore, the ready distinction between physical and mental conditions that is in many ways foundational to much of the modern anti-psychiatric movement is as problematic as the psychiatric establishment's often too-ready acceptance of a medical model of psychiatric disease.

This leaves professional psychiatry and mental health diagnosis at something of an impasse. The anti-psychiatric critique may be wrong in some of its assessment of psychiatric diagnosis, but the movement's questioning of the reasoning behind dividing the mentally "normal" and "abnormal" remains unanswered. As I argue in Chapter 4, I am not necessarily unsympathetic to anti-psychiatric writers on this point. As Joseph Pierre points out, there is real cause for concern that professional psychiatry sometimes does pathologize normal human experience and label it as disease (Pierre 653). Moreover, solidly researched articles without any apparent anti-psychiatric agenda have pointed out the numerous potential conflicts of interest professional psychiatry currently faces because of its dependence on pharmaceutical companies (see, for instance, Cosgrove and Wheeler 645). Much of the data we get on the effectiveness of pharmaceutical products comes through research that is financed by pharmaceutical firms, a problem that is becoming more problematic as the government's share of medical research continues to fall and the corporate share continues to rise. A meta-analysis of studies sponsored by the pharmaceutical industry showed a consistent trend to more positive results for funders' projects than by non-sponsored studies involving the same pharmaceutical products (Schowalter 127–133). Combined with the pressure from insurers on professional psychiatry to define mental illness in terms of some sort of medical, rather than "mental" or nonphysical, condition, and one sees that there is a powerful incentive for professional psychiatry to medicalize an increasing number of life stresses, biological states, or even simply lifestyles that may not be illnesses nor maladaptive nor even distressing to the individual "sufferer." The case of the pathologization of the LGBT community by professional psychiatry is a major case in point.

How then do we define mental disorder? There are a variety of suggestions in the professional literature. One school of thought termed medical naturalism accepts the existing "premise that current medical terminology describing mental abnormality is valid and has global and transhistorical applicability.... Mental disorder is assumed to exist 'out there' and to be independent of its observers or diagnosticians" (Pilgrim 539). Medical naturalism can be faulted for its appeal to transhistorical and global applicability as it fails to note the history of psychiatric medicine itself is rooted in a Western mindset and values, values that, though potentially valuable to the practice of science, do not necessarily have universal applicability to all cultures at all times. A second position, that of the radical constructivists, holds that "diagnoses are context-specific human products. They are deemed to be socially negotiated outcomes that reflect the cognitive preferences and vested interests of the negotiators" (Pilgrim 539). In this system, preferred by the followers of Michel Foucault, mental disorders do not exist as "objective natural entities" but are produced as a "byproduct of psychiatric activity" (Pilgrim 539). The Foucauldian approach therefore tends to focus on the social context in which mental health diagnosis is produced. Critical realism, a third position, argues, unlike Foucauldians, that mental health conditions cannot be dismissed as merely a byproduct of psychiatric activity (they concede that some form of mental health abnormality likely exists), but they also contest medical naturalism in arguing that the term mental illness has "poor conceptual validity" (Pilgrim 539). Critical realists also tend to agree with Foucauldian criticism in arguing that one does need to establish what interests are operating in the relationship between the diagnostician and the person being diagnosed (Pilgrim 539).

My own natural predisposition is towards medical naturalism, but the critical realist position may be more realistic. For the purpose of this book, however, I would like to argue that, to a certain extent, the debate over the etiology or existence of mental illness, though highly relevant to the debates surrounding mental health within the evangelical community, needs to be approached from a different direction than any of the three listed above.

Within an evangelical context, what is important to understand is that regardless of whether mental illness exists or not or has any conceptual validity as a concept in academic medicine, the mentally ill do exist as a socially constituted category within evangelical culture, where their diagnosis (or simply the perception of their being part of a certain diagnostic category of mental illness) marks them as a deviant population. In other words, it is perhaps better when dealing with evangelicals not to consider mental illness as a physiological category (though it may be that as well, as many mentally ill evangelicals believe) but a sociological and cultural identity imposed on those classified as mentally deviant, whether or not they actually exhibit the diagnostic criteria for mental illness. What distinguishes this definition of mental deviance in evangelicalism from most secular psychotherapeutic systems is that it is enforced by an anti-psychiatric establishment, not a psychiatric establishment. Therefore the socially normalizing agent within evangelicalism is not some psychiatric-industrial complex, but an anti-psychiatric industrial complex composed of biblical counselors, deliverance ministers, some professional Christian psychologists and psychiatrists of an anti-psychiatric persuasion, and the publishing companies, churches, and parachurch organizations that support them.

I therefore use the term mental illness throughout this book to describe the life experiences traditionally labeled as conditions like anorexia, schizophrenia, bipolar disorder, etc. I, of course, fully realize that that term is loaded, implying as it does a difference between the so-called "normal" and the "mentally ill," as well as the more problematic distinction between "normal" and "abnormal" psychological states.

I feel sympathy for Foucault's rendering of the history of madness, and I do not think the "illness" paradigm is always the best means of envisioning mental health problems. That being said, this work does assume that whether or not there is such a thing as "mental illness," there are definite subjective experiences individuals go through that produce behavior patterns similar to what is called mental illness. There is of course, infinite room to debate to what extent these behavior patterns are caused by genetics, environment, differences in brain structure, "chemical imbalances," "free will or personal choice," spiritual forces, or a combination of them. What I do find implausible, however, is the hard-line position favored by Szaszians and some more ardent evangelical anti-psychiatric advocates that absolutely no, or only a vanishingly few, of these behavior patterns are caused by differences in brain and bodily function. I am willing to concede that environmental factors may influence human physiology, but this work endorses medical naturalism to the extent that it conceptualizes both bodily and environmental factors as working within a materially bound universe. Let me provide an example of how a contradicting belief within evangelical circles affects mental health treatment. Biblical counselors often offer up the argument that if there are chemical imbalances in the brain, these imbalances are themselves caused by sinful thoughts, which are partly produced by nonmaterial aspects of human beings (the interaction between soul and body, for instance). Their opponents contend that what these counselors label as sinful thoughts may be caused by chemical imbalances (or differences in genetics or brain structure). The argument ends up going in circles. The difference is that proposition two may eventually be subject to empirical verification, while proposition one is clearly an unfalsifiable claim. Therefore, whatever its "truthfulness," proposition one does not seem to be of much help as an organizing paradigm for understanding mental illness.

This work therefore views mental illness as a poor, but currently necessary, organizing methodology for classifying behavior or emotional patterns that human beings find distressing. Ideally, such behavior and emotional patterns should be viewed as distressful only if the individual sees them as distressful; distressfulness should not be a socially imposed category. We should be skeptical, therefore, of governmental, psychological and psychiatric attempts (both historical and current) to classify behaviors such as homosexuality, transgender orientation, female "hysteria," transvestism, and "postabortion syndrome" as "real" disorders, as these categories of behavior are clearly used to pathologize unpopular social groups. Arguably, of course, this can occur even in mental illnesses that are still commonly acknowledged as psychopathologies by most of the psychotherapeutic community. The debate over whether schizophrenia is a political or psychiatric diagnosis is an interesting case in point.

I do not, however, argue that there is an essentialized "thing" in the body called "OCD" or "anorexia" or "bipolar." These are organizing schemas to explain sets of behaviors that many people have in common and they are useful as such. But to turn them into a self-definition can be problematic, since then one "becomes OCD" or defines oneself as "I am bipolar" rather than as "I have bipolar disorder." Therefore, while I acknowledge the reality of mental illness as a subjective experience based on *real* behavioral and emotional patterns, in most cases caused by *real* psychological distress, which may very well have some biological causal factors, I do not argue that one needs to believe in the "illness" paradigm of mental distress or "madness" in order to agree with the argument I make in this book.

Definitions of Evangelicalism

One of the favored definitions for evangelicalism is one used by British historian D.W. Bebbington. Bebbington outlines four distinguishing characteristics of evangelical belief: "conversionism, the belief that lives need to be changed; activism, the expression of the gospel in effort; biblicism, a particular regard for the Bible and what may be called crucicentrism, a stress on the sacrifice of Christ on the cross" (Bebbington 2–3). Although Bebbington's work in evangelical studies is valuable and this definitional system may be one of the best available, it ultimately leans too far in the direction of privileging right-wing explanations of evangelical belief. The biblicist element, in particular, simply does not seem as relevant to a modern evangelicalism that is starting to form both conservative and liberal forms of postmodernist scriptural critique that bring into question the traditional literalist hermeneutic that has characterized twentieth-century evangelicalism. Bebbington's definition also ignores the significant similarities that exist between traditional evangelicalism and mainline Protestantism (particularly the 19th-century variety of that cluster of religious beliefs).

Similarly, as I have argued in *Evangelicals and the Arts in Fiction* (2013), denominational definitions are a problematic tool for developing a comprehensive definition of what constitutes evangelicalism. Many denominations have both evangelical and mainline wings, those denominations ranging from the Mennonites to the Southern Baptists. Similarly, even groups which are traditionally thought of as mainline denominations have large evangelical wings, including the Anglicans, Methodists, and Lutherans (see Sweeney 19). Since denominational identities are not fixed, the historical time period at which one is looking is also important to understanding whether a denomination is evangelical. For instance, the Congregationalist denomination would have arguably been considered evangelical during the early nineteenth century, but few would so define it today. Fixed denominational definitions of evangelical belief therefore simply do not work (Weaver, *Evangelicals and the Arts in Fiction*, 11).

I therefore personally have come to prefer the system offered up by Fritz Detwiler (with a few caveats mentioned below). Detwiler divides the religious right into six parts (one of which is Catholicism). The five major divisions of evangelical belief that Detwiler argues for are fundamentalists, Holiness, Pentecostal and Charismatic, born-again (who in this work are referred to as neo-evangelicals, a change of terminology that would perhaps meet with Detwiler's approval) and Reformed Christians. Fundamentalism is a theological movement originally characterized by its opposition to theological modernism and evolutionary theory (Marsden 3–4). Holiness Christianity is notable mainly for the primacy it places on the pietistic life as the mark of true Christian behavior (Detwiler 152). Neo-evangelicalism is largely distinguishable from fundamentalism, its spiritual progenitor, by a greater willingness to embrace a diversity of hermeneutical viewpoints concerning scripture and by a tendency to try to engage with culture instead of to fight against it. Reformed Christianity is a theological system that is much too complex to simply and neatly define. However, in popular evangelical usage today, it typically refers to those evangelicals who draw their theological inspiration from the "teachings of John Calvin" (Detwiler 154). The Emergent church, not much referenced in this work, is a liberal body of evangelicals distinguished from other left-wing evangelicals by a devotion to a postmodernist, usually nonliteral reading of scripture, as well as a tendency to combine ancient and modern religious practices (Weaver, *Evangelicals and the Arts in Fiction,* 193–194). Another ill-defined group of evangelicals, the seeker-sensitive church movement, has no set denominational affiliation but concentrates mainly on gaining new followers and creating elaborate, massive megachurches. As a general rule, if seeker-sensitive churches do have a denominational or theological leaning it is to the Word of Faith movement (Prosperity Gospel), which has its roots in Charismatic teaching, or to the Third Wave Charismatic movement, its most influential contemporary figure being C. Peter Wagner.

The one significant difference between this work's definition of evangelicalism and the one presented in *Evangelicals and the Arts in Fiction* is that the difference between Charismatic and Pentecostal belief (two theological systems characterized by a devotion to the "gifts of the spirit") is much larger than most scholars have previously realized. In popular evangelical lingua franca, churches are often labeled Charismatic as a means of distinguishing them from what many see as the more extreme Pentecostal brand of Christianity. In fact, if one looks into the history of the Charismatic movement as it has developed over the last fifty years, the very opposite image emerges. While the initial impetus towards Charismatic belief arose in mainline Protestantism during the 1960s and was therefore seen by some as a liberal alternative to the then disreputable mainstream Pentecostal churches, the Charismatic Renewal became increasingly hard-line over the course of its existence. When the Renewal eventually hit non-mainline churches—that is, mainstream evangelicalism—it eventually would morph into what is commonly called the Third

Wave of Pentecostalism. This wave, by the 2000s, would evolve into the New Apostolic Reformation, a form of Charismatic belief based on a pan-denominational system of leadership that bypassed the traditional denominational hierarchies of mainstream Pentecostal (and later on, even some Charismatic) denominations in favor of a top-down system of almost dictatorial control on the part of certain "apostolic" leaders. The New Apostolic Reformation (NAR), contrary to its attempts to soft-sell itself as a benign religious movement, is quite possibly the most dangerous theological development in mainstream evangelicalism in the last century because of the movement's alignment, beginning in the 1990s, with a radical form of mid-century Pentecostal revivalism called Latter Rain theology.[2] While a detailed description of the NAR is beyond the scope of this particular work, interested readers are encouraged to consult the writings of Political Research Associates researcher Rachel Tabachnick, as well as the groundbreaking scholarship of Rene Holvast, for information on this movement. For the purpose of this work, what is important to realize is that the development of modern Charismatic and Pentecostal deliverance (aka exorcism) practices is intimately linked to the evolution of Latter Rain theology into the modern NAR movement.

The distinctions between these theological systems are vitally important to understand. Pentecostal and Charismatic churches tend to promote different forms of questionable mental health treatment than the alternative mental health systems advocated by the Reformed or fundamentalist movements. While there is occasionally some overlap—for instance, deliverance supporter Neil Anderson sometimes finds fundamentalists willing to accept his mixture of Charismatic and neo-evangelical theology—overall the division between these alternate mental health treatment programs is remarkably stark. What is important to understand is that these systems, when taken as a whole, provide a virtually entirely different mental health treatment system—or to be more accurate, systems—from that offered to most secular individuals. Regardless of whether one is mentally ill, gay, or female and regardless of one's denominational affiliation, the mainstream alternative mental health treatments evangelicalism offers are flawed in conceptualization and dangerous in operational practice. It is these flaws that form the main subject of this book.

The Pastoral Care Tradition

Finally, it is important to note the historical tradition from which biblical counseling, deliverance ministries, and, to a lesser extent, integrationist Christian psychology, descend: The pastoral care tradition. The pastoral care tradition has "historically included the collective duties of the clergy aimed at healing, guiding, and sustaining a congregation" (Mitchell 832). Both biblical counseling and deliverance can be seen as forms of pastoral care, though deliverance tends to be more a specific rite thereof, while biblical counseling traditionally conceptualizes itself as a part of an overarching schema of pastoral care in which biblical counseling is linked to other forms of pastoral care, notably church discipline (see, for instance, Adams, *Christian Counselor's Manual,* 55).

The pastoral care tradition is rooted deep within church history. The early church fathers promoted the idea that "physicians of the soul" were needed who could care for spiritually infirm members of the community (Yarhouse, Butman, and McRay 17). They also concluded that suffering, disability, and trials could in the end "be traced back to sin" (Yarhouse, Butman, and McRay 23). Early in church history, classificatory systems for sin were drawn up. These lists of sin became the foundation for pastoral care. Hermas, for instance, identified twelve specific sins that required pastoral care and treatment, while Cyprian, a third-century bishop of Carthage, established a classificatory system that included eight main sins (Yarhouse, Butman, and McRay 24).

By the second century, pastoral guidance consisted mainly of confession to one another and repentance (often termed "reproof and correction" today), a formula that would provide the foundation of pastoral care until the modern era. Initially, such confession was in all likelihood public, but increasingly the church moved from public to private confession. With this move, there was a rise in the use of the confessional as a major tool of soul care, and a corresponding greater emphasis on penance as "a part of the process of confession" (Yarhouse, Butman, and McRay 27–28). The move to penitential theology corresponded with a growing attempt to use the "metaphors, ideas, and language of then current models of medicine" to describe the pains of the soul. By 1215, the Fourth Lateran Council had dictated that every person "must confess their sins to their local priest at least once each year, and by the twelfth century a full sacramental theory of priestly absolution was developed" (Yarhouse, Butman, and McRay 29). During the sixteenth century, the Catholic moral theologians of the period completed this process by establishing a "complex body of casuistry—the application of general principles to particular cases—which promised to solve every spiritual dilemma that anyone could imagine" (Holifield 17). After the Reformation, four major traditions— the Lutheran, Anglican, Reformed, and Catholic—each went their separate way in developing a system for the cure of souls (Holified 17).

For the purpose of understanding pastoral counseling as it has developed in the evangelical tradition, it is important to focus primarily, though not exclusively, on the Reformed tradition. The Reformed tradition conceptualized sinfulness as being rooted in disobedience to God, or idolatry, as they often preferred to call it (Holifield 22). According to the Puritan theologians who so influenced American Reformed theology, "idolatry was the refusal to observe God's law, and the Puritan theologians ... believed that the Bible minutely defined unlawful acts ... thus specifying as it were the content of the disobedience" (Holifield 22). Puritan pastoral care was centered on this concept of idolatry. Puritan pastors specialized in analyzing their parishioners' motives and feelings in an attempt to "discern hidden intentions" and thereby, they hoped, direct their counselee into the path of the good Christian life (Holifield 23). This led eventually to a form of Protestant casuistry, where examples and rules were developed for "cases of conscience" that any potential counselee might bring (23).

Calvinism decreed that God preordained some for eternal life and others for eternal damnation. As hard as it is for some moderns to understand, this was meant to be a comforting doctrine. Calvin believed that in propounding his particular form of predestinarian thinking, he was removing "the anxiety inherent in the struggle to earn salvation through meritorious activity" (Holifield 23–24). Calvin wanted to direct Christians away from "introspective self concern" to a sole focus on Christ as redeemer (Holifield 24). The problem was that the doctrine of election left one uncertain of one's salvation. The elect therefore alternated between a feeling of blissful tranquility and intense anxiety about their future state (Rubin 27). Because of the doubts of salvation that Calvinist doctrines produced, a huge body of pastoral literature developed to guide ministers in how to heal people afflicted with troubled minds (Rubin 35). A great deal of pastoral care ended up being devoted to people who had fallen victim to an oversensitivity of the soul (Holifield 63).

Much of this pastoral literature was devoted to conditions that might now be seen—quite possibly anachronistically—as originating in mental health problems. It also sometimes sought to distinguish between physical diseases and spiritual conditions. Famed Puritan thinker Richard Baxter, for instance, was willing to adopt the medical understanding of his time in seeing melancholia as being rooted in a "humoral imbalance"—in short, a physical disease. William Perkins, similarly, distinguished between normal religious "affections" and melancholy, contending that melancholy represented a physical condition, while the former condition was rooted in mankind's sinful nature (Rubin 37). The Puritans spent their lives in a perpetual process of self-examination, in which they consistently tried to defeat the sinfulness arising from the "natural self" (Rubin 12, 44) in order to gain again the sense of peace that distinguished their "first conversion" (44).

The Puritans' inability to come to terms with this issue led to the development of a sense of religious melancholia that persisted from the sixteenth to the nineteenth centuries. According to Rubin, as "a form of madness, religious melancholy entailed extreme guilt about sin—obsession with having committed unpardonable sins through blasphemy against the Holy Spirit" (Rubin 5). The only cure for this form of melancholy, and also the demonic influence occasionally associated with it, was to find "assurance of grace" and one's status as one of the elect. But the structure of Puritan theology paradoxically made this a very difficult, almost impossible, process. The Puritan saints could never overcome their natural selves, and therefore were constantly prone to self-condemnation due to their inability to measure up to their own exacting standards. Doubt of one's salvation therefore became a periodic and persistent feature of evangelical life (Rubin 55), a fear that is seen in Puritanism's modern evangelical descendants to this day.

The entire history of pastoral care is beyond the purview of this book. As David Powlison points out, the history of pastoral care had liberalized slowly for more than two centuries following the close of the 18th century (Powlison, *Biblical Counseling Movement*, 11). This was perhaps best evidenced by the work of Anton Boisen and the two movements that arose out of Boisen's work: clinical pastoral education (CPE) and the pastoral counseling movement (Beck, *Baker Encyclopedia*, 836; Myers-Shirk loc 202). The pastoral counseling and clinical pastoral education movements sought to find a "rapprochement between religion and science" and this of course influenced their philosophy of pastoral care (Myers-Shirk loc 202–207).

Both biblical counseling and the early forms of Christian integrationist psychology (described in Chapter 9), arose as a response to concerns about the growing secularization of pastoral counseling, at that time mainly dominated by theological liberals (Myers-Shirk loc 3888–3894; Powlison 8). Adams felt that pastoral counseling was largely allowing itself to be supplanted by secular psychotherapy, leading to "jurisdictional" battles between the church and psychiatry over who had the right to counsel (Powlison 8). Adams arguably may have borrowed some from the liberal pastoral counseling tradition. In particular, Adams's consistent distinguishing between organic and nonorganic diagnoses (see Adams, *Competent*, 28–29, for a representative example) seems to owe a good deal to Boisen's distinction between functional illnesses of the mind or soul and organic illnesses of the body (see Myers-Shirk loc 383 on Boisen's distinctions between these forms of illness). But Boisen differed significantly from Adams in how he interpreted functional illnesses. For Boisen the functionally ill, though suffering perhaps from an illness of the soul, were not preternaturally great sinners but tortured saints. Boisen's work fundamentally challenged the then-current notion that "mentally ill people were depraved" (Myers-Shirk loc 392). Adams, by contrast, viewed those diagnosed with mental illness (whom he himself would not label as mentally ill) as suffering from an "autogenic" problem: themselves and their sinful fallen human nature (Adams, *Competent,* 29).

Adams's theology therefore in many ways deliberately sought to hearken back to the Reformed movement's Puritan and early Presbyterian roots. This is vitally important to understand because Adams's form of neo–Puritan "soul care" attempted as much as possible to recapture the diagnostic criteria and methods of the Puritans. The biblical counseling movement sought to place the pastor and the church at the center of the treatment of the mentally ill. Problems that were being interpreted by professional psychiatrists as originating in disorders of bodily function were usually reinterpreted in terms of pathologies of the soul. The biblical counselor, as had his Puritan pastoral ancestors, sought to be a "soul surgeon" who diagnosed in terms of faulty or sinful patterns of behavior or both.

A critical and consistent problem that biblical counseling had in distinguishing itself from professional psychology and psychiatry was that biblical counselors often used psychotherapeutic language and terms, only to try to recast them in biblical garb. Perhaps the most graphic example of this is the *Christian's Guide to Psychological Terms* (2004), by Mary and Marshall Asher, which lists the *DSM* terminology for an illness, and then (in almost all cases) lists the actual sin diagnosis of the illness. The more mainstream *The Christian Counselor's Medical Desk Reference* (2000) exhibits a similar inability to separate psychiatric and Calvinist diagnostic criteria, as does the recent biblical counseling anthology *Counseling the Hard Cases* (2012). Such terminological uncertainty has led to a great deal of tension between those evangelicals willing to endorse traditional psychiatric terminology and those who seek a return to a model more in line with Puritan and early evangelical assumptions about the nature of spiritual and mental disquiet. For those evangelicals endorsing traditional psychiatric views, most human problems requiring extended counsel are typically (though not exclusively) the by-product of mental illness, or perhaps sexual or physical trauma. Therefore, building on this assumption, evangelicals approaching psychiatry from this assumption tend to endorse an empathy-based approach to counseling, one that may or may not include spiritual succor as well. The biblical counseling approach, by contrast, though not necessarily always punitive in its methods, tends to approach counseling in a directive and corrective fashion, assuming that the problems the counselees have are of their own making, a byproduct of their inherent sinful nature. Unlike traditional psychology, which emphasizes self-actualization and self-acceptance, biblical counseling sees the "self" in negative terms. For the Puritans, selfhood was something to overcome. Therefore, for the biblical counseling movement likewise, self-esteem is a bankrupt moral concept (see Holifield 58).[3] This profoundly affected the biblical counseling movement's approach to mental health problems.

Movement opponents tended to focus on the fact that biblical counseling reclassified mental health problems as sins as their main concern in addressing the movement. But there was perhaps an equally fundamental issue that separated biblical counseling from traditional psychiatry, and that was that biblical counseling understood mental health problems as essentially ecclesiological and corporate in nature. In short, these problems were often reconceptualized as matters of church discipline. This can be seen in works as early as Adams's *Christian Counselor's Manual* (1973) (see Adams 52–54) and *A Theology of Christian Counseling* (1979) (see Adams 286–293). What is problematic in this context is that Adams conceptualized church discipline as extending beyond the immediate church in question, so that a pastor from one church should report on church discipline in his church to another church. While this in and of itself is not unheard of in evangelicalism, the extent to which later Reformed proponents of biblical counseling have promoted such models of church discipline has tended to lead to rather extreme applications of church discipline as a form of purported soul care. Sovereign Grace Ministries, covered in Chapter 4, is perhaps the most graphic example of this, but there is a general trend in the Reformed and fundamentalist world to a greater degree of church discipline, exemplified most notably by Mark Dever's 9 Marks Campaign, which seems to be almost monolithically focused on church discipline and discipleship, with a focus on the local church (see Dever, *Nine Marks*, loc 2276–3464, for representative examples). Almost every church investigated in the current Reformed revival (often termed New Calvinism) which practices strong church discipline also features a pastor who either is openly aligned with the biblical counseling movement or allied with one of its members. There are many disturbing but unconfirmable reports of potentially abusive uses of biblical counseling within New Calvinist circles, most of these reports tied to the major churches which most strongly aligned themselves with the current revival in church discipline. Therefore, while biblical counseling definitely has its origins in the more restorative aspects of pastoral care—namely a conservative variation of pastoral counseling—it is not unknown for it to be used, as in the case of Sovereign Grace Ministries, as an ancillary mechanism for helping maintain church authority. As Chapters 5 and 6 highlight, such authority is most likely to be exercised when evangelical women are put in pastoral care or pastoral counseling conditions.

Deliverance also has its roots in soul care, in a more round-about and desultory fashion which I will, for the sake of brevity, only briefly outline here. In early modern Europe, the idea of demonic possession made perfectly good sense. For early modern Europeans the afflictions suffered by so-called demoniacs resulted from the Devil's "entrance into the inner caverns" of the demoniac's bodies, by which he controlled physical and mental bodily functions (Levack 143–147). This was of course consistent with the considerable power attributed to the Devil in early modern culture (Levack 147). Brian Levack points out that the two dominant explanations of possession among skeptics has traditionally been deliberate fakery and mental illness. Levack makes a convincing case, however, that these explanations likely cannot account for all cases of possession—though they may explain some cases—and instead offers up a more culturally situated approach to understanding possession, seeing the possessed as "performers in religious dramas who were following scripts they learned from others" (Levack 160–161). This explanation is very likely to be true, if for no other reason than that the large number of people claiming to have been demonically delivered in the contemporary Charismatic movement alone, for instance, seems to negate the possibility of either mass fakery or mental illness in all cases.

Tales of demonism served an important role in the sixteenth and seventeenth centuries, as instructive and admonitory warnings and, more rarely, as lures to tempt the faithful (Levack 230). Crucial for our understanding of modern deliverance and exorcism, however, is that during the Reformation era claims of possessions and exorcisms were typically designed to induce someone towards Catholicism or alternately a particular Protestant denomination (Levack 268). According to Levack, "Christians of all denominations believed that ... demons could be expelled from bodies they had invaded and occupied." For Catholics, exorcism took the form of an "elaborate, public ritual." Protestants, by contrast, objected to Catholic ritualism because they felt it had no scriptural basis and tended to overemphasize the role of the exorcist while undermining the role of God. Protestants instead supported a simpler method of prayer and fasting to expel the Devil, though a few occasionally resorted to Catholic methods (Levack 648).

Both Protestants and Catholics have historically claimed to root their deliverance and exorcism practices in the Bible and the history of the early church (see Levack 864). The biblical accounts, however, told relatively little about the demonic possessions that Jesus terminated and in many ways the "possessions" of the early modern period bear little resemblance to those cases reported within the Christian scriptures. For instance, the demoniacs that were cured by Christ did not manifest the same range of symptoms as those demoniacs in early modern Europe (Levack 988). In spite of these hurdles, however, exorcism posed a major problem for early modern Protestants because there was not much they were allowed to do about the situation of a demoniac. Because Protestants relied on scripture alone, they were handicapped in what measures they felt theologically acceptable in taking towards demoniacs (1039–1060).

This handicap, as well as a general Protestant distrust of Catholic mysticism and ritualism, led Protestants to propound a doctrine that is now commonly known as cessationism. This is the belief that a large category of supernatural events, including most miracles and the Catholic form of exorcism, had been made obsolete shortly after the Apostolic Age. Thus Protestants sought to validate their own more modest form of exorcism while simultaneously discrediting the Catholic form of exorcism (1060).

In terms of exorcism's role in soul care, the ritual—whether Protestant or Catholic—was always seen as primarily designed for "the curing of the demoniac" (1971–1972). However, the ritual also was intended to serve a number of other purposes, including converting unbelievers and, perhaps most crucial, providing a form of indoctrination into Christian demonological beliefs (1987–2011). In the early church, exorcism could be performed by any Christian believer, with little regard to age, sex, gender, or position in the clergy or laity (2212). Catholicism gradually restricted exorcism to the clergy. Protestantism, given its general antiauthoritarianism, rejected the Catholic restriction of exorcism to the clergy and claimed that the laity as well as the clergy could perform such a spiritual function. Charismatic practice, despite the popularity of Charismatic teachings within many contemporary Catholic circles, has clearly followed the Protestant example, though it cannot be denied that the clergy are often, if not exclusively, seen as the best practitioners of exorcism or deliverance (2243).

Charismatics, however, differ from most other Protestants in that they promote the idea that many of the more miraculous gifts of the spirit present in the early church age are meant for the present age (Allan Anderson 23, 30). These gifts include the ability to cast out demonic spirits, which Charismatics typically see as a form of healing ministry. They therefore reject cessationism, which still predominates within the Reformed movement and among many fundamentalists as well. It is the division over cessationism that fundamentally divides biblical counseling practice from deliverance ministries.

This means that fundamentally biblical counseling has had a very negative view of deliverance ministries and the inner healing movement that arose from them, which combined Freudian and Jungian ideas with deliverance (for a representative example of inner healing, see Collins 95–99). In the 1980s, biblical counseling supporter Michael Bobick criticized the inner healing movement for an overreliance on the use of "creative imagination" techniques. Bobick saw inner healing as being too devoted to an emotional-based faith (Bobick 26–27). Nelson Hinman, another early biblical counseling advocate, also criticized inner healing for its overreliance on Freudian rhetoric (30). David Powlison, the most important figure in biblical counseling history after Jay Adams, established himself as a major critic of deliverance ministries in his book *Power Encounters* (1995). Based upon his writing on spiritual warfare and deliverance in *Understanding Spiritual Warfare: 4 Views* (2012), Charismatics are right to fear him, as Powlison makes a very persuasive case against the utility, and even the ethicality, of deliverance ministries as practiced in the modern evangelical church.[4] John MacArthur, a major supporter of biblical counseling and a prominent Reformed minister, has been a major critic of the Charismatic movement as a whole since the release of his book *Charismatic Chaos* in 1993.

The main thing to understand here is that the biblical counseling movement, rooted as it is in Reformed cessationism, has historically had a rather low view of the use of exorcism as a contemporary form of soul care. Jay Adams's works portray demonic possession as a rare, if not entirely unknown, force in modern times, and that view has been consistently promoted by the biblical counseling movement since his publication of *The Big Umbrella* in 1972 (Adams, *The Big Umbrella*, 119–120). Therefore, while interaction between biblical counselors and deliverance supporters is not unknown, it is at this time unlikely that these two philosophies will try to fuse their therapeutic methods or do anything more than perhaps politically align themselves in cases when both groups feel under assault by secular political, legal, or credentialing organizations.

What is important to understand about both deliverance and biblical counseling is that both groups tend to see the church and fellow believers as the primary deliverers of what the secular world terms mental health care. This flows out of the assumption, not commonly held by most secular psychological professionals, that only believing Christians can properly distinguish between demonic affliction and mental disorder (as in deliverance) or between biological illness and sin-engendered (*hamartiagenic*) sicknesses of the soul (as in biblical counseling). Indeed, many of the problems that modern secular Westerners think of as mental illnesses or even simply non-diseases in any respect are relabeled as potentially spiritually induced problems or as issues with major sin or demonic components in addition to medical ones. Thus, evangelicals commonly believe that only another evangelical can successfully treat them for problems that involve the spirit or the soul.

Mental health problems are particularly likely to fall under the church's purview then, because both the deliverance and biblical counseling movements reject the prevailing monistic and biologically reductionistic view of the human brain that characterizes modern psychiatry. Instead, the brain is influenced by other parts of the human self, parts that are immaterial, such as the soul. When confronted with each other, therefore, the secular view of mental illness (often held in modified form by some evangelicals themselves)—which conceptualizes mental suffering as bodily disease—and the biblical counseling and deliverance models—which regardless of their differences see mental suffering as being born of spiritual "pathogens" (sin or the devil or demons, respectively)—inevitably conflict. Such a conflict cannot help but occur, since these two paradigms start out from fundamentally different conceptions of how to relieve mental anguish. It is the purpose of this book to delineate some of the limits of these spiritual forms of care, but it is important to remember Levack's wise warning that illness is itself socially constructed (Levack 2657). Biblical counseling and deliverance ministries generate different forms, types, and degrees of diagnoses and treatments, but ultimately both groups' aims are curative. What differentiates them from mainstream medicine is their definition of what constitutes "curative" relief (which does not always involve the relieving of mental anguish, particularly in biblical counseling) and the process by which they conduct their curative programs. Medicine, including psychiatry, generally tries to rely on empirical methods to achieve its aims, while deliverance ministries and biblical counseling, though not always opposed to empirical research as such, in general approach the treatment of mental suffering from a spiritually directed, nonempirically based position. Whether, of course, empirical medicine is ultimately more successful than spiritual methods in treating mental health problems is an open question. It is also in large part an unanswerable one, because no one has developed a reliable method of measuring God's, spirits', demons', or the Devil's physical effect on people's mental well-being. Therefore the history offered here of evangelical mental health beliefs is by necessity suggestive. While there are deep concerns about how these beliefs affect those diagnosed with mental illness, the nature of the various "soul care" methods described herein means that their success can largely only be measured subjectively, on a case-by-case basis. I therefore leave it to the reader to decide whether the concerns I express about evangelical mental health beliefs are worthy of discussion.

Deliverance Movement

History and Foundational Assumptions

In April of 2013, it was revealed that a patient of a British doctor was advised by her doctor to stop taking her mental health medication; the doctor told her there was another way to treat her mental health symptoms. The treatment? Exorcism, better known in modern Charismatic and Pentecostal parlance as deliverance. The woman was subjected to a four-hour "testimony" session, in which an exorcism was performed. The patient claimed that her doctor "specifically told her not to tell her psychiatrist about the meetings and told her 'she would be cursed' if she told the GMC [British General Medical Council]" (*Daily Mail Reporter*, "God Will Heal'"). While the doctor denied the allegations, they were considered serious enough by the British General Medical Council to cause one of its Interim Panels to put a series of restrictions on the doctor's practice for 18 months (*Daily Mail Reporter*).

A British general practitioner performing an exorcism may sound absurd to those without a knowledge of Charismatic and Pentecostal culture. To most people, exorcism and its Pentecostal variant, deliverance, sound like some retrograde healing practices from the 19th century. In reality, exorcism is big business today, with scores of different exorcism manuals in print, many of which, such as the Sozo healing manuals and the classic *Pigs in the Parlor,* attract many people to Pentecostal healing models. How did this practice become so big in American Charismatic circles? The answer is surprising.

We start by looking briefly at the teachings of a supporter of such bizarre concepts as demonic fecal matter and "atomic level" fasting, an improbable place for the beginning of modern exorcism, but such is the fate of social movements. Modern deliverance and its effects on mental health treatment is not understandable without first knowing a little bit about two men: William Branham and Franklin Hall, the latter the originator of "atomic fasting." In 1946, two gauntlets were thrown down against the Soviet Union. The first was Winston Churchill's famous Iron Curtain Speech, which dichotomized the world into two warring factions. But this was not the only act of provocation by a citizen of the West, because in 1946, Hall published his *Fasting: Atomic Power with God* (Hall, *Atomic Power* 1; Churchill 231–232). Hall's book would help birth the Latter Rain revival movement and would, through its influence, end up having major effects on how the Charismatic movement's view of deliverance would evolve. Hall's *Fasting: Atomic Power with God* was part of a long line of early Pentecostal books on healing (Williams 67). Hall "went well beyond his predecessors, however, by employing heavy doses of explicitly naturopathic philosophy in his promotion of bodily discipline" (Williams 67). Hall used a combination of alternative medicine with Charismatic spirituality to promote bodily combat against the deadly toxins found in the body. He literally believed that "evil spirits were attracted to filth and that accumulated toxins in the body invited demonic activity" (Hall, *Glorified Fasting*, 39–40; Williams 67); therefore fasting was a means of bodily combatting demonic activity, primarily through the expulsion of demonic fecal matter (Williams 67).

Hall took the biblical emphasis on fasting and put it above all other areas of his theology. The fasting process was not just a period for reflection, but a literal battle in the spiritual realm against demons and demonic powers. When translated into the realm of foreign policy, this idea would lead to later Charismatics, particularly the followers of C. Peter Wagner and the Kansas City Prophets, to use fasting and "intercessory prayer" as a tool to disrupt the demonic forces in control of non–American countries (Wagner 42, 44, "Spiritual Warfare"; Engle, *Digging the Wells,* 145–156; Bickle and Candler, *Rewards of Fasting*, passim [particularly 10, 63–64]). This type of territorial spiritual warfare[1] had profound implications for the mentally ill (as well as abuse victims) because these unfortunate individuals were often seen as the "ground level" (i.e., individual level) on which deliverance tactics were to be tried and perfected.

Hall's *Fasting: Atomic Power with God* endorses the idea of a literally atomic theology. Hall believed: "when we speak of 'ATOMIC POWER WITH GOD' we are using a term expressing something GREAT, and 'Atomic Power' is as good an expression as we could possibly find to fill the bill. We are not exaggerating in the least when we compare 'FASTING AND PRAYING' with the power of the atomic bomb, because, to the Christian, fasting will truly bring atomic spiritual power" (Hall 11–12, capitalization in original). For Hall, fasting and prayer, particularly the former, implemented a kind of greater spiritual power unavailable to the uninitiated. The power that Charismatic spirituality unleashed, when combined with fasting, gave the movement a deterrent against the anxieties of the nuclear age; moreover it gave the Christian church in general a spiritual weapon that could be implemented against the "fanaticism" of the Soviet Union's Communist adherents.

Fasting not only allowed Christians to have their own spiritual nuclear arsenal, it also allowed them to upgrade that arsenal. According to Hall, "Fasting is the most powerful means at the disposal of every child of God. Fasting literally becomes prayer to the praying Christian, prayer that is as different as an atomic bomb compared to an ordinary bomb. Prayer alone is like the ordinary bomb, and the fast with prayer, is comparable to the Super-Atomic Bomb" (Hall 23). Hall believed that Christ himself was not fully seen as the manifested Son of God until he went into the desert and fasted against Satan. It was Jesus's refusal of food from the Devil that made him into such an effective incarnate warrior against the Devil (Hall 23). Hall therefore advises Christians to follow Christ's example. Fasting allows Christians to quickly and effortlessly compete with spiritual Soviets (demons, "demonized" humans, real-life Soviets, etc.) in the spiritual arms race occurring in the spiritual world. By equipping the United States with effective spiritual warriors the Pentecostal church becomes the testing zone, the spiritual Los Alamos, for the weapons that the church wishes to employ against its enemies, foreign and domestic. It also gives the Pentecostal church a keen sense of its own superiority over allied groups, since it's only the truly devout fasting person who is making the best atomic bombs for God.

Hall might have gone down in Charismatic history as a peculiar but forgotten figure, with little influence on its views of the mentally ill, were it not for his influence on the Latter Rain movement. The Latter Rain movement was "a Pentecostal movement of the mid–20th century that, along with the parallel healing movement of that era, became an important component of the post–World War II evangelical awakening." Though the movement's impact was initially limited (Riss, "Latter Rain Movement," 830), it would end up influencing the modern Charismatic movement through the works and preaching of Bill Hamon, Paul Cain, and other prominent supporters of Latter Rain theology. Their works and sermons, only slightly diluting Latter Rain theology, became some of the central organizing principles of the New Apostolic Reformation (NAR), a movement of Charismatic churches led by C. Peter Wagner that spread the once almost-defunct Latter Rain theology to a literally worldwide audience (Holvast 40, 164–165). The New Apostolic Reformation would end up promoting a form of territorial spiritual warfare with literally devastating consequences for mentally ill people.

Latter Rain theology had several unusual peculiarities to it that made it an unlikely starting point for the growth of a major theological movement. First, one of its major precipitating influences, which even Latter Rain adherents typically admit, is the teaching of William Branham (Riss, "Latter Rain Movement," 830). Branham was an unusual and colorful figure, one of the two giants of mid-century Pentecostal healing revivalism (Oral Roberts being the other) (Harrell Jr. 25; Douglas Weaver 9). As his ministry began to fade, however, Branham taught increasingly bizarre and, to outside minds, extreme doctrines, most famously the doctrine of "the serpent's seed" (Weaver 113), in which Eve had sex with the serpent, which produced all the resulting descendants of the human race who were educated, including scientists (which for Branham was bad) (Weaver 113). Branham's theory was literally a form of genoism, in which Abel's godly seed was superior to the seed of intellectuals. According to Branham "simple genetics determined one's eternal destiny" (Weaver 123). James M. Collins classifies Branham as the "first great evangelist of the post–War period" (Collins 25). According to Collins—hardly a fan of Branham—Branham had an uncanny ability at obtaining so-called words of knowledge. Branham could "identify facts about people that he could have no natural way of knowing" (Collins 28). This "ability," whether obtained through trickery or skilled psychological manipulation, spread Branham's theology of deliverance to a wide audience (Collins 27–29). As later Charismatics would do, Branham divided the world into dualistic spheres: God and the Devil, angels and demons, etc. Therefore, for Branham, "confronting the demonic became a key aspect of his ministry, whether through deliverance or, more commonly, through exposing 'demonic doctrines, philosophies, or behavior'" (Collins 29). This kind of dualistic thinking meant that many subsequent Pentecostals and Charismatics would be unable to differentiate between physical afflictions (especially mental illness) and demonic afflictions. Therefore, there was a marked tendency, though receding somewhat in recent years, to blame illness on the Devil. Mental illness, because no physical etiology was readily apparent to most lay people, proved particularly amenable to this kind of spiritualized diagnosis.

Collins points out two facets of Branham's demonology that occurred again and again in subsequent Pentecostal and Charismatic teaching. The first is "transgenerational demon possession (demon possession is due to sin committed by the victim's forebears)" (Collins 30). This idea, today known under the popular appellation of generational curse(s), is virtually ubiquitous among Charismatics and plays an important role even in some neo-evangelical deliverance ministries. This is important because one crucial type of inherited demon is the class of demons associated with mental illness. This is, for instance, seen within one of the most influential of modern deliverance models, the Restoring the Foundations (RTF) paradigm, invented by Chester and Betsy Kylstra.[2] This model would in turn powerfully influence Nancy Alcorn, a woman responsible for promoting the exorcism of anorexics, bulimics, sex abuse victims, and addicts in order to cure them.[3] As Collins points out, Branham is not the "innovator behind deliverance ministry. Deliverance ministry played a prominent part in the ministry of many of the itinerant Pentecostal healing evangelists and had done for decades" (Collins 30). But Branham's power and sheer influence, as well as "the dramatic nature of his deliverance ministry," were primarily responsible for deliverance's wider adoption among some Pentecostals and the vast majority of Charismatics (see Collins 30).

Some of Branham's ideas either influenced or simply intersected with Latter Rain theology (though not immediately, as Branham's most radical teachings—those on serpent seed—did not totally gel until the 1960s. See Weaver 107–109). Branham's influence, combined with the "unmistakable" influence of Franklin Hall (Riss, *Latter Rain*, 60), impelled the early members of the Latter Rain movement to engage in extreme forms of religiously motivated fasting. Just prior to the revival, some Latter Rain members at Sharon Bible School (the initial center of the revival) fasted for as long as 42 days according to Riss's account (Riss, *Latter Rain*, 61). The revival then spread to several other locations (Riss, "Latter Rain Movement," 831). Hall's influence was immediately and most dramatically seen through George Warnock's book *The Feast of the Tabernacles* (1951). Warnock posited that there were three great historical feasts in history and that the third great feast, "The Feast of the Tabernacles," was "yet to be fulfilled" (Riss, "Latter Rain Movement," 831).

Warnock took Hall's theology and ran with it, arguing for spiritual superpowers that the "Manifest Sons of God" would be able to implement during the age of the third great feast (see Warnock 8, 78). The list of these superpowers was imposing and their effect on later Charismatic teaching on spiritual warfare, including against the mentally ill, was profound. Warnock wrote as follows:

> There will not be a country on earth that will be closed to this Gospel of the Kingdom. It will be just as simple to proclaim the Truth in Communist Russia as anywhere else on earth.... They [Soviets] may rush upon him with sword or bayonet, and their weapon will be blunted as truly as if they had charged an armored tank; for no weapon that is formed against him shall prosper.... The most powerful atom or hydrogen bombs ever invented shall be perfectly harmless to the man who is hid away in the secret place of the Most High [Warnock 78].

The perfected manifest sons would be able literally to tear down the Communist empire. Soviet Russia, which up till the time of the publication of Warnock's *Feast of the Tabernacles* had been nearly impenetrable to the gospel, would suddenly and overnight become evangelized by "supermen" missionaries. Not only this, these manifest sons of God would in this last era of the church be capable of superior defensive efforts as well. Warnock literally believed that human beings could survive an atomic blast through faith alone. The heavy emphasis on food still present in *Feast of the Tabernacles,* although somewhat mitigated by Warnock's more charitable attitudes to non-fasters than Hall (see Warnock 36), is evident throughout the text. Fasting leads to spiritual feasting. Moreover, God is a power to be utilized (Williams 49–50), like electric current, and consumed. By fasting in the physical world, the Latter Rain movement hoped to gain the food of spiritual power in the spiritual world. This kind of "bulimic theology" led to a kind of feast-or-famine way of looking at the world, in which hunger for the next revival and the next new system of theological revelation were indoctrinated into each succeeding generation of Charismatics who in some sense subscribed to Latter Rain theology. Warnock's use of manifest sons theology, when combined with broader trends in Charismatic and Pentecostal culture, would reinforce the dichotomous dualism of God vs. Devil and physical and organic illness vs. demonic illness that characterized Hall's and, in particular, Branham's theology.

By the 1960s, Hall was trying to adapt his theology to the changing conditions of the Cold War, specifically the space race. Hall's book *Subdue the Earth* (1966) was the main result of these efforts. By this point, Hall's theology predicted that the "man child" (his version of manifest sons theology) would be able to control gravity through levitation (humorously, he calls levitation in this passage "levity") and have literal control of the elements themselves (Hall, *Subdue the Earth,* 6). Moreover, the saints in the final era would "have faith enough to believe the Lord can adapt them to the necessary condition to become a Holy Ghost powered astronaut, that will travel by teleportation" (*Subdue the Earth* 6). Hall had become a marginal figure, but the fasting theology he had started ended up vitally influencing a wide swathe of the Charismatic church that came after. That he is now forgotten is due more to historical circumstance (and often deliberate historical erasure on the part of Pentecostal and Charismatic historians) than lack of influence.

There was generally not an acceptance of Latter Rain doctrine, including doctrine on fasting, within denominational Pentecostal churches (Riss, "Latter Rain Movement," 832), particularly in the Assembly of God denomination. However, immediately many independent "revival" churches sprang up. In addition, "many of those involved in the Latter Rain [Movement] carried on and developed principles that had arisen in the late 1940s, becoming a vital part of the charismatic renewal in the 1960s and 1970s" (Riss, "Latter Rain Movement," 832). We must turn to the Charismatic renewal movement to see how deliverance ministries first emerged into public prominence, but the reader should keep the Latter Rain in mind, for in the 1980s and 1990s it would reemerge as a powerful influence on Charismatic theology, holding sway over millions of souls.

Deliverance Movement: History, Theology, Worldview and View of Mental Illness

Exorcism, as we have seen, is a practice that dates to the earliest era of the Christian church. As James Collins points out, however, exorcism's popularity had waned by the beginning of the twentieth century (Collins 5). Collins argues that the growth of deliverance and exorcism practices in the twentieth century was the result of a corollary growth in forms of faith he labels "enthusiastic" (Collins 2). As Collins points out, there is no pure enthusiast, but rather degrees of enthusiasm. The more enthusiastic a faith, the greater tendency to accept the deliverance/exorcism model. Enthusiasm can claim a variety of traits, such as "immanent spirituality, anti-rationalism ... ecstatic manifestations ... female emancipation, faddism and schism" (Collins 2). Obviously not all of these values are antagonistic to those seeking mental health treatment (female emancipation, for instance).

Collins is mainly concerned with Christian enthusiasts' "driving assumptions of spiritual immanency and eschatological immanency. These assumptions lead to the tendency towards simplistic spiritualized explanations of experience and events and a further tendency to invest such experience and events with great spiritual significance. These lie in contrast to rational attempts to categorize experience and events in terms of natural cause and effect which would be included in a more balanced faith perspective" (Collins 2). Collins is perhaps too confident in his appeal to rationalism—the biblical counseling movement, for instance, claims to be rationalist as well—but his point is still a salient one. Unlike the fundamentally post–Enlightenment philosophy of the current Reformed movement, which is heavily predicated upon Scottish Common Sense Realism and ponderous but distinguished tomes of Dutch and German Calvinist theology, enthusiastic theological practice, particularly in its Charismatic and Pentecostal varieties, is largely premodern. Indeed, many evangelicals who are adopting Charismatic ideals and practices claim that "the assumptions of animist cultures encountered [by Westerners] are more comparable to the worldview of the Scriptures than that of the Post-Enlightenment West" (Collins 192).

As Michael Cuneo points out, in one sense it was not surprising that deliverance ministries ended up succeeding in Charismatic circles (Cuneo 88). After all, "the charismatic renewal movement was deeply influenced by classical

Pentecostalism ... and deliverance (or exorcism) was commonly practiced among Pentecostals in the United States from the earliest days of Azusa Street" (Cuneo 88). However, the emphasis on demonism in denominational Pentecostalism began to die down in the 1930s and 1940s, as Pentecostalism entered the socioeconomic mainstream of American culture. Pentecostals no longer wanted to be seen as socially marginal, and the emphasis on demonism hurt their public image (Cuneo 88–89). However, in the late forties and fifties there was a "remarkable surge in the popularity of ... itinerant healing evangelists" (Collins 24), many of whom promoted the ideals of healing and some of whom (for instance, William Branham) had created elaborate demonologies (Collins 29).

Particularly influential during this period and subsequently was Oral Roberts. Roberts' chief contribution to the deliverance movement was his ability to take "healing revivalism ... beyond the strictures of the Pentecostal subculture into the emergent Charismatic Movement" (Collins 33). Roberts was able to translate many of the ideas of revivalist Pentecostalism and place them into a Charismatic context (Collins 33). This is important to understand, because the Charismatic Renewal was in many ways much different from Pentecostalism proper. Charismatic theology and practice attracted many mainline Protestants (Synan 150–151), ostensibly (according to the obviously biased Vinson Synan) because of the power of glossolalia and ecstatic Pentecostal worship experienced by those mainline Protestants who felt the call of charismatic ecstasy (Synan 150–151). These new Pentecostals were "less emotional and used their gifts more privately as a prayer language. They also violated many stereotypes about Pentecostalism that had been widely held for decades. They were made up primarily of well-educated clergy and lay professionals" (Synan 154). It would be the leaders of the Charismatic renewal who would provide the wider Pentecostal movement with the intellectual heft, economic influence, and theological sophistication to spread Charismatic teaching worldwide. By the 1980s, Charismatic renewal theology in the mainline churches had already intersected with renewal in non–Pentecostal evangelical denominations (see Synan 177–178, as well as 179–208 passim), creating a powerful syncretic fusion of various theological traditions united by their shared experience of "spiritual gifts."

The two foundational figures for the modern deliverance movement were Derek Prince and Don Basham (particularly Prince), widely seen by deliverance "experts" of the seventies and eighties as being influential on their healing practice (see Collins 44). Both men were crucial figures in the Charismatic renewal through their promotion of a disciplining practice known as shepherding (Synan 353–354). Prince believed that Christian ministry is "superficial" unless the practice of deliverance is used, observing that it was a common practice of Jesus (Collins 47, Prince 18–26). Prince also promoted a highly esoteric vision of demonology. He argued that demons, rather than being fallen angels, are "disembodied spirits of a pre–Adamic race that perished under some judgment of God not recorded ... in Scripture" (Prince 91). Though Prince's explanation of demonology, derived from G.H. Pember's *Earth's Earliest Ages* (1876), is only occasionally adopted by other practitioners of deliverance, his ideas about sin and affliction's relationship to possession were much more widely influential (Prince 95). Prince believed that each demon was associated with a "particular sin or affliction" (Collins 48; see Prince 96–97). Though Prince's list of particular demons is relatively modest, even in his late-career work *They Shall Expel Demons* (1998), later practitioners of deliverance, particularly Frank and Ida Mae Hammond and Chester and Betsy Kylstra, would create demonic taxonomies of stupendous length. The Open Doors to demonic oppression in the RTF manual, for instance, is a three and three-quarter page list of literally hundreds of potential demonic areas of affliction, clearly modeled on Prince's simpler taxonomy, as well as the much more detailed taxonomy of the Hammonds (Kylstra and Kylstra 397–400).

Prince contended that "demons cannot enter humans at will" (Collins 48). However, the number of possible avenues for demonic invasion of the human body were so wide as to be almost impossible to escape. Prince lists seven areas by which "demons ... gain access to human personalities: 'A family background in the occult or false religions'; 'Other negative prenatal influences'; 'Pressures in early childhood'; 'Emotional shock or sustained emotional pressure'; 'Sinful acts or habits'; 'Laying on of hands'; 'Idle words'" (Prince 103). As in the Hammonds and Kylstras demonologies, Prince's demonological system was predicated on a profound fear of the diabolic that in some sense gave the Devil the better end of the stick than it did God. Michael Cuneo, commenting on the Hammonds' demonic taxonomy in *Pigs in the Parlor* (1973), has observed, "Is there anyone who wouldn't be a candidate for deliverance?" (Cuneo 53). Collins comments similarly on Prince: "Although Prince does not explicitly make the claim, it is hard not to draw the conclusion that everyone is demonized to some extent" (Collins 49).

It is notable that here, at the foundations of the deliverance movement, one also sees the association of mental illnesses with demonic manifestations. Prince argued that there were demons of schizophrenia (Prince 200) and that suicide, which in psychiatric terms is often explained as a by-product of mental illness, is almost always "motivated by a demon" (Prince 181). Prince's teaching tapes argued that "compulsions, addictions, many illnesses and emotional disorders are all attributable to ... demonization" (Collins 49). But, whereas the

Reformed psychophobia of biblical counseling was the result of a specific prejudice against the mentally ill as a subset of sinners, Charismatic and Pentecostal psychophobic theological practice resulted from a more generalized fear of the demonic that was directed at almost all human problems, not a specific subset thereof.

Prince also made a crucial distinction, popularized by Don Basham's *Deliver Us from Evil* (1972), between "demonic possession and affliction" (Cuneo 93). As Michael Cuneo relates, Prince held that, "while it was highly unlikely that true spirit-baptized Christians could actually become possessed, which meant falling completely under the sway of Satan, there was no reason to think that they couldn't be tormented or afflicted in some area of their lives by demonic powers" (Cuneo 95). Prince admitted that the biblical "evidence" on this issue was ambiguous, but that pastoral and personal evidence overwhelmingly supported the idea that Christians could be demonically oppressed (Cuneo 95). This issue was crucial because traditionally most Protestants had held (and continue to hold) that Christians cannot be demonically possessed,[4] and the Pentecostal movement was no exception in this regard (Collins 49). Prince argued that the King James Version (KJV) was "erroneous in using the phrase 'possessed by a demon' to translate the Greek verb *daimonizo*" and instead argued that "a better, literal translation would be 'demonised,' which confers a degree of control and influence without the connotation of total ownership" (Collins 49). This distinction was adopted by the vast majority of deliverance supporters who followed in Prince's wake, including even relatively careful studies from within the neo–Evangelical camp, like C. Fred Dickason's *Demon Possession and the Christian* (1987) (Dickason 340–341, passim).

What became immediately apparent to Prince and his followers, and even more so to deliverance's critics, was that the diagnosis of demonization was inherently problematic. How was one to tell who was demonized and who was not, what problems represented demonization and which did not (Collins 50)?[5] As Collins points out, the diagnosis of demonization versus ordinary "illness," infirmity, or life problem was left mainly to the "spiritual gift of discernment" (Collins 50). Someone with the gift of discernment would be able to tell whether or not someone was demonically or only physically, emotionally, or mentally troubled. The inherent problem, of course, was that those with the gift of discernment often lacked any medical, psychiatric, or psychological training.

Thus, behavioral patterns or physical illnesses that might have biological or environmental explanatory factors were typically interpreted solely or primarily in theological terms. In the most extreme cases, this led to extreme and obtuse explanations of mental health problems, such as Ida Mae Hammond's notorious revelation that schizophrenia is a demonically inherited disease involving multiple personalities. Hammond here confuses schizophrenia with multiple personality disorder (MPD) or Dissociative Identity Disorder (DID), leading one to question how much her "revelation" was due to the pop psychology of the seventies and eighties, when films and books concerning multiple personalities were numerous (Hammond and Hammond 123–133).[6] The inability of deliverance ministers to agree on what was demonization and what was mental illness meant inevitably that some exorcisms might be conducted on individuals who were mentally ill, not demonically oppressed (assuming one even believes in demons, which this author does not).[7] While most deliverance manuals offer a somewhat perfunctory caution about being overly quick to associate mental illness with the demonic, almost all such manuals leave open the possibility that many, perhaps most, mental illnesses are the result of demonic oppression or demonization.

Don Basham helped popularize Prince's theology and in practice his deliverance theology differed little from Prince's theology. Basham "went on to join Derek Prince, Charles Simpson, Ern Baxter, and Bob Mumford in [forming] the controversial Fort Lauderdale group who pioneered the Shepherding/House Church Movement" (Collins 54). The Shepherding movement has attracted enormous controversy within evangelical circles for what some considered its cultic practices (Cuneo 123). Basham, Prince, and their fellow leaders "claimed that they had been especially empowered by the Holy Spirit to define strict lines of authority for charismatic prayer groups across the country. And they also claimed that individual charismatics were required to submit themselves, totally and unflinchingly, to the authority of specially designated 'elders' or 'shepherds' from their local communities" (Cuneo 122). The shepherding movement ended up having an enormous influence on subsequent Charismatic theology. For the purposes of this study it had a number of important effects. First, for those within the Shepherding movement who questioned deliverance, there "was better than a decent chance that he or she (especially *she*) would be diagnosed as demonized and subjected to remedial deliverance" (Cuneo 123, italics in original). Cuneo points out that some shepherds engaged in a sort of "spiritual engineering, trying to transform ordinary charismatics into entirely new and submissive children of God" (Cuneo 122). For the mentally ill and for abuse victims, this kind of teaching could become particularly problematic, because the gifts associated with deliverance (especially the discerning of spirits) could be used as a "spiritual cudgel for coercing people into deliverance" (Cuneo 119). The emotionally troubled are especially likely to buy into diagnoses of their afflictions as demonic, especially if such diagnoses are given on "apparently unimpeachable authority" (Cuneo 119). As Cuneo points out, this does not mean deliverance is inherently untherapeutic—a sensitive practitioner could conceivably use the practice to humane effects; however, because the deliverance movement has tended to attract "more than its share of authoritarian cranks" (Cuneo 119), it is quite vulnerable to therapeutic abuse, abuse compounded by the fact that the practice of deliverance is typically unregulated.

The second major effect Shepherding has had on the mentally ill—and, again, abuse victims (especially women)—has been through the practice of church discipline invoked by the Shepherding movement. Even S. David Moore's largely hagiographic telling of Shepherding history, *The Shepherding Movement: Controversy and Charismatic Ecclesiology* (2003), (unintentionally) points out some of the more disturbing elements of the shepherds' control over their disciples' lives:

> Many of the movement's early followers were young people who wanted and needed the discipline the Shepherding relationship brought with its concept of authority and submission. Shepherds were to lead their sheep and provide practical guidance in etiquette, personal dress, management, budgeting and basic home, yard, and automobile care.... Key to understanding how this worked was the recognition that followers were voluntarily to make a definite commitment to a shepherd that included an invitation to be disciple and pastored in all areas of life.... Many of them [disciples] became uncooperative or disillusioned by the degree of authority exercised [Moore 75].

In practical terms this kind of church discipline had two important side effects. First, as Cuneo notes implicitly, when applied to women as well as men, it sometimes led the movement to condone abuse. As with biblical counseling in its fundamentalist and Quiverfull manifestations, the Shepherding movement would prove cruelly irresponsive to both women and children's experiences of sexual and physical abuse. Second, this kind of discipline, when combined with other authoritatarian theological systems, could often provoke disastrous results for the mentally ill. Such would be the case at Sovereign Grace Ministries, an organization that united Shepherding doctrine with biblical counseling.

Shepherding officially folded around 1986, though the handwriting was on the wall for the movement long before then (Synan 354). However, Shepherding doctrine clearly helped provide the emotional context for the acceptance of the New Apostolic Reformation and the subsequent Charismatic acceptance of territorial practices of deliverance (such as spiritual mapping). Within the NAR, prominent leaders "accepted" the role of apostle within their communities (Holvast 38–39), oftentimes gaining immense spiritual power over their disciples. This apostolic role allowed men like C. Peter Wagner, Bill Hamon, and Mike Bickle to turn previously marginal Latter Rain doctrines into the centerpiece of 21st-century Charismatic identity. Because earlier Charismatic leaders, particularly popular deliverance theorists like Don Basham and Derek Prince, had promoted authoritarian church structures, the Charismatic church largely fell into line in accepting this new form of authoritarianism. In practical terms, this would pave the way for the globalization of deliverance practice.

Deliverance's rise to prominence in the late 1960s and 1970s was also due to a number of unforeseeable cultural circumstances. Foremost of these, as Michael Cuneo points out, was the phenomenal success of William Peter Blatty's novel *The Exorcist* (1971) and its subsequent film version. The publication of Malachi Martin's "demon-busting pulp classic," *Hostage to the Devil* (1976), also encouraged the American trend to dwell on the demonic (Cuneo 12–13). Though both works were largely addressed to Catholics, they influenced a much wider audience, as well as predisposing American culture to again dwell on the darker side of spiritual experience.

Blatty and Martin's works were paralleled by a number of other films during this period that explored similar themes, most notably *Rosemary's Baby* (1968), *The Devils* (1971), *The Wicker Man* (1973), and *The Omen* (1976). Though none of the filmmakers who made these works (all of which are arguably cinematic masterpieces) can be categorized as unskeptical, their works all were focused on the impending destruction of Christianity and the triumph of non–Christian, usually neo-pagan or Satanic, belief systems. As evangelical Christianity was at this time beset by the twin "threats" of a reinvigorated American left and a growing trend towards adoption of non–Western religious systems, the threat of a Satanic overthrow of Christian belief was taken quite seriously by many evangelical Christians, particularly in the deliverance movement. As a result, socially marginal groups, be they new religious movements (NRM), rock musicians, or role-playing game enthusiasts, often ended up being the victims of persecution on the part of deliverance supporters. The mentally ill, sometimes cast as members or allies of these groups, or at least as being influenced by them, often bore the brunt of such social stereotyping, as did the persecuted communities themselves.

Much of the early deliverance material was passed around through the "conference circuit" of Don Basham, Derek Prince, and Catholic deliverance supporter Francis MacNutt (Cuneo 206). By the seventies, a flurry of books appeared on the subject. As Michael Cuneo correctly writes, "For the most part they were tedious, slipshod, deadeningly repetitive, a patchwork of shopworn anecdote, wooden testimonial, and play-as-it-goes theology. With very few exceptions, to have read one is to have read them all" (Cuneo 107). Don

Basham's *Deliver Us from Evil* (1972) and *Can a Christian Have a Demon?* (1971) were among the most erudite, but perhaps more influential on the popular consciousness was the Hammonds' *Pigs in the Parlor* (see Cuneo 107). As Michael Cuneo points out, the Hammonds tried to create an "intoxicating new world, a thoroughly desecularized and reenchanted world.... The Hammonds (and many charismatics with them) were committed to a project of historical reversal, trying to bring demons and spirits back into the equation after science and technology had spent centuries knocking them out" (Cuneo 109). Faced with what they saw as an increasingly ungodly secular culture, Pentecostals and Charismatics reacted by assigning to that culture the values of the diabolic. Social and psychological ills no longer needed to be explained in structural, socioeconomic, or even theological terms. Now everything could be blamed on demons. And as Cuneo points out, mental illness was one of the areas often associated with demonism (Cuneo 109). James Collins' reading of *Pigs in the Parlor* is even more blunt in assessing the danger the Hammonds' theology poses to the mentally ill: "There are very serious consequences to attributing the cause of such a mental illness [schizophrenia] to the work of demons. The Hammonds effectively imply that ... there is no role for psychiatry—instead the treatment of mental/emotional disorders appears to primarily (if not exclusively) require deliverance ministry" (Collins 69). What made *Pigs in the Parlor*'s position on deliverance (and by extension, mental health) so dangerous was that by taking such an extreme position, and gaining such popularity and sales by doing so, it forced other deliverance ministers and promoters to adopt even more radical theological positions in order to promote themselves (Collins 69). The faddism in enthusiastic religion that was noted by both R.A. Knox and Collins thus led to an ever increasing number of mental health difficulties (and, for that matter, "problems" that were not problems at all, like homosexuality) being attributed to demons (see Collins 2 on faddism). Worse, the Hammonds promoted an idea of demonic stigma, arguing that Christians did not come forward for deliverance only because they felt a "stigma attached to having demons" (Hammond and Hammond 22). Translated into a mental health context, such an idea had the potential to influence people away from submitting to professional mental health treatment and towards accepting a different type of stigma: instead of having a mental health condition, the mentally ill were labeled as "demonized."

Even at this point, however, deliverance of the mentally ill, LGBT people and abuse victims might have faded away were it not for one of the most well-known moral panics in American history: the Satanic panic, also known as the Satanic Ritual Abuse (SRA) scare. The first public charge of satanic ritual abuse occurred in *Michelle Remembers* (1980), a book "co-authored by

Michelle Smith and her psychiatrist, Dr. Lawrence Pazder" (Nathan and Snedeker 44–45). Debbie Nathan and Michael Snedeker note with typical—and justified—journalistic skepticism that "the book [*Michelle Remembers*] is filled with graphic description of little Michelle being tortured in houses, mausoleums, and cemeteries, being raped and sodomized with candles, being forced to defecate on a Bible and crucifix, witnessing babies and adults butchered, spending hours naked in a snake-filled cage, and having a devil's tail and horns surgically attached to her" (Nathan and Snedeker 44–45). There were numerous problems with Smith's testimony, however. For instance, Smith claimed to have been involved in a fatal traffic accident sometime around 1954 or 1955, yet there "are no newspaper accounts ... of any fatal traffic accidents resembling the one in the book—and the local newspapers from the time gave detailed coverage to even the most minor mishaps" (Nathan and Snedeker 45). Michael Cuneo is even more blunt in his assessment of *Michelle Remembers,* saying, "Read this tale of woe now and almost nothing rings true; it makes *Hostage to the Devil* [a book known for its extreme dubiousness] look like a textbook study in fact-based reporting. Never mind the cameo appearance of Satan or the two-decade-long memory blackout. All of this abuse apparently took place without leaving any significant physical traces, without Michelle's sisters having the slightest hint of it, and without Michelle herself having to miss any time at school" (Cuneo 204).

But the ridiculous charges made by Smith and Pazder did not die. Phobia about the satanic, coupled with a growing concern about child abuse, morphed in the mid-eighties into charges of large-scale ritualistic abuse. The first major charges were made during the McMartin scandal, which started off as a typical (and false) charge of mass ritual abuse, but later morphed into a major satanic conspiracy theory, thanks in large part to the efforts of Lawrence Pazder, who theorized that "the children had been molested as part of an international satanic cult conspiracy" (Nathan and Snedeker 89–92).

Nathan and Snedeker point out that the exact web of ritual abuse theorizing was a complex one which involved "social workers, therapists, physicians, victimology researchers, police, criminal prosecutors, fundamentalist Christians, ambitious politicians, anti-pornography activists, feminists, and the media" (Snedeker and Nathan 5). A "veritable industry" surrounded the attempts to verify ritual abuse. Proof was obtained through ambiguous child behaviors and "verbal disclosures" from children that have subsequently been labeled "as dangerously coercive and suggestive" (5). Prosecutors "exploited popular anxieties about sex to perform character assassinations on defendants" (5). Feminists, in the meantime, "espoused the existence of Satanist sex conspiracies characterized their belief as a political attempt to give children a civic voice, analogous to the effort to gain one for women" (6). A particularly influential text for healing from child abuse, *The Courage to Heal* (1988),[8] promoted the idea of repressed childhood memories, along with Satanic (later sadistic) ritual abuse (Rothe 117–118).[9] Anne Rothe points out, with some acerbity, that *The Courage to Heal* provides a checklist with no less than some 78 phenomena which can be signs of abuse, including "the need to be perfect, a lack of a sense of one's interests, trouble expressing feelings, feeling alienated, or lonely, the inability to say 'no,' and the over protectiveness of one's children" (Rothe 118). Coming at abuse from such a wide-ranging ideological perspective, it became possible for authors Laura Davis and Ellen Bass to find abuse anywhere (who would not fit these criteria?).

And in the eighties, being an abuse victim became, as both Anne Rothe and Cuneo point out, trendy. Michael Cuneo states "there were also undeniable benefits to 'coming out' as a ritual abuse survivor. Within evangelical circles especially, survivors were lavished with attention and prestige. They were invited to tell their stories at conferences, where they were often treated as martyr-saint figures.... For some people, arguably, survivorship may have been a role well worth cultivating" (Cuneo 207). And it is here that SRA's fatal combination with mental health diagnoses becomes readily apparent in a number of revealing ways. First, any cultural movement associated with SRA charges, or with Satanism itself, became immediately suspect. In the eighties and up until today, a fairly wide swath of movements therefore was held under suspicion. For instance a wide variety of seemingly innocent children's programs—*The Smurfs, He Man*, the *Star Wars* movies, etc.—now came to be seen as purveyors of New Age witchcraft.[10] In an even odder circumstance, role-playing game enthusiasts also were routinely persecuted in this era, as RPGs were seen as leading children into occultism (Waldron).

The end result of this movement against imaginative products of the culture industry was twofold. First, the derision many evangelicals felt towards toys and RPGs led to a more general fear of the imagination. As a result, those particular elements of evangelicalism with a strong anti-intellectual tradition—particularly Pentecostalism—became intensely xenophobic towards any cultural product outside of the mainstream, whether it was science fiction, Harry Potter novels, or sometimes even Christian fiction, like the novels of C.S. Lewis. The intellectual dissonance this created for thinking evangelicals over the next several decades, while not necessarily directly contributing to every case of mental illness, certainly could not have helped. Worse, attraction to these media forms, or use of them, was often seen as evidence for demonization. *Restoring the Foundations* (2001), for instance, classifies playing *Dungeons and Dragons* as an "Open Door" to demonization, one that might very readily require deliverance (Klystra and Klystra 400). Neil Anderson is equally convinced that *D & D* is a particularly dangerous sin in need of renouncing, in his more gentle evangelical deliverance system (Anderson, *Bondage Breaker*, 203). Since often, like LGBT people, the mentally ill in evangelical communities are seen as creative and intelligent, it would not be surprising if a disproportionate amount of the persecution of budding evangelical intellectuals and gamers fell on the mentally ill.

However, the effects of SRA charges were more damning than this. These charges had wide-ranging effects on sexual abuse victims (often extending well beyond the evangelical community). First of all, the charges of sexual abuse made by the SRA recovery movement as Anne Rothe points out about the recovery movement in general, may have been embraced by women because it was the "dominant narrative among the few culturally available paradigms to express female suffering" (Rothe 118). As a result, ritual abuse survivors may have honestly been dealing with real mental health or even abuse issues, but those issues may have been masked under the banner of ritualistic abuse, with its never-ending promise of failure, triumph, and recovery (see Rothe 55–56).

In the process of such recovery, however, there was a danger of therapists imposing a mental illness on their patients rather than helping them heal from such illnesses. As Michael Cuneo points out, SRA was most likely a product, "at least in part, of the therapeutic process itself" (Cuneo 206), particularly since much of the therapy used in the SRA recovery movement involved untested or dangerous techniques like "subtle cuing, hypnotic suggestion, and other therapeutic equivalents of leading the witness'" (Cuneo 206). Therefore treatment for SRA seemed in the final analysis to largely merely reproduce more SRA, a cyclical process that cast doubt on the process as far back as the early 1990s and which today makes the diagnosis of SRA largely verboten outside of a small subset of the Charismatic community.

But perhaps the most damaging and dangerous aspect of the Satanic ritual abuse scare was how it interacted with the treatment of schizophrenics. The Hammonds' "classic," *Pigs in the Parlor*, was largely responsible for this. As mentioned before, within that text, Ida Hammond has a personal revelation that schizophrenia is the result of "split personality," a diagnostic criterion that, as James Collins points out, is fundamentally wrong (Collins 68; Hammond and Hammond 123–133). James Collins reflects that the "lengthy process of deliverance ministry for schizophrenics advocated by the Hammonds appears to be almost a prototype for the approach adopted a few years later by some Christian psychiatrists to treat Multiple Personality Disorder" (Collins 68). Collins also apparently suspects that this process could have occurred in reverse—in other words, schizophrenics being misdiagnosed as having MPD (today known as dissociative identity disorder) (Collins 68). Given the widespread popularity of *Pigs in the Parlor* among Charismatics during the seventies and eighties—indeed, a popularity that extends to this day—it seems all too likely that this kind of misdiagnosis was frequent, if not necessarily habitual, among Charismatic deliverance practitioners treating schizophrenics.

By 2000, SRA was falling out of favor as a diagnostic tool, but one could still find it being talked about in Neil Anderson's *The Bondage Breaker* (2000) (Anderson 207–209) and even (shockingly) in the pseudo–DSM of truly professional Christian psychologists (not simply counselors), the *Baker Encyclopedia of Psychology and Counseling* (1999) (Hanson, "Satanic Ritual Abuse," 1053–1054), which, to Christian psychologists' everlasting shame, gave credence to a fair number of these claims (Hanson 1053). With the inability to view evidence skeptically—or simply critically—both mainstream deliverance supporters and many Christian psychologists and counselors were, as the new millennium dawned, increasingly lumping several disparate diagnostic criteria into one, provoking potentially disastrous results. But there would be one more ingredient needed to ignite the explosion. That ingredient would be the New Apostolic Reformation. When this movement combined its teachings with those of Latter Rain, the tragic results would spread literally worldwide, affecting everyone from anorexics in Australia to "witch children" in West Africa.

In the early 1980s, a syncretic group that fused Charismatic and evangelical theology started what came to be known as the "Third Wave" of Pentecostalism. Perhaps the most characteristic theological idea of the Third Wave was its emphasis on disempowering "'strategic level' territorial spirits that hold sway over social groups or the geographical locations with which they are identified" (Collins 103). This led to the practice of "Strategic Level Spiritual Warfare" (SLSW), which became wildly popular in part due to the success of Frank Peretti's fictional *Darkness* series (1986, 1988) (Collins 103).

This belief was originally formulated in John Wimber's course "Signs, Wonders and Church Growth," which he taught alongside C. Peter Wagner and Charles Kraft between 1982 and 1985. Wimber's course argued that mainstream evangelicals, as well as Pentecostals and Charismatics, must begin "regularly healing the sick and casting out demons" (Cuneo 202). Eventually faculty opposition to the course shut it down (Cuneo 202), but by that point John Wimber had started the Vineyard Christian Fellowship (VCF), a quickly growing evangelical movement that soon spread Charismatic teaching worldwide through its influence on the Toronto Blessing (Poloma, "Toronto Blessing," 1149–1152). But more significant even than Wimber's initial efforts was his influence on C. Peter Wagner. Wagner was the most influential proponent of the practice of spiritual mapping, a direct outgrowth of the belief in strategic level spiritual warfare. In spiritual mapping,

> the new paradigm entailed that missionaries had to "identify" and "bind territorial spirits" and "unleash" divine power. Evangelism was to be preceded by "prayer walks," and prayer was considered best if done geographically "on-site," within a "target area." Prayer became defined as the identification of and confrontation with demons. The new "technique" was meant to enhance new church planting projects in areas hitherto without Christian churches [Holvast xiii].

This new form of Charismatic practice was no longer diagnosing simply individuals as demonized; now demonization extended to whole groups of people. While in theory such demonization was spread to all parts of the world, in practice the "per-capita" rate of demonization was different from culture to culture (see C. Peter Wagner, "How Deliverance Sustains Revival," 88). Thailand, for instance, was more demon-inhabited than the United States; apparently demons also tended to congregate in urban areas and preferred New Orleans over Cedar Rapids, Iowa (C. Peter Wagner, "How Deliverance Sustains," 88). What this led to in practice was an increasing interconnection between the global and local within Charismatic ministry. Organizations like Mercy Ministries (which mainly treats women with eating disorders as well as sex abuse victims), for instance, would promote themselves in countries like Uganda and Australia, despite the fact that they were ostensibly engaged in "ground level spiritual warfare" (that is, individual, rather than territorial, deliverance) ("Unforgettable Message of Hope"). Similarly, organizations like Exodus Cry, a ministry ostensibly to abolish sex trafficking overseas (and therefore more engaged in SLSW deliverance practices) but which actively promoted the "deliverance" of prostitutes from demons, would do much of their marketing to individual teens and young adults within the United States (Nolot).[11]

The spiritual mapping movement would eventually evolve into the New Apostolic Reformation, which, as we have seen, was influenced by Franklin Hall's now-distant descendants. Holvast sees the spiritual mapping movement as having crested in the early 2000s, though that is not the same thing as to say it faded away; instead it morphed into the various subsets of influence that one sees today (Holvast 148), with the New Apostolic Reformation at this point clearly being the largest such element. By 2013, the NAR had largely taken over the majority of the Charismatic movement while promoting increasingly bizarre forms of spirituality. In practical terms what this meant was that, because deliverance was now seen as one of the primary tools of SLSW, its reach had become global, affecting not just vulnerably physically and mentally ill Americans but also people from practically every other nationality. For instance, Mercy Ministries' close ally, Lou Engle, a prominent NAR supporter and a devotee of the writings of Franklin Hall, would use his Call ministry to promote death penalty legislation for gay people in Uganda (Kron), at a time roughly coinciding with Mercy Ministries' trip to that country to see Gary Skinner, a pastor of somewhat shady allegiances within Uganda ("Unforgettable Message of Hope"). Deliverance practice had come full circle; the personal was now political, the political now personal.

A Brief Note on Evangelical and Fundamentalist Deliverance

Evangelical and fundamentalist deliverance ministries have had less of an influence on the treatment of the mentally ill than Charismatic practices have, so they will only briefly be touched on here. As early as 1912, Evan Roberts and Jessie Penn-Lewis were promoting a form of evangelical deliverance ministry. Ironically, this form of deliverance was predicated on the philosophical presupposition that many of the "spiritual gifts" being exhibited by the early Pentecostal and Holiness movements were "either the product of, or leave believers open to, demonic deception" (Collins 118). However, true evangelical and fundamentalist deliverance did not really arise till mid-century, when it was "pioneered by Kurt Koch and Merrill Unger (largely it seems as a result of the influence of overseas missionaries) and came of age in the seventies parallel to the Charismatic form of the same ministry" (Collins 120).

Koch was an extremely well-known figure among evangelical supporters of deliverance in the early 1970s and 1980s. Like most evangelicals,[12] Koch was more erudite in his support of deliverance than were most of his contemporaries in the Charismatic movement (barring Prince). Koch's *Christian Counseling and Occultism* (1972) makes a brave though foolhardy attempt to justify evangelical deliverance practices through the lens of contemporary science (Koch et al.). Koch, also unlike many Charismatic deliverance ministers, was careful to distinguish between those labeled mentally ill and those "suffering demonic subjection" (Collins 128), though ultimately he encountered the same diagnostic problems that plagued Charismatic and Pentecostal practitioners of deliverance (Collins 127–128).

In America, the initial centers of evangelical and fundamentalist deliverance were Moody Bible Institute (MBI) and Dallas Theological Seminary (DTS). The three most significant advocates of deliverance among evangelicals and fundamentalists were Merill Unger, Martin Bubeck, and Fred Dickason.

Unger was perhaps the most interesting of the three, as his view of deliverance was very optimistic (Collins 130–131) and he argued that demons, contrary to beliefs of most other deliverance theologies, were not "degraded and inveterate liars" (Collins 133) but "nice, refined, religious and 'good' in a self-righteous sense" (Unger 116; Collins 133). Fred Dickason, as James Collins points out, is one of the most ethical writers on deliverance, dealing with the "biblical data conscientiously" (Collins 135). Dickason fully acknowledges opposing viewpoints to his pro-demonization position. Indeed, nearly half of his *Demon Possession and the Christian* (1987) is devoted to exploring those viewpoints (Dickason et al. but particularly 81–100 and 129–149). Bubeck is, in this author's opinion, less theologically sophisticated than Dickason but more influential on later deliverance practice because of an idea he promoted called "doctrinal prayer" that influenced Neil Anderson, who was a primary influence on Mercy Ministries founder Nancy Alcorn's thinking (see Collins 133–134, which traces Bubeck's influence on Anderson). Also influential in evangelical circles for promoting supernaturalistic explanations of the demonic, complete with elaborate conspiracy theories, was Mike Warnke, whose vision of Satanic cults lurking in the shadows contributed greatly to evangelical cultural paranoia in the seventies and early eighties (Ellis 185–192).[13]

Late in the twentieth century, two other significant voices were added to the deliverance movement. Ed Murphy's *Handbook for Spiritual Warfare* (1992) promoted the claim of Third Wave Charismatics (a movement from which the NAR is largely descended) that animist cultures have a better understanding of the spirit world than first worlders. For Murphy "there is no natural-versus-supernatural dichotomy. The supernatural directly involves the natural" (Murphy 3–4). Murphy therefore adopts the three-tier system of interpreting the spiritual world advocated by Bryant Myers. In the Western worldview, the "spiritual and real worlds do not touch" (Murphy 5). Myers contended that in the actual world there was also a middle level of reality, in which there were "witch doctors, shamans, curses, idols, household gods, and the evil eye" (Murphy 6).

This idea would be adopted by Neil Anderson in *The Bondage Breaker* as a justification for his rejection of Western rationalism (Anderson, *Bondage Breaker,* 30–31; see also Collins 192). Anderson is notable for focusing more on sin as the root cause of suffering than the actual demons associated with demonization, and therefore tends to focus more on repentance than deliverance (Collins 194). Anderson promotes a distinctly theistic view of mental illness. He claims that the first demonically plagued Christian I counseled was diagnosed paranoid schiz-ophrenic by medical doctors.... We should not be surprised when secular psycholo-gists limited to a natural worldview attempt to offer natural explanations for mental problems. Their worldview does not include God or the god of the world.... Research based on the scientific method of investigation of human spiritual problems is not wrong; it's just incomplete. It ignores the influence of the spiritual world, because neither God nor the devil submit to our methods of investigation [Anderson 21].

Anderson believed that such thinking created a "false dichotomy" between "the human soul and spirit.... There is no inner conflict which is not psycho-logical, because there is never a time when your mind, emotions, and will are not involved. Similarly there is no problem which is not spiritual" (Anderson 21). In contrast to Koch—whose theology tends to carefully delineate between the demonized individual and the mentally ill patient (see Collins 128, who also points out that Koch is not always consistent in this regard)—Anderson's theology indicates that the demonic and the psychological interpenetrate each other. Those who are mentally ill therefore are not necessarily any worse than "neuronormatives," as often seems to implicitly be the case in biblical coun-seling material[14]; however, because Anderson's theological paradigm assumes that all inner conflict is spiritual, there is a tendency in his theology to associate mental illness with sin or Satan's mental battle with us. For instance, he argues that "hearing voices," a phenomenon the popular mind commonly associates with schizophrenia (West, "hallucination"; Barlow and Durand 409), may in fact be due to the influence of Satan (Anderson, *Bondage Breaker*, 65). And because God and the devil are not amenable to scientific investigation, ulti-mately diagnosis tends to presume the potential deliverance participant is demonized, regardless of the proof for or against that assertion.

Anderson, along with the various members of the Third Wave charismatic Deliverance Ministry, represents some of the more relatively current trends in Charismatic and evangelical and fundamentalist deliverance ministry. The rest of this chapter will be devoted to exploring the fundamentals of deliver-ance ministry in the following areas: Its theory of the body; its vision of gender; its relationship to the Enlightenment and to the scientific method it promoted; its relationship to governmental systems; and its theory of psychology, par-ticularly in relationship to demonic personality.

Theological Distinctives of Evangelical and Charismatic Deliverance

The deliverance movement, being drawn from a wide range of charis-matic, neo-evangelical, and occasionally even fundamentalist church groups, is not always reducible to any one set of theological ideals. However, there are, broadly speaking, certain distinctive beliefs that seem to unite the movement as a whole. Most of the ideals pronounced by the movement are broadly compliant with the overall worldview of the evangelical movement, but some more specific ideas about the demonic are mainly confined to the deliverance movement. The following section is primarily garnered from the major deliverance manuals this author has perused for the purpose of this study, dating from the late 1960s to the present.

State and Politics

Derek Prince, the nominal founding father of modern deliverance, promotes one of the more consistent analogies that the deliverance movement uses to support its position: that of an oppressed people facing off against a totalitarian state. Prince writes that, "first, some people are under demonic oppression who do not know how to get free and are enduring the various degrees of torment that demons inflict. In some cases, the mental, emotional and physical torment is as severe as that of people imprisoned and tortured in totalitarian prison camps or gulags" (Prince 11–12). For Prince, the place of the believing Christian versus the demonic is a precarious one. The demonic has overwhelming power in the spiritual world, and without God's protection, the Christian will quickly end up being the tramped-on face that Obrien in George Orwell's *1984* (1948) so savagely critiques. Prince, by valorizing tramped-upon Christians, raises them to an equal level with the victims of Stalinist (and perhaps Nazi) aggression. The root cause of both of these oppressive systems, for deliverance supporters, is the same: the Satanic. Prince, of course, should be commended for his condemnation of the Soviet penal system, were it not for the fact that this passage reads more like a queasy equating of the suffering of victims of the Cold War with the demonically delivered. In short, deliverance here becomes a method of promoting a conservative demonology in keeping with Western foreign policy objectives.

Even more direct in his assessment of the totalitarian nature of demons is deliverance theorist Don Dickerman, who writes as follows:

> It has been my experience that the oppressor never voluntarily releases the oppressed! ... That is true in the physical realm and in the spiritual. If you want freedom, then you have to make an effort. Often, you must demand it.... Most believers know that they suffer from the oppressing hand of Satan through his demon powers, but they choose to call it something else. "It's just the way I am." "It's just the way life is" [Dickerman 38].

For Dickerman, Christians are spiritual revolutionaries, the founding fathers of a heavenly state; only here the state is a divine monarchy reinstated to its proper glory, not an actual democracy. Freedom comes through servitude to divinity, oppression ironically comes from rebelling against the rebellion. Satan, who from a theo-political standpoint would seem to be the more truly radical political party, is transmuted into a force of oppression. God, by contrast, a being that even by a charitable reading of the Bible is something of a despot, is valorized into the ultimate figure of "freedom," the promoter of what some radical evangelical organizations have called a "reverse rebellion" ("Battlecry Music Video") for godliness. Satan, as a dictator, seeks to breed political apathy into Christians. Therefore the lesson Christians must learn from previous rebellions is to rebel against Satan and his despotically demonic system. Human beings therefore, like the founding fathers in the political realm, must take action in the spiritual realm to combat Satanic totalitarianism. Thus, exorcism becomes a means of relieving spiritual apathy on the part of Christians and urging them towards greater spiritual action versus oppressive theological and political systems.

There are obvious potential politically radical interpretations of seeing the demonic as a totalitarian system, since such an interpretation of the demonic could also lead one to see totalitarian systems in the "physical" realm (material world) as demonic, and therefore worthy of destruction. However, this is an interpretation that Christian Right thinkers seem at pains to put down. In perhaps the longest statement on politics in any deliverance manual, Timothy Warner takes Liberation theologians to task for promoting a socialistic antitotalitarian gospel:

> They [liberation theologians] say that the social and political structures are demonic, but then they propose that the way to bring them down is with social, political, and even military action. If these structures are really demonic, they will be brought down by spiritual weapons, not by the weapons of the world. Some structures do in fact need changing, but good structures do not make bad people good, though good people can redeem even bad structures. The most basic consideration, then, is not in changing the structures, but in bringing people into touch with the power which enables them to rise above any set of circumstances. The Church in Communist China is a prime example of this. Without overthrowing an oppressive political system, one of the greatest revival movements in history has taken place; a powerful Church exists in spite of the system.... This is not to say that we shouldn't work for the establishment of justice. It is to say that demonic forces, whether those in a system ... like the government of Communist China or those that attack us personally, must be overcome with the power that comes from God, not the weapons of the flesh or of the world [Tim Warner, *Spiritual Warfare*, 52].

Warner's real concern here, of course, is painfully transparent. As a World Missions specialist (Warner back cover), he does not want the Latin

American or African canaille getting the wrong idea. Rebellion, for Warner, is solely a spiritualized state. The rebel is only the individual willing to rise up for the kingdom of God when the kingdom of God is threatened by spiritual, and not physical, oppression. The typical evangelical emphasis on personal, rather than structural or superstructural, forces is evident here (Smith and Emerson 104). Real political change, according to Warner, cannot happen through force of arms or intimidation of existing governmental systems, but instead must come from changed hearts and minds. If totalitarianism is demonic, it can only be resisted with spiritual weapons. Moreover, changing the structure of government, according to Warner, will not truly heal a governmental system if the people within that system have not learned to be "good." Warner's individualistic bias therefore leads him to reject liberation theology's more communalist-oriented theology and political philosophy.

The right to work for justice, the right to even define what justice is, becomes for Warner a condescendingly race-based and gender-based ideal. Warner, a white male ("Meet Timothy Warner"), dictates to liberation theologians from Latin America and Africa what kind of theology is and is not a proper exercise in the promotion of social justice. By truncating the call for social justice from the call for salvation, Warner creates a false dichotomy that evangelical leaders have long exploited for their own political ends. In this reading of contemporary culture, the "social gospel" and the attendant sins of liberalism, Marxism, and the like that go along with it are responsible for the current sad state of the world. Only by rejecting political solutions to the world's problems and embracing theological ones can the church redeem the world.

The problem here, of course, is that evangelicals have never been consistent about which national problems are spiritual and which are political. There has been a marked tendency among evangelicals of all stripes to promote political solutions when it suits their own personal theological agenda, and to promote theological solutions when it does not. Jerry Falwell's condemnation of civil disobedience during the civil rights riots of the 1960s, for instance, was followed by a convenient about-face when he decided to support Operation Rescue and similar antiabortion groups in the 1980s (Martin 57–58, 322). Similarly, while men like Warner urge liberation theologians to cool their heels overseas, they often simultaneously promote a conservative theological agenda both at home and abroad. The end result is that evangelical and Charismatic theologians end up offering theological stones to the Third World instead of the real bread that it needs.

ENLIGHTENMENT, SCIENCE, PSYCHOLOGY AND
DELIVERANCE SYSTEM THEORY

Perhaps the most important philosophical point the deliverance movement has sought to make is that it is profoundly anti–Enlightenment and
"anti-humanist." This point is particularly true of evangelical writers within
the wider movement. Ed Murphy writes, "In the wake of the eighteenth-
century rise of rationalism known as the Enlightenment, Western theology
lost an intuitive, historic understanding of the spirit world" (Murphy xii). Similarly, Neil Anderson (an important influence on Mercy Ministries) has contended that

> in stark contrast to Western rationalism and naturalism, other inhabitants of the
> world have a different view of reality. The reality of the spiritual world is part of
> their culture and worldview.... In many Third World nations religious practice or
> superstition has more practical relevance in daily life than science does.... It is easy
> for those who are educated in the West to dismiss Eastern worldviews as inferior on
> the basis of our advanced technology and economic success. But why then do we
> have the highest crime rate of any industrial nation and the greatest distribution of
> pornographic filth? Neither worldview reflects biblical reality [Anderson, *Bondage
> Breaker* 31].

For both Murphy and Anderson, Western theology has essentially hit a
dead-end. The promises of science and technology have left Western man spiritually empty, unable to encounter the "realities" of the spiritual world that
the Third World deals with on a daily basis. On the other hand, the Third
World's problem is that it is too attuned to the spiritual forces at work in the
world. If the West is despiritualized, the East is overly spiritualized. Where
the West needs soul, the East needs the biblical message that is the primary
tool by which the West has successfully defeated its own demonic realm. But
the East and Africa must defeat the oppressive Satanic system confronting
them without sacrificing their inherent indigenous connection to the spiritual.
The condescension here, is of course, evident. While Western man has
"thought" and "science," Asians and Africans have "spirit" and "soul." Neither
Anderson nor Murphy realize that by African and Eastern standards, the West
may look equally superstitious, with its tales of cannibalistic Christians sym-
bolically eating their deity every Sunday. Superstition, after all, is a relative
concept, often in the eye of the beholder.

To be fair, however, Anderson and Murphy are largely sympathetic to
Eastern and African worldviews, insofar as they confirm the deliverance movement's narrative of dualistic spiritual warfare; it is their precise theological
content, not their spiritualist orientation that concerns the two men. Anderson
and Murphy, operating from a Western evangelical subject position that has

long been seen as socially and economically inferior to that of Western elites, long for a return to a semi-mythic time when religious practice was at the center of American life. Scientific naturalism—by promoting the idea that human beings are no more than biological machines—strips the world of the magic, the previously mentioned "enchantment" that the deliverance movement sees.

What's worse, as far as Murphy at least is concerned, is that without such a magical worldview, not only is life purposeless, it is morally rudderless as well. The Enlightenment, he feels,

> rejected God and all normative ethics based on divine revelation. Individualism, human progress based on reason and not revelation, and total commitment to naturalistic science undermined religious and, particularly, Christian faith. All objective foundation for morality was removed. Whatever human beings enjoyed and found meaningful to their life was acceptable, if it did not directly hurt other people [Murphy 128].

The trade-off for technological progress in the West has been too steep in Murphy's estimation. Because Enlightenment man rejected God and normative ethics, cultural egoism and self-centeredness came to dominate Western culture. Without the barriers of a Christian moral code, "objective" morality was rejected for a more subjective cultural experience in which a liberated sexual ethic flourished (Murphy 128). Murphy feels the result of this theological training and indoctrination is that sexuality has become unrestrained except for the constraints of the "consent of the persons involved and precautions against disease and unwanted pregnancy" (Murphy 128). With progress guiding human beings, not revelation, humanity left itself open to the new "triplets of naturalism, humanism, and materialism" that promoted atheism (Murphy 128). The church that "was supposed to change the world, is becoming changed by the world" (Murphy 128). The Enlightenment's pro-science worldview changed the evangelical church from a dominant cultural force to a peripheral one, largely by altering the cultural *volksgeist* towards a more hedonistic, pleasure-oriented worldview.

Of American deliverance theorists, Neil Anderson probably has the most nuanced vision of science. Anderson gives the following warning:

> The scientific method of investigation by definition leaves out the reality of the spiritual world. God does not submit to our methods of verification. We cannot scientifically prove the existence of God to the satisfaction of the skeptic.... Rest assured that the god of this world is not going to cooperate with our research methods. He is the prince of darkness and the father of lies. He operates under the cloak of deception and will not voluntarily reveal himself for our benefit [Anderson, *Discipleship Counseling*, 28].

Anderson here expresses an understandable distrust of deliverance systems like Kurt Koch's that predicate themselves on scientific testing (see Koch 21–25 in *Christian Counseling and Occultism*). Though Koch's system should be credited for its valiant if futile attempt at scientific respectability, Anderson's point is still a salient one. Since science, by definition, only studies the physical, it is unlikely that it will find any proof of the metaphysical that cannot be discounted as mere ephemeral sense phenomena. Anderson draws from this conclusion a subsequent conclusion that since secular research excludes "the reality of the spiritual world and special revelation" and puts too much faith in the social sciences as "precise and therefore authoritative" explanatory systems, it is not the final arbiter in explaining human psychological and behavioral patterns (28–30). Of course, a case can be—and often has been—made for Anderson's point here. The attempt to reduce human beings to simple automatons without any free will or social responsibility is a serious ethical issue that engages more than just deliverance ministers. Indeed, communities as diverse as the biblical counseling movement, the secular legal community, and artificial intelligence researchers all worry about the inability to create an exact science of the human mind—to, in other words, turn psychology from a social science into a physical science. Such a physical science may indeed prove to be out of our reach.

But the alternative that Anderson offers us looks even worse. In replacement of a system that is at least predicated on scientific proof and verification, Anderson offers up a counseling system based on metaphysical propositions that can be neither proven nor disproven, a system that explains human psychology through the lens of diabolic agency and thus makes human beings little more than demonic pawns. The consequence of such a system is that one is ultimately never able to trust one's own senses. How does one know, in embracing secularism, or simply psychology, that one is not listening to a demon of fear or skepticism? For many of the more extreme members of the deliverance movement, as we will see, this is a very real question.

There is no real, formal system codifying deliverance ministers' beliefs concerning health care delivery itself; in any case, deliverance is practiced by such a wide range of differing evangelical (and even non-evangelical) faith traditions that it is unlikely one would come to a definitive take on this matter. But one can get an idea of the models preferred by looking at more ideologically defined subsets of the Charismatic population, particularly the New Apostolic Reformation. In much of the scholarship and books preferred by the NAR, there is a distinctive stance against Enlightenment-derived models of health practice. Much of the NAR's vision for healing is, for instance, if not based on the scholarship of Candy Gunther Brown, at least influenced by it (see, for instance, "Christian Healing Certification"). Brown is sufficiently in favor with the NAR that her books *Global Pentecostal and Charismatic Healing* (2011) and *Testing Prayer* (2012) are for sale through the Global Awakening Bookstore (an important site for NAR books), which would be an unusual honor for someone whose scholarship the NAR did not trust implicitly ("Global Awakening Online Bookstore").

For Brown and, to a lesser extent, for some Reformed scholars such as David Powlison (see Powlison, *The Biblical Counseling Movement*, 25), a crucial turning point in how human beings view science occurred with the publication of Thomas Kuhn's *The Structure of Scientific Revolutions* (1962). As Brown relates, Kuhn's work "argues that the major 'paradigm' shifts in science are 'not the sort of battle that can be resolved by proofs.'" This is because researchers "invested in the current paradigm great 'novelty' in scientific research with 'resistance' since the new paradigm threatens to invalidate much of the research conducted under the old paradigm" (Brown, *Testing Prayer*, 11). Because of this, Brown's work tends to concur with medical anthropologists like Elliot Mishler and Robert Hahn and sociologists Meredith McGuire and Debra Kantor in seeing "biomedical" medicine as *a* model of reality, but not necessarily *the* model of reality (Brown, *Testing Prayer*, 11–12).

This assumption about reality, not in and of itself necessarily without merit, leads Brown (and more so those Charismatics who follow her line of reasoning) to make profound and far-reaching conclusions about how healthcare is distributed and implemented. For Brown, the

> pattern that emerges in the following chapters [of *Testing Prayer*] is that individuals perceived themselves healed through prayer by members of their social networks. Those who experience healing attribute their recoveries to divine love and prayer and consequently feel motivated to express love for God and other people in part by praying for others' healing. The effects of even a single healing experience reverberate across global networks, as recipients of healing turn their attention to others and become partners and leaders of efforts to expand the reach of healing prayer [Brown, *Testing Prayer*, 14].

Deliverance practice for Brown is therefore a globalized practice, insofar as it seeks to take advantage of transnational networks to effect healing. Motivated by love, the practice, rightly or wrongly, is "self-perpetuating," since it encourages both leaders and followers in such movements to "experience love through their involvement in healing rituals" (Brown, *Testing Prayer*, 14). While Brown does admit that sometimes such healings can take advantage of the unfortunate (Brown, "Introduction," 6), her overall message, to Western readers in particular, is that to downplay or criticize such healing practices is a thinly veiled form of elitism which has "the unfortunate effect of increasing the suffering of those who have already suffered from illness, pain, and, in many instances, social and economic marginalization" (Brown, "Introduction," 6). Completely missing in Brown's analysis is the possibility that deliverance itself may not simply be in reaction to "illness," "pain" and "social and economic marginalization" but also a major contributor to it. Brown also seems tone-deaf to the possibility that many people, particularly LGBT individuals and the mentally ill, may actually be coerced into deliverance, a practice that does in fact happen fairly frequently (as Chapters 3 and 8 point out by looking into Mercy Ministries and ex-gay deliverance ministries, respectively).

Brown's ultimate conclusion about using deliverance practice therefore is that it may prove to be a delivery system for healing where other resources are lacking. As Brown posits it in her study of proximal intercessory prayer (which involves deliverance):

> Future study seems warranted to assess whether PIP may be a useful adjunct to standard medical care for certain patients with auditory and/or visual impairments, especially in contexts where access to conventional treatment is limited. The implications are potentially vast given World Health Organization estimates that 278 million people, 80 percent of whom live in developing countries, have moderate to profound hearing loss in both ears, and 314 million people are visually impaired, 87 percent of whom live in developing countries, and only a tiny fraction of these populations currently receive any treatment [Brown et al. "Study of the Therapeutic Effects of Proximal Intercessory Prayer"].

Brown, in other words, seems to suggest that in addition to putting money into traditional health care, we devote some of our resources into alternative practices such as healing prayer and deliverance. The problem is that it would be almost impossible to empirically prove whether these practices have any scientific validity or not. What "units," for instance, does one use in measuring prayer? How does one tell sham prayer from "real prayer"? Brown's study does not even get close to addressing these issues, instead suggesting that we have faith that deliverance will produce good results.

In the mental health world, studies like Brown's unfortunately can have enormous implications in how Charismatics perceive treatment. Neil Anderson, an evangelical who is well respected by the Charismatic community for his work in deliverance, complains that traditional managed care tries to promote a "values-neutrality" concerning treatment that is ultimately not sustainable (Anderson, Zuelhke and Zuelhke 17–19). Anderson and his collaborators bemoan the fact that mental health professionals "have become the primary caregivers and dispensers of moral guidance in our society" (Anderson, Zuelhke and Zuelhke 18). Because of this role, therapists have an ability to alter people's morals in a way that many Christians feel is not conducive to the survival of their faith.

As a result, Charismatics today, particularly in the NAR, prefer a system of health treatment that is focused more on preventive medicine than on a disease-based model. As NAR supporter Abigail Abildness writes, "Healthcare today should be a health-based program rather than [a] disease-based program. We should be finding ways to create an environment for health and healing" (Abildness pg. 81 Kindle). Abildness is, of course, not wrong to point out that there are potential benefits to preventive health care, particularly as it cuts down on the hefty insurance costs many Americans are yearly forced to pay. But such preventive medicine also runs the risk of ignoring real disease-based health patterns when they do not conform to a more health-based health management delivery system. This is in fact very likely to occur in the United States in particular because of our country's long history of attraction to mind-over-matter, "health and wealth messages" that have been a large part of the American health care ethos since the beginning of the New Thought movement over a century ago. In the meantime, focusing solely on the healthy and increasing the value and worth of healthy people's lives, may in the end leave those who receive Charismatic or Pentecostal deliverance lacking any hope for effective medical recourse when these programs fail, as they almost inevitably do.

PRINCE/BASHAM THEORY OF BODY AND DEMONIC PERSONALITY

One area that should be briefly touched on is the interesting analogies Derek Prince made between spirituality and the body (analogies evidently supported by Don Basham as well) (Prince 99, Basham 107–108). Prince viewed a healthy spiritual life as a "spiritual immune system" (Prince 99). When "demons continually seek to invade a person, but when the person is healthy spiritually, the spiritual 'immune system' within the person identifies and attacks the demons and they are not able to move in and take control. Any kind of unhealthiness, on the other hand, makes a person vulnerable to demonic attack" (Prince 99). For Prince, as for most Charismatics, the body operates in a theo-physiological state, and in turn the spiritual world operates much like the body. There has long been a tendency among Charismatics to spiritualize the physiological. For instance, William Branham's "Serpent Seed" doctrine taught a kind of theological survival of the fittest in which he promoted the idea that Satan had intercourse with the Devil, creating Cain and all his scientific and educated descendants (C. Douglas Weaver 98, 113). Thus, for all three men Christians were at the very least biologically set apart from the world by their rejection of the demonic. At worst, this theology took on quasi-racialist overtones, with the term "Christian" being substituted for race; such a reading again reflected the profoundly American origins of Branham's theology and the influences that theology had on subsequent generations of American Charismatics. And even in Prince's and Basham's formulation of demonic "germ theory," there is more than a hint of the kind of biological metaphors used by German racialists at the turn of the 20th century—particularly in the overlapping of the spiritual health of a person and his biological health.

Prince, Basham, and Timothy Warner all express concern at what is for them a crucial question. How can a Christian, who is filled bodily with the Holy Spirit, have any part of his physical space inhabited by demons (see Warner 83)? The question is in a sense, of course, a rather silly one from a secular point of view, but it is one that has perplexed some Christians. Warner, who wants to promote the theory that Christians can be demonized, warns the reader that "the fallacy with the argument is that spirits do not occupy space, nor is being Spirit-filled a matter of space. It is rather a matter of the degree to which all of my life is lived under the guidance which comes from God through the ministry of 'the Spirit of wisdom and revelation'" (Warner 83). Indeed, Warner assumes as a matter of course that demons also have access to human minds (85). Prince argues that in a certain sense demons cannot inhabit the same space when the Christian is in "perfect health," though he dodges the pneumatological issue of whether the Spirit can occupy the same space as a demon. Prince argues that the reason demons are able to inhabit this physical space, even after salvation, is because Christians do not yet know how to gain authority over demons (Basham 107–108). The problem, of course, is that one has to follow Prince's mind-numbingly complex vision of how to avoid the demonic in order to gain the assurance of being free of possession.

Much could be made of this obsession about demonism and physical space. It is worthwhile to point out that in some of the Charismatic treatment programs aimed at women, especially at Mercy Ministries, there is an intense focus on physical space—on the physical space women do or do not take up, on whether that space is or is not inhabited, on the physical amount of food (calorie space) that women are ingesting. While Mercy's founder, Nancy Alcorn, does not necessarily derive her theology directly from Prince or Basham, it does seem likely that this obsession with demonic space influenced Mercy's theology, if through nothing other than the metaphor of territoriality and demonic geography that characterizes Third Wave Pentecostalism. If, as Rene Holvast has indicated, spiritual mapping is a geography of fear, then deliverance theology's bodily philosophy represents the physiology of biological terror.

Prince's theory of demonological physiology, which Basham seems largely to have agreed with (Basham 105, 107–108),[15] goes hand in hand with his theory of demonic personality. Based on his presupposition that demons were actually disembodied spirits, Prince believed that in their past, pre–Adamic selves these earth-bound demons, referred to as daimonions by Prince, had doubtlessly "led ungodly and sinful lives" (Prince 94). Prince believed that these demons, in their present condition, had "no way to give expression to the various lusts and emotions they developed in their former bodies. It is conceivable that they could find some kind of vicarious release by acting out their lusts or passions through human bodies. This would explain one dominant characteristic of demons: their intense craving to inhabit and work through human flesh" (Prince 94–95). Again, notice the rhetoric of "craving" that surrounds these daimonions and demons. For these beings, the flesh becomes something to be consumed. They are cannibalistic, predators hunting human prey. Prince's rhetoric here is meant to evoke visceral responses in his audience. People have a natural aversion, on one hand, to being eaten. But on the other hand, there is an element of salaciousness to Prince's rhetoric. Partly this is because he is revealing "hidden" secrets about demons, secrets that certainly seem to go counter to the recorded history of Christian demonological speculation.[16] But there is also a certain sexiness, a certain joie de vivre in consorting with the demonic, in learning and interacting with it. The demonic gives free play to the spirits of lust, lasciviousness, fornication, and other vices evangelicals believe exist in their inner psyche. Within the safe confines of a deliverance session, evangelicals can admit their innermost sexual fantasies, even indulge in talking about them, while also still being safely within the bounds of acceptable Charismatic or evangelical behavior. They have all the benefits of therapy, and an exorcism in the bargain. What deliverance supporter could ask for more?

GENDER

The issue of gender in deliverance manuals will reappear in Chapters 2 and 3, but it warrants a brief mention here because of its effect on deliverance ministries like that of Nancy Alcorn's Mercy Ministries. Gender is not directly addressed in most of the deliverance manuals I have read. There are likely a number of reasons for this. Even among some relatively conservative male evangelicals today, there is a desire not to offend the opposite gender by siding with the most antiquated views of sex and sexuality. Disapproval of women, therefore, primarily comes through condemnation of demons of "whoredom," "fornication," or "abortion," which usually, though not always, seem to prefer female habitations. One useful example of this trend in deliverance ministries is a section of Doris Wagner's deliverance anthology *How to Minister Freedom* (2005), in which Peter Horrobin writes, "The first time I ministered to a prostitute, I was aware of an inner anger at what this 23-year old woman had done to men" (Horrobin, "Sexual Sin," 171). Though Horrobin relates quickly that he ended up being mad at the men who had "damaged" this young woman, the point is that very few people outside of evangelical culture would have made such an assumption about a prostitute in the first place (Horrobin, "Sexual Sin," 171). For an evangelical man, the first thing he thinks about when seeing a prostitute is the damage she is doing to young men's sexuality, not the damage being done to her by a patriarchal society.

Horrobin's fascination with sexuality and deliverance is hardly unique, however. Most deliverance manuals deal extensively with deliverance from sexual demons. At their most extreme, as in the case of *Restoring the Foundations,* there is actual talk of succubui and incubuses who can potentially inhabit (or seduce) the bodies of believing Christians (Kylstra and Kylstra 399). Such rhetoric indicates that the sexualized body is indeed a site of contention for the deliverance movement, one that causes a great deal of concern. Perhaps the most repulsive aspect of deliverance rhetoric, from a secular perspective, is the belief held by some deliverance supporters that abuse victims form "soul ties" with their abusers. According to Nancy Alcorn, founder of Mercy Ministries, a "soul tie is the knitting together of two souls. This tie can bring either tremendous blessing in a healthy, Godly relationship or tremendous destruction when made outside of marriage.... In the case of sexual abuse, your soul has been violated, along with your body, and mysteriously knit with the soul of your abuser. The unhealthy connection affects the way you think and feel and the decisions you make" (Alcorn, *Violated*, 25–26). What the exact consequences of this odd fusion of two souls results in is often hard to decipher, but one clear result of it is the possibility of passing down generational curses, as Alcorn makes clear towards the end of *Violated* when she suggests "A Prayer for Parents to Break Generational Patterns" alongside a prayer for one's daughter (Alcorn, *Violated*, 49–50).

Generational curses represent one of the most controversial elements of deliverance ministry. Generational curses in the RTF and Mercy model, alternately referred to as Sins of the Father, or simply generational curses, represent, according to the Kylstras, the "accumulation of all sins committed by our ancestors. It is the heart tendency (iniquity) that we inherit from our forefathers to rebel (i.e., be disobedient) against God's laws and commandments. It is the propensity to sin, particularly in ways that represent perversion and twisted character" (Kylstra and Kylstra 104). What makes this idea so unusual is that the Kylstras, as well as many other Charismatics, apparently believe not only that these curses are passed down but also that the demons attached to them literally descend through the family tree, as mentioned previously. The end result of this is that mental illness, in the particular Charismatic circles Nancy Alcorn and the Kylstras are operating in, is a diabolo-genetic phenomenon, making it very hard for the clients, survivors, and supporters of organizations like Mercy to trust their own judgment, especially when Mercy—and sometimes even their parents—are telling them that any voice they hear contrary to "God's will" is diabolically inspired. In such a theological environment, it is hard for anyone to develop a position of self-trust or even clinical awareness of one's surroundings, since those surroundings are imbued with a spiritual, supernatural power that those outside Charismatic circles simply do not see. The demons Nancy and her "girls" encounter may not be real. What's important, however, is that for both supporters and survivors, those demons often feel real to them. For the supporters this leads to the aforementioned magical worldview that colors Mercy's thinking on most political, theological, and psychological issues. For Mercy survivors, it leads often to extreme PTSD-like symptoms once the support of the ministry has been withdrawn.

Conclusion

Deliverance theology has evolved a long way in the last century, but its roots in premodern thought and anti–Enlightenment rhetoric remain fundamentally as real today as they were fifty years ago. As we will see in Chapter 2, deliverance techniques have now morphed into subtle variations of Freudian psychology, all the while maintaining their focus on the demonic, as well as pseudoscientific concepts like multiple personality disorder (MPD).

2

The Complementary Mental Health Care of Charismatics

From the Sandfords to Sozo

In 1992, the British public was confronted with the shocking story of Jennifer, a woman who claimed before a national television audience that she "was forced to kill her own baby during a devil worship ceremony." Scotland Yard initially wanted to conduct a murder inquiry. But reporters at the *Mail on Sunday* (*Daily Mail*) were suspicious of her claims. The *Mail's* report on the woman, whose real name was Louise Errington, concluded that her confession of murder was "almost certainly not true." Instead, the *Daily Mail* found that Errington's tale of ritual abuse and horror started only after she attended Ellel Grange, a Charismatic healing center in the United Kingdom. Before her admittance into Ellel Grange, Louise's marriage was rocky. Her husband drank and she had been seeing a psychiatrist. At one point she considered committing suicide. The leaders of Ellel Grange told Louise that she was possessed by demons because of the sins of her father and mother. According to Louise, Peter Horrobin, the leader of Ellel Grange, told Louise that he had experienced a "mind-picture" of her being engaged in satanic ritual abuse. Overcome by guilt for this "crime," Louise confessed to these murders. Yet, as the *Mail* concluded, there was no credible evidence for either Louise's story or the two other main stories featured in the British documentary (Jones et al. 8–9). The *Mail* was not alone in finding Horrobin's ministry lacking in credibility. His own wife, Margaret, divorced him, claiming that Horrobin's obsession with the demonic had caused many people considerable pain, even causing some to need long-term psychiatric help. She was particularly upset that Horrobin had subjected one of her daughter's boyfriends to an exorcism as Horrobin poured communion wine over him (Jones and Allen 10).

One might be tempted to pass Horrobin off as an extremist, but he continues to have an enormous amount of influence. Horrobin was the UK's most prominent supporter of exorcism (Howard 90), and reporter Roland Howard estimates that in the mid–'90s, Ellel was the UK's, and possibly the world's, biggest exorcist organization (94). Horrobin's *Healing Through Deliverance* (2008) remains one of the most respected exorcism manuals in the Charismatic movement, gaining recommendations from Charismatic luminaries such as C. Peter Wagner and Dr. Alistair P. Petrie (Horrobin, *Healing Through Deliverance,* Blurbs). Horrobin's work is noted here for the transitional role it played in the development of a newer form of Christian healing ministry, primarily though not exclusively Charismatic in orientation, that also focused on the demonic: inner healing ministry. Horrobin himself used much of the terminology of the early inner healing movement, but criticized some of its early leaders for not sufficiently utilizing deliverance practices (see Collins 90).

During the seventies and eighties, this new therapeutic paradigm arose in America (and was also soon exported overseas). Although it based itself partially in psychological ideas (mainly Freudian or Jungian in origin, see Collins 95), inner healing was still essentially a form of deliverance, albeit sometimes—though by no means always—toned down in rhetoric. In order to survive, deliverance needed to adopt the psychotherapeutic language prevalent at the time but translate it into Charismatic language. This transition proved surprisingly easy for Pentecostals and Charismatics to effect, in part because the movement had inherited so much of the psychotherapeutic positive self-talk language of the New Thought movement. But in the process the movement would promote the then in vogue recovered memory therapies of the seventies, use shockingly ill-informed treatment methods to treat mentally ill patients and trauma victims, and even promise to cure AIDS through the benefit of deliverance ("Healing Room Testimonies").

A number of deliverance healers came to the forefront in the 1980s who practiced inner healing, or inner healing prayer (IHP), as it was also known. Perhaps the earliest practitioners of this method were the Sandford family (John, Paula, and, later, Mark Sandford). Their approach to deliverance was "innovative in that they incorporate deliverance ministry into a Freudian/Jungian psychotherapeutic model of Christian discipleship and sanctification" (Collins 95). The Sandfords borrowed much of their methodology from Agnes Sanford,[1] their mentor and friend, who had pioneered a way of "healing memories" (Collins 95). Agnes Sanford's methodology of prayer and healing had emphasized strongly that individuals' energy reserves were depleted severely by having to deal with painful unconscious memories (Hunter 23). Sanford taught that healing was a three-fold process. First, Jesus must be asked to abide in oneself in order to obtain healing. Second, one "must ask Jesus to touch the memory" (Hunter 25). Finally, one must imagine Jesus working in oneself (Hunter 25–26). This last idea would become increasingly crucial to the inner healing model after the 1980s. Sanford did not dismiss psychology outright, but she did believe that counselors are "quick to dismiss the importance of personal responsibility, confession of sin and repentance" (Hunter 27). Later work in inner healing would selectively combine therapeutic ideas and deliverance, while still maintaining a basically prejudicial, if not always deliberately punitive, approach to the mentally ill.

The Sandfords' early work, building off that of Agnes Sanford, "hardly mention[ed] deliverance" and when it did, "marginalized its significance in the counseling process" (Collins 95). Their later publications, however, tended to emphasize demonization much more, as they created a system in which demonization combined with an "increasingly idiosyncratic psychotherapeutic pastoral model and methodology" (Collins 96). For the Sandfords, people have preexisting "inner spirits" that have a "separate form of consciousness from that of the soul" (Collins 96). That inner spirit, usually referred to as "the inner man or the inner child," often ends up developing a number of diseases, including mental or emotional conditions (Collins 96).

The Sandfords believed in sending all sins to the cross (Frecia Johnson 104). The deliverance healer therefore would focus on praying for the person to be lifted free of their hurts and to "bind the lies" in their life (Frecia Johnson 104). The Sandfords seldom mention deliverance openly in their talks, but their deliverance methodology can be ascertained if one looks at a significantly wide body of their writings and videos. According to Frecia Johnson, the Sandfords frequently pray against generational sins and sometimes command demons to leave (Johnson 107–108). Although they send sins to the cross, they do not send demons there, as the Catholic Macnutts do (108); nor do they believe in talking to demons, one of the more exploitative methods of showmanship favored by some earlier, more colorful deliverance methodologists (this view is not universally shared, however, in the inner healing and modern deliverance movement) (Johnson 108). This kind of mixture of psychotherapeutic discourse with outright deliverance appealed to the increasing middle class sensibility of many Charismatics and even some evangelicals. It also would help fixate the evangelical movement on issues of childhood trauma, in which at the height of the eighties "Satanic panic" would prove deadly when their methodology was adopted by even less scrupulous practitioners of inner healing such as Ed Smith.

By the 1990s, however, the Sandfords were seeking to reestablish their credentials as legitimate deliverance ministers. Like other deliverance proponents at the time, the Sandfords emphasized the intensely anti-rational aspects of deliverance ministry. They did, however, argue that discernment needed to be practiced more carefully if people were to be effectively healed (Collins 98). After outlining "4 levels of demonic activity (infestation, inhabitation, obsession and possession)," the Sandfords defined inner healing "as 'evangelizing unbelieving hearts'" (Collins 98). Collins argues that though the Sandfords definitely represent an attempt at a gentler form of deliverance ministry (a debatable point), they are prone to "indulge in theological eccentricity" (Collins 99). Such eccentricities include promoting the idea of incubuses that molest women and the Sandfords' "experience with a cat working as a warlock's familiar" (Collins 99).

The Sandfords' ministry evolved alongside a number of similar inner healing ministries, most apparently influenced by major Charismatic leader John Wimber and his Vineyard churches (Johnson 5). Each practitioner had a slightly different definition of what inner healing entailed. For David Seamands, a prominent inner healing supporter, healing memories was defined as "a form of Christian counseling and prayer which focuses the healing power of the Spirit on certain types of generational/spiritual problems" (Johnson 11). The Sandfords saw inner healing more simply as a "transformation of the inner person," according to Frecia Johnson (11). And Charles Kraft, one of the most prominent inner healing supporters, defined his own version of inner healing, deep-level healing, as "a ministry in the power of the Holy Spirit aimed at bringing healing to the whole person.... [I]nner healing invites a special focus on what is sometimes called 'the healing of the memories'" (Johnson 12). The inner healing methodology that developed in the eighties therefore was intensely centered on the healing of self and the care for self. This would prove to be highly ironic, in that the various healing systems that came out of the inner healing movement could often be extremely abusive to the mentally ill, and later to abuse victims as well. In attempting to cure these problems, the inner healing movement, with its focus on deliverance, generational curses, and the peculiarly repulsive concept of "soul ties" often made preexisting mental health problems much worse than they originally were, and even managed to effectively create previously nonexistent problems out of whole cloth.

Frecia Johnson, herself a believer in inner healing, lists 11 key components of the practice: Forgiveness, Picturing Jesus, Audibly Hearing Jesus, Sensing Jesus's Presence, Sensing Jesus Speak, Interacting with Jesus, Inner Child, Back to the Womb, Deliverance, Talking to Demons and Discerning Lies (Johnson iii). Johnson also argues that, like any sin, unforgiveness must be handled within the process of deliverance (Johnson 63). What makes this position problematic is that many Charismatics and Pentecostals do not differentiate between types and degrees of sins that must be forgiven, leading them to sometimes expect, for instance, sexual abuse victims to forgive their abusers.[2] Similarly, the recent fascination in Pentecostal and Charismatic circles with promoting racial reconciliation ministries often comes out of a desire to deliver Native Americans, blacks, and other groups of their intergenerational "demons," than out of true desire for repentance.

The process of picturing or sensing Jesus, which is an element of almost all inner healing practice, can become particularly troubling at times, though this is not readily apparent to someone outside Charismatic or evangelical circles. According to Johnson, picturing is "encouraged by prayer ministers by their simply asking the person to picture the event and ask if Jesus is present in the picture. Properly used, picturing is a way of having the person see or bring to mind, the memory" (Johnson 64). The theory behind the practice of picturing Jesus appears to be that since Jesus is a perfect being and perfectly forgiving, his presence within the individual's life can ultimately heal them of the trauma of past experiences. In Kraft's system, for instance (an influential model of IHP), such picturing allows Christians to confront their "spiritual inheritance," which is "usually carried by demons" and gets passed down generation after generation by the sufferer (Kraft, *Deep Wounds*, 79). What makes IHP practice dangerous is that many practitioners, including Charles Kraft, support the existence of repressed memories (see Kraft 81), memories that the inner healer can help uncover. The recovery of such memories even by legitimate psychologists is considered very controversial. As Anne Rothe points out in her book *Popular Trauma Culture* (2011), "while 'recovered' memories tend to be subjectively experienced as reliable ... after large scale legal investigations and extensive scholarly analysis, no empirical evidence that they reflect actual experiences was found" (Rothe 119). Instead, such memories are a therapeutic co-creation of the therapist and the patient, as they mistake popular recovery narratives for real memories of what the patient has gone through (Rothe 119). This, of course, in no way means that real cases of abuse do not occur. Indeed, they occur often. Rather, it suggests the extent to which a therapist or other health provider can influence a client, particularly a client who is emotionally vulnerable or highly susceptible to external influence to begin with.

The idea of picturing Jesus falls under the paradigm of "guided imagery," despite the claims of many supporters to the contrary (see Frecia Johnson 113). Guided imagery is a process in which clients are "encouraged to visualize episodes of violence or abuse during therapy." Oftentimes clients may have "difficulty separating these imaginary events from reality. Researchers have found that people who 'recover' pseudomemories of trauma are often more suggestible and more prone to dissociate—that is, to feel separated from their actual experiences—than most other people" ("false memory syndrome"). Kraft argues that the majority of painful memories occur in episodic, "picture" memory (Kraft, *Deep Wounds,* 84). Therefore, when picturing Jesus, Kraft brings people "back" to a painful event in their past and asks them to imagine Jesus there (Kraft 90). The problem is, of course, that the guided imagery technique often encourages even trained therapists to unintentionally find memories when none were there; the whole Satanic panic was based on such assumptions. What is worse is that such a process, like the hypnosis and guided imagery used by disreputable professional therapists in the eighties and nineties, can lead to a general societal shift away from trusting the testimony of victims who really have been sexually abused and raped. This process is made even more complicated by the fact that guided imagery methods like "picturing Jesus" and hypnosis can often distort real cases of abuse into wild fantasies of satanic affliction and ritual abuse, leaving true victims doubly traumatized, both by events that actually occurred and events that are fantasized.

For Kraft, the therapeutic process is strangely aesthetic. He argues that "picturing brings the Scriptures to life as we contemplate the great events of salvation history.... With all the pictures in Scripture, plus the insights of science into how we use picturing to store personal information, we should not think it strange when God seeks to free people" (Kraft 89). Kraft's therapeutic methodology suggests, in essence, that people enhance their memory collection by trading in all those terrible Kinkade memories for high-class Titians. But our memories are not an art show, and trading in bad memories for good ones often leads to a paradoxical inversion, where good or average memories are distorted into horrible visions out of some nightmare Edvard Munch painting. While, in a sense, most human activity can be reduced to aesthetic appreciation—that's what human beings do anytime they are attracted to a mate, for instance—it is dangerous to bring such aesthetic distinctions into the process of retrieving or reliving memory. If people start making aesthetic distinctions about which memories to relive or experience, they may start seeing memory itself as simply an aesthetic experience, in which they are allowed to create any memory they want, even if that memory brings enormous pain to those accused of inflicting it on them.

According to Johnson, most of the early inner healing ministries accepted the Sandfords' concept of the inner child or inner man. The child-self here often interferes with the life of the adult self, creating a situation which is difficult for the adult self to live through (Frecia Johnson 66). Though the adult self may be fine, the inner child is in need of healing (Frecia Johnson 66), healing provided in a number of fashions, but most of the time involving deliverance. The Back to the Womb exercise focuses on leading the individual back to their place of origin to experience Jesus's love; deliverance sometimes occurs at this time (Frecia Johnson 67). Talking to demons is a more controversial practice. Kraft supports it (Frecia Johnson 69); others however, have deep problems with the idea of engaging in any discourse with the beings of the underworld (69). Discerning lies from truth is a process "pioneered" by Ed Smith, the very controversial creator of theophostic prayer ministry (Johnson 69). This a process by which Jesus replaces lies with the truth (Johnson 69). This process would become the centerpiece of Smith's ministry, perhaps the most controversial inner healing ministry of its time, and a practice that now, even past its zenith, continues to provoke outrage among evangelical Christians.

Ed Smith started Theophostic Ministries in 1996 (Frecia Johnson 111). According to Johnson, theophostics is "a lie-based approach to healing that operates on the assumption that the emotional pain experienced in the present triggers a lie from the past that transfers its pain into the present event" (Johnson 111). As Johnson notes, there have been efforts by Smith to reach out to scientists for empirical verification of his methodology (Johnson 111). As of 2001, a total of 300,000 Christians had received the treatment (111). Theophostics is in ten countries as of 2003, and estimates as of that year show that more than 100,000 people had been trained in its methodology, showing its significance and widespread effect (Fletcher 13–14).

Like Kraft, Smith claims not to believe in guided imagery. Instead he "invites Jesus into the picture" and then asks Jesus "to speak to the person" but does not "generally tell Jesus what to do" (Johnson 113). How any of this differs significantly from typical guided imagery is difficult to discern, since the invitation into the memory would seem to be fairly open to therapeutic manipulation. Indeed, David Entwistle convincingly argues that theophostic prayer ministry does use guided imagery, also pointing out that certain interpretations, especially early ones, of the ministry that rejected the idea it was guided imagery could lead to the even more unsavory possibility that clients would see the imagery as divine revelation (Entwistle, "Shedding Light 2," 37). Typically within a theophostic context, a facilitator will "encourage the person to go back to the memory, and then allows God to reveal the lie. Proponents claim immediate relief from a variety of emotional problems. Smith believes the lies within these memories may also give demons a place from which to oppress the person, and until the lie is removed, the demonic presence may persist in the person's life" (Fletcher 13).

Smith's model, therefore, like Kraft's, is centered on memory and issues of memory fairly specifically; it also couples itself to a truth/lie dichotomy that is fairly typical of evangelical theology as a whole. Only through removing false ideas and beliefs can truth be brought to the surface. Smith is also on record as having spoken of conspiracies of Satanic Ritual Abuse, "where perpetrators are 'careful to strategically fill the trauma moment with false identities, images, and fabricated locations,' so that the victim will not remember the assault" (Fletcher 24). Given the well-known history (already recounted here) of false charges of SRA, especially when coupled with sincere religious belief, it is not surprising that many individuals, including even some within the evangelical community, remain deeply skeptical about the effectiveness of theophostic prayer (Fletcher 24–25).

Indeed, it is not surprising that Smith's methodology has already been linked to at least one fairly widely reported false abuse charge. In early 2002, Thomas Wright was charged with abuse after a church member recovered memories of Wright supposedly abusing a child (Fletcher 29). In June 2002, Stephanie Anderson, the local district attorney, refused to prosecute Wright. In fact, not only did Anderson refuse to prosecute, she also "dis-missed charges against Wright and, instead, publicly accused Harris of 'spiritual abuse,' in a press conference covered by local and state media. At a press conference before television cameras, she called Harris's brand of therapy, 'trance-therapy'" (Fletcher 38). According to Fletcher, "another attorney, Ken Altshuler, who interviewed Anderson and Martemucci, wrapped up the news segment by saying that 'this is a civil lawsuit just waiting to be brought'" (39). Indeed, ministries that use theophostics or other RMT-like methodologies (for instance, the model used by Neil Anderson) do have a suspicious tendency to accuse first and ask questions later. Mercy Survivor advocates, for instance, have told me of cases of parents being falsely accused of abuse, based on recovered memory therapies being used by Mercy. Given the therapeutic influences on Mercy, that hardly seems to be an unlikely situation to have arisen.

Disturbingly, Smith does not seem to care about the difference between real memories and possibly therapeutically implanted ones. Smith believes a person should heal "whatever the cost" (Fletcher 50). To Smith, the feelings of the purported victim are all that matter, and the truth-value of their statements seems to be largely irrelevant within his writings. Indeed, he goes on the offensive against people who question any traumatic memories at all. He has stated, "I have always questioned the possible hidden agenda of those out there who feel obsessed with making other peoples traumatic memory false. If I were seeking to hide my evil deeds I might want to discredit the reliability of what others remember."[3] As Fletcher points out, Smith essentially "insinuates that anyone who questions the scientific validity of recovered memories has a 'hidden agenda,' and is just trying to hide his own evil deeds. Therefore, anyone who questions Smith's theories falls under suspicion of being a sex abuser too" (Fletcher 32). In such a therapeutically created hostile environment, it is difficult to judge the veracity of those making abuse charges, *even if the charges turn out to be true.* The theophostic paradigm therefore muddies the water not just between religion and psychotherapy, but also between the vast majority of valid abuse claims and the small minority of claims that do not turn out to be reflecting reality. In the process, not only does Smith do a massive disservice to the people falsely accused, he also does a disservice to the real victims of sexual abuse themselves and (ironically) the very clients he is supposedly helping (who may or may not be victims).

Smith today ostensibly does not believe he can heal memories, only bring mental renewal (Hunter 28). He also argues that he is moving away from guided imagery (29) to focusing on the memory and feelings associated with Jesus rather than the actual image of him (Hunter 29). Smith's model in many ways borrows from Agnes Sanford (Hunter 29–30). But whereas Agnes Sanford gave more realistic and theologically plausible reasons for her therapeutic method not working (namely that some suffering is redemptive, as well as the possibility that there are unconfessed sins in a person's life), Smith offered a wide variety of differing explanations for why his therapeutic methodology did not work (see Hunter 29–30), most of which deflect attention away from the inadequacies of the therapeutic method itself and towards either the patient or the facilitator.

One of the basic flaws of theophostic prayer ministry (TPM) is the sheer number of basic principles on which the therapy rests. The full list of principles follows:

1. Our present situation is rarely the true cause of our ongoing emotional pain.

2. Everything we presently know, feel, or are mentally aware of has its roots in a first-time experience.

3. If we try to resolve our present conflicts without resolving our historical lie-based woundedness, we will find only temporary relief. At some point the lie-based pain will be triggered again and the pain will resurface. However, if we find renewing truth for our past lie-based thinking, we can redeem our present.

4. Since many of the negative emotions we currently feel are reflections of the past, they provide opportunities for the lie-infested wounds of our lives to be exposed, and thus for mind renewal to occur.

5. To facilitate emotional renewal and restoration, we need to identify the four basic elements in the renewal process: 1) the present emotional pain 2)

the original memory container 3) the original lie(s) implanted in the memory container 4) the receiving of truth from the Holy Spirit.

6. People are in emotional bondage due to two basic factors: belief and choice.

7. If we believe a lie, it might as well be the truth because the consequences will be much the same.

8. To be free of the lies we believe, we must identify and own the lies rather than suppress or deny that we believe them.

9. In the midst of our "darkness," we must come to realize how utterly bound we are to lies, and how helpless we are to overcome their debilitating grip on our lives apart from God's divine intervention.

10. No person, including we ourselves, is capable of talking us out of the lies we believe. We will be free only when we receive the truth from the One who is Truth.

11. When we know the truth experientially, having received truth from God in our memory experience, we can walk in genuine maintenance-free victory in these areas of our lives.

12. In times of crisis or emotionally charged life situations, our experiential knowledge tends to override our logical truth.

13. The only cure for sin is the cross.

14. Mind renewal is a lifelong process [Smith, *Theophostic Prayer Ministry*, 31–38].

The sheer length of this list makes it intimidating to comment on, but permit me a few remarks on some of its key aspects. First, one can see that, despite theophostic prayer ministry's claim to be able to deal with almost all issues, including mental illness (Entwistle, "Shedding Light 1," 26), it is a therapeutic methodology which is primarily geared to trauma and largely influenced by Freudian and psychodynamic considerations. This can be seen by Smith's contention that "the present situation" is rarely the reason for pain. Such a contention is frequently made in reference to issues of trauma, post-traumatic stress disorder, and abuse, and not necessarily incorrectly. What is troubling, however, is that Smith's methodology assumes it can treat a wide range of mental health issues when the therapeutic practice itself does not seem ideally suited to approaching every one of these issues. One is only left to wonder, for instance, how this therapeutic practice would be of much use to obsessive-compulsives, who historically have tended to respond better to behaviorist, present-oriented therapeutic methods (Entwistle, "Shedding Light 2," 39). Similarly, mental health issues whose primary cause is simply genetics and not any external childhood trauma are unlikely to be helped by Smith's methodology.

More troubling is Smith's second contention that what we are presently aware of always has roots in a "first-time experience" (Smith 32). In a sense this should be an uncontroversial assertion, because we know that past events do affect present experience. Indeed, how can they not? But the myopic focus on the past that is characteristic of the TPM methodology, much like that of RMT therapies in general, is prone to find associations between present and past events where none may exist, as well as invent new pasts out of whole cloth.

Ironically, too, Smith puts too much of the burden for emotional health on the part of the person being "ministered" to. For Smith, "emotional bondage" comes from either belief or choice. This idea is already problematic in the area of trauma, because many trauma issues have nothing to do with either of these factors, but simply the belief and choice of others. With mental illness, of course, belief and choice become close to irrelevant. While a few mental health theorists (such as Thomas Szasz) outside the evangelical world have in recent times argued for a "choice-based" model of mental illness, this paradigm of mental illness has few backers in psychiatry or neuroscience and is likely to have even less as new discoveries in neuroscience are made, which are all too likely to link various mental health and behavioral patterns to genetic, bodily, social or environmental variables or a combination of them. Smith's methodology, therefore, would seem of little use to such people, except as a model for encouraging guilt for feelings that are beyond the person's control.

Smith ironically half admits this only to practically take back the admission. He argues that "the Theophostic Prayer Ministry method will not eliminate the symptoms that are genuinely rooted in genuine mental disorders or brain damage" (Smith 259). However, at the same time, Smith believes that the mentally ill can get relief and "mind renewal" from his sessions (259), because whether they are mentally ill or not, they need relief from "lie-based thinking" (Smith 259–260). But as Smith admits, it is hard to distinguish between the "truly mentally ill" and those that "are merely in bondage to faulty thinking" (Smith 260). He therefore simply says, "Why not start with the lie issues and then work toward the medical condition—if one exists? ... What is certain is that not every person with lie-based thinking is chemically imbalanced, but every chemically imbalanced person also has lie-based thinking" (Smith 260). Though Smith commendably claims not to diagnose (260), one is only left to wonder how much harm has already been done by the time the facilitator takes this information to a psychologist.[4]

Another major problem with Smith's therapeutic methodology is Principle Twelve. Smith argues that "in times of crisis or in emotionally-charged life situations, our experiential knowledge tends to override our logical truth" (Smith 36). Smith perhaps here borrows from (or at least is influenced by) Charles Kraft's anthropological distinction between experiential knowledge and factual knowledge (see Kraft, *Anthropology of Christian Witness,* 21). Kraft assumed the existence of a real world (as presumably does Smith) but believed that we "have to distinguish between that reality and the human perception of it" (Kraft 21). Thus human perception is problematic because it can never perceive the whole truth, but only portions of the truth (Kraft explains this by an allusion to the parable of the elephant and the blind man) (Kraft, *Anthropology of Christian Witness,* 21). While Smith should be commended for promoting the idea of a rationalistic approach to healing trauma, one must remember that his idea of logical truth involves such nonscientific ideas as satanic ritual abuse, the existence of demons, and the reality of repressed memories. It is therefore questionable of what use such an idea of logic is going to be in promoting "realistic" or scientifically verifiable knowledge over the lies of experience. Furthermore, since Charismatics are likely to be more attracted to theophostics than other evangelicals, because of its "demon-centrism" (to coin a neologism), the group most likely attracted to theophostic ministry is the group least likely to be able to discern between the diabolic and the ordinary, between fantasy and reality.

There are also serious professional concerns with theophostics. As Hunter points out, theophostic prayer ministry was originally known as theophostic counseling, until the name was changed, as "legal and ethical questions arose" (Hunter 98). Nonetheless some prominent critics within the evangelical community argue that theophostics is still counseling, just done under a different name (Hunter 98). The use of a professional counseling methodology without adequate licensure or oversight renders the methodological procedures developed within that system vulnerable to abuse. This is readily apparent in theophostic teaching in particular because TPM, despite its "deceptively simple" description of its basic practices, in reality involves "techniques similar to those of cognitive restructuring, exposure and desensitization therapies, identifying psychodynamic defense mechanisms, the use of rating scales, and healing of memories" (Entwistle, "Shedding Light 1," 27). Given the wide abuse of such methodologies by various cults and even governments, which typically lacked professional oversight and almost always ignored what ethical professional advice was offered, it does not seem particularly surprising that theophostic ministry has been prone to charges of abuse.

Still more disturbing is the seemingly never-ending number of problems theophostics is supposed to be able to cure. Smith originally admitted that his healing methodology was primarily addressed to sexual abuse survivors

(Entwistle, "Shedding Light 2," 39). However, he was soon arguing that the methodology was available to heal a wide variety of mental health issues. At one point, "the Theophostic Ministries' website claimed that TPM has been 'highly effective' in the treatment of 'Sexual Abuse Issues,' 'Marital Issues,' 'Substance Abuse and other addictive behaviors,' 'Traumatic memory,' 'Post traumatic stress syndrome,' 'Grief and Loss,' 'Eating Disorders,' 'Children's issues,' 'Dissociative Disorders,' 'Homosexuality,' 'Satanic Ritual Abuse,' and 'All lie-based issues.'" (Entwistle, "Shedding Light 2," 39). While Smith, as we have seen, claimed to distinguish between lie-based thinking and mental illness, Entwistle points out that his actual writing tends to be quite contradictory on this point (see Entwistle, "Shedding Light 2," 39). Such a wide-sweeping curative model essentially created a situation where TPM practitioners could claim that they had the solution to every psychological and physical ailment. This is a claim that, despite some evangelicals' claims to the contrary, ethical psychology and medicine seldom makes; but it is also a claim that many suffering individuals are desperate to hear, regardless of the truthfulness of such claims.

Smith also claims that God literally revealed the theophostic methodology to him (Entwistle, "Shedding Light 2," 36). While later writings deny this interpretation of his writing, it is, as Entwistle points out, disturbing and quite telling that Smith even had to issue such a denial (see Entwistle, "Shedding Light 2," 36). Smith's claims of healing also have little empirical basis in support (Entwistle, "Shedding Light 2," 38), and the handful of scholars who have backed up his methodology have a vested interest in seeing it succeed (for instance, Charismatic sociologist Margaret Poloma, see Garzon and Poloma et al.). That the TPM method was ever used in Christian healing, let alone Christian clinical practice, is deeply troubling. What is even more disturbing is that when Smith saw he could no longer use the practice within traditional psychology, he simply changed the name from theophostic counseling to theophostic prayer (see Entwistle's comments on this in "Shedding Light 2," 39). Entwistle points out that simply changing the name of a practice does not change what one does. As he puts it, "counseling does not cease to be counseling by calling it 'ministry' any more than surgery ceases to be surgery by calling it by another name. The issue is not what it is called, but what it is" (Entwistle, "Shedding Light 2," 39). Entwistle's arguments are, of course, based on the assumption that counselors will operate with clinical and professional integrity, as he clearly believes they should, regardless of whether they have a doctorate in psychology or counseling. But what is depressing, as Entwistle himself points out, is that Smith not only does not operate with such an assumption, but even offers advice on how to avoid lawsuits while still practicing

TPM. What is his solution? As we will see when dealing with the much differently oriented biblical counseling movement, Smith seeks the "safety" of the supposedly constitutionally protected field of pastoral counseling. Smith believes that ministers are unlikely to face the same kind of lawsuits that professional psychologists do and therefore suggests TPM be used as pastoral ministry (Entwistle, "Shedding Light 2," 38). As would many evangelical therapeutic practices before and after it, TPM would seek the shelter of the First Amendment and pastoral counseling when criticism of it became severe.

Sozo Healing Methodology

The newest and most radical form of inner healing and deliverance practice currently being promoted (almost exclusively among Charismatics and Pentecostals) is the *sozo* methodology. For many Charismatics, sozo represents nothing new. The term sozo[5] means "to save," which evangelical scholars interpret as having a variety of meanings in the New Testament, including to "save from disease," "to save a suffering one from perishing," and "to preserve one who is danger of destruction" (Thayer and Smith). Charismatics, particularly those associated with the current manifestation of the sozo movement, interpret the word as meaning "salvation, healing and deliverance" (Reese 11). This lines up well with classical Charismatic and Pentecostal understandings of salvific experience. Charismatics and Pentecostals have "boldly made divine healing an aspect of their 'full gospel,' rooting healing in the victory of Christ on the cross and in the latter rain of the Spirit that came to restore the full power of the cross and the resurrection over the forces of sin and darkness through the mission of the church" (Macchia 1135). For Pentecostals and Charismatics, though salvation is not dependent on healing, salvific experience is often reflected in healing experience. Therefore, when the current sozo movement claims to be returning to a more authentic gospel, this can be interpreted as somewhat true within the Charismatic context, to the extent that the sozo model seeks to return to the roots of authentic original Pentecostal experience.

But this kind of simplistic reading of the current sozo phenomena elides real significant differences between sozo and the rites of healing traditionally practiced by Charismatics and Pentecostals. In my discussions with Charismatics in my community who are involved in sozo practice, there also seems to be a disturbing lack of awareness of how much affinity sozo has with previous deliverance and inner healing practices, practices that have been critiqued by psychologists, theologians, and reporters as to their efficacy, quality of care, and theological validity.

The current practice of sozo began sometime around 1997 (see McMichael and McMichael 1, Reese 15). The practice was brought to America by Randy Clark, one of the six main leaders of Revival Alliance, an organization deeply embedded in the New Apostolic Reformation and its quasi-theocratic goals (McMichael and McMichael 1). This model was based on healing methodology first developed in Argentina (McMichael and McMichael 1). Pablo Bottari, a leading deliverance supporter in Argentina, developed a model of "prayer for deliverance" called the four doors (McMichael and McMichael 1). These four doors were "sexual sin, occult, fear, and hatred." According to the McMichaels, "The four doors, when they have been opened by you or someone else, allows the enemy to have legal access to you" (McMichael and McMichael 1). After this, the McMichaels say, "Dawna" (presumably Dawna De Silva, who is the biggest player in the expanding sozo market) and a friend "attended a seminar taught by a brain scientist, Aiko Horman, where other tools were acquired: the wall, divine editing, and how to cure post-traumatic stress" (McMichael and McMichael 1). Two other tools were also acquired for this method borrowed from Pastor Alan Ray and the aforementioned Ed Smith: the "Father Ladder" and "Presenting Jesus" (McMichael and McMichael 1–2). According to Andy Reese, "thousands have found increased peace and freedom, and experienced the freshness of encounters with a loving, living God" thanks to sozo. Reese claims

> there is no single training manual, proponent church or ministry or certification process for sozo. Instead, sozo is more like Alcoholics Anonymous and less like "Sozo Inc." It makes the best use of tools and approaches developed by others and modified for our use and to fit our DNA. No minister is a "professional"—though many have had years of training and experience in Christian ministry. Some are psychiatrists, some are certified counselors who use the tools on a daily basis, and most, like me, are just compassionate knuckleheads [Reese 25–26].

Reese's claims here are for the most part dubious and even more damning when they are not. Reese is correct in stating that there is no one single sozo training manual, although the manuals I have seen all reference the influence of the '90s "revival." Randy Clark's own sozo model is based on Pablo Bottari's model, which would line up with the McMichaels' description of the historical evolution of the sozo movement (see Clark 91, Reese 178). What is even more problematic is the fact that the ministry is not based on professional therapeutic practice or counseling but on the use of paraprofessionals. Again, as is typical in deliverance methodology, the manual officially denies that it means to treat mental illness (Reese 29). However, it also contradicts that position, asking, "Is everything a disease, a syndrome or a disorder? Does everything require multiple counseling sessions or mood-altering drugs? ... Emotional needs are, in many ways, like medical needs. Ninety percent of the need is satisfied by home-based lay-administered first aid and over-the-counter medicine" (Reese 23). The sozo model presents itself as "first aid for the soul" (Reese 23–24). Again, as in Smith's practice, how does one distinguish between regular "problems of living" (to borrow a phrase from Szasz) and actual distinguishable mental health problems in need of professional psychiatric treatment? Reese apparently does not ask, nor care about, that question.

In any case, Reese's view of deliverance is only the public face of the new sozo model. In Appendix E of the McMichaels' manual, they clearly state that some of the possible, though not necessary, indicators of demonic manifestation include "anorexia or bulimia," "behavioral extremes," "addictions," "compulsive behavior," "depression," "emotional disturbances or long-term unbalanced emotions," "hearing internal or external voices," "undiagnosable symptoms," "nightmares," and "suicidal tendencies" (McMichael and McMichael 13). Read literally, virtually any problem can be a demonic manifestation in the McMichaels' sozo model. However, the vast majority of problems listed as symptoms of demonic manifestation are either symptomatic of mental illness or heretical or false religious belief (which to some Charismatics is much the same thing) (see McMichael and McMichael 13). That Reese was not aware of the McMichaels' interpretation of sozo is unlikely in the extreme. The McMichaels' sozo training manual is sold by Healing Rooms Ministries, one of the main healing ministries using sozo practice. It is used by permission of Bethel Church (McMichael and McMichael title page). Bethel is where the model first took form in the United States, as Reese himself tacitly admits (see Reese 9, 15).

Appendix A of the McMichaels' book lists some references for further reading for the prospective deliverance minister. The listing of Carlos Annacondia and Pablo Bottari assures the reader that the list meets with the McMichaels' approval, as well as the Healing Rooms' approval at large (led by Cal Pierce). *Everyone* listed is a supporter of inner healing or deliverance (see McMichael and McMichael 8). The list combines old stalwarts of inner healing, such as John and Paula Sandford, Leanne Payne, and Charles Kraft, with some of the more popular supporters of the deliverance and inner healing methodology, including Neil Anderson, whose writing blurs the boundaries between Charismatic and more skeptical neo-evangelical views of deliverance (McMichael and McMichael 8). Most of these individuals' therapeutic methodologies have at best questionable assumptions and practices.

For instance, Anderson's main deliverance manual, *The Bondage Breaker,* which is one of the more ethically and theoretically sound of these texts, expresses the same degree of skepticism about mental illness found within the sozo model. Anderson admits that people's "body chemistry can get out of balance," only to ask the inane question "how can a chemical produce a personal thought?" (Anderson 65). This is followed by a more bizarre question: "How can our neurotransmitters involuntarily and randomly fire in such a way that they create thoughts that we are opposed to thinking?'" (Anderson 65–66). Anderson then goes on to argue that, since the only way to "physically hear" is through a "sound source" and to see is to have "a light source reflecting from a material object to our eyes," one possible explanation for a person being able to hear voices and hallucinate are "Satan and his demons" since "they do not have material substance, so we cannot see them ... nor hear them with our ears" (Anderson 66). Anderson ignores the fact the we have known the body is composed of chemicals since at least the time of Justus von Liebig and Louis Pasteur ("biochemistry"). He also ignores the fact that neurotransmitter firing—indeed the whole evolutionary process, though not guided by a supernatural agent—is not totally random either.[6] But for Anderson these facts are immaterial. What matters for him, as for sozo supporters, is that 2,000 years of Western science be replaced with the premodern healing techniques of the New Testament, all in the name of supposedly curing the mentally ill.

We could examine the whole list of influences on the sozo model, but most have already been covered in this chapter (for instance Charles Kraft, Ed Smith, and the Sandfords). What is important to understand in the context of sozo ministry is that all of these healers shared a number of common assumptions, methodologies, and psychotherapeutic ideas that define them as a school of thought, and definitely not as any spontaneous outpouring of the Holy Spirit, unless spiritual spontaneity is defined today by cynically organized revivalism aimed at exploiting the mentally ill and abuse victims. But what is more concerning even than the sozo methodology's theory of mental illness is the actual training and practice of sozo healers. It is to this we now turn.

Sozo Healing Theory and Practice

The first element of the Bethel-inspired sozo methodology used in the Healing Rooms is the Father Ladder, which is defined as "the connection between our relationship with our earthly family and how we view the Godhead" (McMichael and McMichael 29). Reese's model uses the same concept with similar terminology. He writes that the Father Ladder tool "has as its primary focus the establishment or restoration of relationship with Father God, Jesus, and the Holy Spirit through dealing with earthly familial relationship issues and letting God bring a present revelatory picture of Himself to the person" (Reese 101). The Father Ladder has six questions attached to it, which are used to help the individual: "How do you view Father God or what do you think about when you think about Father God?" (McMichael and McMichael 30). The second question is, "How does Father God see you, or what does He say about you?" (McMichael and McMichael 30). Both picturing Father God here and listening to his voice are seen as acceptable methods, much as in the methodology outlined by Felicia Johnson (McMichael and McMichael 30). Then the same two questions are asked again, except Jesus and then the Holy Spirit are named instead of God, for a total of six questions (McMichael and McMichael 30). Reese's model seems fairly similar, albeit with a slightly different wording.

In Reese's description of sozo healing, we see God through "our relationship and experiences laid in when we were young and in the presence of our earthly Father" (Reese 204). Again, the same idea is seen in the McMichael's model (McMichael and McMichael 31). Similarly, one's view of the Holy Spirit is influenced by "the nurture we received from our mother or mother figure(s)" (Reese 204). The McMichaels also here concur (McMichael and McMichael 31). One's relationship to Jesus is based on sibling and peer relationships. Therefore, negative relationships in these areas affect how Jesus is viewed (McMichael and McMichael 31).

The sozo methodology externalizes blame, which one might think (particularly after seeing the horrendous internal blaming encouraged by biblical counseling) is a good thing for an evangelical counseling ministry to do. And of course in cases of real sexual abuse or PTSD such externalization of blame is usually of value, especially since it discourages people from feeling false guilt for what others have done to them. But such a methodology becomes more problematic when dealing with mental illness, not because the mentally ill are responsible for the illnesses they suffer from, but because the blame for such illnesses not only does not lie with the individual sufferer but oftentimes does not lie on the sufferer's family or friends either. The sozo methodology therefore shifts the focus of treatment away from dealing with symptom alleviation and management towards labeling one's mental "oppressor." While this may occasionally be of use to people suffering from mental illness—for instance, those who have trauma issues coexisting with their mental health conditions or those sufferers who have undergone significant external mental, physical, or sexual oppression from powerful external agencies (governments, churches, etc.)—overall this methodology appears likely to merely reenact the theophostic tendency to target innocent parties for abuses or crimes they may not have committed.

The second element of the Healing Rooms model of sozo ministry, as learned from Bethel, is the wall. The wall is a "structure that we have erected to protect ourselves from others and from pain" (McMichael and McMichael 30). According to the McMichaels:

> The Holy Spirit may lead you to say: "Do you have any walls?" And if the person says "yes" then you say: "What I want you to do is tell me how high is that wall, how wide is it, where are you in relationship to the wall, what's the wall made out of?" Through that description you are going to see what some of the issue is. You are going step by step. When you are asking the person the question you're reminding them that they need to hear the Holy Spirit and then speak it out loud to you [McMichael and McMichael, 32–33].

This is quite clearly guided imagery practice, not simply because the McMichaels ask the client to envision the wall, but also because they ask the client to relationally interact with it. From a theological standpoint, many Christians would feel deeply disturbed by the formulaic idea that the Holy Spirit will lead one to ask a specific question or type of question to each and every client they deal with, as if these clients had no spirit or soul about them. Again, such a practice has more in common with behaviorist management techniques than it does with any traditional practice of spiritual healing within the Christian church. Whereas a psychotherapist is bound by the ethical regulations of their profession, and is usually trained in effective, clinically tested methods of psychotherapeutic interaction, there is currently no reputable peer-reviewed literature on the effectiveness or noneffectiveness of sozo healing methods. The closest equivalent to such literature one can ferret out is in the scholarship of Candy Gunther Brown, whose writings on deliverance are so methodologically flawed and ethically tainted as to be worthless.[7]

The purpose of finding the wall is ultimately to have the person get down to their root issues (McMichael and McMichael 34), which seem to be rooted in childhood, as in Smith's model.[8] Wall forgiveness also has to be extremely specific; the McMichaels encourage sozo practitioners to make sure they have encouraged the clients to engage in as specific a form of forgiveness as possible (see McMichael and McMichael 36–37).

Also important in the sozo model is "Presenting Jesus" (McMichael and McMichael 44). The idea of "Presenting Jesus" is found in both the McMichaels and Reese (Reese 217). Reese attributes the idea very clearly to Ed Smith, though he claims the sozo methodology has since taken the "best of these streams" to now mix "with our DNA and foundations" (Reese 217). In the sozo version of "Presenting Jesus," one brings "Jesus into memories in which there's pain or wounds that have occurred and inviting Jesus into the memory to identify what the lie is, and to reveal the truth" (McMichael and McMichael 44). The McMichaels point out that this process may involve God and the Holy Spirit as well. Their contention is that they use Jesus because

"Jesus is the one who paid the price for us and He's the one who, more than likely, would be seen in a situation" (McMichael and McMichael 44). Without being unduly cynical of the McMichaels' motives, it is perhaps easier for one to visualize Jesus than it is an invisible Holy Spirit or the abusive God with lightning bolts that people typically associate with God the Father. Since God and the Holy Spirit are not typically portrayed as incarnate, Christ is much easier for sozo facilitators to aestheticize for their clients (McMichael and McMichael 44). The process of presenting Jesus encourages the client to "define feelings of pain and wounding," "find the origin of the pain," and then "Hear Truth, Bless, Fill, Proclaim" (Reese 219–223). According to Reese, when "present in the memory, we ask Jesus to bring truth, to tell what He thinks, to show where He was or what He was doing" (Reese 223). Again, the McMichael's model is very similar, practically identical. It too asks "where is Jesus?" within traumatic situations (McMichael and McMichael 42–43). At no point does either Reese or the McMichaels make clear to their readers or listeners that the practice they are teaching them has definite affinities with guided imagery and given its association with the teachings of Ed Smith, would likely be labeled as such a practice by most competent psychotherapists.

But where sozo turns truly bizarre is in the process of divine editing, which significantly receives no mention in Reese's quite public *Freedom Tools* (2008), but only in the more hard-to-access work of the McMichaels. According to the McMichaels, divine editing is based on the scientific ideas of "Aiko Horman [Hormann]." Hormann argues that

> there's a place in the back of our brains basically at our brain stem where it meets the neck. There is actually a place in our brains called the reticular formation and what that area of the brain does is from the time that we are conceived till we go to be with Jesus it records things that are happening. From the time we are in the womb it could be recording if we have a very pleasant environment around us—if our parents are joyful about our birth and so forth. It's recording that. It's also recording if there is strife and division in the household. Every area of our life is being recorded in that place called the reticular formation [McMichael and McMichael 43].

According to the McMichaels, in divine editing the facilitator and client are

> breaking a lot of lies and things and at the end of the Sozo we are going to pray for that portion of the brain so that all of those things associated with the negativity no longer seem normal. There is a reason why it's called Divine Editing, it's because we're asking God to do it. He's the only one who can. In the natural we can't overcome that, we just have to ask God to remove it. We actually pray for people and put our hands on the back of their head, after we've asked permission to do that, and we pray: "Lord, would you please remove every thought, every thought pattern, everything in this portion of the brain that seemed normal to this person, but was not from you" [McMichael and McMichael 43].

Thus, the divine editing process literally promotes the idea of healing memories through the application of prayer to a specific area of the brain. Not only that, but the sozo methodology also promotes the idea that this can't be done in the "natural," thus minimizing the possibility of secular therapies or medications being used to minimize the symptomologies and mental pathologies previously listed in Appendix E (McMichael and McMichael 13).

Why physically touching a part of the brain stem is likely to bring healing is not explained. There is obviously no physical or clinical reason for this belief, but even the theological justification for it is dubious. While other Christian traditions have emphasized the "laying on of hands," most of these traditions, even among Charismatics, have not taken that belief to the extreme of arguing that one can literally heal memories through selective divine editing. What is more problematical, as Mikhail Gofman, a computer scientist at Cal Fullerton points out, is animals also have a reticular formation (Gofman personal e-mail May 8, 2013). Do we then practice the art of healing animal memories? How far down the evolutionary tree does one go? Why is Jesus apparently interested only in healing human memories as opposed to the memories of a gorilla or a chimpanzee, both species which are sentient and both of which often suffer more pain at the hands of humans than we inflict on ourselves?

Nor is that the only problem with the divine editing concept. In divine editing, the individual is encouraged to ask the Lord "to take out anything that the person has thought was normal that was not normal to God and to replace it with Godly principles—with the truth" (McMichael and McMichael 85). The problem is that oftentimes there are things people think are normal *that actually are normal* but that Charismatics and Pentecostals think are mental abnormalities. Other things are not normal. But telling people that one can edit out manifestations of hallucinations or anorexia, for instance, is unlikely to be of much practical benefit and may indeed actually hurt the suffering individual.

The last step of the intricate sozo program is deliverance, which is a 10-step process based, as in the Clark model, on the deliverance ideology of Pablo Bottari (McMichael and McMichael 94–95, Clark 91). The exact principles of this model vary little from previously described models, but it should be emphasized that, as in the aforementioned models, it involves a literal casting out of unclean spirits (McMichael 96–97). Reese's model of sozo is similarly concerned with the demonic,[9] and like the model offered by the McMichaels argues that "someone strongly influenced by the demonic may chronically experience" such mental health problems as "addictions," "anorexia and bulimia," "behavioral extremes," "compulsive behavior," "depression," "emotional disturbances or long-term unbalanced emotions," "hearing internal or external voices," "hereditary illness or chronic repeated sickness," "irrational behavior," and "suicidal tendencies" (Reese 165). What the McMichaels and Reese are promoting may not center on any one particular training manual, proponent church, or ministry, as Reese claims, but the assumptions of the various sozo methodologies seem to be virtually identical, leading one to question how sincere Reese is in this belief (Reese 25).

Bethel Church, the major promoter of sozo practice in the United States, has added another element to the methodology, *shabar* healing. As Teresa Liebscher describes it, "shabar is a ministry to what we call fragmented people" (De Silva and Liebscher "Session 8[qm] audio). The ministry is aimed at "those that have a dissociative degree in their life" (Session 8). Liebscher's aim in this therapy is "integration," which is what she would like to see happen to these individuals. Why do they need to integrate? Because "some people have people inside of them" whom she labels "parts." To put it simply, Liebscher and those using her methods—which is a huge subset of the Pentecostal community right now—are effectively treating people for DID, using spiritual therapy. Indeed, the shabar healers hardly even bother to change the language of DID, leaving them potentially legally vulnerable to charges of practicing psychotherapy without a license, despite their claim that they do not diagnose (see De Silva and Liebscher "Session 8"). Indeed, listening to Bethel's sozo lectures, it is difficult to shake the impression that their form of sozo is not deliberately inducing DID symptoms in order to treat them.

Liebscher also says that she has seen "the shabar process minister to people with bipolar; it has been effective and it has worked and we have dealt with the parts that present themselves." Then she cautions her listeners that she is not a doctor and cannot diagnose (De Silva and Libescher, "Sozo Q +A," Session 9). The problem here is that her shabar methods—which are largely thinly rehashed inner healing methodology mixed with a tinge of Freudian thinking—are mammothly unlikely to help someone with bipolar, since bipolar sufferers do not have little people inside them nor parts, but suffer from mood swings which seem probably, if not conclusively, to have fairly definitive physical causes (Barlow and Durand 200). Were a professional therapist to use a technique like shabar, they would be committing malpractice. But because sozo healers claim to be faith healers—even as they use what are clearly tools garnered from psychology—they manage to escape from government regulation.

What is rapidly becoming clear is that the sozo model, like the theophostic model, is in many ways what psychiatrist Robert Jay Lifton called a "sacred science." In a sacred science, totalistic philosophies hold out "an ultimate vision for the ordering of human existence" (427). The sacred science argues that it both transcends "ordinary concerns of logic" yet "at the same times makes an exaggerated claim of airtight logic, of absolute scientific precision" (Lifton 428). The end result is that people come to believe that an "absolute science of ideas ... exists ... that this science can be combined with an equally absolute body of moral principles; and that the resulting doctrine is true for all men at all times" (428). Though the concept of sacred science has occasionally itself been turned into a form of sacred science, the concept is still of great explanatory value in discussing sozo. As with other sacred sciences, the sozo method creates exaggerated claims of healing based on an "absolute science of ideas" that masks the truly often painful, hesitant, and seldom complete process of healing into a formulaic path of total life transformation by one particular healing paradigm.

For Protestant fundamentalists, the sacred science is biblical prooftexting, a practice that also has some relevance to Pentecostals and Charismatics. However, Pentecostals and Charismatics combine this kind of sacred science with an intuitive moralistic approach. For instance, a typical approach to intellectual matters is exhibited by Paula Kilpatrick—a deliverance minister whose book and deliverances Mercy Ministries founder Nancy Alcorn endorsed (Kilpatrick and Kilpatrick v)—when she stated, "Based upon the years that I have been ministering deliverance and observing, what I am giving right now is from my heart. It is not from reading books, because very few people know very much about deliverance. Or if they do, it is all messed up.... I didn't read many books because I found that they just messed me up. I found out if it works, do it. Just go with what works for you" (Kilpatrick xi). For Charismatics, the sacred science is both pragmatic and intuitive, as opposed to the more rigid system of hermeneutical sacred science practiced by fundamentalists. This is clearly seen in the increasingly pseudoscientific claims made by healers like the McMichaels. Whereas traditional psychology and psychiatry limit themselves to testifiable results and when ethically practiced do not promise 100 percent cure rates, deliverance practitioners feed on the desire of Charismatics and Pentecostals for quick effortless healing of physical and emotional distress.

The results of such practices can be disastrous. The Healing Rooms ministries that are promoted by the McMichaels and run by Cal Pierce feature testimonies of healing from illnesses that range from cancer to depression, paranoia, bipolar, and even AIDS ("Healing Room Testimonies"). Though the ministry does not directly claim on these Web pages to be responsible for these healings, this is the obvious implication, particularly since the healings almost always reference a local healing room. Even if it is somehow ethically justifiable to claim one can alleviate mental health problems through inner healing and deliverance, it very clearly is unethical to promote the idea that one can heal maladies like cancer and AIDS through faith healing. Even though Pierce's ministry wishes to work concurrently with the medical establishment (Cal Pierce, *Healing in the Kingdom,* 121–122), its promotion of the sozo methodology within its healing rooms is at best extremely dubious. Worse, these healing rooms' widespread nature (there were at least 1300 Healing Rooms worldwide as of 2010, in 52 countries) (Gaines) means that potentially millions of people are being told that their physical or mental healing is as much, perhaps even more, a result of divine intervention than biological intervention. Healing rooms can take the credit for medical improvements, even if there's no proof that they had anything to do with these improvements. But the reverse situation would never be countenanced by the healing room movement or by other practitioners of sozo methodology.

And we do know that sozo has potentially dangerous effects. Bill and Beni Johnson's practice the supposed spiritual healing of autistic children ("About Bethel Sozo"). The ministry has made claims about being able to raise people from the dead, though these claims have been good-naturedly denied by Marty Best, manager of the Mason County Department of Emergency Management located near Johnson's ministry (Winters "Faith Healings"). While no Lazarus events have been recorded, there has been one rather notorious example of Bethel's faith healing ministry allegedly almost causing a death when two students at Bethel waited to call for help for an injured man because they thought they could raise him from the dead. The man alleges that he is a paraplegic as a result (Sabalow "Faith Healing or Foul Play").[10] Such an event was practically destined to happen, given Bethel church's belief in such miraculous apparitions as the spontaneous falling of gold dust and sometimes feathers from heaven, and death-raising practices themselves (Winters "Bethel Signs and Wonders"; Winters "Faith Healings").

Why, then, promote sozo? Well, one reason may be that Bethel Church sells its DVD curricula to churches, controversial even among evangelicals, for upwards of $7,000 (Robertson). Bethel promotes its sozo curriculum, which focuses on "inner healing" and "deliverance," throughout the United States ("Sozo overview"). And, of course, there is usually a charge for sozo "services." Sozo sessions of two to three hours typically cost $75 ("Sozo overview"; "FAQ Sozo: Questions and Answers"). Whether or not Bethel church seeks to directly profit from the practice, it is clear, given the widespread popularity of sozo nationwide, that sozo healing keeps more than a few deliverance supporters gainfully, even wealthily, employed. Sozo is big business. And it looks like it is here to stay.

3

Mission Without Mercy
Mercy Ministries and Deliverance

At age 21, Naomi Johnson was working on a psychology degree at Edith Cowan University in Australia. She worked part time and managed to maintain a fairly independent life despite struggling with an eating disorder. Johnson could not afford entrance into a specialty clinic for dealing with her anorexia, something she wanted to get under control. Because she did not have access to private health insurance or publicly funded service, she decided to go to Mercy Ministries, flying thousands of kilometers away from her family to enter this Christian live-in program. Nine months later she left extremely distraught, feeling little more than a child and terrified to leave her bedroom because she was afraid of the "demons" (literally) that were causing her anorexia. A few months afterward, Johnson entered a mainstream psychiatric unit (Pollard, "They Prayed to Cast").

But Johnson eventually fought back against those who had labeled her struggles demonic. Along with Meg Smith (pseudonym) and Rhiannon Canham-Wright, Johnson went to the media with her story. The three women's description of their time at Mercy Ministries read like some tale out of the Dark Ages. The women had been promised psychiatric treatment and clinical support, but instead were put in the care of Bible students, many of them under 30 years of age and many with their own mental health issues. The counseling the program offered involved prayer readings, exorcism of clients, and tongues-speaking (Pollard, "They Prayed to Cast").

Being a thoroughly secular culture, Australians were scandalized by the goings-on at Mercy. The Australian Medical Association immediately voiced concern about Mercy's practice of forcing "vulnerable patients to see a doctor in the presence of an unrelated third party [as being] both dangerous and potentially unethical" (Pollard, "Ethics"). Allan Fels, former chairman of the Australian Competition and Consumer Commission, warned Mercy that its "misleading and deceptive conduct" could lead to injunctions, damages, and fines ("They Sought Help"). Australian cultural critic Tanya Levin, a former member of Mercy's major Australian supporter, Hillsong Church, voiced the opinion that Mercy Ministries was a godsend for Hillsong, allowing the church to claim it helped young women outcast by "the world," while simultaneously enhancing Hillsong's recruitment and fund-raising efforts (Levin). Australian consumers soon found out that Gloria Jeans Coffees' cofounder, Peter Irvine, who was the director of the Australian Branch of Mercy Ministries, was promoting Mercy through both Gloria Jeans and Borders bookstore. This campaign even included Borders employees being asked to "page customers, every hour, about the coffee emporium's 'Cappucino for a Cause' day in which 10 cents, from every Gloria Jean's cappuccino was donated to the charity Mercy Ministries" (Capone).

The controversy soon spread when the exorcism manuals that Mercy Ministries used were leaked to the media. On November 26, 2008, Tim Brunero reported that "handbooks allegedly used to perform exorcisms on sick girls at the controversial Mercy Ministries residences in Sydney and on the Sunshine coast have been leaked" (Brunero). The exorcism manual, according to Brunero, had sections like "Identifying Additional Demons...." Later, the book, *Restoring the Foundations,* published by an American Christian group, warns those exorcising demons to be firm. "The ministers' commanding attitude [towards demons] resembles that of a person speaking to a little 'yappy dog'" (Brunero).

The controversy next made its way to the American Mercy homes. Nancy Alcorn claimed that the Australian operation had been rogue, operating independently of American control. A significant number of American graduates disagreed, as Caleb Hannan related in the October 2, 2008, issue of the *Nashville Scene*: "While the Australian press devoured the scandal's juiciest morsels—the money and the exorcisms—several former Nashville graduates were drawn to the familiar stories of neglect: the threats of expulsion, and the use of prayer as a substitute for psychiatric care" (Hannan, "Jesus RX"). Jodi Ferris, one of the older survivors and one of the initial leaders in raising awareness about Mercy's therapeutic methodology, related how Mercy had gradually acculturated women to the Restoring the Foundations therapeutic approach that was at the heart of the ministry, the last step of which is casting out demons, "a process that sometimes involved the bedrock of charismatic Pentecostalism: speaking in tongues" (Hannan, "Jesus RX"). Hannan's article also suggested that Nancy Alcorn might be gay, a literally explosive charge in evangelical culture, not only because of evangelicalism's traditional antigay bias, but also because Mercy Ministries promoted itself as a healing center for those "suffering" from homosexual attractions (see Hannan, "Jesus RX"). Alcorn eventually responded to the charges with denial in a February 25, 2009, blog post (Alcorn, "Nancy Alcorn Sets the Record Straight"). In the "post comments" section, Alcorn allowed opponents to dialogue with her significantly for the first time, with the supporters and detractors of Mercy Ministries quickly dividing themselves into diametrically opposing ideological positions. While detractors (including this author) tried to point out the "rational" reasons for opposing Mercy's therapeutic practice, supporters of Mercy and Alcorn challenged detractors with such warnings as this: "I rebuke you trolls in the name of Jesus. Go back to the pits of hell where you belong" (Alcorn, "Nancy Alcorn Sets the Record Straight").

Though Mercy Ministries managed to preserve its reputation in the States, even with supporters claiming Mercy Australia had no links to Mercy America, its reputation was largely in tatters in Australia.[1] Because of Mercy's poor Australian reputation, the homes in Australia eventually closed (Pollard, "Mercy Ministries Home to Close"). The American homes still remain open, as do Mercy "affiliates" in the UK, Canada and New Zealand (See "Locations"). Mercy Ministries now uses a curriculum called *Choices That Bring Change* ("FAQS Mercy"), which is apparently self-generated since, unlike *Restoring the Foundations,* it is not readily available for sale in the United States.[2] Since the closing of the Australian homes, Mercy has aggressively tried to rebrand itself through several tactics, most notably promoting the trendy evangelical cause of sex trafficking abolitionism (Mercy Ministries Web site; Sweatte). But for many of the ministry's critics, particularly the Mercy Survivors organization, this is too little too late.

The question remains: why did Mercy Ministries prove so successful in courting powerful Christian backers? Why was *Restoring the Foundations* (2001), one of the most extreme deliverance manuals produced by the Christian right, used for so long by Mercy? What was the underlying ideology of Mercy Ministries and its founder, Nancy Alcorn, and how did that ideology affect the ministry's operations? To understand why Mercy became the way it is, indeed perhaps even to feel compassion for Alcorn, in spite of the horrendous things she did (and very likely continues to do) to Mercy clients, we must step back and look at Alcorn's own life and how Mercy Ministries started. In the process, we will find that Mercy Ministries has close ties to some of the most extreme elements of the religious right, particularly the New Apostolic Reformation. In the process of casting out demons, Alcorn made alliances with much more earthly forces of evil. And Mercy Ministries' clients were the ultimate victims of these all too earthly moral compromises.

"Mercy Ministries' History"

Alcorn dates her "salvation experience" to 1972, and says it is thanks to the efforts of a friend from high school who took her to a youth service (Alcorn, *Mission of Mercy*, 12). Alcorn was early on influenced by the work of Teen Challenge. Her book *Mission to Mercy* (2013) relates how she showed the film *The Cross and the Switchblade* (1970), a popular film and book about David Wilkerson, Teen Challenge's founder, to an audience at a state juvenile facility in Tennessee where she worked for five years (Alcorn, *Mission of Mercy*, 23–25).

Understanding the view Alcorn developed of the state during this period in her life is crucial to understanding the direction Mercy Ministries' efforts eventually took. Alcorn mixes classic evangelical anti-stateism with a very particular dislike of the state's relationship to "troubled" young women. In *Echoes of Mercy*, Alcorn writes as follows: "Not only must we share the Gospel with our words, but we must address with our actions the hurts and needs that confront us daily. We, not the government, are commanded to support the unwed mothers. We, not the government, are commanded to release the young women in bondage to drug addiction, promiscuity and other sins.... We, not the government, are commanded to bring restoration to broken lives" (Alcorn, *Echoes of Mercy*, 170). Alcorn positions the Christian gospel as being antithetical to government involvement in people's daily lives. It is the Christian's responsibility, not the state's, to administer economic and social relief to the common person. By taking the church's place, the government usurps Christian authority over the private and domestic sphere of people's lives. Worse, because government intervention is based on secular principles, it is unlikely, from an evangelical perspective, to do much good in treating mental health, sexual, or addiction issues. The secular world, not recognizing the true underlying spiritual problems that in the Charismatic worldview characterize many mental illnesses and other traumatic problems, is unequipped to deal with the true root causes of these issues. Alcorn therefore sees Mercy Ministries and other church programs resembling it as essentially serving as evangelistic arms of the church.

Alcorn expresses frustration in *Echoes of Mercy* (1992; revised 2008) that her early work with teenage girls was restricted by her working in a secular treatment facility (Alcorn, *Echoes*, 23–25). As Alcorn writes, "Yet no matter what kind of programs the government offers, no matter how many tax dollars it spends, and no matter how many experts it hires, the government cannot forgive their sin—not even one" (Alcorn, *Echoes*, 25). Alcorn felt that secular therapeutic systems being offered during her work with the State of Tennessee represented a form of behaviorist or biological determinism or both. According to Alcorn, "the experts" argued that the girls she treated were "the way they were because of their parents' and grandparents' backgrounds, they would always be this way, and it would be the same for their children. They were giving them nothing but a doom and gloom picture of the future" (Alcorn, *Mission of Mercy*, 24–25). For Alcorn this kind of deterministic view of human behavior prevented people from transforming themselves, through Christ, into healthier and happier human beings.

The quite consistently anti-determinist elements of Nancy Alcorn's thought might shock those readers who are aware of her ministry's long-standing support of generational curses, an idea that seems itself to be quite predeterministic.[3] It's even more surprising in light of Alcorn's close alliance with Bill Hamon and Christians International, who borrow strongly from Calvinist-like, though not Calvinist, elements of restorationist Latter Rain and NAR thinking. There's no easy way of explaining this paradox, but two things should be noted. First, Alcorn would, like any good Christian, distinguish between biological and behavioral determinism and theistic determinism. Second, strictly speaking, while the idea of generational curses is predeterministic, the cure for these curses is not. Through intercession and processes like identification repentance, Charismatics and Pentecostals, particularly within the NAR, believe they can stand in the gap for demonically or sin-oppressed individuals or populations (including even, within the NAR, whole nation groups) and achieve victory over the curse that dooms them. This element of "the curse is broken in Christ" runs throughout Alcorn's writing and speeches[4] and contrasts strongly with the more strictly deterministic (in genetic terms) thought of the early healing revivalists like William Branham.

In any case, the government's error, for Alcorn, is fundamental: It misdiagnoses a sin problem as a problem rooted in socioeconomic and nonmoral factors. Alcorn's diagnosis of the cultural issues facing the young women she deals with is a moral one. Regardless of whatever socioeconomic factors these women face—misogyny, a culture of sexual violence, lack of economic parity in the workplace, patriarchal attitudes within the church itself—Alcorn commits herself to a reading of young women's problems in individualistic, rather than structural, terms. Indeed, Mercy's entire reading of cultural problems is in general anti-structural. Alcorn's primary problem with the church, as it is, is this:

> When people hear about troubled youths, runaways, teen drug users, and victims of physical and sexual abuse, they commonly assume that it is the government's responsibility to take care of them and restore their lives. Even Christians sometimes over-

look their biblical responsibility, leaving it to the government.... The state cannot bring restoration to broken lives—it is unequipped for the task. The reason is simple: God has not anointed the government to "bind up the brokenhearted" or to "proclaim liberty to the captives." He has anointed the church. We are to set them free [Alcorn, *Echoes*, First Edition, 30].[5]

For Alcorn, the nexus of the problems that "troubled youth" deal with lies not in structural inequalities caused by a capitalist system, but in personal moral problems ("broken lives") that only the church is equipped to heal. A more structuralist Christian approach, like the one favored by liberation theologians, would emphasize the liberating aspects of government involvement in "redeeming" culture. Such an approach has even been approved of by some conservatives, for very different ends: compassionate conservatism, for instance, is a good example. Alcorn's ministry stands in stark opposition to such an approach. So long as the church assumes that the problems of troubled youth are solely those of the community at large, it will do these youth a disservice, since government is not equipped to heal personal problems. Only the church is. It is likely that Alcorn's attraction to the New Apostolic Reformation (through the ministry of Bill Hamon), which heavily focuses on church intervention into, and dominion over, social problems, has its roots in her profound—even for evangelicals—dislike of stateism.

It must be emphasized here that Alcorn's vision is by no means wholly negative or cynical. She has shown a consistent, and probably sincere, concern about the lack of Christian engagement with young women's mental health problems. Thus, her statements in *Echoes of Mercy* are as much a condemnation of the apathy of the church towards young people's problems as they are jabs at the governmental approach to mental health treatment. It is also important to contextualize how Alcorn formed her opinion of the governmental mental health treatment system. Her work at the correctional facility for troubled girls in Tennessee lasted for five years. According to Alcorn, several young women were assaulted during this time period (Alcorn, *Echoes*, 21). She expresses her distress at the facility's use of "behavior modification" (26), which she felt produced only "temporary" healing and left girls fundamentally "the same on the inside. Once they returned to their same friends and environment, they began living as they had before" (Alcorn, *Echoes*, 26). For Alcorn, behaviorism failed to help young girls because they "needed transformation, not *modification*" (27). Secular treatment methodologies, besides being unbiblical, were unable to effectively change the environments young women lived in. Personal change, for Alcorn, *brings about* structural change. Behaviorism, though rooted in a structuralist government approach, is actually to Alcorn a more individualistic approach to mental health treatment than that advocated by Mercy, since Mercy's goal is to redeem the community through redeeming the individual. The government's goals can never be so lofty. Alcorn's analysis of mental health treatment during her formative years[6] hardly seems an inaccurate one either. The overly behaviorist approach of much of 1970s mental health treatment, based in secular behaviorist methodologies hardly less cruel than the deliverance model,[7] could have very easily convinced a woman like Alcorn that she could offer both a better and kinder treatment approach than that available from the state. Even principled, reasonable authors such as feminist novelist Marge Piercy expressed concern about such treatment methods during the seventies.[8]

Alcorn was also clearly, and possibly quite sincerely, traumatized by her later work with child protective services (CPS). Alcorn relates the following:

> There were many, many nights when I met the police on emergency calls and saw firsthand little girls and little boys who had been horribly sexually abused by grown men and women who should have been their protectors. There were many little children who had been physically beaten.... I spent three years investigating child abuse cases and seeing this awful stuff. The sexual abuse was the hardest for me. We had to sit across the table from the perpetrators and gather details for the case records. It was very, very difficult, and I was very conflicted as a Christian. We're supposed to love and care for everybody, but it was almost impossible. I was so angry with the people I had to look at and talk to because of the unthinkable things they had done to a child. I began to have nightmares [Alcorn, *Mission of Mercy*, 31–33].

While I do not wish to offer a diagnosis of Alcorn, she herself clearly feels that her work with these young women left her traumatized. Alcorn talks about her experience with a therapist who seemed to feel that Alcorn was dealing with post-traumatic stress (Alcorn, *Mission of Mercy*, 67). In what is surely one of the most revealing vignettes in her writings, Alcorn talks about how her therapist viewed her trauma as resulting from Satan's wish "to use these [traumatic] 'openings' to torment you" (Alcorn, *Mission of Mercy*, 67). Alcorn's treatment method for herself, in other words, is not much different from that she promotes for her clients. Though Alcorn does see a professional therapist (there is a great deal of debate about whether Mercy has always offered the same option), the therapy she receives is predicated on the same basic assumptions about demonic and Satanic influences on mental health that have traditionally informed Mercy Ministries' own therapeutic practice.

Alcorn's anger and feelings of hopelessness at the mistreatment of abused children during the seventies and early eighties mirrors that of the well-meaning feminists who ended up initially promoting the ritual abuse panic during roughly the same period. Debbie Nathan and Michael Snedeker, in talking about the Arizona Children's Home, the workplace of one of the panic's early leading voices, Kathleen MacFarlane, express how employment at the home during the late sixties and seventies "took on an almost missionary aura and fostered an intense camaraderie. The paraprofessionals [who worked there] spent their leisure time at the same bars, and as a group took the children on long camping trips. They spoke about stopping the war, about opposing Richard Nixon, and about the problems of the youngsters in their care" (Nathan and Snedeker 13). Early advocates for abused children, just like Alcorn herself, did not promote structuralist solutions for the issue of child abuse and did not cast the problem as one of socioeconomics, despite the fact that later research showed "that just as with physical abuse and neglect, sex abuse was linked to poverty" (Nathan and Snedeker 17). Nathan and Snedeker's book, particularly its first chapter, meticulously highlights how time after time during the 1970s well-meaning children's and women's advocates made crucial, and clinically unsound, mistakes concerning how to deal with the problem of sexual abuse, particularly in families (Nathan and Snedeker 11–28). Particularly damaging were the efforts of politicians and children's advocates during this period to keep abusive fathers in families while using therapy to treat them. Not only did this put young women at risk, but the use of the "therapy model of sex-abuse intervention replaced skilled forensics personnel with social workers and others who knew nothing about how to test the validity of criminal sex-abuse charges and who unstintingly believed all of them" (Nathan and Snedeker 28). Thus, paradoxically, both victims of sex abuse and those falsely accused of abuse were put at risk.

Alcorn's concerns with the child protection system at the time therefore had a quite real basis in fact. And it is easy to see, given the numerous missteps made by feminists during the initial stages of child protection activism, why Alcorn came to believe that she had a better treatment plan to offer than her contemporaries. Indeed, while the same could not necessarily be said of her staff, Alcorn herself was in some ways as qualified to treat abuse victims as early advocates like MacFarlane, both women specializing in social work (see Snedeker 13; Campbell). The problem with both MacFarlane and Alcorn's methods was not so much their native intelligence as their foundational presuppositions concerning young women's problems. For MacFarlane, trauma took on an individualistic character, largely free from social, economic, or cultural influence. Alcorn's presupposition, concerning both the traumatized and the mentally ill, was that both populations suffered from Satanic or demonic affliction and therefore could be liberated through a gospel message. In both cases, harm was done by, at least at the time, well-meaning trauma and illness advocates, because these advocates did not support their ideas with well-researched scientific or scholarly evidence.

Roughly in between her work with the state and Mercy Ministries,[9] Alcorn began working with both Teen Challenge and an Illinois ministry called Team Thrust for the Nations.[10] Alcorn was clearly impressed by a federal government survey, later backed up by a dissertation by Aaron Todd Bicknese, that Teen Challenge was more effective than similar secular programs. Teen Challenge credited this success to the "Jesus factor," which in Alcorn's personal interpretation seems to mean that the only "identifiable difference between the two [secular and Christian programs] was the inclusion of teaching Christian values" (Alcorn, *Echoes*, 41; Goodstein). Similar claims, modeled doubtlessly after Teen Challenge, were later made for Mercy Ministries itself, which claimed that Mercy Ministries, in 93 percent of cases, helped transform girls' lives and restore their hope ("Results"). However, as a *New York Times* report pointed out, such claims, particularly for Teen Challenge, are deeply misleading. Social scientists argue that Teen Challenge's claim of an 86 percent success rate distorts research evidence, because it does not count people who dropped out of the program. In addition, like many religious and private charities but unlike many secular treatment facilities, Teen Challenge "picks its clients" (Goodstein). David Reingold, a researcher at the Indiana University School of Public and Environmental Affairs, after working on research concerning religious charities' effectiveness, argued that "It's an extreme exaggeration to say that religious organizations are more effective" (Goodstein). Alcorn's work with Teen Challenge and Team Thrust confirmed her belief that she needed to work in a "Christian environment" if the young women she treated were to "have a chance to live joyful, fulfilling lives and not end up on the streets" (Alcorn, *Echoes,* 42). For Alcorn, this was a Manichean conflict between good and evil: Secularist treatment led to poverty and death, while Christian treatment offered the only means of hope available. This kind of dichotomous division between one's chances for success at Christian treatment centers versus secular treatment centers came to characterize much of Mercy rhetoric over the next 30 years.[11]

Alcorn founded Mercy Ministries in 1983 (Alcorn, *Echoes of Mercy,* revised edition, back cover). Over the course of the eighties the ministry gradually consolidated. The Monroe, Louisiana, home opened first, in 1983. This was followed by Nashville in 1996, the international headquarters for Mercy in Nashville in 2001, the St. Louis home in 2005, the Bradford, UK, home in 2006, the Auckland, New Zealand, home in 2007, the Sacramento home in 2009, and the Vancouver, British Columbia, home in 2010 (Alcorn, *Mission of Mercy*). The Australian homes are now closed down.[12] Before the Mercy scandal in Australia, there were also plans afoot to open homes in Lima, Peru, and Johannesburg, South Africa, thus widening Mercy's clientele into the developing world (Alcorn, *Echoes*, 2nd edition, 206).

Alcorn's early efforts were in a wide variety of areas. Like many evangelical ministries to "troubled" youth, Mercy tended to try to minister to a range of problems, from mental illness (especially eating disorders), cutting, and drug addiction to sexual abuse.[13] Mercy has at times also treated people for same-sex attraction, as well as promoting the teachings of Sy Rogers, one of the more extreme members of the ex-gay movement (Alcorn, *Echoes* 114–115; Pollard, "God's Cure for Gays"). Although in recent years the eating disorders and abuse aspects have appeared to have taken more center stage, Alcorn's efforts, particularly (from what the scant historical record can tell us) in the ministry's early years, involved pro-life activism as well. According to the *Nashville Tennessean,* Alcorn, along with Richard Crotteau of Bethany Christian Services of Tennessee, was directly involved in a 1992 attempt to challenge the legality of abortion by asking to be appointed guardians of "all unborn children who might be affected by abortions" in Tennessee. Alcorn and Crotteau's lawyer cited a "1988 proclamation by then president Ronald Reagan as the basis for his argument that fetuses should be considered people with legal rights under the U.S. Constitution" (Loggins).

Alcorn's ministry works closely with crisis pregnancy centers to "aid" young women considering alternatives to abortion, and women are recommended to Mercy Ministries frequently by crisis pregnancy centers (CPC). Mercy's adoption efforts have been promoted by powerful Charismatic leaders, including Joel Osteen. It was thanks to Mercy's efforts that Joel's sister Lisa was able to adopt three Mercy children ("Pastor Joel Osteen"). While Alcorn's individual efforts to "minister" to young women seeking abortion may not be problematic, it is troubling that she is uniting her efforts in helping crisis pregnancy centers with similar efforts to find adoptive parents for children. As Kathryn Joyce meticulously documents in *The Child Catchers* (2013), adoption efforts in evangelicalism have turned frequently into something of an organized racket (Joyce et al.), to the point where evangelical adoption agencies are often serving as virtual human traffickers themselves (see Joyce 93–114 in particular).

It is unclear from the available historical evidence how long Mercy Ministries has practiced deliverance as its counseling methodology, but evidence suggests that it long predates the Australian controversy. Alcorn explicitly endorses the deliverance manual of Paula and Charlie Kilpatrick, published in 1995, in its foreword (Kilpatrick v).[14] Kilpatrick even "ministered" to young women at Mercy Ministries, which, given the context of the foreword, likely means that she herself practiced deliverance at Mercy, in addition to having Alcorn endorse her deliverance ministry. Indeed, there is recorded audio proof, now freely available online, that Nancy Alcorn herself has helped perform an exorcism (Alcorn, "Keys to Walking and Living in Freedom").[15]

Just when Mercy Ministries started using the Restoring the Foundations program is a little harder to tell, but it dates to at least 2000 or 2001, as Jodi Ferris confirmed to the *Nashville Scene* that she received the Restoring the Foundations manual from Mercy around that time (Hannan, "Jesus RX"). There are two reasons why the manual is disturbing, both of which will be discussed in great detail, as understanding the truly disturbing nature of this manual is vital if one is to understand why the Mercy controversy so shocked and divided the evangelical community and so outraged Australians when parts of the manual were made freely available to the public. The first reason is Restoring the Foundations' particular method of "ground level" deliverance. The second reason is how that practice of ground level deliverance, as practiced by both the Kylstras and Nancy Alcorn, was fueled by the New Apostolic Reformation. To understand the first practice, we must look at *Restoring the Foundations,* as well as some of the deliverance and evangelical material with which Alcorn has publicly identified in the past, and also her own writing. Works that Alcorn has referenced include her own *Mercy for* Series (*Violated, Starved, Cut*) and *Echoes of Mercy,* the Klystras' *Restoring the Foundations* (cited in all three of the former books, see *Violated* 61, *Starved* 81 and *Cut* 85), Neil Anderson's *The Bondage Breaker* (cited as an important text in *Cut* 85, *Violated* 61, and *Starved* 81), Charles Capps' *God's Creative Power for Healing* (1991) (cited in *Violated* 61), and the writings of Linda Mintle, who according to Alcorn herself "played a key role in training our counselors and staff, and has provided resources that are used daily in our Mercy Ministries' homes" (Alcorn, "Beauty Is in the Eye of the Beholder").[16]

Given her anti-psychological position, Alcorn's position on the life of the mind can be roughly characterized as anti-intellectual. In *Echoes of Mercy,* she contrasts the "big medical terminology" and "expensive medication" of the world with Mercy Ministries program, which "makes things very clear" (*Echoes of Mercy,* 91). Mercy's treatment methodology, therefore, was deliberately marketed as being something simple, a theological system that was easy to decipher rather than a medical practice that takes years of training to master. This problematically positions Mercy as an organization committed to rejecting the "world's" knowledge whenever that "big medical terminology" fails to conform to Mercy's worldview.

Indeed, most of the deliverance manuals Mercy endorses are deeply pessimistic about the value of skepticism and questioning in the life of the mind. *The Bondage Breaker,* for instance, argues that naturalistic explanations for mental problems often indicate a naturalistic worldview, because they "ignore the influence of the spiritual world" (Anderson, *Bondage Breaker,* 21). Anderson derides the scientific method because its explanation of mental illness goes hand in hand with its explanation of "the origin of the species" (21). Anderson sets himself up against not simply philosophical naturalism, but arguably against any of the theoretical methodologies that are a byproduct of it. Thus, philosophies like behaviorism are rejected out of hand, not because they are wrong, but because they conflict with Anderson's anti-scientific worldview (see Anderson, Zuehlke and Zuehlke, *Christ Centered Therapy*, 31–32).

Far more troubling than *The Bondage Breaker,* however, is the epistemological system in *Restoring the Foundations* (RTF). The RTF manual argues that "our thinking has to be changed so it lines up with God's Truth and not the facts of our experience.... Facts are true, based on experience in the here and now. But: There is a higher level of truth than the facts. And that is God's Truth. The real truth is what He says about the situation" (Kylstra and Kylstra 174). The almost Orwellian nature of this statement is obvious to even the most casual reader. For those who undergo RTF treatment, what matters is not their subjective experience, nor what is true, but the truth that is higher than facts. What exactly such a statement means, of course, is deliberately left open to interpretation. And that interpretive room can be easily utilized to promote an abusive counseling system, when "God's Truth" is identified with the particular teachings of a particular spiritual leader. The truth then becomes not what God "says about the situation," but what that leader says about the given situation. If the leader promotes a strict hierarchized system of obedience, as is quite common in Charismatic organizations, the result can be an extreme form of discipleship that deprives already vulnerable young women of their personal agency in confronting emotional problems.

The Kylstras' epistemological system also encourages their adherents to replace any attempt at rational inquiry with an appeal to divine fiat. What matters to the Kylstras is not the actual truthfulness of a statement, but whether that truthfulness conforms to God's word. There is, in short, truth and Truth, and upper-case Truth is always predominant. If lower-case truth gets in the way, it is to be casually disposed of. What matters is that the ideological system remain uncontested; the actual truth content of that system becomes irrelevant, since lower-case truth does not exist apart from what God "says about the situation."

The Kylstras compound the intellectual problems associated with such an epistemological system by coming up with an even more bizarre theory of demons' influence on the mind. The Kylstras believe "some ... dear people have gone through life as analyzing machines. They analyze everything.... In addition a demon may be empowering the analytical thinking" (Kylstra and Kylstra 220). The Kylstras also promote the existence of "skepticism demons" (227) and "mental-blocking demons" (307). The latter "strategize to prevent deliverance of other demons. They whisper messages to the person's mind such as: 'Demons are not real. This is an outdated concept. My problems are really psychological.' ... These demons work to affect the person's belief system and, thus, his will. The most common blocking demons are doubt, unbelief, skepticism, rationalism, and pride" (Kylstra and Kylstra 307). Thus, for the Kylstras, the very existence of doubt is possible proof of possession. The more a client resists the RTF deliverance system, the more likely the RTF counselor or facilitator is to assume that the demonic, rather than the physical, is involved in the client's mental health problems. Worse, the direct result of teaching vulnerable people to believe in a mental blocking demon is that they may end up believing that they cannot trust any of their own internal judgments, since it is impossible to tell what judgments are and are not being influenced by demons. Whomever one turns to, one cannot trust, because that person may be consorting with demonic forces. Nor can one trust her own senses, since they too may simply be part of this demonic Pentecostal matrix. Of course, it is impossible to disprove the idea of "mental blocking demons." The idea is not amenable to disproof, since any negative conclusion one comes to on the existence of demons, regardless of its validity, could be merely discounted as false sense impressions created by demonic forces. The promotion of the existence of skepticism demons also ensures that Mercy residents will have trouble resorting to secular therapy, since that therapy, from the Mercy standpoint, is based on skepticism and therefore is vulnerable to demonic influence.

As Mercy Survivors have themselves pointed out, *Restoring the Foundations,* much like Ed Smith's theophostic counseling (from which it borrows some ideas, see Kylstra and Kylstra 235–236), represents the kind of "sacred science" that Robert Lifton so deftly critiques in his *Thought Reform and the Psychology of Totalism: A Study of Brainwashing in China* (1961) (Mercy Survivors, "Is Mercy Ministries"). There are an intimidating number of steps, prayers, and ideas that one must accept, reject, or think about in order to receive healing in the Restoring the Foundations system. The system is basically broken into four "foundational Problem/Ministry Areas of: 1) Sins of the Fathers and Resulting Curses 2) Ungodly Beliefs 3) Soul/Spirit Hurts, 4) and Demonic Oppression. The key phrase, Integrated Approach to Healing Ministry, means ministry to all of these areas in concert under the direction and power of the Holy Spirit" (Kylstra and Kylstra xvii). Each of these ideas is important to understanding the complete RTF ideology and its relationship to wider Charismatic and Pentecostal teaching.

The Kylstras define curses as "consequences, penalties of sin, which are put into action when we break God's law. Curses frequently continue from one generation to the next, especially when the original sin involved the occult or when there has been no repentance for the initial sin" (Kylstra and Kylstra 24). Although generational curses resulting from sins of the father need not automatically lead to demonic oppression, in the Kylstras' system—as in other deliverance methodologies that promote the idea of generational curses—they almost inevitably do lead to such oppression. As in other Charismatic deliverance systems, generational curses, when combined with the idea of demonic oppression or demonization, end up operating in a manner strikingly similar to how secularists today perceive genetics, with curses being passed down the family line.

Ungodly beliefs (UGB) are any beliefs, decisions, attitudes, etc., that "do not agree with God" (Kylstra and Kylstra 157). This is, of course, a very nebulous definition, depending as it does upon one's belief in God and the relative merits of differing theistic systems. According to the Kylstras, ungodly beliefs are crucial to the working of demons in people's lives. They "provide legal permission for demons to stay. Why? Because we are in agreement with the Devil—rather than God—when we have an UGB" (Kylstra and Kylstra 159). Taken to its logical extension, of course, this idea would imply that every human being, Christian or non–Christian, is thoroughly demonized, since it would be difficult in the extreme for any human being to measure up to the "biblical" standard of godliness, let alone the standard provided by the Kylstras.

Soul and Spirit Hurts, the third element of the Kylstras system, are "hurts on the 'inside' of a person. They are wounds to the soul or the spirit of man that are carried and experienced within the person himself. They are not physical and they cannot be seen. Their presence is revealed by their symptoms, by the manifested evidence of unhealed emotions, behaviors, and thoughts" (Kylstra and Kylstra 200). According to the Kylstras, demonic oppression relates to this area of their system because "demons do not play fair. When hurt or trauma is experienced by someone, certain demons frequently invade: fear, failure, isolation, loneliness, shame.... Their work does not stop with the invasion. They continue to agitate and stir up the same hurts by 'picking off the scabs,' so to speak" (Kylstra and Kylstra 203). One concept that seems to flow out of the Kylstras' investment in the concept of soul/spirit hurts is their promotion of one of the most extreme ideas within Charismatic circles today: the concept of soul ties.

The Kylstras' system defines a soul tie as "an ungodly covenant with another person, organization, or thing based on an unhealthy emotional and/or sexual relationship" (Kylstra and Kylstra 322). The idea of soul ties is deeply troubling to those working with abuse and trauma victims, because in its typical manifestation concerning sexual abuse, the concept refers to a literal demonic tie between a rapist and a victim. Doris Wagner, wife of C. Peter Wagner (the most powerful figure in the NAR and perhaps in Charismatic and Pentecostal Christianity in general), promotes the idea that when "an injustice or serious sin has been committed, such as child sexual abuse," unforgiveness eventually sets in. Inevitably, this "invites a demon of unforgiveness to set up housekeeping in the soul of that person" (Doris Wagner, "Forgiving the Unforgivable," 99). What is disturbing about Wagner's and the Klystras' position here is that it is all but explicitly endorsed by Nancy Alcorn herself, even as Alcorn's ministry tries to treat trauma victims. According to Alcorn:

> A soul tie is the knitting together of two souls. This tie can bring either tremendous blessing ... or tremendous destruction when made outside of marriage.... In the case of sexual abuse, your soul has been violated, along with your body, and mysteriously knit with the soul of your abuser. This unhealthy connection affects the way you think and feel and the decisions you make. You may have experienced guilt for feeling attached or connected to your abuser or you may have frequent thoughts about him or her or notice strong feelings toward that person. Those are all natural responses to an ungodly soul tie [Alcorn, *Violated*, 25–26].

Assuming Alcorn is using the same definition of ungodly soul ties as virtually every other Pentecostal or Charismatic who deals with sexual abuse, one is forced to conclude that she literally believes rape victims have a demonic attachment to their abusers. One need not even have a particularly negative view of Alcorn to come to this conclusion. For Pentecostals and Charismatics, destroying such demonic attachments is often seen as a key means of helping people achieve normative mental health. Therefore, Alcorn may sincerely believe she is helping people while still promoting this belief.

The fourth element of the Kylstras' system is, of course, demonic oppression. The Kylstras use a softer term than demonization, namely oppression, to convey their feelings of demonic influence (Kylstra and Kylstra 274). Nevertheless, their own demonic taxonomical system is by far the most detailed extant, surpassing even that of *Pigs in the Parlor* (on which it is modeled, as one can see by the demonic oppression groupings the Kylstras provide in their work, which reference the taxonomy of the Hammonds explicitly, see Kylstra and Kylstra 294–295). And the same criticism leveled by Cuneo—that virtually everything would be possession under the Hammond's system—applies even more strongly to the Kylstras' system (Cuneo 108). When combined with the Kylstras' warped epistemology—skepticism demons and deliverances that won't work when people are on medications (Kylstra and Kylstra 220)—the by-product of this belief system is a clientele that are incapable of trusting any action they take, since practically all actions, particularly if they divert from the evangelical norm, have the capability of introducing demons into one's life. Thus, a system that claims to be liberating ends up putting mentally ill and traumatized people's lives in bondage.

The second troubling element in the RTF manual, which directly and intimately relates to Nancy Alcorn's own ministry, is the Kylstras' alignment with NAR theology. Bill Hamon, a major apostle and thinker in the New Apostolic Reformation, wrote the introduction for *Restoring the Foundations* (Hamon, "Foreword," xiii). It's no surprise that he did, either, because the Kylstras freely admit that

> in 1993, they [Kylstras] were called by Dr. Bill Hamon to Christian International in Florida to minister to the CI leadership. This led to the first "Prophetic Counseling" conference in March of 1994, which included the launch of the "Christian International Proclaiming His Word Healing House." The relationship with CI and Dr. Hamon continues as Chester and Betsy are ordained by CI and serve on the CI Board of Governors [Kylstra and Kylstra 423].

The Kylstras established the Healing House Network in 2001 as a "covering membership organization" for RTF ministry teams. In NAR terms, this means that just as Bill Hamon apostolically covers the Kylstras, so too do the Kylstras cover those within the Network. In addition to being under Bill Hamon's leadership and serving on his board of governors, the Kylstras are also part of C. Peter Wagner's Apostolic Roundtable of Deliverance Ministries and hold faculty positions at the CI School of Theology and Ministry Training College, Wagner Leadership Institute, Vision International University, and Christian Life School of Theology (Kylstra, *Biblical Healing and Deliverance* 277–278). They are thus involved in some of the more important ministries in the NAR today, with connections stretching up to chief NAR apostle C. Peter Wagner himself.

However, it is the Kylstras' close ties with Bill Hamon that are the most troubling. Hamon is one of the most fanatic apostles within the New Apostolic Reformation and one of the most influential as well. Hamon promotes an unusually open version of "manifest sons" theology; in his particular formulation of that ideology, the church is equated with the "church race" (Hamon, *Prophetic Scriptures,* 77) in a profoundly racialized discourse of church membership in which there is a racial elite. But that elite is determined not by racial classifications based on physical difference, but rather on religious difference. Hamon's gospel is profoundly restorationist (see Hamon, *Prophetic Scriptures,* 99–100). Restorationism is a set of ideas prevalent within all of Protestantism, but particularly among Charismatics and Pentecostals, that something went dreadfully wrong with the early church, but that the church has been successively reviving itself since the Reformation to a better and better form of Christianity in preparation for Christ's return (Ware 1019). Restorationist thought within the NAR, even more than in most Charismatic movements, is distinguished by an intense hopefulness about the future, which distinguishes it from the pessimistic viewpoint of premillennial dispensationalists.

To realize the importance of Hamon's brand of restorationism, one must understand how NAR churches are structured. In particular, one must understand the concept of "spiritual fathership" that is becoming an increasingly important reason for the promotion of Latter Rain and manifest sons ideology within the NAR. The NAR's belief that the return of the apostolic office to the church has occurred is incredibly important to understanding the movement. As Rene Holvast relates, the

> essential difference between the NAR and the traditional denominational churches concerned leadership and governance. The NAR was led not by a group but by an individual apostle. It was this divinely appointed apostle, as opposed to a board or a presbytery, a democratic vote or institution who was seen bearing responsibility for making decisions and guiding adherents [Holvast 158–159].

What has given the NAR its enormous organizational advantage over traditional mainstream churches has been its ability to mobilize people through transdenominational, translocal groups that focus on relational networks, rather than on denominations, as their chief organizing component (Wagner, *Churchquake,* 126–127). Because an apostle could act quickly, effectively, and (if necessary) outside denominational bounds, new apostolic churches proved to be highly adaptive in their responses to changing cultural situations. Those apostles who proved particularly effective in gaining and maintaining adherents and popularity gained in power, while those who did not lost out, in a free market religious economy. However, the effectiveness of the promotion of the NAR rested on the concept that the role of the apostle had been restored to the church due to the New Apostolic Reformation (see Hamon, *Prophetic Scriptures,* 128). The Latter Rain movement on which Hamon cut his teeth (see Hamon, *Prophetic Scriptures,* 183, for his ties to Latter Rain preacher Reg Layzell) provided the prophetic fervor, ideology, and leadership skills to successfully pull off the promotion of this return to apostolic leadership, and Hamon, as one of the leading thinkers on restorationism within the NAR, was a crucial figure in this process.

It is important to note, therefore, that *Restoring the Foundations* deliberately and specifically invokes restorationism. The following is found in the preface of the book:

> This restoration process [within RTF and the Charismatic movement at large], which is going on in each saint's life, also coincides with the restoration of the Church. It fits in with, and is a part of the restoration of the apostles and prophets. *Restoring the Foundations* ministry ... has been brought forth by God at this time to bring foun-

dational healing and freedom to the Church.... Three levels of foundations are being restored today. The foundation of each saint, the foundation of the local church, and the foundation of Christ's Church universal. As each individual saint is restored, all three of these foundations are being restored, healed, strengthened, enabled, and equipped [Kylstra and Kylstra xvii–xviii].

The Kylstras therefore see their ministry as a ground-level application of the wider church restorationist practices, such as strategic level spiritual warfare and spiritual mapping that are being practiced by the wider New Apostolic Reformation. By helping individual saints, the Kylstras help restore the foundations upon which the Christian church was built, thus promoting a return to a more "authentic" form of Christianity based on a "primitivist" model (S.L. Ware 1019). Healing ministry thus paves the way for spiritual warfare on a grander scale. The Kylstras quote approvingly from strategic level spiritual warfare experts such as George Otis, Jr. (Kylstra and Kylstra 147), and thus seem to be clearly aware of the "spiritual technologies" that characterize the NAR (see Holvast 4–5, on the idea of spiritual technologies). *Restoring the Foundations* serves as a kind of "popular" NAR text that can reach audiences that might be turned off by Hamon's discussions of the "church race" or George Otis, Jr.'s digressions on spiritual mapping and thus sucks people into NAR ideas of spiritual warfare through the back door.

Not surprisingly, despite Mercy's claims to have forsaken the RTF model (Hannan, "Jesus RX"), Mercy still openly aligns itself with Christian International, despite that organization's historically close links with Chester and Betsy Kylstra. Christian International even calls Mercy "our ministers," which denotes that Mercy Ministries is under Hamon's apostolic covering and answerable to him (Christian International Ministries, "Our Ministers: Mercy Ministries"). Apostle Jane Hamon has spoken at Mercy as well, along with her daughter Crystal (Christian International Ministries, "Suicide Bows Its Knee"). Alcorn attended a Watchmen Intercessors Conference in April of 2009, in which Bill Hamon was one of the primary public speakers. Alcorn raved, "It was such a powerful time! It is so very important to learn all we can about how to pray for people, and for our nation" (Alcorn, "On the Road Again"). In fact, Alcorn received an award from Hamon's Christian International for being the "global impact ministry of the year" ("Mercy Ministries Surprised with Prestigious Award"). One must ask why Mercy maintains links to an organization so closely tied to the promotion of Restoring the Foundations when Restoring the Foundations was the very treatment program that got Mercy Ministries in trouble in the first place.

Nor is this Alcorn's only link to NAR theology. Alcorn took a number of her residents to The Call, which she raved was "such a joy for our girls to be personally encouraged and ministered to by Lou Engle's wife, Therese, world-renown [*sic*] author and speaker Cindy Jacobs, and Lou's beautiful parents" (Alcorn, "Thousands Gathered to Pray"). Engle attended a baptism at Mercy's Lincoln, California, home ("Mercy Ministries Celebrates 22 Baptisms"). The Call and Engle have both been associated with NAR theology by the Southern Poverty Law Center.[17] Engle is closely linked to the extremist antigay legislation (including, in some cases, the death penalty for homosexuals) in Uganda and has praised Ugandan leaders for promoting this legislation (Kron). Engle is also famous for his appearance in the documentary *Jesus Camp;* he's the middle-aged man at the end of the film who gets the children in it to wave miniature fetuses around as they shout for "righteous judges, righteous judges!" in the Supreme Court (*Jesus Camp* DVD). Finally, according to Mercy, "Mercy Ministries has had the privilege of financially supporting Watoto ministries through the construction of two homes for orphans, but in July, we actually sent a team to do the work!" ("Unforgettable Message of Hope"). Watoto Ministries Marilyn Skinner has also spoken at Mercy ("Unforgettable Message of Hope"). Mercy advertises Watoto Ministries (apparently also known as Watoto Church) as an organization devoted to ministering to AIDS victims, a claim that, while true, underlies a more sinister agenda ("Unforgettable Message of Hope"). But there's something Mercy leaves out. According to the *Gay City News,* Skinner's church is at the "forefront of the anti-gay movement in Uganda," a country that has narrowly avoided enacting the death penalty for homosexuals (Osborne). And, not surprisingly, Watoto has ties to Mercy's former close ally Hillsong, which donated over $700,000 dollars to the organization (Morris, "Focus on Justice").

Mercy seems to have weathered the scandal that engulfed it, but that does not mean the ministry is free from controversy. Indeed, the Mercy Survivors network has proven to be a very strong and effective voice in countering the pro–Mercy narrative that Mercy has bombarded the Internet with. The survivor network has made skillfully chosen alliances with progressives such as Tanya Levin and has proven to be surprisingly effective in courting media sympathy. No doubt a great deal of the success of the survivor program lies in its ability to work among vastly differing ideological groups. Members of the survivor network can range from Charismatics to atheists. In addition, the survivor network has put out and maintained a consistent ideological message about how to interpret Mercy's activities, focusing on the scholarship of Robert Lifton and the anticult activism of Steven Hassan as exemplified in his BITE model (Mercy Survivors, "Mercy Ministries and Destructive Mind Control"; Mercy Survivors, "Is Mercy Ministries a Cult?"). Though there may be disagreements among survivors and advocates in the network as to the relative merits of individual approaches to combatting Mercy, the network's ability to create and maintain alliances, to, in fact, *network,* should make Mercy Ministries uneasy. It is not often that a survivor network gets a ministry to close down its operations in an entire country. That the Mercy Survivors were able to do so speaks to how powerfully their message has affected Australia. It can only be hoped that message will eventually be heard in the U.S. as well.

Conclusion

In the next section of the book, we will move from deliverance ministries like Mercy to the very different world of biblical counseling. The biblical counseling movement's promotion of an anti-psychiatric message has for a long time dominated fundamentalist and Reformed discourse concerning mental health treatment and mental illness. As we will see, this treatment methodology has proven to be nearly as destructive as the very different deliverance practices of the Charismatic movement.

4

Jay Adams

The Beginnings of Evangelical
Anti-Psychiatry and the Demonization
of the Mentally Ill

Shortly after 9/11, I was in a bad state mentally. My mother had been diagnosed with cancer. I had recently had to leave college because of mental health issues. My family and I were looking for a place that could provide me with the kind of sustained long-term counseling that I could not afford on my own. Eventually we decided on a Christian facility in New England that claimed to offer such treatment. I went into the program understanding that not all the people providing counseling would be professional therapists, or even professionals engaged in any form of psychological practice. What I did not understand, however, was that the treatment model being offered assumed that my mental health problems were spiritual in nature.

After five days in the program, I had my first counseling session. The counselor asked me what I thought the root of my problems was. Since at the time I was diagnosed with obsessive-compulsive disorder, I answered that I thought OCD likely played a role in some of my problems. The counselor responded that my problem was that my mental health issues were rooted in the "sin of pride." I was shocked that someone would claim mental illness is the result of a specific sin and immediately asked to leave. The next day I was forcibly locked in two separate rooms over the course of six hours where I was continuously berated to repent of my sin—that is, repent of the pride that caused my OCD. When I refused to do so, I was expelled from the program.

To this day, I cannot definitively prove what exact counseling model this provider used. However, it is impossible that the institution's counseling was not then heavily influenced by one of the most authoritative evangelical thinkers on mental health: Jay Adams. As we will see, the beliefs of my counselors almost exactly matched those of Adams in all respects, though Adams was perhaps more sophisticated in his presentation of those deemed "mentally ill." But as we will see, even the term "mentally ill" would be for Adams a loaded concept.

The biblical counseling movement Adams founded is the official arm of anti-psychiatry within the evangelical movement. While deliverance ministries often oppose psychiatry as well, there is no monolithic anti-psychiatric position within the deliverance movement, and some deliverance purveyors support limited or even extensive uses of psychiatry. By contrast, the biblical counseling movement, based mainly on the works of Jay Adams, has tended to have a much more negative view of psychiatry and psychology. Therefore, neither evangelical anti-psychiatric practice nor the position of the mentally ill can be properly understood apart from an analysis of Adams's major works.

According to Adams's chronicler, friend, and biographer, David Powlison, Adams was born on January 30, 1929, in the Windsor Hills suburb of Baltimore. His family was working class (Powlison 28). At age 15, Adams converted to Christianity (29). Precociously brilliant, he went on to gain a double undergraduate degree, getting a "two year bachelor of divinity at RE [Reformed Episcopal Seminary] and a four year bachelor of arts in Greek at Johns Hopkins" (29) and then "went on to serve in a series of small conservative Presbyterian denominations during the 1950s and 1960s" (Powlison 30). From the late fifties on, but particularly in the mid-sixties, Adams became increasingly concerned with the state of evangelical counseling practices (28–29, 34). He became suspicious of traditional psychiatric diagnostic labels. As he put it, "If, as James teaches, one's sinful behavior is at least sometimes responsible for physical illnesses, what about the possibility of a similar responsibility for mental illness?" (Adams, *Competent,* xiv). Adams soon came to wonder, "Is much of what is called mental illness, *illness* at all?" (xiv).

Open now to the possibility of sin-engendered diagnoses for what were labeled "mental illnesses," Adams turned to the works of O. Hobart Mowrer, including *The Crisis in Psychiatry and Religion* (1961) and *The New Group Therapy* (1964) (Adams xiv). The extent of Mowrer's influence on Adams will be described later in this chapter. Its immediate effect on him was profound. Adams began to correspond with Mowrer, and Mowrer invited Adams to participate in his Eli Lilly Fellowship program at the University of Illinois. Adams spent the summer of 1965 working with Mowrer at two state mental hospitals in Illinois (Adams, *Competent,* xv), and he "began to see people labeled 'neurotic, psychoneurotic, and psychotic' ... helped by confessing deviant behavior and assuming personal responsibility for it" (Adams xv). For Adams, the lesson to be derived from Mower's counseling movement was obvious: "Apart from those who had organic problems, like brain damage, the people I met in the two institutions in Illinois were there because of their own failure to meet life's problems. To put it simply, they were there because of their unforgiven and unaltered sinful behavior" (xvi).

Mowrer, like many dissident psychiatrists in the sixties, opposed the Medical Model of psychiatry (xvi) but did not go as far as Thomas Szasz (who rejected mental illness entirely). Instead, Mowrer did see neurotics and psychotics as "sick" (Mower, *New Group Therapy* 141). He saw psychological neurosis as deriving from a "*mistake which is then protected and protracted by means of a lie*" (Mowrer, *New Group Therapy,* 138, italics in original). Mowrer promoted a treatment paradigm called Integrity Groups (Mowrer and Vattano 419), He claimed to "have seen persons who have wallowed in neurotic 'illness' for years recover with astonishing swiftness when they are given a little encouragement in admitting the reality of their guilt and making a serious conscious attempt at restitution" (Mowrer, *New Group Therapy,* 129). This moralistic form of therapy sought to heal neurosis by having the client repudiate "the guilt engendering behavior" and enter into "service" in order to help others (Mowrer 129).

Mowrer's therapy had a number of methodological peculiarities that would make it problematic once the biblical counseling movement adopted this paradigm. First, Mowrer's therapy assumed that the guilt his clients and counselees felt was for real "deviant" behavior. The idea that counselees might be admitting guilt for imagined wrongs did not apparently impress Mowrer as a real phenomenon, despite the fact that such behavior is a common facet of several psychological neuroses (particularly OCD). Even more troubling in Mowrer's model was the question of who defined "deviancy." Because the therapist or integrity group leader had control over the session, the integrity group (IG) model could easily be used to socially "norm" people into a form of standardized behavior that they did not feel comfortable with, all in the pursuit of eliminating social "deviancy." In this model, the IG leader, as well as other members of the Integrity Group, would help determine for the individual what his "norms" should be, regardless of whether those norms were in the best interest of the client. Therefore, a hyper-religious interpretation of IG philosophy, could, for instance, be used to "norm" gays into heterosexuality, or to tell obsessive-compulsives that over-washing their hands was a moral failing. Mowrer himself realized the limitations of IG philosophy shortly after Adams's first works came to press. He came to replace the concept of "fixed standards of conduct" that the group set up for a contractual arrangement with a loved one to better the loved one's mental health, in which the individual himself had, it was hoped, voluntarily subscribed to (Mowrer, "My Philosophy of Psychotherapy," 37–38; see also Mowrer, *The New Group Therapy,*

165–166, on false guilt). Furthermore, even as Adams was promoting the idea that most psychiatric diagnoses were not the result of real bodily dysfunction (see Adams, 28–30, *Competent to Counsel,* but keep in mind that such an impression is mainly gained through reading the entirety of Adams's work), Mowrer himself had come to the conclusion that much psychological illness had at least a partial biological basis (Mower, "My Philosophy of Psychotherapy," 39). This change in Mowrer's thinking was seldom disclosed in Adams's writings, despite the fact that the journal articles Mowrer wrote on his changing philosophy of psychotherapy were readily available in the mid-seventies.

Adams came to see the term "mental illness" as a misnomer. He argued that while organic malfunctions caused by brain damage, gene inheritance, glandular or chemical disorders might be termed mental illnesses, the vast majority of human problems labeled as such were not "engendered by disease or illness at all" (Adams, *Competent*, 28). Adams was never clear about how he defined "gene inheritance" or "chemical disorder," but the large number of anecdotes about miraculously cured schizophrenics and depressives within Adams's corpus of writings attests to the probability that his definition of these phenomenon is much narrower than psychiatry's.

Adams asked trenchantly, "What then is wrong with the 'mentally ill'? Their problem is autogenic; it is in themselves.... Apart from organically generated difficulties, the 'mentally ill' are really *people with unsolved personal problems*" (Adams 29, emphasis in the original). Adams argued, in line with Mowrer, that "much bizarre behavior must be interpreted as camouflage intended to divert attention from otherwise deviate behavior" (Adams, *Competent*, 30). Adams assumed that the mentally ill's problems were self-caused. Like many observers of so-called madness or mental illness (including, unfortunately, many psychiatrists), Adams thought that the behaviors of the mentally ill were character flaws or moral shortcomings, even when in reality the supposition that these behaviors were "sinful" had rather scant theological or scriptural support. Everything from homosexuality to a wife not doing her "chores" was seen by Adams as signs of sinfulness (Adams *Competent* 35–36, 135), a result of self-induced mental illness. In the process, Adams typically ignored or downplayed the secular psychiatric diagnostic criteria used in the treatment of these individuals, even when the individuals he treated had been diagnosed with severe mental illnesses. Given that Adams practically never reports a case in which he was unsuccessful, it is impossible to tell how many of these individuals truly met the "sinner, not sick" criteria he set up, even if one assumes, for the sake of argument, that the "sinner" label has any meaningful purpose in the treatment of mental distress.

Adams's theology, though based on predeterministic Van Tillian presuppositionalism, held to the idea that "the idea of sickness as the cause of personal problems vitiates all notion of human responsibility.... People no longer consider themselves responsible for what they do wrong" (Adams, *Competent,* 5). Personal responsibility became a crucial, perhaps *the* crucial, issue defining the biblical counseling movement, particularly as advancements in neurology and psychiatry made the positions of both the anti-psychiatry and biblical counseling movements more and more untenable. If individuals did not have control over their thoughts, then, biblical counselors reasoned, they did not have control over whether they sinned or not. Individuals could therefore not be held personally responsible for the actions they committed while under the sway of a mental illness. Such a position, for evangelicals (indeed for many people, including most of the legal profession), threatened to blur the line between evil and illness. In its most extreme biomechanistic permutations, this new biological paradigm of brain equaling mind threatened to eliminate the existence of soul and spirit altogether. What was at stake here was more than just minor points of theology or the fate of mentally ill evangelicals. For Adams and, even more, for his later descendants in the biblical counseling movement, psychiatry's increasing doubt about the independence of "mind" apart from "brain" called into question a host of theological assumptions that had buttressed Christianity since at least as far back as Descartes.

Undergirding this belief was that human beings were part body, part spirit (dichotomous beings, although Adams prefers the term duplex) (Adams, *Theology,* 109–111). Adams, in line with Descartes, embraced a rather strict theological dualism, in which mind was almost totally separate from body, a position echoed in the writings of many contemporary psychiatrists who were critical of the concept of mental illness, particularly Thomas Szasz. Adams radically disconnected mind from brain, arguing that "mind is probably not to be thought of as an entity in itself (like brain), but as the thought life of the non-material side (or inner life) of man. It is a term used to refer to the subjective experience of thinking, knowing, feeling, willing, etc." (Adams, *Theology,* 117). By contrast, the brain was "the part of the body that stores information for later retrieval and that regulates bodily functions.... The word mind describes a functional aspect of man, not a physical entity" (117). While Adams himself is careful not to create a total (and untenuous) mind/body split, some of his disciples are less willing to keep this distinction clear.[1] Because the mind is something distinct from the brain, biblical counselors reason it cannot be sick, merely sinful. The brain, by contrast, can be sick, but if a brain is sick, it is by definition not a "mental" illness, but a "brain illness." This kind of semantic sleight of hand, also practiced by Thomas Szasz in his influential *The Myth of Mental Illness* (Szasz, *The Myth of Mental*

Illness), makes it literally impossible to define any illness as psychiatric, since all psychiatric illnesses found to have physical causes (the so-called mind illnesses) are reclassified as neurological illnesses (Wiseman). The remaining "illnesses" are therefore assumed to be merely "problems in living" (Szasz, *Myth,* loc 700), which need either moralistic correction (Adams) or no treatment at all (Szasz).

Adams's conclusions about psychiatry were more radical ultimately than Szasz or Mowrer's. While Mowrer admitted the need for some psychiatric treatment (Mowrer, "My Philosophy of Psychotherapy," 39) and Szasz proved willing to allow for at least contractual agreements between psychiatrists and counselees (Szasz, *Myth,* loc 58–59, 1156–1174), Adams argued that "biblically, there is no warrant for acknowledging the existence of a separate and distinct discipline called psychiatry. There are, in the Scriptures, only three specified sources of personal problems in living: demonic activity (principally possession), personal sin, and organic illness.... All options are covered under these heads, leaving no room for a fourth non-organic mental illness. There is, therefore, no place in a biblical scheme for the psychiatrist as a separate practitioner" (Adams, *Christian Counseling Manual,* 9). Adams argued that psychiatry's "legitimate function" is to help people who suffer from "organic difficulties" (Adams 11). The problem for the biblical counseling movement, as we will see in later chapters, is precisely how to define organic brain problems versus nonorganic mind problems. A variety of diagnostic criteria have been suggested, ranging from Mary and Marshall Asher's exhaustive sin-illness correlations in *The Christian's Guide to Psychological Terms* to Ed Welch's more refined speculations about brain vs. mind issues in *Blame It on the Brain* (1998). The inability of the biblical counseling movement to come to an agreed upon standard about what constitutes spiritual versus physical problems remains, to this day, one of its greatest methodological shortcomings, though one that is not necessarily impossible for the movement to surmount.

Counseling Methodology

Adams practices a form of counseling known as nouthetic confrontation.[2] Nouthetic confrontation is a controversial counseling methodology within evangelical circles, even more controversial than Adams's actual views on mental illness. The reasons for this controversy become obvious when reading Adams's description of the nouthetic process: "Nouthetic confrontation, then, necessarily suggests first of all there is something wrong with the person who is to be confronted nouthetically. The idea of something wrong, some sin, some obstruction, some difficulty, some need that has to be acknowledged and dealt with is central. In short, nouthetic confrontation arises out of a condition in the counselee that God wants changed. The fundamental purpose of nouthetic confrontation then, is *to effect personality and behavioral change*" (italics in original) (Adams, *Competent*, 45). Adams goes on to add that "*nouthesis* presupposes a counseling type confrontation in which the object is to effect characterological and behavioral change in the counselee.... Nouthetic confrontation, in its biblical usage, aims at straightening out the individual by changing his patterns of behavior to conform to biblical standards" (Adams 46).

The actual counseling practice of biblical counselors, therefore, has obvious affinities with behaviorism. Adams's obsessive focus on sin, to the exclusion of any other physical or pathological explanation, has earned him criticism from Christian psychologists (the so-called integrationist camp) (Powlison 173). The goal of biblical counseling is to effect change in clients, regardless of their individual will and regardless of their commitment to Christian spiritual values. While Adams presumably meant biblical counseling to be used mainly with Christian and therefore presumably willing clients, he failed to recognize the potential for abuse inherent in his system. Unlike mainstream behaviorism, which did not typically presuppose what in particular ideological direction behavioral change should be taken (and therefore allowed for greater client and counselee autonomy), biblical counseling argued for an explicitly ideological approach to counseling. The client was to be made to conform to Christian standards, whether or not they agreed with those standards as set down by the nouthetic counselor. The most obvious area where this methodology could cause concern was with children and teens, who might not willingly enter into the nouthetic process but be placed in the process by their parents. And along with traditional behaviorism, there is the danger that abusive organizations will use nouthetic confrontation as a means of social control and humiliation. The cult-like group of churches known as the Independent Fundamentalist Baptists (IFB) has used nouthetics for precisely this purpose, as has (reportedly) the hybrid Charismatic/Reformed Sovereign Grace Ministries (SGM), which combined nouthetic practice with extremist Pentecostal church "shepherding" practices.[3]

While traditional behaviorism can be used to make a moral judgment about an individual, its tendency has been simply to see human behaviors as simple reactions to environmental stimuli (see Hunt, *The Story of Psychology*, 276, 291, on this trend). Behaviorism has therefore always had a rather dim view of moralistic counseling, though it ironically has frequently been used to promote such moralism (e.g., Glasser's reality therapy and Mowrer's Integrity Groups). Biblical counseling, however, by definition is a moralistic

enterprise. Adams succinctly states that "judgments of moral value in counseling are precisely what the Scriptures everywhere commend. There can be
no morally neutral stance in counseling" (Adams, *Competent,* 85). For Adams,
the patient exists in an explicitly moral universe. All their actions, therefore,
must be interpreted through a moralistic lens. The problem with such a stance,
of course, is that some human actions may not be motivated by any moral
impulse, but by biological "hardwiring" that has tragically short-circuited or
that simply operates in a way that the biblical counseling movement disap-
proves of. Nor does Adams, like Szasz (from whom he frequently borrows),
question the applicability of stigmatizing behaviors that society deems
"deviant." Therefore, any potential for biblical counseling to be compared with
the liberationist anti-psychiatry movement of R.D. Laing in Britain or Szasz's
less fruitful attempts in the United States falls flat. Biblical counseling, far
from being against social control, *is an agent of social control,* by which evangelical churches seek to minimize dissent among those members deemed mentally ill or deviant.

Biblical counseling also assumes that most mentally ill individuals have
the power to change their behaviors (a belief it derives primarily from Mowrer,
but also William Glasser) (Mowrer, *The New Group Therapy,* 129; Glasser 6,
10–15). While this belief may be true, biblical counseling offers no empirical
evidence to support this belief. Biblical counseling, according to Adams, "must
avoid any notions of genetic determinism that may make parents ... responsible
for the behavior or feeling of the counselee. No, all of these attempts to enlarge
the counseling context fail since, as the Scriptures plainly teach, God holds
each one of us personally responsible for his thoughts, words, and actions
regardless of external pressures and influences" (Adams, *Christian Counseling
Manual,* 3–4). Adams's system offers no excuses: the individual who drowns
her five children because she has a psychotic episode of postpartum depression
is held equally guilty with a serial killer. The effects of environment, genes,
chemical disorders, etc., are deliberately minimized in order that biblical counselors may reach the maximum number of counselees. Personal responsibility
remains paramount in the biblical counseling movement.

Adams rejected the Rogerian counseling methods then popular among
pastoral counselors. For Adams,

> because it is authoritative, biblical counseling is directive.... It has been only in quite
> modern times that the concept of counseling did an about-face so that for some the
> word came to mean listening rather than speaking. Now we hear of nondirective
> counseling. Biblically speaking, those words represent a contradiction of terms. Of
> all of the terms that Carl Rogers might have chosen, this combination is at once the
> most strategic and the most tragic [Adams, *Christian Counselor's Manual,* 17].

Adams here made a quite traditional, though also quite accurate, criticism of Rogerian methodology. Among many mentally ill people, and also among counselors, there has always been a reaction against Rogerianism since it seems to absolve the counselor of all responsibility for the counselee's condition. Counselors are merely to sit and observe, nod at convenient points, and collect their fees. Because of his counseling theory's foundations in behaviorism, as well as his Christian predilections, Adams was uncomfortable with such a model. For Adams, the great counselors of the Bible—the prophet Nathan, Paul, Christ himself—were directive in their methodology. Indeed, Christian scripture does seem to support a directive approach, as the nondirective advice offered by Job's "comforters" has been widely derided by both evangelical supporters and detractors of the concept of mental illness. Therefore, Adams's desire to be directive was in keeping with both traditional Christian theology and behaviorist practice.

However, Adams's interpretation of what "authoritative" counseling meant is more subject to scholarly distrust. His position on counseling authority was predicated on a hyper-legalistic reading of 2 Timothy 3:16–17: "All Scripture is God-breathed and is useful for teaching, rebuking, correcting and training in righteousness, so that the man of God may be thoroughly equipped for every good work" (NIV). Adams interpreted these verses to mean that "just as the Christian counselor knows that there is no unique problem that has not been mentioned plainly in the Scriptures, so also he knows that there is a biblical solution to every problem" (Adams, *Christian Counselors Manual*, 23). For Adams, therefore, the Bible allowed a nouthetic counselor to deal with every form of human mental problem, except those that the counselor clearly believed were biologically derived. Here again, the problem of the qualification of the biblical counselor to diagnose biological vs. sin problems is clearly evident; while Adams himself did recommend that biblical counselors consult with doctors (see Adams, *Competent*, 142, on this score), it is not very clear that MDs are capable of deciphering what is and is not "organically derived" mental diseases. Besides the fact that biblical counselors, like all counselors, are likely to consult only sympathetic physicians, the fact remains that relatively few of the published biblical counselors have degrees in psychiatry or neurology.[4] Indeed, the two most prominent "DSMs" of the biblical counseling movement, the *Christian Counselor's Medical Desk Reference* (2000) and Mary and Marshall Asher's *The Christian's Guide to Psychological Terms*, are not written by psychiatrists or neurologists but by a physician and a dentist (Asher and Asher back cover; Powlison 57–58).[5] While there have occasionally been anti-psychiatric biblical counseling books written by professional psychiatrists, they tend to be a rarity and none of them make the sweeping diagnostic strokes found in, for instance, the Ashers' work. Therefore, the typical biblical counselor is ill equipped to make distinctions between neurological or biological and sin-engendered problems. And, unfortunately, not every biblical counselor consults with an MD in the first place, compounding the potential psychological harm done by untrained "counselors."

But it is not simply in the form of professional credentials that biblical counseling's obsession with "authoritative" counseling can be found lacking. Nouthetic counseling is a presuppositional counseling strategy that bases itself on attacking the foundations of errant worldviews and correcting them (Adams, *Competent,* xxi). Derived from Cornelius Van Til, nouthetic confrontation has a great similarity with another of Van Til's disciples' theological practices: Francis Schaeffer's "taking the roof off" style of theological apologetics (Detwiler 159). In both these presuppositional philosophies, the emphasis is on attacking the secularist and mentally ill person's foundational presuppositions, without allowing for one's own presuppositions to be questioned. While this philosophy does not have to be inherently abusive, it does have a tendency to turn into a cultic one-way discourse, when the nouthetic practitioner is uninterested in mutual dialogue. And Adams seems clearly to be unwilling to engage in such discourse.[6] He argues that "Christian counseling involves the use of authoritative instruction. 'Authoritative instruction' requires the use of directive nouthetic techniques.... Instead of excuse-making or blameshifting, nouthetic counseling advocates the assumption of responsibility and blame, the admission of guilt, the confession of sin, and the seeking of forgiveness in Christ" (Adams, *Competent* 55).

Because of nouthetic counselors' combative, aggressive stance towards sin, they have gained a reputation over the years for being cold, even abusive, to their clients. While this is doubtlessly to a certain extent an exaggeration, especially of second and third generation biblical counselors, there is no doubt that the biblical counseling model is prone to abuse because of the authority it vests in the counselor. As the counselor is seen as the representative of God, his word can be questioned only if it contradicts the "Word of God." The problem here is who controls the interpretation of that word: for vulnerable mentally ill evangelicals, or even more vulnerable LGBT evangelical teens, the biblical counseling paradigm offers a real potential for spiritual and psychological abuse.

View of Other Counseling Systems

David Powlison has pointed out that a frequent criticism of Adams was that he lacked "a profound, comprehensive, and sensitive grasp of human beings in their psychological complexity" (Powlison 173). Adams, for instance, tended to neglect the "interior dimensions of human beings, viewing problems as largely behavioral" (Powlison 173). The exact degree to which Adams accurately assessed the other therapeutic methodologies then extant is difficult to ascertain, and, in any case, can only be subjectively evaluated. Adams, given his behaviorist leanings, tended to be more accurate in his assessment of behavioral psychology than in his somewhat tongue in cheek critiques of Freud and Rogers.

Adams argues that "the Superego is the culprit in the Freudian system. According to Freud, the problem with the mentally ill is an over-socialization of the Superego. An oversocialized conscience is overly severe and overly strict. The mentally ill are victims of the Superego" (Adams, *Competent* 10). This explanation is only partially true. While mental illnesses in the Freudian system can be caused by an overactive superego, they can also be caused by an overactive Id. In other words, not following your conscience enough is as likely to lead to mental illness in the Freudian system as having too strict a moral code (Barlow and Durand 18). Adams concludes from this analysis of Freud that

> if Freudianism is true, the most immoral people, or at best the most amoral people, should be the healthiest, whereas in fact the opposite is true. People in mental institutions and people who come to counseling are people with great moral difficulties... Immorality of every sort, irresponsibility toward God and man (i.e., the breaking of God's commandments) is found most prominently among people with personal problems [Adams, *Competent* 13].

Adams, besides stigmatizing the mentally ill as immoral (a common tactic historically, and one that was thoroughly debunked by the very Szaszian and Foucauldian anti-psychiatric literature that Adams should have read), also concludes that "immorality," in Freudianism, is directly tied to health. Yet even a basic reading of Freud would have shown Adams that Freud was still highly dependent on moralistic language. By turning Freud into the epitome of evil, Adams merely perpetuates a common stereotype of him as a sex-crazed maniac, a stereotype so far antithetical to Freud's actual life that it verges on dishonesty. As Jeanne Rellahan points out in her trend-setting dissertation "At Home Among the Puritans: Sigmund Freud and the Calvinist Tradition in America" (1988), Freud if anything shared with Adams's Puritan forebears a distrust of the "innate corruption of human nature" (Rellahan 78). Freud's own personal attitude to sex, as is well known, was largely negative (Schultz and Schultz 49, Rellahan 86–88).

Adams also expressed concern that both Freudianism and behaviorism attacked humanity's

responsible nature.... Skinnerians say he [man] is inevitably controlled by his impersonal environment and may be manipulated in any way that is consistent with his
physical abilities through rearrangement of environmental contingencies backed by
a proper reward/aversive control (punishment) schedule. Freud's views were no better.
His concept of the irrational unconscious as the mass of the iceberg beneath the surface by which we are controlled and motivated ... again leads to a sort of determinism
that removes all responsible choices from us. Obviously, we only rationalize and act
self-deceptively when we think otherwise [Adams, *Theology*, 118–119].

Adams falls into a deep theological hole here, however, because his own theology is rigidly Calvinist in origin. He explains that Christian predeterminism
is different from Freudian and Skinnerian predeterminism in that "in predes-
tining every man's act, God did so in such a way that He preserved human
moral freedom" (Adams, *Theology*, 124). This is, of course, a contradiction in
terms, a basic tautological statement that most non–Calvinist theologians
would avoid committing themselves to. Adams's theology, however, is dependent on predestinarian thinking. But his counseling methodology, which
emphasizes personal responsibility and "accountability" to God is the exact
inverse of his theology. The conflict between the theology and counseling
methodology of the biblical counseling movement has never been fully
resolved and remains a vexing question to biblical counselors to this day.[7]

Adams's critique of behaviorism, besides embracing his mutually contradictory predeterminist and non-predeterminist ideology, adds a further element of critique, centering on Skinner's view of the environment. For Adams,

in this sense, every unregenerate man, and every system he designs, is influenced by
his sinful failure to describe the environment properly and, as the necessary consequence, his inability to develop a counseling system ... that corresponds to the reality
of the environment as it truly exists. A false view of the environment, therefore can
lead to nothing else but a counseling system that is askew, and that rebelliously misrepresents man and the rest of creation because it misrepresents God [Adams, *Theology*, 41].

Adams, in a theologically sophisticated move, makes the same critique of secular counseling methodologies that these methodologies have been making of
Christian counseling since the time of Freud: "You simply do not understand
the environment you're dealing with." Because secular counseling philosophy
presupposes naturalism, it arrives at only naturalistic conclusions. Christian
counseling, by contrast, presupposes that a theological, metaphysical plane
indeed exists; therefore, anyone not operating from that plane is doomed to
failure. The problem here, of course, is falsifiability. Secular counselors cannot
prove that God does not exist any more than they can prove that angels or
demons or unicorns do exist. While secular counseling does not necessarily
dismiss the existence of such entities out of hand, it cannot build its whole

counseling system on the presupposition of their reality, without verifiable, testifiable results as to the efficacy of the angel-derived or God-derived, counseling methodology. It is of course, quite possible that an unscientifically derived counseling methodology like nouthetics could be more efficacious than secular treatment methodologies. Even if it is not, it doubtlessly helps some people. The question is whether the same results could be obtained from biblical counseling practices without telling clients that they are manic-depressive, schizophrenic or depressed "sinners" with no "excuses" for their "sinful behaviors." In other words, is the assumption that counselees have some inherent sin problem that must be changed a necessary requirement for biblical counseling to succeed?

In one of the strangest, and yet most brilliant sections of Adams's writing, he goes on to state the logical outcome of his beliefs:

> Skinner too talks about the environment. But he is an atheist. How then can he have the faintest notion of what his environment involves? If he cannot even understand the visible environment, because he fails to relate it to the unseen environment which gives it definition and purpose, how can he possibly make good on his grandiose claim to control man by controlling his environment? Can angels, demons and—above all—God be controlled by man? How does one condition an angel? Skinner thinks that he need busy himself only with those things that he can see. But God has revealed that the seen world is inextricably bound to the unseen one. As in this life one cannot separate the body from the soul (another problem of Skinner's) since one is affected by the other, neither can the seen world be separated from the unseen [Adams 41].

Adams's basic objections to Skinner go much deeper than mere moral outrage at the "inhumanity" of behaviorism. Fundamental incarnational issues are at stake. Can God or the Devil or demons or (most dangerous) Christ be behaviorally conditioned? For Adams, the behaviorist model as outlined by Skinner is antithetical to the Christian worldview and can never be otherwise, because it is founded on fundamentally naturalist presuppositions: that the observable world is all that can be properly studied or analyzed. Since Adams does not see human beings as merely bodies, he does not believe human beings can be conditioned simply by reference to physical or psychological control mechanisms. Spiritual or divine mechanisms must also be at work. The only viewpoint one can embrace alternative to this, for Adams, is to admit that people can indeed have their spirits conditioned. In short, spirits become fundamentally not merely tied to bodies but *merely bodies*. Because Christianity is an incarnational religion, this is a fundamental issue: If Christ was incarnate God-made-man, then embracing Skinnerian beliefs would allow an individual to "condition Christ" and break him of his will to be God. This is perhaps the single most brilliant psychological insight Adams makes in all his works.

Unfortunately, just because Adams does not want Christ to break under the weight of behavioral conditioning it does not mean he would not. Nor does Adams's speculations here invalidate behaviorism. Because behaviorism bases itself on science, it measures only the verifiable and the observable. To date, there has yet to be a verifiable miracle that has stood up to sustained scientific scrutiny. Until that event occurs, behaviorism may simply be a better option than the prevailing models of biblical counseling currently used among nouthetics supporters.

As for Rogers, the third member of the psychological trio Adams most frequently invokes, Adams's main problem seems to be that in the Rogers system man is "good, not evil" (Adams, *Christian Counselors Manual*, 84). As Adams puts it, "When man is not responsible to God and is only held responsible to himself, responsibility is swallowed up by anarchy" (Adams, *Christian Counselors Manual*, 85). The Rogerian system, for Adams, besides being too nondirective, puts too much faith in humanity's goodness and tends to see human beings in too positive a light. Unlike Adams's own counseling methodology, there is little room in humanistic psychology for sin or evil, and because of this Rogers is unequipped to attack the roots of human problems: humanity's basic disregard for God and for fellow human beings. Indeed, one could see how "unconditional positive regard" with its "complete and almost unqualified acceptance of the client's feelings and actions" is simply not conducive to the kind of judgmental counseling activity on which biblical counseling is predicated (Barlow and Durand 21). "Reproof" does not play a key part in Rogerianism. Yet Adams's own counseling practice seems to make the opposite mistake of Rogers; instead of judging too little, it judges too much, depending on an arbitrary definition of what constitutes godliness, one certainly not held by all, or even most, Christians.

Adams in the Context of the Anti-Psychiatric Movement

As David Powlison points out, Adams must be viewed in the larger context of the anti-psychiatric movement (Powlison 3). Powlison credits O. Hobart Mowrer, William Glasser, Perry London, and Thomas Szasz (3) as being the main anti-psychiatrists that Adams respected. Adams was part of a larger cultural ferment going on in the sixties that called for a reevaluation of psychiatric practice. He distanced himself from Mower (and by extension, from the virtually identical William Glasser), insisting that there were very real differences between Mowrer's system and his own (Powlison 37). As we shall see, these differences were in fact largely superficial. However, Adams's views about psychiatry did differ significantly from some of the other major anti-psychiatric thinkers, and therefore it is important to understand the context in which he was writing.

Three thinkers, in particular, were at the center of anti-psychiatric criticism, though ironically none of them would claim the anti-psychiatry label: R.D. Laing, Thomas Szasz, and Michel Foucault. Of R.D. Laing, little need be said. As a proponent of the drug culture and, to a certain extent, of looser British social and sexual mores, Laing was anathema to Adams, and he is not listed in any of the indexes in Adams's three major works: *The Christian Counselor's Manual, Competent to Counsel* and *A Theology of Christian Counseling*. In addition, Laing's brand of counseling stigmatized those labeled "mentally ill" even less than the Rogerian method, practically honoring them. In this aspect, it in some ways mirrored Thomas Szasz's strong libertarian critique of psychiatry, whatever Szasz's denials to the contrary (Szasz, *The Myth of Mental Illness,* loc 308).

Foucault is an even more peculiar case. Part of his lack of influence on biblical counseling can be derived from the fact that his works were originally written in French, and until recently some of them had not been fully translated (e.g., *History of Madness* and *Psychiatric Power*). Foucault's avowed left-wing convictions, formidable intellectual sophistication and homosexual orientation also doubtlessly served as a barrier to his wide acceptance among biblical counseling elites. Yet this cannot fully explain his continued disregard today. The biblical counseling graduates of Westminster Seminary, at the very least, are capable of reading and understanding Foucault, and it is probable that even some of their counterparts in the southern and western (as well as at other Northeastern) seminaries might be capable of understanding Foucault and ignoring his left-wing political and sexual convictions.

No, with Foucault, there is a more fundamental issue than merely a disagreement with Foucault's sexuality or trouble with his use of verbiage. For Foucault, unlike Szasz, Mowrer, or Glasser, is completely antithetical to the kind of simplistic binary distinctions between body and mind or sin and sickness that the biblical counseling movement sets up. Nor, unlike with many other anti-psychiatrists (excluding Mowrer), does this position derive from a lack of understanding of religion. Rather, Foucault understands religion far too well for the comfort of biblical counselors. For instance, Foucault turned the sanity/sin paradigm on its head by suggesting, in the good company of Erasmus and Nicholas of Cusa, that by humanity's standard, God was not sane but insane (Foucault 31). Therefore, taking Foucault to his logical conclusion, if anything human beings should conform to insanity rather than to sanity. Moreover, Foucault, like Szasz in the *Myth of Mental Illness* (see Szasz, *Myth of Mental Illness,* loc 2928–3064; note that this theme runs throughout Szasz's works), points out how intimately stigmatization of those labeled "mentally ill" was tied in with cultural mores concerning blasphemy, with blasphemers frequently being confused with the mad until relatively recently in human history (Foucault 92). Foucault, living within a predominantly Catholic culture, sees the foolishness of separating madness from holiness, or even godliness. Foucault's viewpoint therefore threatens to destabilize the binary oppositions set up by biblical counselors for a more productive theological paradigm that questions the whole meaning of sanity and mental health entirely.

At first, Szasz would seem about equally useless to biblical counseling proponents, and indeed the foundations of biblical counseling *practice* owe more to Glasser and Mowrer than they do to Szasz; the justifications for biblical counseling's anti-psychiatric critique, however, owe much to Szasz. Szasz argues that "diseases of the body have causes, such as infectious agents or nutritional deficiencies, and often can be prevented or cured by dealing with these causes. Persons said to have mental diseases, on the other hand, have reasons for their actions that must be understood; they cannot be treated or cured by drugs or other medical interventions, but may be helped to help themselves overcome the obstacles they face" (Szasz, *Myth,* loc 164). Szasz bases this distinction on his definition of illness as a "pathological alteration of cells, tissues and organs" (Szasz, *Myth,* loc 75). Mental illnesses, he argues, "are not, and cannot be, brain diseases: once a putative disease becomes a proven disease, it ceases to be classified as a mental disorder and is reclassified as a bodily disease" (Szasz, *Myth,* loc 330).

Despite Szasz's great erudition, there are a number of basic flaws in his argument. First of all, by always removing mental illnesses to brain diseases, Szasz conducts a semantic sleight of hand. If one simply used a different term, "brain diseases with unknown etiologies," one could then argue that they had met Szasz's criteria, unless Szasz proposes never treating an "illness" before one knows the "cause" (Roth 318). Szasz gets into even further difficulties because many illnesses have historically been treated with effective cures long before people knew the physical causations for such illnesses (Roth 317–318). Szasz's definition of illness based on lesion is blithely ignorant of the fact that many bodily problems, like lower back pain and idiopathic epilepsy, are diagnosed even when their exact causes are unknown (L. Clarke "Sacred Radical of Psychiatry," 449). Martin Roth points out that for Szasz to be consistent, at least as of the 1970s, narcolepsy, migraines, and tic doloureux could not be real illnesses because no "cerebral or biochemical basis has been found for them" (Roth 318). In fact, as Roth points out, since physical lesions were not found for most illnesses until about a century ago, illness before the 1800s was an extremely rare occurrence in Szasz's system (318). Finally, Szasz has been critiqued for getting rid of the term "mental illness" without also getting rid of the term "mental health" (Brassington 123). Arguably Szasz at least tried to get rid of the latter term. In any case, the biblical counseling movement did not. As I.M. Brassington points out, if one is simply a product of "behaviors, attitudes and so on, then it is hard to see how one could be either healthy or unhealthy mentally" (Brassington 123). Therefore, for Adams to adopt Szasz's condemnation of mental illness without also arguing for a condemnation of mental health is philosophically, if not theologically, inconsistent.

Ideally, while biblical counseling could respect these caveats about Szasz's (otherwise) provocative theory of "mental illness," the biblical counseling movement in fact simplifies Szasz's arguments. Ed Welch's *Blame It on the Brain,* for instance, explains Szaszian mind and body distinctions in grossly simplified terms: "At the level of the brain, this unity [between body and soul] suggest that the heart or spirit will always be represented or expressed in the brain's chemical activity. When we choose good or evil, such decisions will be accompanied by changes in brain activity. This does not mean that the brain causes these decisions. It simply means that the brain renders the desires of the heart in a physical medium" (Welch 48). Welch goes on to explain in a later chapter that, "according to our biblical understanding of the heart-body relationship, we would predict that one day researchers will find chemical differences [in the brains of some people with psychiatric diagnoses]. Depression, disobedience, fatigue, dyslexia, and every other human behavior is represented on a neurochemical level. This doesn't mean that the brain causes all these behaviors, but that the brain expresses differences at a chemical level" (Welch 48). Welch's arguments here, usually simplified even further by his everyday interlocutors, is typically reduced to the following formula: "Chemical imbalances are caused by sinful thoughts. Sinful thoughts are not caused by chemical imbalances." What constitutes a sinful thought in the modern formulation of biblical counseling is so abstract that a tone of voice, a compulsion, or a momentary lack of joy can be seen as being rooted in sin, even when the exact reason such behavior would be classified as a sin is never "scripturally," let alone scientifically, justified. This diagnostic lack of specificity is made even more problematic by the fact that though Calvinism typically tends to argue that sin is who we are more than what we do, the biblical counseling system does seem to take on a voluntaristic model of sin, which makes those people who "choose" to sin through obsessions, compulsions, and the like ontologically at their roots spiritually "inferior" to the mentally "normal."

As mentioned before, the problem with Welch's formulation of Szaszian-style arguments is that his analysis is essentially an infinite regression. A psychiatrist could say "chemical imbalances cause the 'sinful' thoughts that cause the chemical imbalances" to which the biblical counselor would simply say "sinful thoughts cause the chemical imbalances that cause the 'sinful' thoughts that cause the chemical imbalances." And on and on the patient goes, in an endless loop. As a basis for counseling, still less for scientific analysis of mental illness, Welch's position makes little sense. Worse, Welch and other biblical counselors twist the essential meaning of Szasz's analysis of mental illness. While Szasz agrees with the biblical counseling movement that some deviant behavior can be controlled by ethicists or politicians (Szasz, *Myth*, 38–39, 900–904), his analysis calls into question why precisely we label people deviant in the first place. Szasz saw the mentally ill as resembling "witches, women, Jews, [and] Negroes" who had been scapegoated in order that society could claim that its problems were "solved" (Szasz, *Myth*, 2929). Szasz, in line with the mental health liberationist movements of the sixties, points out that "even if we do not believe in reducing psychiatry to biochemistry, the notion of mental illness implies, first, that mental health is a 'good thing'; and second, that there are certain criteria according to which mental health and illness can be diagnosed" (3062). For Szasz the involuntarily committed mentally ill are persecuted for not giving in to society's definition of what mental "health" should be (3062). Biblical counseling, by replacing a behaviorist view of mental health with a behaviorist plus biblical view of mental health, is merely stigmatizing those labeled "mentally ill" in a different way. It is not liberating them, unlike what Szasz tried to do, and by combining medicine and theology it merely creates a twisted form of theo-psychiatry that is ultimately neither theology nor science, but a theistiscience that combines the worst aspects of scientific and theological discourse.

From Mowrer, Adams borrows the concept of guilt-inducing counseling. Mowrer relates, "I have repeatedly seen persons who have wallowed in neurotic 'illness' for years recover with astonishing swiftness when they are given a little encouragement in admitting the reality of their guilt and making a serious, conscious attempt at restitution" (Mowrer, *New Group Therapy*, 129). Mowrer, according to Adams, says the patient "suffers from real guilt, not guilt feelings (false guilt). The basic irregularity is not emotional, but behavioral" (Adams xvii). Mowrer opposed the "Freudian notion that man sickens, not from sin but excessive conscientiousness" (Mowrer, Crisis, 66). Yet one must ask how realistic a counseling methodology is that looks for the terrible sins that must cause an eight-year-old to repeatedly wash her hands to the point of bleeding (a frequent occurrence among young obsessive-compulsives). What societal sins is an anorexic teenager atoning for? Even from a pragmatic standpoint,

Mowrer and Adams's emphasis on guilt does not make much sense. It is certainly not likely to be an effective motivational tool for improvement, particularly outside the context of religious cultures.

Mowrer, describing *The New Group Therapy* more than a decade after its publication, wrote "here the supposition was that 'disturbed' persons are disturbed precisely because they have violated the beliefs of conscience and community and instead of admitting and rectifying these errors, have continued to hide and deny what they have done" (Mowrer, "My Philosophy of Psychotherapy," 36). For Mowrer the standard for individuals should be what communities want for them, not what the individual wants. Unlike Szasz, Foucault, the current critical psychiatry movement or mental health liberationists, Mowrer is primarily interested in exerting and maintaining community control, and biblical counseling has built on that principle. The community or God (who is defined by the community) becomes the standard by which all actions are deemed right or wrong. The autonomy promised at the beginning of the anti-psychiatry movement, and in some parts actualized outside of religious contexts, is in biblical counseling turned into a repressive form of stigmatization. Rather than being "sick" (as in biological psychiatry) and therefore offered treatment or "not sick" (as in Szasz) and therefore at least left alone, biblical counseling offers a treatment paradigm for the mentally ill that calls them "sinful" without ever providing convincing scriptural or biological justifications as to why depression, obsessions, mood swings, and hearing voices represent anything other than peculiarities of character. The love of a "mad Christ," like Dostoyevsky's Myshkin, that is promised in Erasmus and even the Synoptic Gospels (witness Gethsemane) is replaced with a Christ who punishes those labeled mentally ill for the sin of their illness that is not an illness, for the sin of the sickness that is not a sickness.

In the final analysis, Mower's compatriot William Glasser does not provide an effective therapeutic model. Glasser's therapy was rooted in a peculiar understanding of the term *reality*. For Glasser, "in their unsuccessful effort to fulfill their needs, no matter what behavior they choose, all patients have a common characteristic: they all deny the reality of the world around them.... Therapy will be successful when they are able to give up denying the world and recognize that reality not only exists but that they must fulfill their needs within its framework" (Glasser 6). Why reality should be the standard is open to question. Plenty of our most enlightened thinkers have not conformed to common definitions of "reality." Moreover, though Glasser ostensibly wants the patient to determine whether or not his behavior is responsible or "irresponsible" (and therefore in keeping with reality), it is most likely the therapist who will determine what is and is not proper reality for the patient. Indeed, reality and choice therapy's marketing to the educational and penological establishment (Mason and Duba et al.; Glasser 67–97) point to the fact that its usage is aimed at social control, rather than the liberationist aims of more radical members of the anti-psychiatry movement.

Nevertheless, reading Glasser is instructive. While it appears Mowrer was more influential on Adams than was Glasser, Glasser's reality therapy approach has real similarities to the nouthetic confrontation process. Both processes, along with Mowrer's integrity therapy, are rooted in a behaviorist reading of human nature that emphasizes authoritarian control of counselors over counselees and, in contrast to Rogerian therapies, an overly directive counselor-client relationship.[8] Because of this, reality therapy and biblical counseling both are utilized as practices within authoritarian contexts, such as the military, churches, and the aforementioned educational and penological establishments. While neither practice is necessarily inherently abusive, the emphasis on both authoritarianism and social control within biblical counseling would end up making the practice a powerful tool for abuse, indoctrination, and social control after the publication of *Competent to Counsel* in 1970. As we will see, individuals ranging from influential former Charismatic leaders to high ranking U.S. army officers would see the potential of biblical counseling to control and oppress the masses. And as a result, the mentally ill, sex abuse victims, and women undergoing or recovering from domestic abuse would become the target of social oppression on the part of the evangelical church.

Finally, Adams was influenced by Perry London. London's analysis of psychiatry is an interesting one, later copied by Adams. London argued that "psychotherapy is a moralistic as well as a scientific undertaking to such an extent that it cannot be properly understood as the latter unless it is also thoroughly evaluated as the former" (London v). Adams argued that such moralizing of the sciences essentially turned psychiatrists and psychotherapists into "part physician ... and part secular priest" (Adams, *Christian Counselor's Manual*, 9). Adams objected to this practice because he felt it effectively gave the domain of the pastor over to the psychiatrist (Adams, *Christian Counselor's Manual*, 9). Problems that used to be handled internally within the church were now being farmed out to the psychotherapeutic community. London's conclusion is in a sense irrefutable: Obviously at some point morality does enter the therapeutic relationship, no matter how much a therapist might wish otherwise. This is a problem hardly unique to psychiatry but is characteristic of at least medical discourse in general. Labeling conditions diseases is by definition pathologizing individuals; like it or not, it is a moral choice, even if we typically do not associate immorality with so-called "physical" illnesses. Indeed, as we have seen, Pentecostals and Charismatics frequently do assess physical illness in such moralistic terms. If biblical counseling is going to argue for the inherent immorality of the behavior patterns that produce "mental illnesses," it is difficult to see why such illnesses receive so much more attention than "physical" illnesses when the etiological diagnosis of both should be, by biblical counseling terms, the same: sin.

Conclusion

In the final analysis, Glasser, Mowrer, and Adams are simply behaviorists who wear an anti-psychiatric badge.[9] Their therapies take advantage of more radical critiques of psychiatry, critiques that were often (particularly in the cases of Foucault and Laing) much more sympathetic to the problems of those labeled with "mental illness." While Glasser promoted norming the mentally ill to reality, and Mowrer the mentally ill to community, Adams simply replaced these terms with God, which was not even a functional change (God being defined by the evangelical community in toto), merely a semantic one. The result, for many evangelicals who are labeled "mentally ill," is that there is a great deal of confusion about who biblical counselors are exactly. People go to such counselors expecting psychological advice or medication, and they receive nouthetic confrontation instead. The result of such treatment can be devastating for those who receive it.

5

Biblical Counseling
The Second and Third Generations

The development of the biblical counseling movement after the publication of *Competent to Counsel* in 1970 is a subject of considerable fascination, though this might not be immediately apparent to people looking at the movement from the outside. The story consists of second generation "theorists" engaged in increasingly rarified critiques of psychology and psychiatry and of one of its leading intellectuals becoming a convicted pedophile. It is also the story of a bizarre combination of legal counsel and biblical counseling being used in the furtherance of domestic and sexual abuse, as well as the story of how one young man's suicide nearly killed the biblical counseling movement before it had time to begin only to end up propping up the biblical counseling movement by radicalizing one of its chief supporters. But in the beginning there were three men: Jay Adams, John Bettler and John C. Broger. And the history of these three men's actions over the next four decades would come to define how an entire social movement perceived not only the mentally ill but LGBT people and abuse victims as well.

The Beginning

In 1966, Jay Adams began attending Trinity Orthodox Presbyterian Church in Hatboro, Pennsylvania. The pastor of the church was John Bettler. A recent graduate of the conservative Westminster Theological Seminary, Bettler was one of Adams's former students (though he had never taken a counseling course with Adams) (Powlison 39). Like many students at Westminster, Bettler was enchanted by the teachings of Dutch Reformed intellectual Cornelius Van Til (Powlison 39; Bettler, "CCEF the Beginning," 47), who promoted the use of presuppositional apologetics, a form of argumentation that was proving to be influential among a wide swath of Reformed intellectuals, especially Francis Schaeffer, the theological genius behind the founding of the religious right. Bettler was the first pastor to learn Adams's counseling methodology at what was then called the Christian Counseling and Educational Center (CCEC), an organization Adams had founded in 1966 (Powlison 38–39).

According to Powlison, Bettler was "second only to Adams in influence upon the nouthetic counseling movement" (Powlison 39). Whereas Adams provided the theoretical vision and intellectual brilliance that would come to define nouthetics and biblical counseling at their best and worst, Bettler was "instrumental in founding and developing many of its leading institutions" (Powlison 39). According to Powlison, Adams tended to promote a form of separatist Presbyterianism (40). Bettler, by contrast, "reacted strongly against separatist, sectarian, and anti-intellectual tendencies" (Powlison 40).[1] Bettler would subsequently serve as the visionary of the "moderate" wing of the biblical counseling movement.

In 1968, CCEC was reincorporated into the Christian Counseling and Educational Foundation (CCEF), which both at its founding and today represents the dominant biblical counseling organization extant. Adams and his followers foresaw a time when they would offer "counseling services, education and training of counselors, publication and mass media and diversified institutions of care" (Powlison 41).

After the publication and widespread acclaim of *Competent to Counsel* among conservative evangelicals, Adams became an associate professor at Westminster Seminary (Powlison 55). The growth of the biblical counseling movement was somewhat slow in the early seventies, at least within the seminary establishment (Powlison 56). However, Adams's Westminster connections undoubtedly brought him a respectful hearing from many pew-sitters, particularly among more conservative Reformed and fundamentalist churches, as Westminster was one of the most well-regarded conservative seminaries in the United States.[2]

In 1972, Bill Goode, a Baptist pastor, and Bob Smith, a member of his congregation, were converted to Adams's cause at a pastoral counseling training conference (Powlison 57). This was important for two reasons. First, Goode and Smith would go on to start Faith Baptist Counseling Ministry (FBCM). This ministry would train more than a thousand pastors and missionaries in biblical counseling beliefs and practices (Powlison 57–58). What was even more important was that as members of the General Association of Regular Baptist Churches (GARBC), Goode and his allies gave the biblical counseling movement a huge inroad into traditional fundamentalist circles, which were often suspicious of Reformed evangelicals like Adams (see Powlison 57–58). Although it cannot be definitively proven, it is likely that the inroads biblical counseling teaching made into more extremist fundamentalist groups, such as the independent fundamentalist Baptists, might very well have resulted from IFB members interacting with Regular Baptists who had bought into Adams's system.

In addition to the sheer prominence of Faith Baptist Counseling Ministries itself, the addition of Robert Smith to the biblical counseling movement gave it its first true medical theorist. Over the next several decades, Smith would publish in a number of biblical counseling outlets, including the *Journal of Pastoral Practice* and the *Journal of Biblical Counseling*.[3] In 2000, Timeless Texts would publish Smith's *Christian Counselor's Medical Desk Reference* (2000). This work would serve as one of the two primary diagnostic manuals for contemporary biblical counselors, along with Mary and Marshall Asher's less skillfully written *The Christian's Guide to Psychological Terms* (2004). As we will see, Smith's work had some rather elementary argumentative flaws in it that makes one question his theoretical sophistication; but to this day his work remains perhaps the definitive expression of scientific anti-psychiatric critique from within the biblical counseling movement and remains influential among the more conservative biblical counseling elements within the right wing of the National Association of Nouthetic Counselors (NANC) (an important organization in biblical counseling circles which is described in the following pages).

In 1975, Westminster Seminary began offering a specialized degree program for nouthetic counseling (Powlison 59). As Powlison points out, this was a significant gain for biblical counseling proponents as it gave them a base of operations and a training facility for new proponents. In 1975 Adams left both Westminster and CCEF to devote himself to spreading the gospel of nouthetics to a worldwide audience (Powlison 59). Towards the end of the decade he also completed *A Theology of Christian Counseling* (1979), which he considered one of his most important works (Powlison 60).

In the meantime, however, there had been a very interesting development in biblical counseling: the addition of John C. Broger to the biblical counseling movement. In terms of American history as a whole, Broger is far more important than any single member of the biblical counseling movement, though less influential on the movement as a whole. This is because Broger was the architect of much of the military's anticommunist indoctrination campaign during the 1950s (Derosa 148). Broger believed that "communists had succeeded because each [communist] was well versed in a simple, accessible ideology that they could explain to others" (Derosa 148). By contrast, the West lacked such an ability to convey complex ideas simplistically and therefore was losing out against the Communists in the race for control of the world. Broger believed that the West needed a "codified system" if it was to beat the Communists.

As a result, Broger came up with a program called Militant Liberty, which revolved around ten basic freedoms and ten responsibilities (Derosa 148–149). Rights included such freedoms as practice of religion, owning property, and the rather ominously entitled "freedom to compete in production and to bargain for goods and services in a free market" (Broger, *Militant Liberty*, 11). Responsibilities including tolerating the beliefs of others, respecting the customs of others, and the "responsibility to assure equal opportunities and to further individual and national wellbeing" (11). As Derosa points out, "the idea [of Militant Liberty] was to get all Americans thinking along on a single, easily grasped ideological axis conceived for an audience with an eighth-grade reading level" (DeRosa 149). In 1955, the Department of Defense hired a prominent merchandiser, Jam Handy Agency (which had marketed Coca-Cola), to sell *Militant Liberty* worldwide (149). Despite the backing of the Joint Chiefs, the Defense Department, and the wishy-washy approval of President Eisenhower, the program ultimately did not get very far because the armed services refused to go along with it, seeing political indoctrination as a line even the military should not cross (Derosa 150–151). The navy's evaluators were particularly scornful of Broger's efforts, seeing them as "crude, propagandistic, and technically flawed" (Derosa 151).

Broger was an ardent evangelical and a graduate of Southern California Bible College. He operated the Far East Broadcasting Company, which during the Cold War was used to "beam Christian and anticommunist radio propaganda at Asian countries" (Derosa 148). Broger's twin passions of anticommunism and militant evangelicalism went hand in hand and he repeatedly searched for venues for spreading evangelical ideals. Therefore, when he heard of Adams's biblical counseling program, he "responded enthusiastically" (Powlison 62).

Broger immediately realized the potential "for inserting a frankly Bible-based counseling curriculum into the military context" (Powlison 62). He therefore arranged for Jay Adams to conduct a two-day training course in peer counseling that would teach military lay men and women to use biblical counseling methodology. Broger had the lecture transcribed and worked it into a two-part syllabus. His *Self-Confrontation Manual* "adapted Adams into a workbook intended to foster self-examination and personal growth; *Biblical Counseling* [the other half of the course] then trained people to help others" (Powlison 62). According to the January 12, 1977, issue of the *Nevada Daily Mail*, these tapes were seldom used afterwards in the military, leading to the suspicion of economic malfeasance (Anderson and Spear 4). In reality, however, while such malfeasance was going on (Anderson and Whitten), Broger was actually planning on using this material for a much wider audience: apparently to indoctrinate the entire U.S. military. According to Powlison, in what is probably the most gossipy passage in biblical counseling history, Broger prepared a nouthetics-inspired

> series of Armed Forces radio and TV spots to be aired over 1100 stations worldwide. The plan also called for overradio spot announcements and written material for 1900 troop newspapers to support the counseling "hot-lines" planned at various U.S. military bases around the world. The theme for the radio and TV spots and troop newspapers was "It's in the Bible" [Powlison 62].

This, unfortunately for the biblical counseling movement, proved to be even too much for the military, especially after the National Association of Evangelicals, using government funds, began hawking the program that Broger had developed (Anderson and Spear 4; Anderson and Whitten). A backlash developed against Broger led by columnist Jack Anderson (Powlison 62). Anderson charged, with considerable justification, that Broger was using his position to "promote evangelical Christianity and right-wing politics" (Powlison 62). While the Justice Department officially cleared Broger of wrongdoing, Anderson makes a very convincing case that this was in fact a whitewash (Anderson and Whitten). Indeed, a management study initiated by Broger himself found that the Armed Forces Radio and Television Services system that he was in charge of was "inefficient and ineffective and not responsible to policy guidance and direction" (Anderson and Spear).

In 1977, therefore, Broger retired and decided to found the Biblical Counseling Foundation (BCF). This organization implemented "his adaptation of Adams to self-counseling and to 'discipleship' for laity and pastors alike" (Powlison 62–63). Broger's *Self-Confrontation Manual* (1978) became wildly popular, selling over 100,000 copies (63). His Biblical Counseling Foundation would in subsequent years become a powerful, though by no means the most powerful, organization within the biblical counseling movement.

The reader should pause to reflect here. The almost-architect of U.S. indoctrinatory policy during the Cold War, a man who was valued highly enough by at least the Joint Chiefs and several successive Cold War administrations, found biblical counseling material sufficiently indoctrinatory to risk his whole career in an effort to make it a major tool of the U.S. military. Not only that, but when he was found out in this role, he decided to make biblical counseling his career. Broger had found his one idea, a simple idea (a *very* simple idea), by which he could now manipulate the masses. Never mind that even the military found Militant Liberty crude and propagandistic and Adams's model "too biblistic for the multi-denominational military chaplaincy to tolerate" (Powlison 62). What mattered was that Broger had an ideological indoctrination system, designed for the military, based on biblical counseling, and now ready for implementation on American civilians whose only crime was being diagnosed as mentally ill. The only point more damning than this is that Powlison apparently does not see the absurdity of using military training methods, meant for our hardiest individuals, as treatment methodologies for the most vulnerable among us: abuse victims, the mentally ill, and children.

Around the time Broger was embracing Adams philosophy, John Bettler was rethinking the biblical counseling system's anti-professionalism. Whereas Broger supported lay ministry and Adams pastoral ministry, Bettler was more concerned with a more scholarly and professional approach to pastoral counseling (Powlison 63–64). Bettler proposed the formation of what would become the National Association of Nouthetic Counselors, which would be officially established in 1976 (Powlison 63–64). Bettler's plan was "to form an accrediting body to set standards both for training programs and for the individual practice of those who would claim to be nouthetic counselors" (Powlison 64). Bettler's goal was practical and largely admirable. Despite being devoted to a system of at best questionable therapeutic benefit, he foresaw that this system would (perhaps unintentionally) promote abuses if it was not regulated. Unfortunately, even by Powlison's admission, the accreditation process for NANC was "not particularly taxing by secular standards" (Powlison 65). It consisted of four elements: a preliminary course, a study of marriage and family counseling, an overview of "counseling case studies, and [a] critique of psychological theories (essentially the Westminster counseling curriculum that Adams had created)" (Powlison 65).

Such a program was immediately problematic because Adams, despite his sometimes profound intellectual insights, did not have a good grasp of the secular psychological theories he critiqued. Therefore, insofar as biblical counseling did critique secular therapeutic systems over the next four decades, it often tilted at windmills, because too many of its proponents read only Adams, or perhaps Adams and a smattering of Mowrer and Glasser, rather than the therapists who influenced them. Even many of the professional psychotherapists and psychiatrists who converted to biblical counseling methods, such as Dr. Richard Ganz, were so simplistic in their rendering of the various psychological schools that their works were little more than formulaic restatings of Adams's largely refutable critiques of Freud, Rogers, and Skinner. Among second and third generation biblical counselors and advocates, only David Powlison and Gary Almy wrote intellectually respectable critiques of mainstream psychiatry and psychology. So pervasive was this intellectual rot at the core of biblical counseling that it was a common occurrence to find Ed Welch's only marginally stimulating *Blame It on the Brain* treated as a profound work of theological exegesis and psychiatric study. In reality, however, the biblical counseling movement often seemed perplexingly anti-intellectual by the high standards of Reformed scholarship that had given birth to it.

However, the biblical counseling movement came dangerously close to self-imploding in the late seventies due to the careless actions of one ministry. In 1979, a depressed young evangelical, Kenneth Nally, committed suicide while being counseled by pastors from the Los Angeles megachurch Grace Community (Powlison 218, Weitz backmatter). The church was led by John MacArthur, one of the most prominent supporters of biblical counseling in the western United States and a man whose influence over the movement (and evangelicalism in toto) has only increased over the years. A crucial arm of Grace Community Church was its pastoral counseling program (Weitz 16), led by Lynn Cory, who was college educated but had no counseling training other than that received from Grace Church. He had no medical degrees and was not certified to be a mental health counselor (Weitz 16).

Ken Nally initially turned to Cory for spiritual guidance, and Cory in turn directed Nally to Duane Rea. As John MacArthur's brother-in-law, Rea was an important member of the church, serving as both a pastor and a member of Grace's biblical counseling center. Like MacArthur, "Rea was a staunch advocate of biblical counseling but had no medical or professional counseling training" (Weitz 17). Indeed, Rea's former occupations were those of mechanic and fireman, not schools of employment ideally equipped to impart doctoral-level knowledge of mental health problems or even the history of pastoral counseling practices (Weitz 17). The counseling team at Grace Community Church claimed competence to treat disorders ranging from standard depression to bipolar to schizophrenia (Burton 488). Nally, who had displayed suicidal tendencies as early as 1973 (Weitz 20), became increasingly depressed as the 1970s rolled to a close. Problems with women and his inability to "reconcile his biblical beliefs with his secular studies" proved detrimental to both his academic and emotional life (Weitz 22–23, Burton 489). When Ken approached Rea for advice on his problems, Rea's answer was simple: sin was at the root of Ken's emotional pain, particularly "his desire for intimacy outside of matrimony" (Weitz 24).

After Ken broke up with his girlfriend, he became utterly despondent. He asked his pastor whether "a person who committed suicide" would "forfeit eternal salvation" (Weitz 24). The pastoral counselor Ken was dealing with answered that one could not lose salvation through suicide. Weitz correctly points out that despite the seeming callousness of this pronouncement it has deep roots in Protestant tradition (Weitz 24–25). Indeed, in the context of evangelicalism, where suicides are often still condemned to hell willy-nilly, Thompson could have quite realistically seen his answer as compassionate advice. Nor is it unrealistic of Weitz to trust Thomson, Rea, and MacArthur in their emphatic denial that they advocated Ken's suicide. Such an idea would be abhorrent to almost any evangelical, no matter how bloodless they might be (Weitz 25). But Ken, still partly operating out of a childhood steeped in Catholicism, may have interpreted this message differently than MacArthur or his followers meant it to be seen.

Nally's condition rapidly deteriorated in 1979. In February, he indicated to Pastor Rea that he had thought of committing suicide in 1974. This is crucial to understand because Grace Community Church staff were aware of Nally's suicidal tendencies but did not share them with Ken's family (Weitz 20, Burton 489). On March 12, 1979, Kenny attempted suicide. His parents were faced with a tough decision, especially in the relatively unenlightened 1970s. Should they admit Kenny to a psychiatric facility, even if he wished otherwise (Weitz 26)? While he was in the hospital, Ken told MacArthur that he wished he had succeeded in his suicide attempt and explained to Pastor Rea that he would try to commit suicide again (Burton 489, Weitz 26). The Nallys were not informed of these statements. Understandably, given the amount of psychophobic and legal prejudice against the mentally ill in the late 1970s, the Nallys were reluctant to admit Ken to a psychiatric hospital. Ken denied to his doctor that he was suicidal. At the time, the doctor believed Ken "was recovering well physically" (Weitz 27). She explained that the paralysis Ken felt in his right arm (which he was concerned about) was a temporary condition caused by his overdose (Weitz 27).

Ken then saw a psychiatrist, Dr. Hall. Hall was unable to figure out exactly the kind of counseling being offered at Grace Community Church, since Ken would say only that he was receiving biblical counseling. However, Hall was concerned with Ken's statement that "my counselors have advised me not to go to a psychiatrist. In fact I did want to check with them before coming to see you, to see if it was all right, but I was unable to" (Weitz 27). Hall then explained to Ken aspects of depression, while his father, Walter (then present), speculated about whether Ken might be suffering from a "kind of chemical imbalance" (28). Again, this therapeutic no-blame approach directly contradicted the guilt-based "sin model" of mental illness promulgated by Grace Community Church and by the biblical counseling movement at large. After Ken left the hospital, he spent most of his time reading the Bible and listening to John MacArthur sermons. Worse, his arm was not getting better (Weitz 28).

The last Walter Nally saw of his son was his son slowly leaving his driveway. Walter begged, as Weitz relates, "to know why Ken was so upset. Ken finally blurted out, 'It's my arm, see how it is?' 'What about it?' Walter asked still walking to keep pace with Ken's car. 'They told me it was because of my sin. They told me it was God's punishment, Dad.' Walter Nally could not believe his own ears. 'Tell me which one of those bastards said it!'" (Weitz 29). But it was too late for Ken. In a spiral of suicidal depression, he drove away. Walter Nally never found out how his son spent his last few days. All he knew for sure "is that sometime between the morning Ken pulled out, March 30, and the knock at the door [from the police] on April 1, he took his own life" (Weitz 29). Walter Nally probably thought his personal hell could not get any worse. But he had not counted on the ministrations of Grace Community Church. Though Catholics, the Nallys allowed Grace to handle the funeral. Duane Rea, the counselor in large part responsible for Ken's suicide in the first place, got up to speak and stated, as Ken's parents looked on, "It is not my purpose to eulogize Ken.... Ken disobeyed God in the final act of his life. He took what did not belong to him" (Weitz 31). Despite the pleas of Walter Nally that no one be told Ken had killed himself, Rea "made it clear to even the most ignorant observer that Ken had committed suicide" (Weitz 31). After the funeral, Rea proved himself to be blindingly insensitive. He showed Walter Nally a testimonial from Ken that proved he had tried to kill himself prior to 1979. Rea then admitted the church had known all about these previous attempts, and indeed that the knowledge stretched to the upper echelons of Grace Church. But for Rea, this was all right, because Ken's death was not the result of poor counseling but of "unresolved sin." Ken simply "could never do what was required to overcome his problems" (Weitz 32).

MacArthur, similarly, in trying to comfort Walter, told him that the fault for Ken's suicide was Ken's entirely, not Walter's at all (Weitz 32–33). Walter Nally, having grown up in the Catholic tradition, which has historically been much more forgiving of mental difference, found Rea's ideas utterly perplexing. When he discussed them with his priest, he found that his priest found them even more troubling (Weitz 35). What Walter did next was unprecedented: He sued Grace Community Church for clerical malpractice, a then unheard of accusation (Powlison, 219; Weitz 48–49). As Powlison relates, the "case was twice dismissed at the trial level, only to be reversed each time in appeals court" (Powlison 219). Eventually, the California Supreme Court ruled in favor of the church (219). As of 1997, "every state that has considered a cause of action for clergy malpractice has rejected it" (Burton 468). As Loue despondingly points out, "Courts consistently have been unwilling to find clergy liable for the adverse effects associated with their mental health counseling activities" (Loue 184). Loue contends the secular state is reluctant to judge clerical competence in counseling (Loue 185). The state's view is understandable because different religious traditions have different ways of interpreting mental illness, and judging between interpretive methodologies may itself be unconstitutional (Loue 185). To get out of that impasse, Loue suggests

> the legal imposition of a requirement of minimum education relevant to the counseling function, with a continuing education requirement, on clergy engaging in counseling activities that encompass the secular functions noted above. The educational requirement would not necessitate the achievement of a particular degree or level of education, but would mandate basic training in the recognition of symptoms that may be indicative of a condition requiring professional mental health diagnosis and treatment [Loue 192].

Loue's idea sounds promising. It might even work with deliverance ministers, who are not necessarily opposed on principle to psychological training, just psychological interpretation. Loue argues that "it [her proposal] would not impose punishment on individuals in connection with their religious beliefs, activities, attendance, or nonattendance" (Loue 192). The problem is that Loue's proposal does in fact tacitly discriminate against at least biblical counselors, since the very foundation of their ideology is a rejection of secular psychology and psychiatry in total. Similarly, Scientologists could equally claim that their counseling methods were being unfairly singled out. Perhaps Loue has a means of avoiding such a constitutional quandary. But since biblical counseling and deliverance proponents have been using first amendment protections successfully for forty years, it seems doubtful that there will ever be a successful legal challenge to clerical malpractice within our lifetime. Walter Nally's efforts to avenge his son's death were heroic and commendable. But they were also largely quixotic. Biblical counseling had survived the most formidable challenge to its existence ever posed. And indeed, thanks to the radicalization of John MacArthur after the conclusion of the legal proceedings in 1989, the main effect of Nally's challenge seems to have been to reinforce the hold the nouthetic model had over MacArthur's powerful and influential ministry. Indeed, Master's College and Seminary, which MacArthur had founded, became "committed to nouthetic counseling" (Powlison 220). MacArthur, along with FBCM's Bob Smith, would replace the psychology department at Master's with a biblical counseling department, and certify its pastors with NANC (Powlison 220). The first prominent manual of biblical counseling not written by Adams would come out of Master's (Powlison 220). In the battle between biblical counseling and its victims, the biblical counseling community had clearly scored its first victory.

One other crucial late addition to the second generation of biblical counselors was Ken Sande. Properly speaking, Sande wasn't actually a biblical counselor at all. Instead, he was a "lawyer influenced by Adams and CCEF"

(Powlison 220). Sande's book *The Peacemaker* (1991) and his Institute of Christian Conciliation (better known as Peacemaker Ministries) promoted "conflict resolution" by bypassing "the adversarial processes of the legal system by helping people and institutions to reconcile and resolve differences privately" (Powlison 220). Unlike Adams's work, Sande's Peacemaker Ministries met with little opposition, as it did not step on anyone's turf. Though Adams was not entirely approving of Sande, he accepted Sande's model into the wider biblical counseling movement; this model allowed a kind of nouthetics "lite" to prosper where it would not have normally been listened to (see Powlison 220). Sande's role here, indeed his mention in Powlison's *The Biblical Counseling Movement: History and Context* (2010) might seem anomalous. In reality, Sande would prove to be a significant player in biblical counseling power politics, though his real significance to the spread of biblical counseling methodology would not become apparent to even Reformed insiders until several decades later.

In the 1980s, the biblical counseling movement seemed to plateau (Powlison xvii). Adams's writing had slowed down, and Powlison apparently feels that Adams lost some of his creative powers during this period (208). NANC, meanwhile, had plateaued at about 100 members, and its accreditation power at the time was proving minimal (Powlison 208). It is clear that a lot of biblical counseling was being done in this period. Indeed, given the popularity of the Adams books (250,000 copies of *Competent to Counsel* were sold in the seventies alone, see NANC, "History."), it would be safe to assume that only deliverance methodology was more popular as an alternative therapeutic system to professional psychotherapy among evangelicals as a whole, but clearly much of the biblical counseling that went on did not even meet the minimum requirements of NANC certification. By 1983, fault lines were also appearing in the movement as a whole. Broger was becoming "disillusioned by NANC's professional goals" (Powlison 209), not surprisingly, considering that his model was predicated upon lay ministry. Bettler was also coming to see NANC as an increasing embarrassment to the biblical counseling movement, despite his critical role in its formation. He thought its "lack of quality control" and inability to evolve beyond a "good old boys club" was jeopardizing his goal "to produce an intelligentsia, a cadre of specialists in pastoral counseling, who could defend biblical counseling to the wider church" (Powlison 209). Eventually Bettler, like Broger, would step away from the NANC board and stop attending its annual meetings (Powlison 209).

What eventually allowed NANC to survive and prosper was the sponsorship of Bill Goode and Faith Baptist Church Ministries (Powlison 209). According to NANC's own Web site, "the church embraced NANC, providing volunteer workers to do mailings, host conferences, duplicate tapes, and support their pastor in his labors for NANC" (NANC, "History"). NANC became particularly involved with Master's Seminary thanks to Faith Baptist's Bob Smith and CCEF and NANC theorist Wayne Mack, who would become the chairman of the Biblical Counseling Department at Master's and served in that capacity between 1992 and 2000 (Mack, Foreword, 2, *Christian's Guide to Psychological Terms*). *The Journal of Pastoral Practice* (now *The Journal of Biblical Counseling*) was forced by financial conditions to cut back, with Adams and Bob Smith taking the lion's share of the writing duties (Powlison 210). Nouthetics practice made only "spotty headway" in academia. Biblical Theological Seminary began teaching the nouthetics model (Powlison 212), as did the fundamentalist Baptist Bible College (BBC) in Clark Summit, Pennsylvania, and Calvary Baptist Seminary in Lansdale, Pennsylvania. However, even fundamentalist Jerry Falwell's Liberty University, which initially favored nouthetics, ended up rejecting the model during Liberty's well-publicized bid for academic respectability (Powlison 212). Therefore, in response to these developments, over the course of the 1980s, CCEF became increasingly "professionalized," though it is doubtful whether the ministry's training ever even approached secular levels.[4]

CCEF also aggressively marketed itself to evangelicals and therefore became quite dependent on counseling fees to meet its budget. By 1991, its fees were already up to $50 an hour (see Powlison 214–215)—and this was for what was essentially, and often remains, nonqualified help, help that is any case opposed to any causal explanation of mental illness not based on its "sin-engendered" nature. Though CCEF is today the most well-respected biblical counseling organization, in the 1980s the Biblical Counseling Foundation and FBCM, according to Powlison, appeared to many people to be more stable, largely because there was a divide between CCEF, which aspired to be the intellectual caste of the biblical counseling movement, and NANC, which viewed itself as the promoter of doctrinal orthodoxy (Powlison 216). This divide can in part be explained by the greater fundamentalist and Baptist character of NANC, which was centered in a Baptist church and whose chief intellectual lights, Bob Smith and John MacArthur, were still essentially fundamentalist in orientation (Weitz 11–13, NANC, "History"). CCEF, by contrast, was essentially a more traditional Reformed initiative and aspired to the intellectual status that Reformed evangelicals have long been accustomed to.

Not surprisingly, therefore, this animus led to a further subdivision in the biblical counseling movement when a group *even further to the right* than Jay Adams and NANC emerged. These new polemicists included such authors as Martin and Deidre Bobgan and Dave Hunt. Though Martin Bobgan had started his professional career as an educational psychologist, his eventual conversion to conservative Protestantism made him highly critical of modern psychology (Powlison 217). Adams initially endorsed the Bobgans' book *Psychoheresy* (1987), and when he had difficulty acquiring "a publisher for one of his books, the Bobgans, who had begun their own publishing house, published it" (Powlison 217–218). The Bobgans became so strident against "integrationist" Christian psychology, however, that they eventually came to see biblical counseling as merely another form of integrationism. In their work *Against Biblical Counseling, for the Bible* (1994) they repudiated the entire biblical counseling movement (Bobgan and Bobgan, *Against Biblical Counseling, for the Bible* 167; Powlison 218).[5] The Bobgans criticized Bettler for his "recycled use of Adlerian psychology" (Bobgan and Bobgan, *Against Biblical Counseling For the Bible*, 158–159) and scored some telling hits on both NANC and CCEF counselors who accepted fees for counseling services, understandably seeing this as blurring the line between pastoral and professional therapy (Bobgan and Bobgan, *Against Biblical Counseling for the Bible*, 83).

Meanwhile, Hunt's sporadic criticisms of Christian integrationism over the course of many decades, though not as heavy-handed as that of the Bobgans, would eventually culminate in the 2008 publication of *Psychology and the Church* (2008), a simplistic but influential evangelical anti-psychology book and DVD documentary twin set, the latter of which, as of April 28, 2012, was still available on YouTube for free viewing.[6] In the early 2000s, Lisa and Ryan Bazler would join the Bobgans and Hunt as the third major force in "psychoheresy-hunting." The Bazlers' book *Psychology Debunked* (2002) and their Web site, "Psychology Debunked: Exposing Psychology, Exalting Christ" (Bazler and Bazler et al.; Bazler and Bazler, "Psychology Debunked: Exposing Psychology, Exalting Christ"), promoted extremist anti-psychiatry sentiments, often trying to link psychiatric medications to mass murder by promoting the idea that mentally ill murderers (not surprisingly) were sometimes on psychiatric medication, but that these medications *were what caused the murders* (Bazler and Bazler "Adam Lanza"). The reader will not be surprised to learn that the Bazlers were members, as of 2008, of the Scientology front organization Citizens Commission on Human Rights (CCHR), arguably the biggest non–Christian anti-psychiatric organization in the world and one co-founded by none other than Thomas Szasz (Anonymous Organization, "Fact Checking CCHR's Board of Advisors"). Though the Bazlers remain a largely marginal force at the periphery of acceptable biblical counseling practice, the fact that the movement as a whole has not more strongly condemned their dangerous opposition to psychiatric medication speaks volumes about the continued anti-biological reading of mental illness that mainstream biblical counseling supports.

By the 1990s, according to Powlison, the biblical counseling movement was seeing a resurgence. The Biblical Counseling Foundation's staff were again appearing at NANC conferences, and CCEF and NANC became less alienated (Powlison 220–221). Meanwhile, a host of new biblical counseling advocates, many out of CCEF, began to publish during this period. The most significant works were Ed Bulkley's *Why Christians Can't Trust Psychology* (1993), Ed Welch's *Blame It on the Brain* (1998), Gary Almy's *How Christian Is Christian Counseling?* (2000), the various works of Elyse Fitzpatrick, and David Powlison's *Seeing with New Eyes* (2003), as well as his updated history of the biblical counseling movement, *The Biblical Counseling Movement: History and Context* (2010). In addition, *Introduction to Biblical Counseling* (1994) and *Counseling: How to Counsel Biblically* (2005) (essentially an update of the former text), biblical counseling anthologies sponsored by MacArthur and Master's College and Seminary, set the strident tone for West Coast fundamentalist biblical counseling, while *The Christian's Guide to Psychological Terms* and *The Christian Counselor's Medical Desk Reference* became the de facto DSMs of the biblical counseling movement, where the movement adopted psychological terminology practically outright (particularly in the Ashers' work), only to cloak it in sin and guilt.

Of these works, Ed Bulkley's *Why Christians Can't Trust Psychology* is the most marginal, though Bulkley himself would play an important part in biblical counseling over the course of the 1990s and 2000s. Bulkley was the senior pastor of LIFE Fellowship in Denver (Bulkley back cover). His *Return to the Word* program, which played from the mid 1990s to the late 2000s, established Bulkley as a nouthetics-inspired James Dobson, only Bulkley labeled everything as sin rather than poor childhood habits.[7] The actual content of *Why Christians Can't Trust Psychology* is an odd mixture of fictional portrayals of biblical counseling and largely rehashed arguments borrowed from Adams. Bulkley also promoted the idea that women should not "cling to victim status" when they were victims of sexual or physical abuse (Bulkley 125). Though Bulkley's statements were made against the backdrop of the Satanic panic, they are nonetheless insensitive to the many real victims of abuse who greatly outnumbered those women making suspect ritual abuse charges in the eighties and nineties. Largely, however, Bulkley's work was simply too marginal to be of any note.

Ed Welch's *Blame It on the Brain* was the first significant single-author, book-length work by a third generation biblical counselor. The purpose of *Blame It on the Brain* was to give the biblical counseling movement a working methodology to distinguish between "chemical imbalances, brain disorders, and disobedience" (Welch, front matter). Despite a scientific veneer to the book, Welch was clearly troubled by the growing prominence of neuroscientific explanations for mental difference that were then gaining currency. He complains that "the Bible has not been defeated, but it has become irrelevant. Many researchers find no more use for the idea of an immaterial soul. All our behaviors are allegedly explained by brain chemistry and physics" (Welch 24). Why was Welch troubled by these developments? For one, he feared that biochemical alterations could affect the state of the soul. He complains, for instance, that in Peter D. Kramer's *Listening to Prozac* (1993) a man's interest in pornography is ended by taking Prozac. To Welch, while it's beneficial to be freed of a desire for pornography, such neurochemical alterations of the brain will convince people that "if the soul exists, it can be changed through prescription drugs, not preaching the Gospel" (Welch 25). For Welch, what is at stake is nothing less than the existence of the soul and the mind as distinct entities, and as for Adams, if the soul can be conditioned or altered biochemically, it can be changed via processes other than spiritual ones.

Welch is what is called an interactionist (Welch 29). Interactionism is "the view that mind and body—or mental events and physical events—causally influence each other" (Robinson "Dualism"). While Welch understandably, and perhaps correctly, takes traditional psychiatry to task for its reductionism, interactionism faces formidable, though not insurmountable, challenges. As Calef relates, "The Occam's Razor argument creates a strong methodological presumption against dualism, suggesting that the mind-body split multiplies entities unnecessarily in much the way that a demon theory of disease complicates the metaphysics of medicine compared to a germ theory" (Calef). The presupposition that there is such a thing as the mind is, in light of Occam's razor, seemingly needlessly complicating. Even more problematically, interactionism conflicts with what we know about human biological development. No one, for instance, seriously argues that embryos have minds (Calef). If we start as wholly physical beings, it is likely that we will continue to be wholly physical beings once we exit the womb (Calef).

Biblical counselors like Welch, of course, will argue that spirits or souls are added by God to the embryo or fetus, thus allowing for the existence of the mind. But contemporary philosophers of the mind, including dualists who would typically support Welch's position, put little stock in such arguments (Calef). The biblical counseling model, which is absolutely dependent on the existence of the soul, and also in many models, on the mind, seems to posit needless additional entities existing within the brain, influencing it in unpredictable ways. Calef, by no means a total critic of mind-body dualism, points out some of the other formidable challenges to Cartesianism and the salvation it would provide to the biblical counseling movement:

Since the mind is, on the Cartesian model, immaterial and unextended, it can have no size, shape, location, mass, motion or solidity. How then can minds act on bodies? What sort of mechanism could convey information of the sort bodily movement requires, between ontologically autonomous realms? To suppose that non-physical minds can move bodies is like supposing that imaginary locomotives can pull real boxcars. Put differently, if mind-body interaction is possible, every voluntary action is akin to the paranormal power of telekinesis, or "mind over matter." If minds can, without spatial location, move bodies, why can my mind move immediately only one particular body and no others? [Calef].

Essentially, if Welch is going to take a mind-over-matter approach, it is difficult to see why he does not go all the way and embrace the kind of paranormal and healing powers typically associated with the deliverance movement and its various proponents. Welch cannot adopt that position because of his alignment with the specifically cessationist Reformed movement. He could conceivably argue that there is only mind, not matter, and this is in fact where the biblical counseling movement could eventually be forced to end up, philosophically, as neuroscience leaves smaller and smaller amounts of room for the soul within the neural framework of the brain. Even if Welch adopted a non-cessationist position, he would face formidable philosophical challenges, as Dean Zimmerman, writing for the *Encyclopedia of Philosophy,* points out:

Even if property dualists are right and some psychological phenomena cannot be reduced to or exhaustively explained in terms of properties similar to those now ascribed to physical bodies and their parts, nothing would be gained by supposing that these irreducible mental properties belong to some new entity.... One must now explain why the exercise of the soul's mental powers depends so heavily upon a properly functioning brain. Perhaps hard evidence of spirit possession, reincarnation, veridical out-of-body experiences, and the like would change the situation. But, in its absence, respect for parsimony in theory construction provides a powerful reason to reject souls [Zimmerman].

If the soul does exist, why does it seem to exactly resemble the brain? Why do behaviors labeled sin seem to be so keenly affected by extreme brain injury? Welch really has no good answer for this.

Welch argues that when one makes a decision for good or evil that decision "will be accompanied by changes in brain activity" (Welch 47). However, the brain does not cause the decision but is affected by the heart, a concept Welch leaves nebulous but which roughly corresponds to a combination of the spirit and the mind (despite his denials to the contrary) (see Welch 47). The body is "equipment for the heart. It does what the heart tells it to do" (Welch 40). The problem, of course, with this argument, is that it violates Occam's razor. Welch believes that since the heart is the seat of the body, the brain ultimately "cannot make a person sin or keep a person from following

Jesus in faith and obedience" (Welch 49). Welch's claim here takes biblical counseling's peculiar version of Cartesianism to new lengths.

As the brain cannot be the center of sin, the heart is now the center, leading to ridiculous situations like the nouthetic admonition of Alzheimer's patients and the demented, when their problems are spiritual instead of physical (Welch 69). Welch seems to sincerely believe he can tell the difference between spiritually induced mental problems and physically induced ones within Alzheimer's patients. In a passage of somewhat marked cruelty, Welch writes: "Does the disease [dementia] create the sinful behavior? Absolutely not. Is the sinful behavior a reaction to a body that is wasting away.... Perhaps. More often the sinful behavior is the person's heart being revealed" (Welch 78). Welch honestly believes that many of the hallucinations, angry outbursts, and other typical behaviors of demented patients are a result of their *personal failings being now revealed to the world.* He even advocates nouthetic rebukes of lewd language used by such patients (Welch 81). In Welch's system it is a sin for an 80-year-old Alzheimer's patient to make a pass at a nurse, but it is not a sin for a biblical counselor to berate that person for behavior that most sane neurologists would tell them is beyond the patient's control.

Compared to Welch's work, Gary Almy's *How Christian Is Christian Counseling?* (2000) is a masterpiece of erudition. One way this is immediately apparent is Almy's greater engagement with European philosophy and culture. For instance, Almy draws some interesting links between the notorious Ernst Haeckel and Sigmund Freud (Almy 97–99) and also tries to more thoroughly and honestly acquaint lay biblical counseling advocates with what he sees as the major defects of traditional "Christian psychology."[8] He also states what is only implicit in much other biblical counseling material—its application of pro–Augustinian and anti–Pelagian theology to issues of psychotherapy. That Calvinism tends to be Augustinian should, of course, surprise no one familiar with that philosophy, but that Almy respects his audience enough to expect them to know who Augustine and Pelagius were, rather than offering the extremely dumbed down exegesis present in *Blame It on the Brain,* speaks to his greater sense of scholastic honesty. Almy also makes a semi-plausible, though ultimately not convincing, case for a return to Puritan-like forms of "soul care" (Almy 206–211). All in all, therefore, while his critique of traditional psychology is ultimately trapped in the same Cartesian bind as Welch's (see Almy on 123–126 particularly), he makes a more convincing case for that position than any other biblical counseling supporter I've encountered.

What is troubling in Almy isn't his neo–Cartesianism, as shortsighted as it is, but the fact that he is a convicted pedophile (Kim; Long, Gutkowski and St. Clair). But that is not all. Almy, perhaps the most literate and persuasive of the biblical counseling movement's supporters outside of David Powlison and Adams himself, was also demoted from his position as chief of the medical staff at the Veterans Affairs Medical Center in North Chicago and reassigned to an advisory position after it was revealed that poor care at the hospital led to the death of patients. Fifteen patients in all died, an achievement that would, one might think, not endear him to a counseling movement that tried to take over U.S. chaplain training (Millenson; Felshman; "VA Acts"). Veterans Affairs secretary Edward J. Derwinski said in reference to the situation at the hospital where Dr. Almy was the *chief of staff* that "this is as bad as anything we've had. It's very disappointing" ("Veterans Groups Alarmed"). Larry Rivers, executive director of the Veterans of Foreign Wars, a prominent veterans organization, said the situation was a "doggone disgrace" ("Veterans Groups Alarmed"). Concerned patients at the Edward Hines, Jr. VA Hospital believed that part of Almy's reason for their lack of care at that institution might in fact be that he did not believe in psychiatry (Felshman).

But the situation unfortunately becomes even more farcical. Gary Almy was also, according to his own allies, a prominent board member of the International Association of Biblical Counselors (IABC). This organization was at the time led by the previously mentioned Ed Bulkley (see Compton's revealing advertisements for Bulkley and Almy, link provided in works cited). Not surprisingly, upon finding out about Almy's unprofessionalism—which had been going on for at least 15 years, including at the time he wrote *How Christian Is Christian Counseling?*—Ed Bulkley "declined to comment" (Susnjara). Bulkley is, of course, the same man who said that sex abuse victims—which he seems to sometimes argue are women who had affairs and other times true victims depending on the "age of the female" and the amount of consent involved—should not "cling to victim status" (Bulkley 125). It is not surprising, therefore, that Dr. Almy would gravitate to the teachings promoted by Bulkley.

Almy also worked with some Lydia home patients at a place called Salem Ranch, though he was not on staff (Salem4youth, "Counseling"; Blatter). Salem's Ranch, formerly known as Salem's Children Home, claims to provide biblical counseling (Salem4youth, "Counseling"). This site had incurred abuses before, including the accusation of manslaughter of a young boy who had been handcuffed in order to restrain him (Karwath). A 1985 *Chicago Tribune* report on the review of the organization stated the following: "A DCFS review committee described it as a 'caring and loving environment' with an excellent vocational skills program and living quarters that were 'spacious and homelike.' ... But the review also noted that youths 'in need of intensive mental health counseling or a tightly structured environment' don't belong in the Salem home.

The year-old report also said that the child-care staff tended 'to be young and have limited previous child-care experience or training'" (Smith and Franklin).[9] Therefore, we have the rather awkward situation of having one of the biblical counseling movement's most formidable intellectuals being a pedophile, a convict, and an abuser of veterans at least indirectly responsible for 15 deaths (Millenson), and one who also happens to be linked to a provider who claims to do a form of biblical counseling (nouthetic or otherwise) and who has a long history of questionable practices towards "troubled youth." Much of this abuse can be directly linked to the philosophy of "no accreditation" or professional training that is at the heart of the biblical counseling movement.

Powlison's work would prove to be initially less scandalous, though currently he finds himself, along with Ken Sande, near the center (though fortunately not a direct participant in) of one of the biggest sex abuse scandals in the history of the Calvinist church, if not evangelicalism as a whole. In *Seeing with New Eyes,* Powlison seeks to provide a systematic model for biblical counseling consisting of four components: A conceptual framework, a methodology, a social structure, and an apologetic component (Powlison, *Seeing with New Eyes,* 3).

Powlison feels that concepts "are the first and defining ingredient in any system of counseling. Every theory defines its version of human nature and the dynamics of human motivation" (Powlison, *Seeing with New Eyes* 3). Powlison's conceptual orientation towards counseling sharply contrasts with the more emotionally laden definition of counseling prevalent among Pentecostals and Charismatics. This is not particularly surprising. As a general rule, the Reformed movement has tended to prefer a more rationalistic theology, while the Charismatic movement has always been open to manifestations, sometimes very extreme, of great emotion. The Van Tilian element of Powlison's conceptual framework of biblical counseling is quite pronounced, first in its emphasis on rationalism and second in the scope of authority it grants to the Bible. For Powlison, the "Bible's truth competes head-to-head with other models. God speaks a truth that is intended to make sense of us and change us. It is not truth about how to find a job, or how, genes transmit eye color, or how to fix a clogged drain. The truth that is in Jesus reveals and changes what we live for" (Powlison 3).

For Powlison, the biblical model is more than just a model because Truth is mediated through "a Person, a working Redeemer" (i.e., Jesus) (Powlison 4). Powlison here directly builds on Van Til and Schaeffer, who advocated a radically transformative vision of Christian culture in which it eventually pervaded and saturated a secular culture with the truth of "Christian worldview thinking."[10] This philosophy, originally rooted in the thinking of Dutch politician and Reformed thinker Abraham Kuyper (who very well might not have agreed with its application in modern day America), in the American context has been used to justify Christian takeover of social venues normally meant to be free of control by any one religious or ideological group (most notably, in this context, the courts and the health care system). If truth is defined through the mediation of Jesus, then secular individuals are, by the biblical counseling model's definition, at a distinct disadvantage in attaining any form of truth.

Powlison's comments about methodology are largely banal, but his idea of the "delivery system" or institutional framework for purveying biblical counseling are of keen interest to any concerned reader:

> In modern America, the "mental health system" is a vast complex of higher education, hospitals, publishers, third-party insurers, drug companies, licensing boards, and private practice psychotherapists. But the loving truth and truthful love of Ephesians 4:15 come embedded in a different social system: The ekklesia of the people of God.... The most magnificent institutional structure imaginable is a community living up to how Ephesians 4 weds pastoral leadership with every-member mutuality. Both the special gifts from God and the general call to all God's people traffic in the cure of souls, as each part does its part.... Whether finding expression in local church, regional church, or para-church, God's new society is called to develop and provide radical alternatives to the current system of autonomous counseling professions licensed by the state, creedally committed to the secular psychologies, and funded on a for-profit, fee-for-service basis. God's wisdom has institutional implications [Powlison 6].

Powlison's position here is both troubling and perplexing and should be so even to people normally sympathetic to the biblical counseling movement. First, Powlison assumes that the church is the group of people best equipped to treat mental health conditions. In keeping with biblical counseling theory, Powlison provides no empirical evidence for this belief. Nor is it immediately clear why groups like "higher education" (which supports CCEF and Powlison itself through their close connection to Westminster Seminary), publishers (which Powlison also has), and private practice psychotherapy (which is what, whether Powlison wants to admit it or not, is providing, only unlicensed and unregulated) are all that different from what biblical counseling itself provides. What distinguishes secular psychotherapy is that it does generally support psychiatric drugs, licensing boards, and third-party insurers. But even here, for instance, biblical counselors are far from united against psychiatric medication, not because they like it—they clearly do not—but because they also clearly do not want to be sued for suggesting to mentally ill people that they go off their medications.

Almost every major biblical counseling manual warns not to use its information as an excuse for suggesting to clients to stop taking their medication. For instance Robert Smith's *The Christian Counselor's Medical Desk Reference* strongly admonishes readers that "one strong caveat is necessary for the correct use of this book. At no time should you use the information to make a diagnosis or attempt to influence a physician's diagnosis" (Smith xiv). And Powlison's complaints against licensure are transparently self-serving. As we have seen, he himself has pointed out John Bettler's contention that biblical counseling licensure never was what it should have been (Powlison 63–65). Secular licensure hurts Powlison's cause because it keeps biblical counselors away from more high-paying and lucrative clientele. It also ensures that secular psychotherapists, as bad as they sometimes are, tend to operate with higher ethical standards, and certainly higher accountability to state authority, than the biblical counseling movement.

Even more perplexing are Powlison's complaints against the for-profit, fee-for-service basis of secular psychotherapy since whether or not CCEF is for profit it clearly does charge fees for its services, quite significant ones as we have seen. An average CCEF session today costs $95 per hour (CCEF, "Hours, Fees, Directions"). Since CCEF offers faith-based counseling, none of that money is likely to go to any insurer, since insurers wish for such crazy requirements as empirically based counseling methodologies and professional training in psychology or social work. The former requirement is almost never provided by CCEF, the latter only occasionally.[11] One does wonder where CCEF's counseling fees do go. As of 2007, 25.9 percent of its employees made $50,000 or more a year ("Christian Counseling and Educational Foundation in Glenside, Pennsylvania"). Compared to similar programs, CCEF allocated 66 percent of its income to program expenses, while other programs usually allocate over 82.0 percent ("Christian Counseling and Educational Foundation in Glenside, Pennsylvania"). Therefore, while CCEF from its financials does not appear to be much worse than secular organizations in fee charging, it is hardly better either.

What can we then conclude from Powlison's critique of the secular institutional framework for counseling? Mainly that Powlison offers a number of complaints about secular psychology that actually apply at least as much, and often far more, to his own theoretical framework than they do to psychology. The only place that he might be right is in arguing that psychology is by definition creedally different from biblical counseling and therefore (one presumes, given biblical counseling rhetoric) from Christian theology in general. But this is far from a universal belief even in the evangelical church and would not be shared at all by most non-evangelical Christians. This, in the final analysis, leaves Powlison with nothing. The apologetic function of his counseling, the fourth element of his framework, will not work at all if the conceptual presuppositions on which it is based are wrong. Powlison can assert, as many in the Van Tilian school do, that the assumption of the truth of Christianity is foundational and known to all people, whether they admit it or not. But how Powlison can then prove that subjectively within any other individual's own experience, when he is not that person, is a point that seems to elude most presuppositional thinkers. It is the fatal flaw at the heart of modern Calvinism, as true today as it was when Van Til began teaching at Westminster more than eight decades ago.[12]

Powlison's other main area of scholastic inquiry was into how specifically health care was to be delivered within this emerging biblical counseling mental health system. Powlison's methodology here in many ways was closely modeled on that of Adams. For Adams, counseling was "fundamentally a pastoral activity and must be church-based" (Powlison, *Biblical Counseling Movement: History*, 130). Therefore the health care delivery system that Adams proposed for the mentally ill—whom, we must remember, he did not consider mentally ill—was the local church. The pastor was the "therapeutic agent" who gave treatment, while the church was the institution of choice for giving treatment (131).

It must be understood by secular readers that, for Adams at least, this was not necessarily an entirely cynical ploy. Adams believed that his "model of pastor-counselor could draw upon an entire congregation to help him. Others in the community might pray for his counseling, might aid counselees financially or medically, might take a troubled person into their home or shelter a battered spouse, might provide a job for a counselee or financial counsel or friendship or modeling" (Powlison 133). For Adams, the great advantage of having the church as a mechanism for counseling was that it could draw on resources that other institutions could "barely dream of" for the aid of patients (Powlison 132). In the 1970s, as Adams's counseling ministry was hitting its stride, the dominant therapeutic practice was behaviorism. Despite behaviorism's eventual successes as a therapeutic practice, it cannot be denied that it did have a negative reputation among many "caring professionals" at the time, not always for bad reasons. We have seen, for instance, how deeply impacted Nancy Alcorn was by her encounters with behaviorism within a penal environment. Therefore, Adams's system may have seemed to him to offer up real therapeutic hope in a way that secular behaviorism did not.

The problem was, unfortunately, that this delivery system was also based on a largely behaviorist-oriented vision of the world, specifically one revolving around church discipline. Adams's model of counseling was "public." Therefore, his model conceptualized people's lives as containing "no ultimate secrets" (Powlison 133). As a result, Adams's therapeutic program sought "to solve problems by involving as small a circle of people as possible and as large a circle of people as necessary. When an individual refused to change in order to resolve problems, Adams gradually brought larger community resources to bear" (Powlison 133). As Powlison points out, this was a radically different conceptualization of mental health treatment delivery practices than that practiced by secular institutions. Secular institutions were voluntaristic and largely overseen by a "fee-for-service" model; by contrast the model practiced by the biblical counseling community (especially outside of heavily specialized counseling centers like CCEF) was "constructed along premodern communitarian lines" (Powlison 133). Personal problems, including mental health problems, were ultimately not merely an individual's failings but reflected on the spiritual health and reputation of the entire community.

Because of this, and because of the extremely disciplinarian nature of much of Reformed church discipline, particularly after the entry of C.J. Mahaney into the movement (whose shepherding practices undoubtedly unintentionally influenced the way many major Calvinists viewed church polity), the tendency in much of Reformed—and also conservative non–Reformed Baptist circles—was to not operate under secular standards of best clinical practice. For instance, there was no promise of "absolute confidentiality" and the information one divulged in counseling could be brought up as a matter of church discipline (Powlison 134). Similarly, counselees could be taken into the pastor-counselor's home and have dual formal and informal relationships, something absolutely frowned upon by secular clinical practice (Powlison 136). The biblical counseling movement conceptualized this as an improvement upon traditional secular best-practice therapeutic models since it allowed for a pastor to work particularly efficiently with his congregation (Powlison 135), and presumably therefore to model Christian love and best care practices to the wider community. However, in practice, the biblical counseling movement's model of communitarian mental health care proved to be badly flawed, because the secular assumptions about the need for confidentiality and, in particular, the assumption of formality in counselor-counselee relationships were not met.

Powlison returned to the subject of institutional delivery systems in his essay "Cure of Souls and the Modern Psychotherapies."[13] Powlison believed that the role of "cure of souls" did not belong to psychotherapeutic professions, which "should not have the rights and honors to practice the cure of souls. They have the wrong knowledge base, the wrong credentials, the wrong financial and professional structure" (Powlison, *Biblical Counseling Movement: History*, 295). The church, in Powlison's opinion, had the responsibility for such curative practice, and indeed there was "no legitimate place for a semi-

Christian counseling profession to operate in autonomy from ecclesiastical jurisdiction and in subordination to state jurisdiction" (Powlison 295). In short, not only was the church to be the mental health delivery system for mentally ill evangelicals, it also was the only organization that could claim that right. "Secularists" were by definition deficient in their ability to treat and interact with the mentally ill.

Powlison freely admitted that the church was not yet ready to be the delivery system it needed to be. He proposed a number of standards, therefore, to make the system better. However, arguably these ideas were more aimed at making the system more reflective of Christian doctrine than they were at actually helping counselees. For instance, Powlison advised that the current system needed "creedal standards for the care and cure of souls, or at least a widely recognized corpus of practical theological writing" (Powlison 297). It is not very clear why having one particular set of creedal standards will make biblical counseling practice effective, particularly since creedal standards are here interpreted in an explicitly ideological, rather than scientific or empirical, sense. What is even worse is that Powlison explicitly endorses the idea that churches should enact "ecclesiastical supervision" over "the faith and practice of cure of souls, both in local churches and at higher ecclesiastical levels. It matters what theories and ideas are being mediated to counselees. A secular psychotherapist can freely adopt any of many theoretical orientations.... The church does not believe in such theoretical diversity but aims to refine its doctrine to cohere with the gaze of God revealed in the Bible" (Powlison 298). Problematically, therefore, what became important to the biblical counseling movement, especially as Powlison's influence over the movement has grown in recent years, is that the movement be concerned primarily with the ecclesiastical health of the church rather than with the health of the church's individual members. This increasing focus on ecclesiology, though always an important element of biblical counseling, also meant that churches that supported biblical counseling were often more than willing to sell out less powerful members of the ecclesiastic structure if the health of the church polity as a whole was at stake. Many lives were harmed in the process.

Actual Diagnoses and Treatment Methods

The supporters of the biblical counseling movement have built their movement on normalization. They have set up their own classificatory systems, from which they deem what behaviors are considered spiritually normal and which are not. For instance, Robert D. Smith, a leading biblical counseling advocate and medical doctor, claims the manic phase of bipolar is "a faulty, sinful attempt to overcome the depression one feels, fears, and unsuccessfully seeks to alleviate"(Smith 217). A tic exhibited by a Tourette's syndrome patient is "sinful if it is a response to life, if it turns the one with it away from pleasing God, or if it is disruptive to others" (Smith 355). Marshall and Mary Asher's *Christian's Guide to Psychological Terms* presents an extensive catalogue of this kind of normalizing rhetoric. Anorexia is considered a sin because anorexics are "dominated by the fear of man" (Asher and Asher 10). Children with Asperger's syndrome sin when they fail to develop "mutually supportive interpersonal relationships" (Asher and Asher 14). The volatile mood swings caused by disorders like bipolar 1 are the result of "bitterness and despair" (Asher and Asher 49). Obsessive-compulsive disorder is a manifestation of "ungodly fear" (Asher and Asher 114). Perhaps most disturbing is the Ashers' tendency to doubt the salvation of certain groups that they deem mentally ill. A schizophrenic, for instance, should be considered an unbeliever "until proven otherwise (even if he has a history of effective Christian ministry)" (Asher and Asher 164). Like much antigay rhetoric, the Ashers' view of salvation divides the world into the normalized evangelical "us" and the abnormal homosexual or mentally ill "other."

The Ashers' beliefs are quite widespread in the biblical counseling movement, though others in the movement are less likely to express their views so bluntly. John MacArthur argues that psychotherapy is embraced by the spiritually weak—those who are not stoical enough to accept that life's pain leads to a better relationship with God (MacArthur, "The Psychology Epidemic and Its Cure," 18.). David Powlison proclaims that "Galatians 5:19–21 says that the manifest lifestyle of sin is 'obvious.' ... Those 'works of the flesh' are sinful; they arise casually from various 'lusts of the flesh.' ... What about problems like those labeled 'eating disorders' or 'obsessive-compulsive disorders' that do not appear on the representative list in Galatians 5? 'Obvious' (and close study will unpack the details to show the how and why of those works of the flesh)" (Powlison 281). OCD and anorexia, in Powlison's estimation, are sinful "lusts" rather than diseases or psychological aberrations. Michael Emlet, another third generation biblical counselor, writes that "it is that very sacrifice [of Christ] that can embolden you to step into the light to forsake the real sin: the self-absorption in which an OCD sufferer is caught" (Emlet 15). Emlet is relatively understanding by biblical counseling standards, but he apparently does not recognize that calling OCD "self-absorption" and a "sin" may make the counselee feel worse. Winston Smith, in the *Journal of Biblical Counseling*, asks, "Why is the obsessive compulsive person so prone to adopt the standards of the world rather than God's standards?"(Winston Smith 27).

OAIM, an online ministry influenced by the biblical counseling movement, argues that depression, suicidal tendencies, schizophrenia, panic disorders and eating disorders are all the result of an unbiblical response to our personal sinful behavior ("OAIM: What is Biblical Counseling?"). Perhaps the cruelest comments are reserved for bulimics. Elyse Fitzpatrick, commenting on this group of sufferers, mournfully asks, "What precipitates these [bulimic] binges? You may discover lusts both of the body and the mind" (Elyse Fitzpatrick, "Helping Bulimics," 16). Fitzpatrick goes on to state that bulimia is influenced by "greed" and "idolatry" (16, 18). Still other populist biblical counselor supporters argue that the root of all our problems is sin (O'Hara) and that insanity is often a judgment for pride and sin ("Idolatry of Christian Psychology").

The actual cures proposed for individual disorders vary only slightly from individual theorist to individual theorist. The Bobgans, for instance, argue that depressives must be confronted biblically rather than psychologically (Bobgan and Bobgan, *Psychoheresy: The Psychological Seduction of Christianity*, 198). Robert Smith warns that "the Bible is the only solution for a depressed person" (Robert Smith, *The Christian Counselor's Medical Desk Reference*, 216). Adams, too, eschews chemical relief for depression in favor of "scriptural" therapy (Adams, *Competent to Counsel*, 93). Asher and Asher provide the most extensive list of biblical counseling treatments. For obsessive-compulsive disorder, Asher and Asher suggest the condition will improve as the counselee repents and "is willing to endure the fear experience if that is what God has sovereignly and lovingly planned for him" (Asher and Asher, *The Christian's Guide to Psychological Terms*, 114). For dissociative identity disorder, Asher and Asher suggest that the counselor teach the counselee with the gospel and confront the counselee with her sin (Asher and Asher 106). The bulimic must "repent, confess her sin and study the Scriptures to understand how she can learn to fear God, not man" (Asher and Asher 31). An anorexic must "recognize her sins and repent" (Asher and Asher 10). Schizophrenics must be confronted with their sins (Asher and Asher 164). Lisa and Ryan Bazler, at the edge of the biblical counseling movement, claim that anorexics can "trust God" to get control of their "sinful nature" (Lisa Bazler and Ryan Bazler, *Psychology Debunked*, 96). People with OCD or OCPD (obsessive-compulsive personality disorder) can gain victory over their illnesses by calling "Jesus the Lord of our lives" (Bazler and Bazler, *Psychology Debunked*, 97).

Some in the biblical counseling movement might claim that these approaches do not represent the mainstream of the movement, but the foreword to Asher and Asher's book was written by Wayne Mack, a former board member of the National Association of Nouthetic Counselors, the foremost biblical counseling association in the country outside of CCEF (Mack, "Foreword," unpaginated). And Robert (Bob) Smith's description of mania, for instance, as "unbiblical behavior in the face of a serious dilemma," coming from the leading medical "authority" in the biblical counseling movement (Smith 218), also shows not only a basic misunderstanding of human decency but also a basic misunderstanding of mania, since there is nothing in the manic phase that is necessarily inherently sinful even by biblical counseling standards (often the phase is just marked by excessive energy, though sometimes displayed to dangerous levels. See Barlow and Durand 184 on mania's contribution to hyperactivity). It is hard to believe that Smith can seriously see excessive physical energy, stamina, and endurance as inherent sins, even if brought on by mania; rather Smith's vision of mania is predicated on an antiquated view of what symptoms bipolar people actually exhibit.

None of these arguments by biblical counseling proponents appear to make rational sense. Sometimes, of course, biblical counseling curative methods may actually work. It would not be surprising that, among Christian patients at least, the curative rate was almost as high for biblical counseling as it is for secular counseling. The problem is, however, that for people who do not wish to undergo such therapy it may prove extremely damaging, especially for the mentally ill and victims of sexual abuse (as we have seen and shall see again). And it is certain that such therapy will be used against people's will, even people who are not a danger to themselves or others (which is often the secular rule of thumb for treatment). Children, for instance, typically have no say about receiving faith-based treatment. LGBT people are likely to be pressured into the therapy as well, especially teens and young adults. While not all mentally ill people are pushed into biblical counseling, many mentally ill people, particularly those suffering from psychosis or extreme manifestations of bipolar disorder or OCD, will likely have very diminished capacities to judge what is efficacious treatment for their condition. The same is even more true of already suffering anorexics and bulimics. Just as the belief in demonism would be particularly dangerous to people suffering from mental psychoses, an excessive focus on guilt (which is more a preoccupation of biblical counseling than deliverance) is a very risky way of treating anxiety and eating disorders, because both of these types of disorders, by their very nature, tend to attract anxious and guilt-ridden people. With all the associated scandal surrounding biblical counseling, is it really worth risking a treatment whose proponents specifically avoid testing for scientific efficacy and who consistently fail to meet the most basic of supposedly inferior secular ethical standards? In my opinion it is not. There is one more scandal to relate in this chapter that explains why.

Sovereign Grace Ministries

Here we come to perhaps the strangest story in the whole of mental health treatment within the evangelical movement. It is a tale of how a charismatic ministry that gave birth to such famed charismatic leaders as Che Ahn and Lou Engle (Charlton) ended up turning from Charismatic teachings to a strident form of Calvinism. It is a tale of how that ministry has been accused of repeated sexual abuse, massive cover-ups, and discrimination against the mentally ill (Charlton; Kris, "What Sovereign Grace Ministries Teaches"),[14] charges that gained such widespread attention that they were reported in secular national news services (Charlton). And as we will see, this Calvinist ministry, Sovereign Grace Ministries (SGM) to be precise, was closely aligned with CCEF, David Powlison, and Ken Sande. We will see how Ken Sande's practice of promoting extra-legal contracts became a tool for silencing Sovereign Grace's victims, and how Powlison continued to work amiably with both Sande and Sovereign Grace's leader, C.J. Mahaney, when, unless he was blind, he had to have known about the widespread charges of corruption going on.

Mahaney started off as a former drug user turned Charismatic preacher (*Washington Times*, "Keeping Their Eyes on the Cross"). By 1974, he was "alternating teaching assignments with Larry Tomczak ... an intern with the AFL-CIO" (*Washington Times*, "Keeping Their Eyes on the Cross"). In 1977, Mahaney and Tomczak cofounded Covenant Life Church (Charlton). Five years later, "the church launched what would become its overarching ministry, Sovereign Grace, originally called 'People of Destiny International'" (PDI) (Charlton). Initially Charismatic, the PDI ministry gradually shifted into Calvinism but blurred it with Charismatic practices. In the mid-nineties, Mahaney began promoting the doctrine of "biblical womanhood" that would become so prominent in Calvinist churches (*Washington Times*, "Keeping Their Eyes on the Cross"; Charlton). At the same time, he acquired a powerful and influential protégé, Joshua Harris (Charlton). Harris's book *I Kissed Dating Goodbye* (1997) was popular among homeschoolers and fueled the so-called courtship movement, which was devoted to, among other things, abstaining from dating relationships and often waiting till marriage for one's first kiss (see Charlton). For evangelicals in the courtship movement, courtship relationships were frequently arranged or at least heavily monitored during this period, and oftentimes it would be the father who chose whom a girl would marry; her own choice in many cases (and the same applied for men sometimes) was immaterial (see Joyce, *Quiverfull*, 231–232, on courtship).

With Sovereign Grace's mid-nineties promotion of Reformed theology, the ministry soon had some powerful allies, "including Albert Mohler, president of the country's largest Southern Baptist seminary, and Seattle's 'cussing pastor,' Mark Driscoll. Harris and Mahaney are also board members of influential, staunchly conservative organizations like The Gospel Coalition and the Council on Biblical Manhood and Womanhood" (Charlton). The Council of Biblical Manhood and Womanhood (CBMW) is largely controlled by Reformed evangelicals, including John Piper, who has contributed multiple articles to the *Journal of Biblical Counseling*.[15] Tomczak left the church in 1997 after the church punished him for his son's "teenage rebellion" (Charlton). Starting in 2007, a number of "survivor blogs" started up, the most influential of which were SGM Survivors (Charlton) and SGM Refuge. In 2011, a former prominent SGM leader, Brent Detwiler, accused C.J. Mahaney of having blackmailed Tomczak (Charlton). Mahaney confessed to the blackmail, took a brief leave of absence from the ministry, and then was restored to his position of power, over the objections of Joshua Harris (Charlton). In October 2012, Covenant Life Church (CLC) and Sovereign Grace Ministries were named as defendants in a class action lawsuit that charged "that a pastor and church volunteer together operated a 'pedophilia ring' at CLC and its school" (Charlton). At the current moment, the suit alleges that there are simply too many victims to name because Sovereign Grace Ministries cultivates a culture of abuse (Charlton). T.F. Charlton's excellent article on the Sovereign Grace debacle points out the literally devastating impact of the culture of abuse that was promoted at Sovereign Grace:

> The stories from plaintiffs who are included describe a church culture where pastors' sympathies routinely lay with male perpetrators of sexual abuse, particularly married fathers, who were allowed continued access to victims and other children in the church. Victims' families were deliberately misled to keep them out of legal proceedings, while pastors provided perpetrators with legal support. And families were pressured not to report abuse and to "forgive" perpetrators, with even children as young as three being forced to meet their abusers for "reconciliation.... Women and children who came forward were threatened and ostracized if they resisted efforts to "restore" their abusive husbands and fathers to a position of "leadership" in the family [Charlton].

In one particularly despicable case, a mother was told to send the victim away so the father could return as "head of the household" (Charlton). And this testimony comes from the victim's sister, not the victim herself, giving it added credibility. Larry Tomczak, the former coleader of the ministry, was formally charged with abuse, including spanking a young woman, over a period of 25 years, after each time forcing her to undress (Charlton). As Charlton points out, this seems to be hardly an unlikely accusation against a man who writes a book entitled *God, the Rod, and Your Child's Bod* (1982), where he talks gleefully about giving children "posterior protoplasmic stimulation" (Charlton). Indeed, SGM promotes a book that calls for spanking children as young as 8 months (Charlton). Not surprisingly, the book is written by a biblical counseling supporter, with two *Journal of Biblical Counseling* articles to his credit: Ted Tripp ("Communicate with Teens"; "Dazzle Your Teens"). Adding weight to these charges was the fact that Nathaniel Morales, a Sovereign Grace worker, was indicted for sexual abuse ("Md. Church Members"). In addition, at least one other person accused of abuse in the lawsuit has already been convicted, and possibly two ("Second Amended SGM Lawsuit," 12, 36, 39).[16] Note that the patriarchal orientation of SGM's teachings are in line with the rhetoric of John Piper and other proponents of both Quiverfull and biblical counseling methodology (see Charlton).[17]

But how exactly do Powlison and Sande and their allies fit into this mess? Well, it turns out they fit in plenty. After Mahaney was found to have blackmailed Tomczak, he reached out to Powlison and fellow Reformed thinker Mark Dever and "asked them to review the charges and provide me with their counsel and correction" (Taylor; Charisma staff, "C.J. Mahaney"). This was widely seen by critics of SGM as a whitewash of the ministry without which Mahaney could not survive. At the same time, Mahaney was also receiving Ken Sande's "correction" (Taylor).[18] As of May 2, 2013, C.J. Mahaney was not only being promoted on CCEF's Web site, *but was also being used to promote CCEF* (CCEF, "What Others Are Saying").[19] Al Mohler, in a video made with CCEF alumnus John Bettler, praised Mahaney for being a "man of great faith" (SGM Survivors). Mohler argued that C.J. Mahaney will tell you the truth and maintained his support for Mahaney even after he was charged with blackmail (SGM Survivors).[20] Biblical counseling guru John Bettler, meanwhile, is on record stating that Mahaney is one of the most "brilliant men" he has ever known (SGM Survivors), a position CCEF largely continues to have to uphold because Bettler's protégé David Powlison, not to mention the entire biblical counseling movement, was deeply embedded in the Sovereign Grace scandal.

Biblical counseling, including its anti-psychiatric tenets, was a crucial part of Sovereign Grace teachings.[21] Andy Farmer, a leader at Sovereign Grace, taught as follows: "But, uh, I think in generally speaking, we can engage people in their medications in a very helpful thoughtful way and they could—and they could—they could be, ah—and—and—and—we can become part of that process of the management of it" (Kris, "What Sovereign Grace Teaches"). This sermon occurred at the Sovereign Grace Pastors Conference in 2009 (Kris) at a time when Mahaney was actively promoting Powlison's teachings to his Sovereign Grace audience. But as Kris, a commentator on SGM Survivors, points out, does SGM seriously believe pastors are equipped to be giving informed advice on medication management—to be involved in the process of diagnosis itself (Kris)? We have seen that even fanatic biblical counseling supporters like Robert Smith did not go this far in their pronouncements, arguing that medication should be the domain of the doctor, not a pastor (and preferably not psychiatrists). Yet Pastors College, the faux seminary set up by the SGM denomination, taught biblical counseling as a core part of its curriculum, something that's admitted on C.J. Mahaney's own blog (Purswell). After the charges of sex abuse, as of May 2, 2013, I could not find a single post by Powlison nor by his close ally Al Mohler condemning Mahaney or saying a single negative thing about him. This might be for the very inconvenient reason that Dave Harvey, who had the very important position of being in charge of church planting at Sovereign Grace, was also on CCEF's board of trustees (and still was as of September 1, 2013) (CCEF, "Board of Trustees"). Needless to say, Mahaney and his followers had Powlison and CCEF so thoroughly tied up that any hope of CCEF distancing itself from him was effectively futile (CCEF, "Board of Trustees").

Powlison's cause was made even more difficult by the fact that Ken Sande was involved in the whole Sovereign Grace debacle. Sovereign Grace wanted to use Peacemaker Ministries as a means of resolving a disagreement between the bloggers on SGM Survivors and Sovereign Grace (Kris, "SGM Seeks Peace with Noel and Family"). This conflict that needed peacemaking was an allegation that a woman with the user name "Noel" had a 3-year-old child who was raped by the son of a fellow member of her church. Sovereign Grace then allegedly proceeded to blame the mother for making too big a problem of the issue and *demanded that she apologize for complaining too much about her daughter being raped* (Kris, "Noel's Story"). The SGM church that initially handled this tried to use Christian conciliation tactics (solving legal matters without the benefit of the courts)—basically what had been promoted by Peacemaker ministries to begin with, in substance if not in exact form—to silence Noel. And when the ministry was found out in this role, suddenly the epitome of Christian conciliation tactics, Ken Sande, offered himself up as a "peacemaker" for the situation (Kris, "SGM Seeks Peace"). Yet it was these very peacemaking–Christian conciliation tactics many SGM survivors were concerned had so influenced SGM in the first place (Kris, "Noel's Story"; Kris, "An Open Letter").

Ken Sande, of course, was also the public cover, along with Powlison, for the blackmail whitewash that occurred in the case of Brent Detwiler (Charlton; Taylor; Charisma Staff, "C.J. Mahaney Takes Leave"). The foremost legal mind of biblical counseling therefore used his skills to definitely play down blackmail allegations against SGM and, if the allegations on SGM Survivors are true (and both the course of the case so far and the respect the SGM Survivors blog has been accorded by both the media and the survivors community would greatly dispose unbiased observers to believe them), in all likelihood also tried to discourage sexual abuse accusations that hurt SGM's image. To add final insult to injury, the actual civil lawsuit against Sovereign Grace Ministries was tossed out, not because the purported abuse did not happen (the court remained neutral on this count), but because the statute of limitations had expired ("After Judge Dismisses Sovereign Grace Lawsuit, Justin Taylor, Kevin DeYoung, and Don Carson Explain Their Silence.")

The only question left to ask is this: who is nouthetically confronting the biblical counseling movement for its sins? Apparently no one in Reformed leadership, though plenty of so-called discernment bloggers and survivor networks have done so. What kind of healthy counseling practice promotes the sexual abuse of children, the abuse of the mentally ill, the suppression of women, all in the name of maintaining some abstraction of doctrinal purity that not more than a fourth of the evangelical church thinks is even necessary? Unfortunately, however, the scandal does not end here, for, as we shall see in the next chapter, biblical counseling made inroads into at least two other evangelical movements, the Quiverfull movement and the Independent Fundamentalist Baptist group of churches. Here the exploitation of the mentally ill, particularly women, through biblical counseling methods, and sometimes methods even more primitive than biblical counseling, would take on such crude and despicable forms of sadism that it scarcely can be believed.

6

Patriarchal Counseling

Teresa Frye was sent to an evangelical tough love home, New Bethany, in her mid-teens. The camp was part of a group of loosely affiliated fundamentalist churches now commonly known as the Independent Fundamentalist Baptists, or IFB for short (an entity which will be covered later in this chapter). Most of the children sent to the home had done nothing more than be rebellious teens. Frye, for instance, had resisted the strict discipline of her Baptist upbringing. The home was advertised as a place where girls could ride horses, read the Bible, and grow in their Christian faith. Instead, the girls found themselves at "a remote compound bordered by a rural highway and ringed with barbed wire.... Their studies consisted of memorizing Scripture (mistakes were punishable by paddling) and a rote Christian curriculum." Discipline could be anything from belt whippings to being forced to scrub pots with undiluted bleach to running in place while being beaten from behind with a wooden paddle. Another New Bethany alumna, Lenee Rider, described one young woman, Angela, who arrived at New Bethany right out of a mental institution and was punished so severely she twice attempted suicide. When saved from possible death by Rider after the second attempt, Angela asked Rider why she had not let her die. Angela's response to Rider is not perhaps as surprising as we would wish. Angela was beaten immediately after her suicide attempt (Joyce, "Horror Stories").

The scandal at Sovereign Grace Ministries was only one of several scandals associated with Christian patriarchal counseling methods in recent years, as the story of New Bethany's survivor community shows. In this chapter, several of these particular patriarchal counseling methods will be examined. Most of the methods used by these ministries have more in common with biblical counseling than with deliverance ministries[1]; this is not particularly surprising, given the greater visibility of women within the Charismatic movement. This is not to say, however, that there are not abuses of women within Charismatic or Pentecostal circles (Though in its origins it may have been more pro-woman than the feminism of its time, Charismatic practice has not been that forward thinking in several decades). At its most extreme, the patriarchal counseling described in this chapter could lead to unbelievably cruel treatment, including a rape victim having to apologize to her church for being raped ("Man guilty of raping teen"). Patriarchy had returned with a vengeance in evangelicalism, leaving wrecked lives in its wake.

The Quiverfull Movement

The impetus for the modern Quiverfull movement lay in the writings of Mary Pride, particularly Pride's controversial *The Way Home: Beyond Feminism, Back to Reality* (1985) (Joyce 11). For Pride, feminism was responsible for evils ranging from communism to "self-worship" to witchcraft (Joyce 11). In both *The Way Home* and in her book *The Child Abuse Industry* (1986), Pride critiques what she sees as a contemporary victimization attitude (Joyce 11; see, for instance, Pride, *Child Abuse Industry,* 61). For Pride, the ongoing crisis produced by the increased awareness of child abuse in the eighties—and the corresponding rise in unfounded allegations due to the misfortune of the SRA scandals—was an attempt by over-reaching governmental institutions to extend their jurisdiction over the family. This is the way Pride puts it: "First, the child abuse industry is in the process of replacing or co-opting all traditional family and community support structures. Those who detect or suspect abuse are never encouraged to confront the suspected perpetrator directly, hear his or her side of the story, or offer him or her advice or help.... The role is reserved exclusively for government employees and contractors, under penalty of law" (Pride, *Child Abuse Industry,* 61). For Pride, the growth of groups like child protective services (CPS), the Department of Education, and other bureaucratic U.S. governmental institutions threatened traditional American gender and familial norms. Her book was therefore deeply (and, as it turns out, rightly) suspicious of some of the more extreme child abuse charges being made at the height of the 1980s (see Nathan and Snedeker 231–232).

Thus, from the beginning of the Quiverfull movement, the movement had a built-in prejudice against secular counseling services. Many evangelicals, particularly in the homeschooling movement, developed a profound distrust of secular child protection services that often translated into a general distrust for secular psychology in general. So pervasive were these fears that Michael Farris, a leading advocate for the homeschooling movement, published an anti–CPS thriller, *Anonymous Tip* (1996), in the 1990s that even caught the attention of some secular critics, such as Sarah Diamond (Diamond 120).

The larger patriarchal movement's general opposition to secular counseling services also undoubtedly benefited from the formation of the Council on Biblical Manhood and Womanhood (CBMW), a group founded in 1987 whose goal was "fighting feminist or egalitarian influences in the evangelical church" (Joyce 13). Many of the Reformed leaders in the CBMW, particularly those associated with Reformed Baptist belief, were also associated with the biblical counseling movement, such as John Piper,[2] Russell Moore,[3] and Heath Lambert.[4] The larger Christian patriarchal movement had deeply Reformed roots, with many of its major leaders—Piper, Joshua Harris, John MacArthur Jr., R.C. Sproul Sr., D.A. Carson, Albert Mohler—hailing from Reformed traditions, usually Baptist or Presbyterian in origin (see Joyce 13). The Reformed movement's general orientation to antiegalitarian gender roles probably played a large role in the relative prominence of Reformed-oriented institutions in the Quiverfull and pro-patriarchy movements.

Piper, who stands at the center of the current revival in Reformed Baptist theology, promotes "his complementarian theology through his popular 'Desiring God' ministry, church 'plants' (expanding a network of churches like a franchise from his own Minnesota-based church), and conference series" (Joyce 14). Shortly after the council was formed, Piper and Wayne Grudem published an outline of their plan for the new form of biblical womanhood, *Recovering Biblical Manhood and Womanhood: A Response to Evangelical Feminism* (1991). The council's position on psychology was conveyed through the work of George A. Rekers, who used much of his writing to critique the gay rights movement (Piper and Grudem; Rekers 299–319).[5] According to Rekers, the "idea of natural sex-role boundaries embedded in creation is anathema to the relativistic humanists" (Rekers 299). For him, as for much of the Christian patriarchal movement, gender distinctions were God-given and inviolate. Therefore the promotion of feminism became not simply a matter of personal choice but a life and death struggle for the "soul" of a nation.

In Rekers's case, he saw feminism as emblematic of a wider struggle against the effeminization of American males, played out against the context of debate with the gay rights movement (Rekers 299–313). Unfortunately, as is all too common in the gay rights debate, Rekers turned out to hail from the very groups he oppressed. In 2010, he was forced to resign from NARTH, one of the prominent providers of the pseudoscientific ex-gay therapeutic process known as reparative therapy, after a male escort admitted to giving him naked massages (Coscarelli, Olbermann; Bailey). Equally troubling was the presence of another representative of questionable Christian counseling methodologies who was also involved in supporting Piper's politics: Gary Almy. Almy was involved in the Danvers statement that gave the council its official ideology (Piper and Grudem 479). Richard Mayhew, the vice-president of the pro–biblical-counseling Master's Seminary, also played a part in the Danvers statement as well (Piper and Grudem 480). Also, John MacArthur Jr., certainly no fan of traditional psychology in the late 1980s, was on the Board of Reference that the CBMW set up to oversee the construction of the Danvers statement (Piper and Grudem 481).

But to really understand how pervasively linked the patriarchal movement is with biblical counseling, one must look at the links between Southern Baptist Theological Seminary (SBTS) and the biblical counseling movement. In 2005, Russell Moore declared that the SBTS would shift its counseling training from psychology to biblical counseling, thus giving the biblical counseling movement a powerful new ally in its desire to spread its counseling method globally. Al Mohler, who had already allied himself closely with the Calvinist movement and would subsequently promote such Reformed leaders as C.J. Mahaney and David Powlison, stated, "In this psychotherapeutic age, it is really important that we think as Christians ... that we employ authentically Christian thinking, biblical thinking, to human life, and that we do this in a way that, without apology, confronts and critiques the wisdom of the age and seeks the wisdom that can come only from God and God's Word" (Robinson; Allen).

Southern put two men in charge of the biblical counseling program: Stuart Scott and Randy Stinson. The history of these men is very interesting. Stuart Scott was a former Master's Seminary professor and a prominent integrator of biblical counseling with the patriarchy movement. His works included books like *The Exemplary Husband: A Biblical Perspective* (revised edition, 2002), a book with clear similarities to Martha Peace's *The Excellent Wife* (1999), another biblical counseling text (Jeff Robinson).[6] Randy Stinson, meanwhile, was a senior fellow for the CBMW and a prominent player in evangelical gender politics ("JMBW Journal Spring 2012"). The naked union of biblical counseling with hard-line evangelical gender conservatism is clearly part of a bigger objective within the SBC. As Mohler has as much as admitted, his goal is to push the Southern Baptist denomination back to a more conservative and Reformed path.[7]

Why use biblical counseling in this process? In part it's used because the philosophy can utilize many of the effective tools of behavioral conditioning to produce desired submission on the part of evangelical women, and it has the added benefit of not suffering from government oversight or secular credentialing standards. In addition, because much of the biblical counseling movement, particularly the third generation of the movement, practices a form of very strong church discipline, it is a counseling movement conducive to the patriarchal movement's view of women. By focusing on solving problems internally—either through the family (as in the teachings of the more extreme proponents of biblical counseling) or through the use of supposedly biblically endorsed methods of conflict resolution (such as Christian conciliation tactics and "peacemaking")—the Christian patriarchal movement helps minimize the chances of women effectively complaining to church authorities or going to secular authorities for help. This is bad enough with "mainstream" Christian patriarchy supporters, like John Piper, who contends that "if it's not requiring her to sin but simply hurting her, then I think she [an abused woman] endures verbal abuse for a season, and she endures perhaps being smacked one night, and then she seeks help from the church" (Piper, "Does a Woman Submit to Abuse?"). But the attitude that Piper exudes is expanded tenfold when dealing with more extremist elements of patriarchal counseling ideology. Taken outside its original Presbyterian confines, where this patriarchal ideology at least had to deal with a generally highly educated body of female believers, this new form of Baptist and ex–Pentecostal (as in the case of SGM) Calvinist patriarchalism is extremely dangerous because it takes on all the cult-like elements of fundamentalism, Pentecostalism, and the biblical counseling movement itself, but without the intellectual brakes on the movement that Presbyterian and Dutch Reformed intellectualism put on the more extreme elements of biblical counseling ideology.

Two biblical counseling supporters—both of them women—have helped in particular to spread biblical counseling methods to the wider patriarchy movement: Martha Peace and Elyse Fitzpatrick. Perhaps the most well-known biblical counseling proponent of the patriarchy movement is Martha Peace. Peace is an author on "biblical womanhood and Titus 2 ministries" (Joyce 51).[8] She wants women to solve their problems through "strictly biblical means" (51). As Joyce points out, Peace's biography is filled with colorful stories of supposed adultery and substance abuse, actions she lays at the feet of former feminist attitudes (52). As Joyce points out, such "taming of the shrew" biographies are a frequent motif within the patriarchy movement, with Mary Pride being one, and not even the most prominent, example.

For Peace, as for much of the patriarchy movement, women are primarily meant to be homemakers. Among purists within the Christian patriarchy movement, women are supposed to make a list of daily activities that they submit to their husband for approval. Sexually, too, they must be available at all times for all activities (barring "ungodly" "homosexual acts") (Joyce 53). Even among more liberal conservative Christians, this means that a husband ultimately has the final say on most matters (Joyce 53). Peace's teachings not only emphasize female submission but characterize feminism as literal idolatry (Joyce 56). As anyone with any awareness of the biblical counseling movement knows, the theme of idolatry has been a fairly constant one throughout the movement, used to characterize both those who suffer from mental illness and women.[9] While the theme is perhaps strongest in the writings of David Powlison (see Powlison, "Idols of the Heart"), references to it can be found in other writers, particularly Elyse Fitzpatrick, the other bête noire of feminists opposed to patriarchy ideology (Fitzpatrick, "Helping Bulimics").

As Kathryn Joyce points out, Peace's position on gender is not incidental to her counseling methodology. Rather, the "Christian counseling movement that Peace comes from doesn't just seek to provide a Christian gloss on normal counseling but to use that counseling for God's glory. For those coming from a fundamentalist reading of gender roles, that means counseling women by transmitting the theology of headship and submission" (Joyce 56). Because the goal of nouthetic counseling, as Joyce relates and we have seen, is first the glorification of God and only second the well-being of the counselee or client, it is a system that is likely to put the well-being of God first, religion second, church third, and the client last of all. Such a system tends to reinforce existing social structures that support traditional ideas of gender relations. And because biblical counseling is, as Joyce correctly points out, often committed to maintaining traditional gender distinctions, the practice also tends to inherit many of the biases against women found in the wider contemporary society, as we will see once we turn to Elyse Fitzpatrick's work.

Perhaps the most distinguishing feature of Peace's writing, and the clearest sign of Jay Adams's close influence on her work (Adams read the manuscript and gave her comments on it) (Peace acknowledgments), is the emphasis on "reproof" within her writing, which appears roughly equivalent to Adams's similar development of that concept in his model of nouthetic confrontation. The following is an example:

> How you [a wife] respond to your husband's reproof is a reflection of your desire to become more godly. Begin with considering his reproof to be, at the least, possibly valid. Next consider the following right ways to respond to reproof ... (1) Take the time to think about what you have been told ... (2) Search the Scriptures to determine what the sin is and how to "put it off" ... (3) Ask your husband to give some specific examples of how you could have better responded to his reproof ... (4) Confess your sin ... (5) Show the fruit of repentance. Stop doing the sin and start doing the right thing ... (6) Do not justify or defend yourself... If you know that our husband's reproof is valid or even partially valid, then heed his advice and change your sinful way [Peace 40–41].

Peace's methodology of conflict resolution presupposes that a woman may likely bear partial guilt for the situation she finds herself in. The woman is supposed to give the man the benefit of the doubt in disagreements between them (Peace, *The Excellent Wife*, 40–44). Thus, as in nouthetic confrontation, the reprover (here the husband, in counseling itself the nouthetic or biblical counselor) is given the benefit of the doubt, with the reproved individual (the woman in this situation, in counseling the counselee) being seen as in all likelihood the wrong party. But because the nouthetic method is being applied to a noncounseling relationship—specifically, the relationship between husband and wife—there is tremendous potential for abuse. The husband in such a relationship can use nouthetic methods as a tool of psychological indoctrination and conditioning, forcing his wife to take on the role of an abused woman.

Because Adams's counseling methodology is modeled on Glasser's and Mowrer's behaviorist-like applications of Skinnerian counseling methods, there is enormous potential here for women to be exploited; the methods Peace advises men to use are not simply "bad advice" but badly misused applications of behaviorist ideology which force women into the role of the conditioned client. And make no mistake: the role women are being conditioned for in this counseling, though not by Peace's will, is the role of victim. As biblical counseling presupposes both the guilt of the counselee and the subordination of women it is a philosophy ideally suited to serve the interests of physical and sexual abusers. When one adds to this the fact that biblical counselors are not effectively regulated by any state or federal agencies and have virtually no professional oversight, biblical counseling becomes the ideal practice by which abusers can take advantage of women and children whose only crime is being born into a religion they believe will protect them.

Peace, of course, is smart enough to know domestic and sexual abuse occur. Indeed, to her credit she has claimed to have counseled women to leave their abusers, though she believes that a woman must be in physical danger in order to qualify for that protection (see Joyce 56). The problem here is with the coded message behind the external message. Peace's writings maintain that a woman can "know that you [the woman] are receiving reproof from your husband sinfully when... 1. You become angry and lash out at him... 2. You feel hurt, resentful, and unforgiving... 3. You focus on the things he is doing wrong... 4. You suffer intense personal hurt" (Peace 45). Peace's statement here is, unfortunately (despite her provision for much weaker-stated reproofs of husbands by wives), tailor-made for exploitation by abusive husbands and parents, especially when taken in the context of her previous defense of a husband's right to biblically reprove his wife.

The reactions Peace lists here are natural reactions most women would have to any number of significant disagreements with their partners, including but not limited to sexual and physical abuse. What makes matters worse is that Peace's counsel here seeks to minimize women's own emotional involvement in their life situations; in other words, women are discouraged from becoming emotionally invested in their own fate, instead trusting in God for providence. Women cease to be personal actors and agents in history and instead are encouraged to step aside as men take from them control of their personal destinies. Again, here biblical counseling and Christian patriarchal ideology work as one. Both philosophical systems, operating out of their commonly held Calvinist frameworks, stress God's sovereignty. That sovereignty is communicated to humanity through divinely ordained societal hierarchies, including that between God and man, man and woman, and parent and child. Abuse, particularly when physical and not sexual, can in such a system all too easily be seen as just a more extreme form of nouthetic confrontation, a form of biblical reproof different only in form, and not kind, from everyday arguments.

Even worse than Peace is Elyse Fitzpatrick. Not only does Fitzpatrick promote, as we have seen, some of the worst imaginable advice for anorexics and bulimics, she also extends such patriarchally oriented advice to the realm of sexual abuse. In Fitzpatrick's estimation, the term victim is not really necessarily "an appropriate label for a Christian who believes in a sovereign God. Victim is synonymous with other words such as casualty or fatality—accidents.... The reality for every Christian is that there is a God who is able to control every circumstance and could have prevented or stopped the abuse if He had chosen to do so.... The sovereignty of God should stop a person from believing that he or she is inherently a 'victim'" (Fitzpatrick, "Counseling Women Abused," 345). For Fitzpatrick, being victimized does not automatically or inherently make one a victim. Not only that, because God is a sovereign God there is a sense in which one's abuse was supposed to happen and there is some good that God wants to get out of that abuse.

This is not a misreading of Fitzpatrick, unfortunately. Later on in her essay, she declares that one of the reasons there is suffering in the world, is to "drive us to His mercy and to free our hearts from self-deception.... Let us teach our counselees [specifically referred to here as women abused as children] to be thankful for their suffering because they serve as sweet alarms that wake us from hazy dreams of independence and self-sufficiency" (Fitzpatrick, "Counseling Women Abused," 353). Fitzpatrick literally believes that the abuse of children, though clearly wrong in her eyes, can teach them valuable lessons later in life, and that might explain why God allows abuse to happen. Suffering, as in all Christological systems, is for Fitzpatrick redemptive. And this is one of the main problems with biblical counseling's relationship to women. The Christian theological system has always had a tendency to accept the sacrifice of scapegoats, willing or unwilling. One can look first to Christ himself, whom Christians willingly accept as their blood sacrifice for redemption. But when Christ did not come back on his appointed timeline, Christians of various stripes ended up sacrificing a wide number of innocent proxy victims in his place; Jews, witches, women of all stripes, Satanists, homosexuals, and free-thinkers have all paid the price for this kind of twisted martyrology. Not only does the biblical counseling version of evangelical Christianity encourage women to embrace the role of scapegoat, it also asks that they be denied the honor of being acknowledged as the actual sacrificial victims being offered up to the patriarchal desires of this particular version of God.

But Fitzpatrick is actually far more unbelievable than this. She does not simply believe that child abuse victims should not be referred to as victims. Nor does her teaching stop at the idea that abuse may have some redemptive role in the real world. No, Fitzpatrick also believes that abuse victims should feel guilty for their supposed sinful responses to their abusers' sins. She gives an elaborate theological justification for this belief:

> We have heard so much about how a victim tends to believe her abuser's sins were her fault that we shy away from addressing her personal sin. First, let me remind you the Bible clearly teaches that we all sin. You must spend time gently teaching her [the abuse victim] the difference between her sin and the sins of others.... Is she sinfully worried, angry, or afraid? Does she try to manipulate circumstances or function as super mom so she might control the future? She is not responsible for being sinned against, but she is responsible for her response to that sin. You must point her to verses on confession and repentance of sin.... You must also teach her that before she can confront her abuser (or anyone else who has sinned against her), she must remove the log from her own eye [Fitzpatrick, *Counseling Women Abused*, 355].

Fitzpatrick's philosophy of counseling equates the man with a log in his eye with the abuse victim; by definition, that would seem to imply that the abuser has only a speck in his eye, if one takes the biblical parable at its words. In what moral universe can anyone honestly claim that being a sexual or domestic abuse victim is morally more problematic than being a rapist or domestic abuser? For that matter, in what moral universe can one argue that being the survivor of sexual or physical abuse is the victim's fault at all? Somehow, in the world of biblical counseling, being angry at an abuser, or feeling bitterness or regret at what happened, is morphed into a sin of gargantuan moral proportions. Why this is the case is not clear. Of course women get angry about abuse. Of course they lash out at times. Why that has anything remotely to do with sin is not clear to the Quiverfull and IFB female survivors I have talked to nor to myself. Given the marked cruelty of this passage, it is likely that were evangelicals more aware of Fitzpatrick's view of sex abuse victims, as well as of anorexics, the biblical counseling movement would not have as much support among women as it does today.

But Fitzpatrick has one last cruel twist in her teaching. She believes that "confrontation and forgiveness are always to be for the sake of the Lord and the offender [the abuser]—never so that the one forgiving will feel better" (Fitzpatrick, *Counseling*, 358). Not only does Fitzpatrick expect abuse victims to forgive their abusers (although only if they ask for forgiveness) (Fitzpatrick 358), but she also argues that forgiveness must be undertaken for the sake of the abuser, not for the abused. Thus, Fitzpatrick encourages the victim—who, remember, she does not even consider a victim—to revictimize herself by forgiving the victimizer for the sake of the victimizer himself. Nor is it very clear how Fitzpatrick's counseling methodology would effectively shield these victims from those who were shamming repentance in order to regain access to their victims, and re-perpetuate the abuse their victims had already undergone. In short, Fitzpatrick's counseling method is tailor-made to perpetuate abuse.

Before closing this section, a brief mention should be made of one other very important figure in the history of Quiverfull ideology, though he is not a proponent of the Adams model of biblical counseling: Bill Gothard. According to Powlison, though Gothard did not directly influence Adams's development he could legitimately be considered a "forerunner of Adams" (Powlison 72). Like Adams, Gothard was "biblistic" in his theology, though from Powlison's standpoint Gothard's model is "simpler" and "less systematic" than Adams, with a focus on pragmatic issues. Therefore as Powlison points out, Gothard was not really worried about institution-building in the same way Adams was, still less about developing a coherent evangelical counseling ideology (Powlison 72). Gothard was primarily concerned with results.

Gothard is well known as an opponent of psychiatry and psychology (Megan). He claims that, in many cases, clients of psychological professionals simply get worse (Megan). Yet the curriculum that Gothard's own Advanced Training Institute offers has found itself twice at the center of national controversy due to the extreme reactions people have had to the curriculum. In the first instance, "Matthew Murray ranted about his super-religious, rule-driven home schooling, which used Gothard's curriculum, in web postings before he opened fire on two Christian centers, killing four people and then himself" (Megan).[10] According to Murray, his mother used psychiatric drugs to control him (Blumenthal), while forbidding him from listening to almost all Christian or secular music. Murray felt constantly spied on in this environment (Blumenthal). While Gothard's teaching was not the sole contributor to Murray's rampage, Gothard's anti-psychiatric ideas and pronouncements certainly could not have helped (these ideas, for instance, may have influenced Murray's decision not to receive psychological help from a concerned counselor who had offered it) (see Blumenthal).

According to Joy Solano, an M.A graduate in counseling psychology from Bowie State University and a "survivor" of Gothard's ministry, Gothard emphasizes that mental health problems are "caused by guilt. Gothard emphasizes that guilt is a main reason that people feel stress, which develops into mental dysfunction, such as depression or anxiety. Finding the root of the problem and fixing it will alleviate the guilt, leading to moral freedom" (Solano). For Gothard, mental health issues are a by-product of stress. One must first find the roots of a problem and then fix the problem in order to achieve true moral and spiritual freedom. Solano also speaks of a video (which is referenced on multiple other Web sites but has since been taken off YouTube) of Gothard referencing an unnamed "Jewish psychiatrist" who influenced his work (Solano). Solano postulates that, given Gothard's views, the psychiatrist he was talking about was likely Thomas Szasz (Solano).[11] If Solano is correct, and she almost surely is, given the likely possible anti-psychiatric influences on Gothard, this would point to a commonality between Gothard's anti-psychiatric views and that of Jay Adams. One should not, however, make too much of this. Adams, to his credit, has condemned Gothard's teachings (Veinot, endorsements).

It does not require much intelligence to realize that supporting Bill Gothard's view of mental illness is not in the best long-term interest of any social movement attempting to gain intellectual legitimacy. Among Gothard's most famous teachings is his assertion that Cabbage Patch dolls can be responsible for "strange and destructive behavior in children" (Fisher; Veinot). Yes, according to Gothard, those cute little Coleco dolls from the 1980s are responsible for mental health aberrations. That Gothard's views were taken seriously at all does not speak well of the intellectual maturity of the evangelical movement during the formative years of the religious right; that Gothard still manages to use powerful political muscle among a certain segment of the evangelical populace[12] speaks to how far the religious right still has to go before it achieves intellectual respectability.

But for some of Gothard's students it may be too late. As Solano relates, Joshua Komisarjevsky, a young Gothardite, ended up killing three people (Solano; Beach). Although Joshua's case was desperate to start with, due to the sexual abuse he suffered from a foster child in his home, his parents' beliefs on mental illness and psychiatric medications—that the former did not exist and the latter should not be used—likely in part contributed to the eventual escalation of his violent tendencies (Solano; Beach). Yet, despite the influence of Gothard's teaching on the Komisarjevsky family, and previously on the Murrays, the guru of evangelical child-rearing was nowhere to be seen as the victims of his ministry continued to pile up year after year.

Independent Fundamentalist Baptists

According to the admittedly biased account of IFB survivor Jocelyn Zichterman,[13] IFB teachings can be traced back to the influence of Bob Jones, Sr. and Bob Jones, Jr., who held that "all churches and Christians not associated with their ideology were 'compromising' and 'liberal' and needed to be completely shunned by the Jones' followers" (Zichterman, 25). Bob Jones University has always been famous for its cultural separatism. The university was involved in some famous conflicts with the government, including the IRS's decision to deny the university tax exempt status because it refused to admit African Americans, and for many of its extremist cultural policies, including its long-standing and infamous ban on interracial dating, lifted only in 2000 (Zichterman, 27; Dallhouse 156–158). These policies were meant to isolate Bob Jones and its students from the wider fundamentalist world. What distinguished independent fundamentalist Baptists, who borrowed much of their ideology from Jones and who continue to be profoundly influenced by his university, from traditional Baptists was the doctrine of separation.

As historian George Marsden relates, "By the late 1950s, strict fundamentalists split with Graham and the new evangelicals, insisting that complete separation from any alliance with doctrinal impurity should be a test of true faith. Often they demanded double separation, breaking fellowship not only with liberals but also with those who fellowshipped with liberals" (Marsden 233). This latter position would tend to characterize the doctrinal rigidity of the IFB. According to Zichterman, in modern IFB churches there are now three degrees of separation, the third degree being not simply "disfellowshipping" evangelicals who fellowship with liberals, but disfellowshipping evangelicals who fellowship with evangelicals who fellowship with liberals (Zichterman 27). Another characteristic of IFB churches, noted by Zichterman and anyone else who has had contact with them, is their tendency to accept what is called "KJV-only" beliefs. In its more "liberal" forms, this belief system expresses the belief that churches should use only the King James Version (KJV) of the Bible, with all versions other than the KJV (and perhaps the NKJV) being heretical. In its most extreme forms, KJV-onlyism can literally promote the idea that only those who read the KJV version can be saved (Zichterman 28–29). As Zichterman points out, at this point in time IFB belief is more a mindset than an affiliation with Baptist tradition; indeed, Bob Jones, Sr. was a Methodist at the time of his death (Zichterman 30).

For Zichterman, much of the problem within IFB churches lies within their organizational structure. As Zichterman relates, "IFB churches deny adamantly that their ministers wield absolute power because almost all of them have church constitutions mandating congregational government. However, corrupt pastors skilled in control have little trouble stacking their deck of deacons with men who will do as they are told, especially if these sycophants have skeletons in their closet that can be used as blackmail" (Zichterman 35–36). As we have seen with Sovereign Grace Ministries and to a lesser degree with the wider Christian patriarchy movement, a predisposition to rigid authoritarian structures is a common characteristic of many of the counseling methodologies used by supporters of patriarchal counseling. In the IFB, as in (ironically) the New Apostolic Reformation (one of the IFB movement's arch-enemies), the focus on powerful leader figures tends to delegitimize the power of congregational methods of church discipline and control. These congregational methods, though not always able to prevent authoritarianism within evangelical circles, for a long time limited the extent and speed with which such authoritarianism could seek to control the wider evangelical movement.

It is not surprising therefore that Zichterman believed in her childhood that mental illness was the result of sin. According to Zichterman, such beliefs were ubiquitous in the IFB (Zichterman 143). Indeed, Zichterman's sister Melissa told her that as a nurse studying at Bob Jones University, she was taught "'that mental health issues were a sin...' Her psychology 'professors' had lectured that bipolar disorder, depression, anxiety, ADD, and ADHD were spiritual problems, not worthy of medication or therapy" (Zichterman 208). Whatever the IFB survivor community's (or that of the IFB churches) opinion of Zichterman, here the evidence amply backs her up. Bob Jones University utilizes a number of biblical counseling teachers' works in the course offerings it sells, including Adams's *Christian Counselor's Manual* (1973), Ed Welch's *Blame It on the Brain,* various works by NANC hard-liner Wayne Mack and a premarital counseling book by Howard Eyrich (Berg, "Biblical Counseling Series"). Bob Jones professor Jim Berg is the lead promoter of these courses (Berg, "Biblical Counseling Series"). Berg's teachings on mental illness tend to be hard-line even by biblical counseling standards. For instance, Berg promotes the idea that depressed people would do better if they started thinking about their issues from God's perspective. He advises them to ask, "What choices have you made while you were depressed that have further complicated your situation? Does anything (thought or choices) need to be repented of and forsaken?" (Berg, "Basics for Depressed Believers," 6).

But, not surprisingly, Berg, like many members of the Christian patriarchy movement, is at his most punitive in his approach to women—or to be more precise, towards a mental disorder he clearly (and wrongly) associates exclusively with women. He writes of anorexia and bulimia: "Anorexia and bulimia always have destructive effects on the body's health but are not diseases in themselves. Rather, they are sinful patterns of misdirected control that the counselee has developed in order to solve problems that have arisen in her life" (Berg, "Biblically Overcoming Anorexia and Bulimia," 8). Also not surprisingly, Berg credits this conceptualization of anorexia to Fitzpatrick's equally extreme vision of anorexia (Berg, "Overcoming Anorexia and Bulimia," 8). And as with Fitzpatrick's views, there are basic methodological flaws within Berg's counseling system that even a freshman counseling major would catch, the most obvious of which is that Berg and Fitzpatrick appear not to realize that anorexia and bulimia often are not reactions simply to poor body image issues, but can result from a variety of outside stressors. As with Mercy Ministries material,[14] there seems to be a lack of acknowledgment in Fitzpatrick's and Berg's writings about the possible influence of sexual trauma and physical abuse in causing or at least aggravating eating disorders. This disinclination to deal with trauma stems not just from Fitzpatrick's poor understanding of gender politics, but also from the basic logic of the patriarchal movement, which believes that all female problems must stem from women yearning for male attention rather than recoiling from it.

Bob Jones University's history does not give one much hope about the counseling efficacy of Berg or his fellow IFB nouthetics supporters. In 2010, Tina Anderson accused Ernest Willis, a congregant of Trinity Baptist Church in Concord, New Hampshire, of sexually abusing her when she was a teenager (Leubsdorf). Willis was then being pastored by the Reverend Chuck Phelps. What was interesting about the case was not so much Willis's actions as his church's reactions to them. In an act of congregational love and compassion straight out of Margaret Atwood's *Handmaid's Tale* (1985), not only was Anderson forced to endure the pain of being raped, she was also forced to apologize to her congregation for her "part" in the sin of "having sex" with Willis. In other words, she was forced to apologize for being raped ("Man guilty of raping teen"). Chuck Phelps, the pastor overseeing this modern day reenactment of Salem, was a board member of Bob Jones University at the time of Anderson's accusations, but he subsequently was forced to resign from the board (Riddle). Similar sex scandals twice struck the prominent IFB First Baptist Church in Hammond, Indiana. In the second scandal, Pastor Jack

Schaap was accused of kissing an underage girl during counseling sessions (Bryan Smith). Schaap's father-in-law, Jack Hyles, suffered similar charges of sexual impropriety. Indeed, such improprieties, including rape and sexual abuse, were allegedly systematic throughout numerous IFB churches, according to Detroit's WJBK station (Gruszecki).

Charges of sexual and physical abuse were not lodged solely against houses of worship, however. Like the wider biblical counseling movement, members of the IFB frequently set up "homes" in which to provide their particular form of counseling. The most infamous of these homes were the Roloff homes run by Lester Roloff, who claimed to change "parent-hating, Satan-worshiping, dope-taking immoral boys and girls" into "faithful servants of the Lord" (Colloff). According to Pamela Colloff, "Roloff's method of Bible discipline, which he said was rooted in Scripture, meant kneeling for hours on hardwood floors, licks meted out with a pine paddle or a leather strap, and the dreaded 'lockup,' an isolation room where Roloff's sermons were played for days on end" (Colloff). During his career as a revivalist, Roloff managed to parlay his salesmanship skill into the creation of numerous homes, most built on a particular model of community he wanted to "help": adults, pregnant young women, troubled teens, and the like (Colloff). He would end up refusing governmental oversight of his homes despite repeated pressure and even prosecution.

In the seventies, as they would be for many years, the Roloff homes were literally torture chambers, where children could be whipped, handcuffed to drainpipes, or paddled to within an inch of their lives for such minor infractions as being unable to remember a Bible verse (Colloff). As Colloff relates, while some of the girls in the Roloff homes were genuinely "troubled"—involved in drugs or prostitution, for instance—many others were simply in the homes for having sex or for the "crime" of growing up in abusive households (Colloff). In any case, the abusive mentality promoted at the Roloff homes was applied to all these young women, regardless of the circumstances of their near-literal imprisonment (see for instance Susan Donaldson James). The Hephzibah House has garnered some of the worst accusations of any Roloff home, ranging from a young teenager being beaten by a board to another young woman being given a forced medical examination in which someone at the institution stuck a speculum in her. Young women could go to the bathroom only when they were told they could; if one had to go at another time, she would be paddled ("Hephzibah House—Ungodly Discipline"). And again, not surprisingly, the leader of the Hephzibah house, Ronald E. Williams, claims to have received "specialized training in biblical counseling" ("Hephzibah House: Serving Christ Since 1971").

There are several schools accused of being IFB–leaning that can be confirmed as using some variant of biblical counseling as part of their curriculum, often a crucial element of it.[15] Bob Jones University is the primary one, but I also found that Boston Baptist College, Faith Baptist Bible College, Trinity Baptist College, Detroit Baptist Theological Seminary, and Pacific Baptist have also used biblical counseling material (Boston Baptist College, "Our Faculty"; Faith Baptist College and Theological Seminary, "Minors/Biblical Counseling/Faculty"; Faculty, Detroit Baptist Theological Seminary, "Basic Library Booklist"; Trinity Baptist College, "Trinity Baptist College: Graduate Studies"). Given the low educational standards of IFB institutions, the continued existence of these training centers should be a matter of grave concern not simply to society as a whole but also to the supporters of biblical counseling themselves. Opinions of the biblical counseling movement's moral integrity aside, it is doubtful that most lay supporters of biblical counseling would countenance domestic or sexual abuse. While it is completely understandable for the evangelical movement to show some caution in making child abuse charges after the SRA scandals, the church needs to show discernment between what appear to be unreasonable charges (as in the SRA cases) and what charges make logical sense. Regardless of one's opinion of Satanism, the SRA scandal had serious markers of false accusation right from the beginning.

First of all, the very first charge made in the scandals, from which practically all subsequent SRA narratives derived, has been conclusively proven to have been a fraud (see Nathan and Snedeker 45, which thoroughly debunks the Smith case; Cuneo is even more scathing: see *American Exorcism* 204–205). Second, many of the charges made during the SRA period were not simply outlandish, they literally were almost beyond belief, involving actual spiritual and sometimes physical communication with demonic or supernatural beings (Cuneo 204). While this kind of belief is unfortunately all too ubiquitous among Pentecostals and Charismatics, one would assume that the more intellectual and skeptical Reformed denominations would not be a safe haven for such credulous theological silliness. And while the recent charges made against organizations like Sovereign Grace Ministries, Bob Jones University, and the First Baptist Church of Hammond carried enormous financial and personal risk for the accusers, due to the power of the individuals being accused, the SRA charges were directed against a despised cultural minority, and those falsely caught in their net typically hailed from down-and-out or disprivileged (though totally non–Satanist) elements of society (see Nathan and Snedeker 130).

The time has come for the evangelical church to stop taking SRA seriously and start taking real cases of real sexual abuse seriously. But this requires a rethinking of how evangelicals do church, a rethinking that may radically call into question existing definitions of the mentally ill, women, and trauma victims. If the church is to cut down on the epidemic of abuse and sexual trafficking occurring in the world, the first place to look is in the pews and the pulpits. This can only be accomplished if evangelicals of varying convictions—including perhaps, biblical counselors—learn to rethink how they approach society's most vulnerable members. Whether or not one agrees with the practice of biblical counseling, Jay Adams himself would likely not approve of the uses to which many IFB and Quiverfull churches appear to be putting nouthetic practice. And here there is room for Jay Adams to nouthetically confront "sinners" who really do need to repent, for crimes much worse than the nonexistent ones of being schizophrenic, bipolar, or anorexic. It is to be hoped that Adams will indeed do this, but perhaps it is too late to ask an old nouthetics supporter to change his ways.

In the final analysis, then, what is the social effect and reach of patriarchal counseling methods? Clearly within the IFB churches, these methods are far-reaching, though still largely shrouded in mystery. Because relatively few IFB members successfully exit the movement, and even fewer are able to maintain scholarly objectivity regarding it, it will continue to be difficult to garner 100 percent accurate information on IFB theology and practice. But most of the evidence to be found largely confirms Zichterman's narrative of IFB theology, albeit with minor caveats. The IFB's promotion of apparently abusive practices may make the movement ultimately unsustainable in the long term. Certainly, its advocacy for a brutal theology towards abuse victims and anorexics will not endear it to more moderate evangelicals, or even to the Charismatic movement, which does not want that kind of bad press. And much the same thing might be said about the Reformed patriarchal movement, which at times recently has seemed dangerously close to imploding, due to its links with the worst elements of SGM. However, feminist strategists should still be very concerned about the Reformed patriarchal movement. Elyse Fitzpatrick and Martha Peace have a wide following, as does the slightly more secularly palatable but still basically biblical-counseling supporter Nancy Leigh Demoss, who reaches even wider audiences than Peace and Fitzpatrick. The counseling advice of these women, particularly Fitzpatrick (by far the most prominent female biblical counselor), gives the patriarchs of the Reformed movement— men like John Piper or neo–Confederate patriarch extraordinaire Doug Wilson—an open cover by which they can promote the marginalization of women within their ministries.

But there's also a wider and more sinister sense in which the rhetoric of IFB churches and the Christian patriarchy movement make sexism palatable:

They give cultural legitimization to the rhetoric and extremist tactics of anti-reproductive rights organizations, particularly crisis pregnancy centers (CPC). Crisis pregnancy centers are "nonprofits set up by antiabortion groups to offer free pregnancy tests and dissuade pregnant women from having abortions" (Joyce, *Child Catchers*, 100). Crisis pregnancy centers are the pro-life equivalent of abortion providers, and many receive copious financial support from the government (Joyce 101). Although most people do not typically think of crisis pregnancy counseling in terms of counseling "theory," such as it is, there is a very real need to do so, for both the pro-choice movement and even pro-lifers. Because, quite simply, what psychological advice crisis pregnancy centers provide is not based on science or best counseling practice.

As Ziad Munson points out in *The Making of Pro-Life Activists* (2009), the actual counseling theory used by crisis pregnancy centers varies from center to center. Some use entirely secular reasons to argue against abortion, while others support counseling through biblistic arguments (Munson). Many pro-life movement leaders also push for CPC counseling that includes pictures of fetuses in development; other pro-lifers, including CPC centers, push adoption as an alternative to abortion (Munson). For pro-lifers, CPCs have long played an important ideological role, serving as a mark of dedication by which the movement can justify that it does care about the "unborn" (and occasionally the unborns' mothers). Much of this concern is, of course, totally sincere. Undoubtedly, many in the pro-life movement sincerely believe that the providing of adoption services, pregnancy testing, and abstinence education is reducing the number of abortions performed in the U.S. and paving the way for the eventual repeal of *Roe vs. Wade*.

But even leaving aside the deep moral problems inherent in repealing *Roe vs. Wade*,[16] the simple fact is that crisis pregnancy centers' counseling services do little to further this goal. Indeed, as Kathryn Joyce points out, at several Carenet CPCs alone there were accusations that CPC staff had "held an infant under false pretenses while they hounded its unwed parents to relinquish [it for adoption], detained a woman in labor in the CPC offices for hours in the same effort, pressured new mothers to sign unidentified papers while they were under heavy medication shortly after they gave birth, failed to provide legal counsel for surrendering parents, and badgered one young couple with pressure tactics that a psychiatrist compared in court testimony to brainwashing" (Joyce, *Child Catchers*, 106). As Joyce relates, CPCs do not simply support the pro-life movement; they also serve as an arm of the increasingly aggressive Christian "adoption" movement, which seeks to justify pro-life ideology, not simply through adoption, but often also through what amounts to the forced kidnapping of infants (see Joyce 112–113). This is not surprising, given that the pro-life movement promotes the idea that women who would consider abortion are already unfit parents to begin with, regardless of whether they choose "life" or not (113).

As a result, CPCs promote "biased counseling" in favor of adoption, even though relatively few women actually want to give their children up for adoption (Joyce, *Child Catchers*, 113). The idea of the mythological millions of women waiting to give up their children to strangers is as ubiquitous in the pro-life movement as the equally bizarre belief that there are millions of willing evangelical families waiting to receive these children, regardless of their race or physical condition. Indeed, the very nature of CPC counseling is by its nature biased, since CPCs presuppose that abortion is not, or should not be, an option. And here, regardless of the pro-life movement's concerns about Margaret Sanger and Planned Parenthood's "eugenic" past, is the essential difference between CPCs and the modern abortion providers. Planned Parenthood advocates for the right of its clients to receive reproductive health care, including abortion. It does not, as the pro-life movement claims, advocate for abortion itself. This therefore means that counseling practice at any reputable reproductive health care institution is not directive in the sense that it tries to force a woman to make one type of decision or another about carrying her pregnancy to term. By contrast, the pro-life movement, including CPCs, are deliberately directive in their methodology. In this, they share the element of moralism common to biblical counseling, Mowrer's integrity groups, and reality therapy. And as in all these methodologies, there is enormous room for abuse of the counseling practice, because behaviorist practice here is integrated into a counseling methodology typically unconcerned with maintaining any professional code of ethics or standards.

Thus one ends up with, as Joyce notes, the pro-life movement promoting the idea to clients that abortion "increases their risk of breast cancer, depression and suicide—claims that are not accepted by the medical establishment" (Joyce, *Child Catchers*, 104). Another typical claim is that women suffer from "post-abortion syndrome," as a result of the supposed trauma that occurs during the abortion procedure (National Abortion Federation, "Post Abortion Syndrome"). While it is of course entirely possible, and even likely, that some women may have had adverse psychological side effects from having undergone an abortion, there is absolutely no scientific evidence—and never has been— for the therapeutic reality of "post-abortion syndrome" (see the National Abortion Federation's "post-abortion syndrome"; see also the APA [American Psychological Association] Task Force on Mental Health and Abortion [2008], *Report of the APA Task Force on Mental Health and Abortion* for the most definitive APA statement on abortion). Indeed, any reasonable pro-lifer should be able to see this. The politicization of post-abortion syndrome and its rapid adoption as a clinical paradigm by various integrationist and biblical counseling counselors speaks to its enormous value as a rhetorical and ideological weapon in the battle over abortion. Yet the history of the use of mental health diagnoses as political tools is a long and sordid one; slave-owners, Nazis and the Communists created new psychopathologies to politically marginalize, and even kill, their enemies. Women have often been the political target of such pathologizing tendencies and there is no reason now to suppose post-abortion syndrome is anything more than another cynical ploy by the leaders of the Christian right to lengthen the conflict over abortion well beyond its natural lifespan.

Unfortunately the mentally ill and women were not the only victims of the evangelical movement, nor even the only group to be deliberately psychopathologized by that movement. The next chapter will explore how the evangelical movement views homosexuality, how it has consistently pathologized LGBT people as suffering from mental health problems, and how the biblical counseling and deliverance movement's answers to the "problem" of homosexuality make the more commonly practiced reparative therapy look positively benign by comparison.

Evangelicals and Ex-gays

The Failure of Praying the Gay Away

Shawn O'Donnell spent time in programs of the ex-gay organization Exodus International, on and off, for 10 years. Exodus International even used a picture of O'Donnell, along with other purported ex-gays, as "proof" of Exodus's success. The problem was that Exodus did not work for O'Donnell. Indeed, once he came out of the closet, he experienced relief and feelings of happiness that had been denied him during his years within the ex-gay movement. O'Donnell grew up Pentecostal. He knew he was gay at an early age, but he was also told by the evangelical movement that homosexuality was a sin. At age 18, he started to receive counseling from Leanne Payne Ministries (Payne is a famous Charismatic inner healing advocate). Over ten years of therapy, O'Donnell was told alternately that "'a bad relationship with his father may have made him gay, that he may have been sexually abused, and that his mother was overbearing." The problem was that none of these counseling suppositions was in fact true. O'Donnell attempted suicide by slitting his wrists, but he still tried to remain in the ex-gay movement. He even checked himself into a around-the-clock inpatient "treatment center" for homosexuality called New Hope Ministries. After his attempts to remain straight again failed, he again tried to commit suicide. O'Donnell eventually decided that the only way to get out of this self-destructive cycle was to reject ex-gay ideology. Fortunately, he did so (Salon staff, "True confessions"). Research has shown that reparative practices "routinely led to worsened mental health, self-harm, thoughts of suicide and suicide attempts" (Strudwick). While the exact number of people who have killed themselves due to reparative therapy is not known— and likely not knowable—the steady drumbeat of stories of failed conversion attempts, dating back to the 1970s and beyond, continue to testify to the danger of reparative practice.

A book on suspect evangelical counseling methods, therefore, would not be complete without a brief foray into the extremely suspect field of gay conversion therapy and reparative therapy. Unlike deliverance ministries and biblical counseling, which at their most honest do not claim to be offering professional psychological help, reparative therapists typically claim to be—and unfortunately often are—licensed psychologists, sometimes with imposing credentials. In addition to explicitly psychologically based reparative therapy, both the biblical counseling and deliverance movement engage in ex-gay conversion processes.

Although the professional literature is not always consistent about the matter, this section will distinguish between psychologically based reparative therapy and other forms of gay conversion therapy, such as deliverance ministries and biblical counseling. It is important to do this because though these therapies invoke similar stereotypical images of LGBT people, they operate out of vastly different theoretical paradigms. The difference between these paradigms significantly affects how ex-gay conversion practice is conducted, as well as the underlying message being conveyed to LGBT individuals.[1] Perhaps the most significant difference is what homosexuality is blamed on. As we will see, quasi-secular versions of gay conversion therapy, particularly reparative therapy, diagnose homosexuality as a maladaptive response to poor parenting and typically see homosexual "behavior" as resulting from mental illness (Erzen 137–145). However, while this vision of homosexuality is inherently homophobic, it is not necessarily, in and of itself, committed to a vision of homosexuality as sinful. Rather, homosexuality is seen as being sexually or psychologically deviant. Homosexuality is therefore typically regarded in this model as a mental illness in need of treatment. Christian or other religious forms of reparative therapy also often diagnose homosexuality as a mental illness, but they also argue that it is a sin as well, one that can be cured through a combination of Christian religious practice and psychotherapy.

Deliverance ministries typically diagnose homosexuality as simply a demonic problem, sometimes resulting from generational curses inherited through the family line.[2] Though Pentecostal and Charismatic Christianity is in some ways the most homophobic forms of evangelicalism extant, ironically their diagnosis of homosexuality places less "blame" on LGBT people for their supposedly sinful behavior than do other forms of conversion therapy. For deliverance ministers, the "responsibility" for LGBT behavior is placed more on the demonic and less on the individual person. However, it is quite doubtful that LGBT people hearing this "diagnosis" will respond to this message of deliverance any more positively than mentally ill individuals being told their schizophrenia or OCD is the result of demons. As with these individuals, the message of "hope" deliverance ministers try to convey is lost in all the crazy talk of demonically inhabited bodies (and in deliverance to gays, bodily orifices, literally) (*One Nation Under God*).

Biblical counseling, given its anti-psychiatric, anti–Charismatic, and anti-gay politics, settles for a simpler explanation of homosexual behavior. It is the result of sin and can be cured through a call to repentance (see Adams, *Christian Counselor's Manual*, 95). Again, there are ironies here. Although the Reformed movement that gives birth to biblical counseling is the most intellectually sophisticated form of evangelicalism, the cures it offers for LGBT "behavior" are the most simplistic. And though individual Reformed evangelicals tend to be much more polite in their distaste for homosexuality than do Charismatics and even sometimes mainstream reparative therapy supporters, they are also often the most likely to offer up bloodthirsty, even murderous, cures to the "problem" of homosexual behavior. The most dangerous threats to LGBT freedom in the last forty years have often resulted from proposals offered up by Reformed evangelicals, especially the writings of Reconstructionists like Rousas Rushdoony.

Nevertheless, the mainstream of gay conversion practice appears to be psychologically based reparative therapy, not because evangelicals particularly believe in reparative practice over the other pseudo-therapeutic paradigms being offered up, but because it has the air of quasi-scientific "legitimacy" that the evangelical movement longs to exude. The public face of ex-gay therapy, therefore, is reparative practice and it is to reparative therapy we will first turn.

Reparative Therapy: Freaky Freudianism in the Service of Fundamentalism

The roots of reparative therapy lie in Freudian psychoanalysis. While there are other forms of "therapeutic practice" that have been used against LGBT people to "cure" them, such as aversion therapies and psychosurgery, reparative therapy has come to be associated with psychoanalysis primarily. Indeed, even into fairly recent times, psychoanalytic practice has been perceived as being relatively hostile to LGBT people (Drescher, "I'm Your Handyman," 6), as opposed to more scientifically oriented therapeutic systems like behaviorism.

Debates about the psychological and biological origins of homosexuality had their beginnings in late nineteenth-century Europe, where sexologists began to debate the origins of a "distinct type of person—labeled at different times and by different people as the homosexual, intermediate sex, invert, urning, and third sex" (Erzen 134). As Erzen points out, however, this debate did not just come as a result of sexologists' research. While historians have shown that medical and scientific dialogue helped classify homosexuality as a distinct entity, there is still considerable debate about whether this discourse was an attempt to define and control already preexisting communities of same-sex attracted individuals (Erzen 134). Sexologists tended to assume homosexuality was a biological phenomenon. Sexology presumed that moral character was inherently tied to biological character, with much of that character being sexually driven (see Erzen 134). Early sexologists such as Karl Ulrichs and Magnus Hirschfield used such arguments to contend that those without heterosexual inclinations, including homosexuals, were neither diseased nor criminal. Instead, they saw homosexuality as part of a "natural variation of human sexuality" (Erzen 134–135).

Another individual who argued for the biological origins of homosexuality was Richard von Kraft-Ebbing. Ebbing's massive work *Psychopathia Sexualis: A Clinical Forensic Study* (1886) offered a huge classificatory system for defining what he considered the major sexual perversions. However, Kraft-Ebbing's views eventually shifted from seeing such behaviors as crimes towards seeing them as diseases. As Erzen points out, this shifted the focus of treatment from "criminality to pathology" (Erzen 135). Homosexuality was here moved from the realm of the prison warden to the realm of the psychotherapist, though often with the implicit threat of exposure and prison if therapy did not work. Kraft-Ebbing's other significant contribution to the pathologization of LGBT people was to "link an insecure gender identity to the homosexual condition" (Erzen 135). Specifically, Kraft-Ebbling was the originator of the infamous term "mannish lesbian," as a descriptive term for women who exhibited "cross-gendered behavior" (Erzen 135). Early case work on same-sex attraction focused specifically on male homosexuals (a trait that would tend to characterize religious reparative treatments as well), but eventually sexologists like Havelock Ellis contributed case studies of women as well. What should be understood, however, is that what united the rather diverse theories of early sexologists was that there was a "biological basis for homosexuality ... and that homosexuals should not be subject to criminalization" (Erzen 135, *One Nation Under God* DVD). Thus, even at its most primitive, sexology and the Freudian psychoanalytic stream that borrowed from it explicitly stood against the most extremist elements of religious gay conversion practice, which sought the criminalization (sometimes the execution of) homosexuals and argued against the biological origins of homosexuality.

Freud's research into homosexuality shifted research on homosexuality away from "biological determinism toward psychoanalytic and later psychological approaches" (Erzen 135). Freud saw sexuality as operating somewhat on a continuum. He thought that normal heterosexuals had to have some subliminal homosexual impulses to exhibit healthy heterosexual behavior. Similarly, all "homosexuals had some heterosexual feelings" (Drescher, "I'm Your Handyman," 8). For his time, Freud was relatively sexually tolerant. In the 1930s he called for homosexuality's decriminalization in Austria and Germany, a brave act considering the sexual and anti–Semitic politics of those countries during that era (see Drescher 7). Freud did not believe homosexuals should be punished for behaviors that he felt were beyond their personal control. Unlike contemporary reparative practitioners, he did not believe that "criminalization and social opprobrium were acceptable therapeutic tools" for "treating" LGBT sexual practice (Drescher 7).

However, this is not to say that Freud endorsed homosexual behavior. His writing would tend to indicate that he did not (see Drescher 8). In his opinion, "early childhood development was organized into psychosexual stages of libido." Freud's theory placed genital (heterosexual) intercourse above what he saw as more infantile forms of gratification, as he set up a hierarchal "ordering of pleasure" in which children moved from oral to anal to genital stages of sexual development. For Freud, therefore, adult sexuality was explicitly "genital to genital ... intercourse." Anal and oral sexual contact were labeled as either "foreplay or immature vestiges of childhood sexual expression" (Drescher 9). He thought that changing an individual's same sex orientation to heterosexuality was akin to helping them attain a "higher level of psychosexual development." For Freud, entering reparative therapy was not about attaining a religious conversion nor even so much about achieving a cure but simply a process of "growing up" (Drescher 9). He felt homosexuality was a mental health problem, a psyche problem, rather than a biological condition or phenomena (Erzen 135). He thought that homosexuality in boys was caused by an unhealthy attachment to the mother during a boy's Oedipal phase or a deep connection to a father or older male or "competition with sibling for a mother's attention" (Erzen 136). Among later reparative therapists, particularly religious reparative therapists, Freud's more complex explanatory theoretical system would be simplified into the simple theory that male homosexuality was caused by an "absent father" and an "overattached mother" (see *One Nation Under God*).

Even though Freud's work saw heterosexuality as a norm, he analyzed it in much the same way as he did homosexuality. He did not believe in keeping LGBT people apart from the rest of society, and he stated emphatically that homosexuals "were not diseased" (Erzen 136). Freud rejected much of the moralism of American therapists who attempted to cure homosexuality. But despite his opinions, in the years following his death, psychological professionals, including psychoanalysts and psychiatrists, revised key areas of Freudian theory to argue that homosexuality could be successfully treated and "cured." This eventually led to the pathological classification of homosexuality within the DSM (Erzen 136).

The main early champions of reparative therapy were Irving Bieber and Charles Socarides. Bieber argued that homosexuality was the result of a "highly pathologic" parent-child relationship, accompanied by early life problems or situations that exacerbated a propensity to homosexuality. Early childhood trauma therefore was at the root of Bieber's theory of homosexuality (Erzen 137). Bieber and Socarides claimed to be able to cure "up to 50 percent of 'strongly motivated obligatory homosexuals'" (Erzen 137). Socarides disagreed with Freud's position that same-sex sexuality is the result of arrested development and sought to redefine it as conflictual. The conflict model that Socarides suggests emphasizes that homosexuality is a "compromise between intrapsychic forces" (Drescher, "I'm Your Handyman," 13). As Drescher points out, this is a "metapsychological" idea rather than a truly scientific one, as it relies on a conflict between three psychological constructs—id, ego, and superego—that, unlike human behavior in behaviorist constructions, are not subject to direct human observation (see Drescher 13). Indeed, this tendency of psychoanalytic theory to devolve into largely mythic explanations for human behavior might be part of the reason why religious reparative therapists have found Freudian theory so attractive to use, despite Freud's well-known opposition to metaphysical explanations of human behavior. For supporters of religious reparative therapy, Freudian psychoanalysis's inherently mythological nature makes it an ideal tool by which to construct their own mythology of sexual behavior, one conducive to both Freud and faith.

As Erzen points out, however, the Bieber and Socarides theories were "as essentialist as many biological studies" (Erzen 138). For Bieber and Socarides, one highly Western theory of child development could explain all parent-child dynamics in all historical eras and all cultures. Heterosexuality was redefined as something somehow "natural and innate." Worse, both men used their theories to pathologize LGBT relationships as unhappy, short lived, and doomed to failure (Erzen 138, *One Nation Under God*). Socarides even made a now infamous link between same-sex attraction and psychosis, arguing that same-sex attraction was accompanied by psychological illnesses such as schizophrenia and bipolar mood swings (Erzen 138).

Bieber and Socarides's therapies remained popular well into the 1970s, but by that time LGBT activists were becoming increasingly outspoken—and, for that matter, simply "out"—in their opposition to reparative treatments. Most professionals in the APA at this time still agreed that homosexuality was a pathology. But there were increasing dissenting opinions. For instance, the work of Evelyn Hooker argued that same-sex attraction did not affect LGBT individuals' well-being and that society should if anything, stop stigmatizing and oppressing LGBT people and promoting treatment to "cure" them. Other psychiatric and psychological practitioners, such as Judd Marmor and Richard Green, also united against what they saw as the abuse of the gay community and allied with Hooker and LGBT activists opposed to the pathologization of same sex attraction. These individuals attacked not only the American Psychiatric Association (APA [2]) as an organization, but the organization's claim that it had a natural and unassailable right to define who and who was not normal and deviant (Erzen 139).

Robert Spitzer, who ironically would gain the gay community's ire three decades later, was a member of the American Psychiatric Association Committee on Nomenclature in 1972. After meeting with concerned gay activists, Spitzer arranged for them to address his committee the next year about the need to remove homosexuality from the DSM as a pathological classification (Erzen 141–142). Spitzer was careful not to argue that homosexuality was a "normal sexual variation" but his committee did argue against any pathologization or discrimination against LGBT individuals based on the idea that homosexuals were somehow mentally ill. By 1973, the American Psychiatric Association had voted to remove homosexuality from the DSM. However, though the gay community was happy about the removal, there were still concerns about the classificatory systems for sexual deviance left in place within the DSM. Spitzer, for instance, continued to refer to homosexuality as a "suboptimal" condition. It became increasingly clear that Spitzer felt the DSM still needed diagnostic criteria for LGBT individuals who felt distressed by their condition (Erzen 142).

In 1992, Joseph Nicolosi, Charles Socarides and Benjamin Kaufman founded the National Association for the Research and Treatment of Homosexuality (NARTH). Kaufman was a psychiatrist at the University of California, Davis. Joseph Nicolosi, the most prominent spokesman for NARTH since its formation, is a clinical psychologist and president of NARTH (Stewart 73–74). NARTH provides "an international referral service for both religious and secular licensed therapists offering sexual reorientation treatment in the United States, Canada, Europe and Australia" (Erzen 143). Ex-gay conversion therapists' assumptions about homosexuality are fundamentally different from the mainstream therapeutic community. Mainstream secular and gay-affirming religious therapists use psychotherapy to help minimize and hopefully eliminate maladaptive psychological symptoms that come from sexual and religious conflicts (Erzen 143). Ethical therapists never assume that homosexuality is the problem; indeed, the American Psychological Association (APA) specifically warns against the dangers of doing so (APA Task Force on Appropriate

Therapeutic Responses to Sexual Orientation). Indeed, sexuality of any sort is generally not judged at all, unless a sexual practice (for instance, sexual harassment) directly harms another individual. By contrast, NARTH therapists assume that homosexuality represents an unwanted attraction and instead use the therapeutic relationship to create a new heterosexual lifestyle or orientation (Erzen 143).

NARTH promotes itself through a number of means: a monthly bulletin, lectures, literature distribution to colleges and high schools, and psychotherapy. Part of NARTH's "research" consists of surveys which are designed to show that "change is possible" for LGBT people (Erzen 143). NARTH has close ties to the ex-gay movement, despite its own ostensibly secular status as a scientific organization. Nicolosi, a practicing Catholic, participated in the conferences of the religious Exodus International organization and endorses the religious component of ex-gay ministries (Erzen 143). NARTH theorists and therapists seek to legitimize the practice of psychotherapy for homosexuals. Joseph Nicolosi's work *Reparative Therapy of Male Homosexuality: A New Clinical Approach* (1991) is one of the major works used by providers of reparative therapy (Erzen 144). Most of the work is dedicated to an explanation of homosexuality's etiology rooted in "gender identity deficits" (Stewart 74).

However, as Stewart points out, Nicolosi's work goes beyond merely an attempt at scientific legitimization of reparative therapy. Instead, Nicolosi specifically aligns reparative therapy with "mainstream values," thereby positioning gays and lesbians as a marginalized, inferior social minority (Stewart 76). Nicolosi's work is explicitly moralistic. Like Jay Adams, he rejects the idea that the therapeutic process can be values-neutral (see Stewart 78). Nicolosi sees male homosexuality as a problem resulting from "incomplete masculinity," an idea that, though consistent with earlier forms of psychoanalytic theory, is often more emphasized in religious forms of gay conversion therapy (see Erzen 144). Nicolosi situates his theory in the "mainstream," as resulting from "common sense" ideas, thus appealing to the American religious base's popular understanding of science (Stewart 78–79). Besides portraying gays as being opposed to mainstream values, Nicolosi also, again like Adams, positions his opposition group (here homosexuals) as lacking in personal responsibility (Stewart 83).

Stewart observes that many of the arguments of Nicolosi—and frankly of the reparative therapy movement at large—share with creation science "an appeal to the 'folk epistemology of science,'" that is, an idea of science that emphasizes common-sense ideas of the world combined with inductive reasoning (Stewart 73). The importance of this idea for the Christian right, as Stewart partly notes, is that it allows supporters of reparative therapy and creation science to position themselves as supporting the scientific method, even as they pursue unscientific goals (Stewart 73). Reparative therapy, more than most forms of Christian therapy, is tied to this folk understanding of science and thus rises or falls on its ability to convince people of the correctness of that folk understanding.

Nicolosi's ideas originated in a work called *Homosexuality: A New Christian Ethic* (1983) by Elizabeth Moberly (indeed, Moberly claims Nicolosi stole many of her ideas and has received undeserved credit for his ideas) (Erzen 145). Moberly, like Nicolosi, felt that homosexuals greatly needed to form "nonsexual same-sex friendships" in order to fulfill "unmet love needs" developed during their early childhood (Erzen 145). Moberly's ideas resurrected the theories of male homosexuality proposed by Bieber and Socarides but now integrated them into ex-gay religious conversions programs, programs that were often residential in nature (Erzen 147, *One Nation Under God,* Robinson and Spivey, 656).

According to Moberly, homosexuality originated from problems developed between the parent and child. Each had "specific emotional needs" that same-sex parents had to address. When these needs were unmet, they became eroticized in puberty. Because of this, in all homosexual relationships children were seeking to fulfill unmet needs for love and attention from the same-sex parents. Homosexuality itself therefore was an innately reparative drive, an attempt by the homosexual to correct an emotional deficit (Erzen 146). Moberly, rather than use the term homosexuality, referred to "same-sex ambivalence" (Erzen 146, *One Nation Under God*). Moberly also referred to what she called "defensive detachment," a concept designed to explain why children sometimes refused "to identify with a parent of the same sex" (Erzen 146). For Moberly, homosexuality was not a sexual orientation, simply a condition. For many ex-gays of the time (Moberly's theories were popular in the eighties and early nineties, before largely being subsumed into the wider reparative movement), Moberly was seen as a relative breath of fresh air, since her theory deemphasized sin as an explanatory mechanism for homosexuality (see Erzen 146). Moberly would help popularize the idea that gender "problems" determine sexuality, with homosexual males having the famous dominant overclose mothers and passive, non-protective fathers (Robinson and Spivey 656).

Moberly's belief that a healthy nonsexual relationship with members of the same sex was the cure for homosexuality was the justification for the growth of ex-gay residential programs (Erzen 147). For Moberly, unlike many of her successors in the ex-gay movement, forming relationships with opposite-sex individuals was not necessarily the solution for homosexuality (Erzen 147). Indeed, she thought it was "completely ineffective" in meeting deficits in same-sex emotional and physical needs. She also "criticized the focus on behavior at ex-gay programs and the idea that marriage would cure homosexuals" (Erzen 147). Also, unlike many other religious supporters of gay conversion therapy, Moberly argued that there was a spectrum of sexuality, and she was open to the idea that there were some biological and genetic factors that shaped whether a person developed same-sex attraction (see Erzen 147).

Moberly's ideas were, as Tanya Erzen points out, "purely speculative," but they were eagerly adopted by "ex-gay-supportive psychiatrists and psychologists at NARTH and elsewhere" (147). Those ideas continue to be the basis for much of the clinical and counseling practice used by many ex-gay programs. What is immediately problematic for many gay men in these programs is that their familial history does not necessarily mesh with Moberly's explanatory schema for homosexuality (Erzen 148). Some gay men, obviously, have very healthy relationships with their fathers that do meet their emotional needs. And of course, not all mothers of gay men reflect the stereotype of being overbearing and domineering that characterizes the explicitly antifeminist discourse of the ex-gay movement. Some gay rights advocates, most notably Wayne Besen, have expressed concern that the underlying message of therapists like Moberly and Nicolosi ends up not only hurting gay men, but also puts enormous amounts of undeserved and unrealistic guilt on their parents, who are unfairly held responsible for a sexual attraction that is neither sinful nor changeable (see *Fish Can't Fly* DVD). Again, here ex-gay therapy replicates biblical counseling and even more so the deliverance movement. Though biblical counseling encourages people to take "personal responsibility" for their "sin" (aka mental illness), many biblical counselors often castigate parents (particularly mothers) for their children's behaviors. And of course, the deliverance movement is even worse in this regard, shifting much of the blame for mental illness and homosexuality away from genetics, biology, and early childhood development to "inherited demons." Thus, while Moberly's theory is actually in some ways marginally better than the even more devolved form of psychoanalytic pseudoscience promoted by the current generation of gay conversion therapists (some of whom eliminate psychotherapy entirely), it is hardly conducive to effecting "change" in LGBT individuals, were that change even possible.

The ex-gay movement's developmental theories do not take women much into account. What literature is out there tends to blame mothers for creating effeminate sons and masculine daughters. Moberly rather implausibly assumed—and wrote as much—that all gay men were effeminate and all gay women "masculine identified or butch" (Erzen 149). Thus, the existence of femme lesbians or butch gay men presents a major explanatory problem for the ex-gay movement, one it simply does not address (149). Ex-gay theories about lesbians assume that the cure to lesbianism is to teach women how to be more feminine (Erzen 149). Thus women are taught how to do their hair, how to put on makeup, how to walk in heels, etc. (Erzen 149, *One Nation Under God*). In one painful scene from the documentary *One Nation Under God,* a woman explains that even though she knew how to change a tire, she asked for a man to do it for her so that she would be more feminine (*One Nation Under God* DVD). At one Exodus conference that Tanya Erzen attended, the positive feminine characteristics listed included "nurturing, weak ... responsive ... delicate ... prudish ... and quiet," while the negative traits included "spiteful, smothering, weepy, clingy, and wishy-washy" (Erzen 150). While many ex-gay women resent these theories of femininity (Erzen 151), they continue to be the explanatory mechanisms offered up for curing same-sex attraction.

The literature on women in ex-gay cultures typifies them as "completely asexual" (Erzen 152). While men are sexual, women are emotional. Men to the ex-gay movement are sexual predators, while women by contrast do not typically experience attraction for one another (Erzen 152). In line with this idea, the ex-gay movement often explains lesbianism as being a by-product of sexual abuse (Alden 87–88). According to ex-gay theory, sexual abuse so traumatizes a young woman that she is frightened away from men entirely and seeks solace in women (Alden 88). As Helena Alden points out, in this system the "lesbian self being constructed is one that is so severely damaged that the only available outlet is another woman. In other words, lesbians are constructed as victims seeking solace as opposed to women actively and passionately seeking other women" (Alden 88). Michael Bussee, similarly, has pointed out that much of ex-gay rhetoric is rooted in a hatred and fear of women (*One Nation Under God* DVD). This is not surprising. For the Christian right, men being attracted to men is bad enough. But the idea that a woman would not be interested in genital-to-genital male penetration, is both shocking and disturbing to many evangelical men. Similarly, as Ralph Blair, a pro-gay evangelical gay therapist points out, what seems to concern the Christian right is not so much homosexuality itself, though that is bad enough in evangelicals' eyes, but specific types of genital acts (*One Nation Under God* DVD). What is disturbing to evangelical Christian men is that men would enjoy the role of "penetrated" rather than penetrator, the former role which the Christian right assumes should only be a woman's domain. Bussee is therefore almost certainly correct in seeing a deeply misogynistic element in evangelicalism's obsession with male homosexuality and its neglect of lesbianism. This misogyny is predicated not only on men's fear of women, but also on the specific fear of men taking on the role of women or acting like women. To evangelical men this is the ultimate shame. This position is further aggravated by evangelical men's relative lack of involvement in church affairs as compared to women, which often leads such men to overcompensate for their perceived lack of authority, by an exertion of redoubled masculinity (see *One Nation Under God*).

Lesbian women, unlike gay men, are still seen as proper women insofar as they are classified as explicitly nonsexual beings by the ex-gay movement (Alden 89). As with male homosexuality, however, lesbian attraction is often explained by contemporary ex-gay theorists as resulting from insufficient attachment or connection to one's same-sex parent (Alden 89). Sometimes this occurs through a lack of identification with the mother or perhaps through insufficient bonding between a mother and an infant (Erzen 153). Fathers, however, are also important in shaping a lesbian's perception of herself, because, according to current ex-gay theorists, they play a crucial role in shaping a woman's view of gender. Fathers directly teach women how to relate femininity to masculinity. But as is typical for the Christian right, women are to be defined not independently, but mainly—even solely—through their relationship to men (Alden 90).

However, because the system the ex-gay movement sets up to explain lesbianism is even less theoretically sophisticated than its inadequate explanation for male homosexual behavior, the ex-gay movement often falls back on the sexual abuse explanation when individual lesbians argue that the parental explanation isn't applicable to their personal situations. At one conference, for instance, Bob Davies, the former president of Exodus International (the largest Christian ex-gay organization in the world at the time), stated that 80 percent of women coming for help from their organization were victims of "sexual trauma" (Erzen 154). As with male homosexuality, there is a focus here on "sifting through the past for crisis points and familial dysfunction as the causes of homosexuality" (Erzen 154).

Both the religious and secular versions of reparative therapy have had notoriously low success rates.[3] What few contemporary studies that support psychotherapy for homosexuals exist are typically methodologically flawed (see APA Task Force on *Appropriate Therapeutic Responses to Sexual Orientation* vii), and often have poor research design and ridiculously small sample sizes (*One Nation Under God DVD*). But the movement has managed to weather this lack of scientific credibility because the desire of society as a whole for a solution to the gay rights debate, as well as the desire for heteronormativity among most religious Americans, the parents of many gay individuals, and some conflicted LGBT people themselves provides the ex-gay movement with an all-too-large body of clientele, even today. As we will see in the next section, the history of religiously based ex-gay treatment, even in its reparative form, bodes even less well for the movement's viability than its questionable theoretical foundations in psychoanalytic theory.

The History of the Ex-gay Movement: Scandals, Leaders (Fallen and Otherwise), and Contemporary Theories (Fallen, Never Otherwise)

Ex-gay ministries were first formed in the early 1970s, primarily in reaction to the depathologization of homosexuality in the DSM (Robinson and Spivey 651). One of the first activists in the ex-gay movement was Frank Worthen. A gay man, Worthen converted to Christianity and turned to Pastor Kent Philpott for support. Philpott, seeking to successfully counsel gay parishioners, saw Worthen as an answer to prayer. He urged Philpott to join his church, Open Door, and aid him in counseling homosexuals (Erzen 24). Open Door's roots lay in the Jesus movement revival of the early 1970s, in which members of the counterculture joined evangelical churches en masse (Erzen 24). Particularly influential in this regard was Chuck Smith's Calvary Chapel church movement. Calvary Chapel's theology, largely Charismatic, appealed to young people and tapped into many of the favorite pastimes and concerns of the counterculture, such as contemporary music (see Erzen 24–25). Smith's movement, along with the Vineyard movement that later sprang off from it, would go on to shape much of contemporary Christianity over the next 30 years and would have a major impact on the growth of the Charismatic movement, thanks to the New Apostolic Reformation (see Erzen 25).[4] As Erzen notes, many of these churches would also emphasize parachurch ministry that stretched across different denominations and focused on issues of concern to the wider evangelical movement such as abortion, homosexuality, and mental illness (Erzen 25).

As Erzen points out, many mainstream denominations in the early seventies would have looked with distaste at the drug addicts, homeless people, and hippies that churches like Calvary Chapel and Open Door embraced (Erzen 27). One of the many ironies of ex-gay therapy is that the initial impetus for its extremely harmful practice among evangelicals sprang from what was probably one of the least homophobic elements of a very homophobic evangelical culture. Unlike the situation with other evangelicals, who even into the 1990s would often claim that homosexuals were automatically condemned to hell simply because of their orientation, reparative therapy at least offered the possibility of change and salvation. This was a radical message in the early seventies, when most evangelical Christians would not even talk about homosexuality at all.

After Worthen arrived at Open Door, Philpott decided to form a ministry devoted to treating homosexuality, under Open Door's auspices. Worthen started meeting with people on a weekly basis for counseling; soon the group took the name Love in Action. In the late seventies, Philpott took over as director of Love in Action, with Worthen serving as assistant director (Erzen 27). Philpott authored two books on homosexuality during this period suggesting that change was possible (Erzen 28–29). He also played a significant part in establishing the narrative of homosexuality that religious ex-gay programs, particularly Love in Action, would adopt. For him, homosexuality could not be changed through counseling alone. A spiritual component was needed as well (Erzen 28). By 1979, Love in Action had established itself as the first residential ex-gay program; it was only a short matter of time before the program had ten to twenty men and women living in the home at one time (Erzen 28). Although Love in Action opened its "first house of women" in the summer of 1986, by the early 1990s the women's ministry had ended, as the program was unable to find anyone willing to be a house leader. Some of the members of the women's program became prominent in the ex-gay movement, particularly Anne Paulk, wife of John Paulk (Erzen 30).[5]

In the mid-seventies, Worthen found out about the Melodyland Hotline, a "ministry" of Melodyland Christian Center, a California megachurch. Worthen met with two ex-gay Melodyland leaders, Michael Bussee and Jim Kaspar. Out of that meeting came Exodus International, a national group devoted to turning LGBT individuals into heterosexuals (Erzen 31). Worthen, Bussee, Kaspar and a woman named Barbara Johnson next organized what became the first annual ex-gay conference. At the conference, Exodus was officially founded, with Bussee and Kaspar elected president (Erzen 32–33). However, Exodus had trouble forming a consistent ideology, with some members advocating the "change is possible" idea and others promoting the more tragic but also realistic idea that only celibacy, not change of sexual orientation, was realistic for ex-gays (see Erzen 33). Though the late seventies was a period of intense antigay activism, notably via evangelical celebrity Anita Bryant, the ex-gay movement did not gain much "benefit" from this increase in homophobia (Gallagher and Bull 16–20). Instead, important movement leaders defected from Exodus when they found they could not handle being ex-gay. The most famous early scandal in the movement was Michael Bussee's very public rejection of ex-gay treatment during a speech he and his future life partner, Gary Cooper, gave in 1979 (Erzen 34; *One Nation Under God*). This legendary event was only the first of many scandals and defections that would rock the ex-gay movement throughout its entire history.

In the mid 1990s, John Smid, who had taken over the directorship of Love in Action from Worthen, moved Love in Action to Memphis, Tennessee, an action that caused considerable friction between Smid and Worthen. Worthen eventually reopened his ministry in California but renamed it New Hope (Erzen 39). John Smid eventually defected from the ex-gay movement in the late 2000s, after an intense national debate over the Refuge program at Love in Action, an ex-gay program directed at teenagers which was widely condemned (*This Is What Love in Action Looks Like* DVD). As of the early 2000s, there were over 200 evangelical ministries under the umbrella of Exodus International (Erzen 42), with these ministries located in the United States, Europe, South America, Canada, Australia, the Philippines, Singapore, Japan, China, and Mexico (Erzen 42).

During the 1980s, Exodus used the AIDS crisis to promote fear about homosexuality and thereby incite interest in its "redemptive ministry" to LGBT people (Grace 549). This marked the beginning of what John Gallagher and Chris Bull call a "cottage industry of antigay research," led principally by Paul Cameron. Cameron was the director of the Institute for the Scientific of Sexuality in Lincoln, Nebraska. This group, which would eventually evolve into the Family Research Institute, produced and distributed a number of inflammatory tracts about supposed social ills associated with homosexual behavior. Cameron spent most of the AIDS epidemic attempting to prove that gay men brought AIDS on themselves, and by extension, the rest of the world. Cameron advocated for the forced segregation of homosexuals and moved openly for the quarantine of anyone infected with HIV (Gallagher and Bull 26).

Despite this, Cameron's theories found widespread support among many mainstream movement conservatives. His studies were cited by prominent conservatives, including movement luminaries William Bennett and Pat Buchanan. Cameron constructed statistics that supposedly proved gays and lesbians were 10 to 20 times more likely to be child molesters than their peers, and five times more likely to engage in acts of bestiality. Cameron distorted research to suit his agenda, including research that sometimes directly contradicted his own, in order to prove the validity of the Christian right's antigay politics (Gallagher and Bull 27). By 1983, "an accumulation of cooked statistics and questionable behavior" would force Cameron's expulsion from the American Psychological Association on ethics charges (28). Yet Cameron would continue to be used as a tool by antigay activists for many years afterwards (Gallagher and Bull 116–118, 245). His studies were used to justify the antigay and ex-gay movement contention that LGBT people are mentally ill. He therefore at least temporarily buttressed up the already flimsy claims of the ex-gay movement (Robinson and Spivey 652).

By the early 1990s, Exodus's membership was declining. In order to revitalize, Bob Davies, then president, focused on "publishing and international outreach" (Grace 549). In 1995, Exodus gained membership in the U.S.–based Evangelical Council for Financial Accountability (ECFA). This allowed the organization to increase its fund-raising efforts and gave it an air of quasi-legitimacy and respectability, as the ECFA is highly regarded by many evangelicals (Erzen 45; Grace 549). Exodus now was seeking new allies in the wider evangelical movement, allies that could give it increased visibility, presence, and funds.

And allies they found. Since the early 1990s, many Christian organizations were taking cues from the ex-gay movement and began switching their rhetoric from an explicitly condemnatory stance to a superficially compassionate one (Erzen 185). While there were some unintended policy consequences to this (notably that the next generation of evangelicals became somewhat less homophobic than their parents), the move was purely political. The Christian right now used the testimonies of ex-gays not just as justifications for opposing LGBT civil rights but also as support for a rearticulation of evangelical identity that deliberately placed the movement in the most flattering—and least realistic—relation to the LGBT community possible (see Erzen 185). During the summer of 1998, some of these ads even appeared as full-page advertisements in the *New York Times,* the *Washington Post,* and other national newspapers as part of a concentrated media blitz against gay rights (Erzen 183). The ex-gay movement's leaders jumped at the chance to become allies with other Christian right organizations which had previously shunned them. In the process, significant friction sometimes occurred between ex-gay supporters, some of whom felt that change was a complex process that did not always work for everyone, and the mainstream evangelical movement, whose vision of homosexuality was much more condemnatory and simplistic (Erzen 189).

The ex-gay movement, as Tanya Erzen notes, is highly testimonial in character (Erzen 205–206). In particular it likes to highlight testimonies of formerly politically active gay men and women whose activism now is supposed to evolve from pro-gay rights politics to an antigay rights message (Erzen 206). Ex-gay celebrities like John Paulk, Mike Haley, and Amy Tracy have at various points in their sexual evolution "chosen to make their ex-gay identities the public vehicle of their activism" (Erzen 207). Frequently, they have allied with the vast empire of Focus on the Family to accomplish this, particularly through the Focus-sponsored Love Won Out conferences (207). Perhaps the most active spokesman for antigay rights politics within the wider ex-gay movement is Joe Dallas. Dallas feels that the ex-gay movement has a "prophetic mandate" to be involved in politics, including such issues as marriage, adoption, hate crimes legislation, and gays in the military (Erzen 209). Dallas's own counseling theory, which may have some mild biblical counseling influences but uses ideas from mainstream psychology as well, insists that becoming ex-gay is the only choice for LGBT individuals (see Grace 554).

The ex-gay movement in recent years has suffered some significant setbacks. The Refuge program's closure and the negative reception it received for admitting young gay teenager Zach Stark against his will cast a major shadow on the movement (*This Is What Love in Action Looks Like*), as did John Smid's defection from the movement and his subsequent adoption of a seemingly more gay-affirming philosophy (*This Is What Love in Action Looks Like*). Also, in 2012 a significant rift opened when Alan Chambers, long-time leader of Exodus International, distanced himself from reparative therapy (Burroway). Although Chambers's move to this observer initially seemed to be mainly tactical—it is proving increasingly hard to justify "mainstream" reparative therapy, both scientifically and in the court of public opinion, which means that deliverance and pastoral and biblical counseling methods will likely gain increasing prominence—it nevertheless seems to have pushed some ex-gay leaders to split from Exodus to form a more hardline organization, the Restored Hope Network (Burroway).

But, in fact, Chambers's change of heart turned out to be sincere, as Exodus closed its doors in 2013, dealing the ex-gay movement a major setback (Do, Mather, and Mozingo). To add to the problems the ex-gay movement faces, other evangelicals are promoting different paradigms for "treating" homosexuality that, while still problematic, are different from those being currently offered by reparative therapists. The most well-known of these paradigms is promoted by Warren Throckmorton, a psychologist at Grove City College, who argues that "reorientation" therapy should focus more on helping religious LGBT individuals live in accordance with their beliefs but puts the decision whether to change in the hands of the patient, not his community (Kwon). While in reality Throckmorton's paradigm seems to this observer little more than window dressing for the continuation of antigay politics, its existence will likely push much of the evangelical movement to at least temporarily moderate some of its more hostile rhetoric, thus again leaving room for liberal evangelicals to take a more active role in challenging all conversion therapies, including Throckmorton's, en masse. Whether that can successfully stop reparative therapy remains to be seen.

The actual science of reparative therapy continues to be viewed as being dubious at best. A study by several Ohio State researchers notes the following:

> Scientific estimates of effectiveness of conversion therapy are essentially nonexistent because of difficulties obtaining samples, following individuals after they exit therapy, defining "success" and obtaining objective measurements of behavioral and psychological change [Drescher, 1999; Haldeman, 1991, 1994; Isay, 1988; Tozer & McClanahan, 1999]. Existing evidence on reorientation attempts suggests that, while behavior change is possible in some cases, actual alteration of one's underlying sexual orientation is not possible [Ritter & Terndrup, 2002; Weiss et al. 292].

As Weiss and her collaborators point out, even if change is possible, the fact remains that empirical study shows that the "vast majority of people" who attempt to alter their sexual orientation fail. More important, current research, popular media publications, individual accounts, and available empirical research suggests numerous negative results of conversion therapies, including "depression, anxiety, sexual difficulties, sexual difficulties with partners of both sexes, problems expressing affection, professional difficulties ... religious and spiritual crises, and significant life losses (marriage, family church, community, etc.)" (Weiss, et al. 292). A study by Shidlo and Schroeder in 2002 was among the most comprehensive to date and argued that conversion therapy typically involves a common starting point that can deviate into one of two paths. According to Shidlo and Schroeder, all clients within such therapy processes experience a "honeymoon period" where they feel "hopeful and positive" about altering their sexual attraction. After this, participants come to see themselves either as "self-perceived failures" or "self-perceived success[es]." People who see themselves as failures typically pass through a period of reflection in which they question the process of conversion and the ideology behind it. They therefore may eventually return to a gay identity, in either a healthy or unhealthy way. Those who perceive themselves as successes, may identify themselves as successful but struggling or alternately successful without any sexual struggle (Weiss 293).

In any case, even if one assumes that reparative therapy can occasionally work, one must ask whether the therapeutic process is worth its inherent social cost. As we have seen, the therapy greatly harms the majority of same-sex clients. It is also likely that among clients who claim to have been successfully treated through reparative therapy, unnecessary harm has been done since the only justifications currently left for reparative therapy or other gay conversion practices are (1) the bogus idea that homosexuality is a mental illness and (2) religious arguments against same-sex sexual contact. Both of these positions on homosexuality, whether right or wrong, are unprovable and purely ideologically grounded, rather than based in science. As we have seen, it is difficult enough to prove that even truly "legitimate" mental illnesses exist, since the classification of mental disorders is based partly on societal assumptions about "normality." But whereas most mental health conditions defined by the DSM—particularly major disorders like schizophrenia, bipolar disorder, and OCD—result in behaviors that are not only intrinsically distressing to those without such diagnoses, but also to those who suffer from these disorders, homosexuality is by definition distressing only to individuals living in or influenced by a homophobic society. A society without a notion of homophobia or sexual intolerance would simply not understand our culture's disdain for same-sex sexuality. By contrast, most cultures have a concept of mental unwellness, even if phrased differently from our own.

But to go even further, even if we could find cases of reparative therapy that were totally successful in changing sexual orientation, what would that mean? In all likelihood such changes would merely reflect the fact that the person one was treating did not have strong same-sex attractions in the first place, either resulting from a bisexual predilection or perhaps sexual confusion unintentionally brought about during sexual experimentation. It is difficult to see, therefore, how reparative therapy could ever claim to be science at all, since sexual orientation, unlike human behavior, is not an observable phenomena and therefore cannot be meaningfully quantified. It is therefore not surprising that, to date, every major U.S. mental health association has issued position statements that warn that reparative therapy is dangerous and can potentially harm clients. The American Psychological Association, in particular, has explicitly argued against any reorientation treatment that a priori assumes that homosexuality is a mental disorder or that a patient "should change his or her sexual orientation" (APA Task Force on Appropriate Therapeutic Responses to Sexual Orientation).

Andre Grace points out the ultimate dangers of pathologizing homosexuality. According to Grace, "to date, all major U.S. mental health associations have issued position statements warning that reparative therapies can possibly harm clients, given the lack of evidence to support their efficacy.... Notably, the American Psychiatric Association issued a position statement in 1998 opposing any sexual reorientation treatment 'based upon the assumption that homosexuality per se is a mental disorder or based upon the a priori assumption that a patient should change his or her sexual orientation'" (Grace 558). Given, therefore, reparative therapy's continued lack of clinical success, it seems difficult to fathom why the therapy is even legal, let alone practiced. And recent court challenges to the use of reparative therapy point to the fact that such pseudoscientific counseling may come under increasing legal scrutiny in the years to come.

Biblical Counseling and Homosexuality

From the start of the biblical counseling movement, there has been an interest in homosexuality. Not surprisingly, Jay Adams outlined the movement's initial approach to homosexuality. As with the mentally ill, Adams believed that using mental health diagnoses to treat homosexuality did not help prospective counselees. He argued that "to call homosexuality a sickness, for example, does not raise the client's hope. But to call homosexuality sin as the Bible does, is to offer hope" (Adams, *Competent,* 139). Adams therefore from the start clearly rejected the medicalization of homosexuality that provides the basic diagnostic system for the reparative therapy movement. Instead, he sees homosexuality as simply a deviant sin-based behavior.

This affects Adams's vision of homosexuality in several interesting ways. First of all, because he does not appear to believe in the concept of sexual orientation, he argues that "homosexuality is not considered to be a condition, but an act" (Adams, *Competent to Counsel,* 139). Therefore, for Adams homosexuality is not so much a state of being, though it can evolve into one, as a series of temporary acts that can be reversed or not reversed, depending on one's obedience to Christ and the effort one puts into "healing" oneself of homosexuality. In a sense, Adams's position here is more sophisticated than the reparative therapy movement's, since Adams, like some pro-gay theologians, focuses more on homosexuality as an act and seems to be at least dimly aware that the medicalization of homosexuality as a deviant sexual behavior is the product of late–19th and 20th century psychiatry. Unfortunately, however, Adams simply remedicalizes homosexuality in biblical counseling's quasi-medical, quasi-theological terms, refusing to acknowledge that homosexuality is neither a medical condition nor a sin but a sexual state of being that has no inherent moral pathology, good or evil, attached to it.

Early biblical counseling theory tends to be slightly less hardline about homosexuality than the theorists who followed in their wake, despite the modern CCEF claim that they represent the progressive wing of biblical counseling. Wayne Mack, writing for the *Journal of Pastor Practice,* states that

> since homosexuality is not a genetic or endrocinic inevitability, but rather an acquired or learned habit, it follows that it may be prevented. This is not to deny that certain males are born with physical and emotional dispositions which would make them likely candidates for homosexuality. Nor is this to rule out the possibility of birth trauma influencing a boy toward homosexuality. But these constitutional and birth trauma experiences can certainly be counteracted with proper educational, intrafamilial, and environmental helps [Mack, "Preventing Homosexuality," 43].

Mack very clearly sees homosexuality as a sin, one in need of biblical counseling. But, unlike future biblical counselors, he is more willing to admit to biological and environmental influences that might motivate LGBT individuals to, as evangelicals terms it, "become homosexual." Also, Mack's language about the LGBT community would prove to be much milder than that applied by later theorists in the biblical counseling and reparative therapy movements, particularly during the panic over AIDS in the eighties and nineties.

Howard Eyrich, a prominent early member in the biblical counseling movement, in 1977 wrote one of the first "theoretical" papers on homosexuality for the biblical counseling movement. He argued that there were three basic presuppositions for counselors "approaching the problem of homosexuality. The first is the absoluteness of the Word of God.... Second, growing out of the first, is the fact that homosexuality is sin.... The third presupposition is that homosexuality is a learned behavior" (Eyrich 29). Eyrich's view on homosexuality, not surprisingly for a supporter of nouthetics, was biblicist in orientation, locating the solution and diagnosis of homosexuality as sin from a literalist reading of the biblical text. A natural corollary to this presupposition was that homosexuality must be a learned behavior. The biblical counseling movement was even at this time profoundly uncomfortable with the idea of biologically derived homosexuality, since the movement feared that this kind of explanation for same-sex attraction would undercut the basis on which the movement built both its condemnation of the mentally ill and the LGBT community.

In the late eighties, the biblical counseling movement even argued that it was possible, though not certain, that AIDS was God's judgment on homosexuals. The movement was cautious on this point, however, because they argued homosexuality itself might be the judgment on LGBT people (Franklin Payne, "God's Judgment and AIDS," 13–15). Thus, the biblical counseling movement can hardly claim to have developed a compassionate approach to LGBT people at a time when such an approach was desperately wanted in the evangelical church.

By the mid 1990s, the major biblical counseling theorist concerning homosexuality was Ed Welch, whose chapter on same-sex attraction in *Blame It on the Brain* remains one of the longest and most detailed descriptions of the biblical counseling movement's view of same-sex attraction. Welch, like Eyrich, starts with the biblicist presupposition that the Bible should remain the center-point for determining whether or not homosexuality is considered an acceptable behavior by the church as a whole. He therefore argues that the Bible "is unambiguous and consistent in its prohibitions against homosexuality. At every mention, it is condemned as sin" (Welch 154). Welch therefore feels that Christians cannot accept the "pro-homosexual" hermeneutic—that is, the concept furthered by some pro-gay theologians that the Bible speaks only of noncommitted, non-loving, same-sex relationships, unlike those practiced today (see Welch 155).

Welch argues that such arguments rely heavily on the idea that homosexuality is "natural." He claims that the LGBT community sees homosexuality as "not something that moderns *do,* it is who they *are*" (Welch 157, italics in original). The problem Welch sees with allowing such an argument any place in the evangelical church is that the church "cannot live with the idea of a natural homosexual orientation without, at some point, altering Scripture to fit our sense of God's character" (Welch 157–158). Thus, for Welch, the issue of homosexuality is not so much one of homophobia or hatred—though these may or may not exist in his mind—but of hermeneutics. In Welch's mind, the evangelical movement is in danger of losing its literalist hermeneutic identity—its single-minded devotion to a biblicist reading of scriptures—if it accepts a pro-gay reading of scripture. This argument, to those outside the evangelical community, may seem absurd. Yet, in reality, it is the way many evangelicals honestly approach not just the subject of homosexuality but also every other "behavior pattern" condemned by evangelicalism (including depression and some forms of mental illness). A behavior pattern that is seen as inherently violating this hermeneutic is almost always rejected, regardless of whether that behavior pattern is seen as morally permissible by the rest of society (including this author). Because biblical counseling is so inherently biblistic, and also because it has a heavy fundamentalist constituency that is unwilling to adapt as readily as its Reformed founders, it is very unlikely that the movement's basic foundational approach towards homosexuality will change in the near future.

This presents real problems for the LGBT community, because with the recent downturn in the number of therapists willing to do traditional reparative therapy, as well as the welcome closing of Exodus International in 2013,[6] increasingly ex-gay therapy will be in the hands of biblical counselors and deliverance ministers, individuals who are even more likely to damage LGBT individuals than the supposedly professional clinicians who treated them before. Because of the biblical counseling movement's overcommitment to a literalist hermeneutic when looking at the issue of homosexuality, the likelihood of the antigay element of the evangelical movement's increasing alignment with biblical counseling is quite troubling. Welch's *Blame It on the Brain,* for instance, a book still immensely popular in the biblical counseling world, promotes the idea that biblical counseling can not only root out actual same-sex "behavior," but also can help an individual battle and root out "sin at the level of the imagination" (Welch, *Blame It on the Brain* 158). Welch argues that it is possible not only to vanquish "homosexual acts" but also "homosexual desire" (Welch, *Blame It on the Brain*, 173). Yet Welch, even compared to Adams, leaves little effective counseling theory as to how exactly to achieve such miracle cures, relying primarily on paeans to following Christ and the importance of Christians forming effective relationships with LGBT individuals at the expense of effective theory.

To this day, Welch's work remains the most well-known biblical counseling work to deal with LGBT behavior. One recent anthology of biblical counseling articles has also attempted to handle the issue: *Counseling Hard Cases* (2012). Though there were some slightly welcome modifications to previous theory, most notably the volume's willingness (through an article by Kevin Carson) to focus more on homosexuality as one of a spectrum of "sin problems" that an LGBT person "suffers from," rather than as one's root issue, overall the volume largely rehashes previous biblical counseling theory on homosexuality, showing little nuance or understanding of same-sex attraction and, again, providing no meaningful theoretical framework, let alone testable system, for effectively treating LGBT individuals for their supposedly deviant behavior (Kevin Carson in Scott and Lambert, *Counseling Hard Cases,* loc 3865–4339).

Whatever its effectiveness for the mentally ill, biblical counseling seems to have little hope of dealing efficaciously with same-sex attraction, even if one accepts the idea that same-sex attraction is something that has to be "dealt with" in the first place. But it is interesting to note how central the rejection of the "homosexual hermeneutic" is for the biblical counseling movement, and how closely this rejection parallels their rejection of the "psychiatric hermeneutic." Indeed, with the biblical counseling movement, one could argue that the movement rejects the mentally ill mainly because an acceptance of the mentally ill's claim to diminished moral culpability for certain actions will undercut the rejection of homosexual behavior on which the biblical counseling movement's antigay stance is based. Similarly, allowing acceptance of LGBT behavior might force Adams and the modern generation of biblical counselors to accept the mentally ill as well. Thus, these two communities' fates within evangelical religion are tied together, whether they wish them to be or not.

Deliverance and Inner Healing

This section would not be complete without a brief section on the deliverance and inner healing movement's view of homosexuality. Despite the fact

that many deliverance ministries and deliverance theorists do address the subject of homosexuality, the actual theoretical approach to how homosexuality
is treated is not markedly different from the theories the deliverance movement
provides for other "sexual sins." Occasionally, Pentecostals and Charismatics
will speak of soul ties between LGBT people and their lovers or former lovers.[7]
As with sexual abuse, there is an idea here that an unholy person—here one's
gay or lesbian lover, in sexual abuse one's rapist—can pass on to oneself evil
through the transmissions of demons. Homosexual contact therefore becomes
a spiritual pollutant. To be fair to the mainstream of the deliverance movement,
they are perfectly consistent with their literalist reading of scriptures in also
applying this standard to premarital sex, adultery, and numerous other
frowned-upon sexual behaviors.

The major deliverance works outside of the ex-gay movement that address
homosexuality at any length (at least in the writer's own voice) are Doris Wagner's *How to Minister Freedom* (2005) and Ed Murphy's *Handbook for Spiritual
Warfare* (1992). Murphy argued on one hand that most homosexuals "are not
interested in flaunting their sexuality before the media and the masses.... Thus
they are people who merit our love compassion, and gentle, but firm Christian
witness" (Murphy 143). Murphy therefore rejected the then-prevalent idea
among evangelicals of a uniformly united and pedaristic gay community. However, while Murphy was somewhat sympathetic to closeted or "quiet" gays, he
saw the gay rights movement as "demonic" (Murphy 142). Murphy did qualify
this statement, however, by arguing that this was not true of necessarily all
members of the gay rights movement, and he was willing to acknowledge that
"some members of the Gay Rights Movement are loving, kind, and compassionate people" (Murphy 143). Nevertheless, the portrait Murphy offers of
the LGBT community is depressingly similar to the typical Sodom and
Gomorrah, hell-fire and brimstone mentality that characterized so much of
1990s discourse surrounding homosexuality. While Murphy put a much gentler face on this discourse than did many evangelicals, the fact remains that
his work was mainly just copying the complete pathologization of same-sex
attraction being promoted during the early 1990s.

David Kyle Foster's "Freedom from Homosexual Confusion," an essay in
How to Minister Freedom, represents the other major piece of mainstream
deliverance theory on same-sex attraction. Foster argues that "homosexuals
are internally driven to self-destructive behavior as a result of the lies that they
have believed about themselves, about God and about the purpose of life"
(Foster 211). Foster uses the writings of Dr. Jeffrey Satinover to support this
position, arguing that homosexuals are prone to AIDS, rectal cancer, bowel
disease, a high suicide rate, and a 25-year decrease in life expectancy (Foster

211). However, besides the fact that some of Satinover's claims are demonstrably false—AIDS, for instance, is an equal opportunity killer—there is real reason to doubt his professional credibility. As Wayne Besen points out, Satinover was even willing to countenance the idea that homosexuality could be cured through Prozac (Besen 137). He also promoted the long-discredited idea that pedophilia and homosexuality are linked ("The Problem of Pedophilia"). The same article that contains Satinover's statements about pedophilia also makes a rather unfortunate choice in its concept of who promotes the homosexual agenda: John Money, a sexologist initially favored by some left-wing groups but later justly vilified by the LGBT and intersexual communities for his surgical mutilation of David Reimer.[8]

Basically, Foster's theoretical position on homosexuality is not particularly unique, except that he does not believe there is any one "demon of homosexuality" that is the sole cause of someone's sexual identity (Foster 216). Instead, homosexual desire is caused by "a unique and complex matrix of elements that must be uncovered and dealt with in an appropriate fashion" (Foster 218). Foster promotes a three-stage level of deliverance:

> Homosexuals receive a degree or dimension of deliverance when they repent and give their lives to Christ. Even so, as the Holy Spirit continues to unveil the secret roots of their condition, they continue to be delivered to a greater and greater degree. Then, on the last day when Christ appears and transforms them into His image completely, they will be delivered fully and for all time [Foster 217].

Foster's cure for homosexuality is depressingly cynical. The ultimate "cure" appears only when Christ comes back or they die and enter heaven, thus leaving LGBT people in a constant state of anxiety about their spiritual destiny, afraid that one slip back into same-sex attraction or sexual behavior will permanently damn them and cut them off from God's love. The idea of progressive sanctification implicit in Foster's rendering of ex-gay deliverance theory is even more problematic because it allows the ex-gay movement the ability to push back the promised cure to any date it chooses, and because it makes the success or failure of the therapy totally dependent on the client's ability to sanctify himself before God. It is, in evangelical terms, an intensely "works-based" system.

Perhaps the most famous deliverance ministries for LGBT individuals are Desert Stream, run by Andy Comiskey, and Joanne Highley's Life Ministry. Comiskey's Desert Stream represents (in *highly relative* terms) the more "respectable" front of evangelical deliverance practice for homosexuals. Desert Stream Ministries was influenced by the inner healing movement teacher Leanne Payne (who also influenced the sozo movement). Payne wrote several books that provided the framework for the Christian inner healing movement's understanding of homosexuality. As with the sozo movement, Payne promoted the idea of the healing of memories (Payne, *The Broken Image*, 9). Payne also used quasi-visualization techniques, including the inviting of the Holy Spirit to help heal memories (Payne, *Broken Image*, 29).[9] She felt that the healing of memories occurred at "the deep heart (the deep mind, or unconscious)—the level, I must add, for which, it was always intended" (Payne, *Crisis in Masculinity,* loc 374). Despite her rather transparent attempts to distance herself from Freud, Payne's rhetoric in both *The Broken Image* (1995) and *Crisis of Masculinity* (1995) bore many similarities to the popular Freudian therapeutic systems of the 1980s, particularly the growing segment of the feminist movement that appropriated Freudian ideas about the unconscious.[10] This was not particularly surprising. Both the recovered memory and the mainstream ex-gay movements concentrated on blaming parents for the problems of their children. But whereas the feminists who recovered memories of (usually) non-existent abuse during the Satanic panic and Memory Wars of the 1980s and early 1990s are largely culpable for the pressure and pain they caused their families, the same cannot be said so easily for the blame ex-gays directed at their parents. In many cases, these parents were the ones pushing LGBT people into getting deliverance sessions in the first place. Even when this was not the case, the inherent culture of the ex-gay movement, despite its outward appearance of psychotherapeutic discourse, has always been one of self-blame; this is the complete opposite of the cultural identity that was promoted by the feminist ritual abuse recovery movement of the 1980s and 1990s, which was a culture of self-exoneration even when, as with the notorious tome *The Courage to Heal,* feminists were clearly culpable for promoting deeply unscientific, nearly criminal, theories about the prevalence and means of detection of sexual abuse (see Rothe 117–118 on *Courage to Heal;* see Cuneo 204–209 on recovered memory theories).

Comiskey's organization allegedly was responsible for a case of teenage sexual abuse, a charge made more plausible by the organization's willingness to conclude the lawsuit against it in an out-of-court settlement (Besen 39). According to Peterson Toscano, a professional playwright and one of the most influential and respected survivors of the ex-gay movement, Desert Stream Ministries did exorcisms and healing prayer, complete with a belief in the influence of generational curses (Toscano; Burroway, "Surviving an Exorcism"). Again, this charge seems quite likely given Comiskey's explicit endorsement of "demonic" homosexual emotional attachments (Comiskey, *Pursuing Sexual Wholeness*, 103). With the growing upsurge against Exodus International that culminated in its recent closing, Comiskey became one of the most prominent supporters of continuing reparative therapy—this, despite the fact that his form of conversion therapy is closer to the rough-and-ready school of schlock

Pentecostal exorcism than it is to the damaging but marginally more scientifically aspiring reparative models offered up by the mainstream of the reparative therapy movement (Rattigan).

Highley's organization, Life Ministries, is largely famous for her infamous appearance in the documentary *One Nation Under God* (1993), in which she stated that she has the ability to "cleanse and bind demonic powers ... out of genitals, of course out of anal canals, out of intestines, out of throats and mouths if there's been ungodly deposit of semen in those areas—we cleanse with the blood of Jesus, and we cast out the demonic powers" (*One Nation Under God*). Highley's Life Ministries promotes the idea, consistent with more traditional reparative therapy, that "the primary cause of homosexuality is ungodly reaction to pain in childhood" (Robert Schaeffer). The ministry also draws inspiration from one of the earliest supporters of deliverance in the 20th century, Jesse Penn-Lewis, a fundamentalist who was at the forefront of normalizing deliverance practice within a limited number of fundamentalist churches (Collins 120; Robert Schaeffer). Overall, however, after extensively reviewing nearly the entire article base of material that Highley has on her Web site (which is quite considerable), Highley's deliverance system—like so much of reparative therapy, deliverance theory, and biblical counseling—offers nothing more to homosexuals than a slightly exaggerated form of "pray-the-gay away" methods, only this time complete with exorcisms.

In recent years, one other theorist within the inner healing and deliverance school has gained attention: Richard Cohen. Wayne Besen's *Anything but Straight* (2003) provides an excellent dissection of Cohen's troubled past. In 1988 Cohen joined a cultic Charismatic church that, among its many bizarre practices, had indulged in "therapy sessions" in which "men, women, and children breast-fed on women who had stripped to the waist" (Besen 161). The pastor of the church claimed that this physical contact helped improve people's lives. The group eventually turned into what Besen characterizes as "an eclectic mix of puritanical Christianity, pop psychology, and survivalist dogma" (Besen 162). In 1984, three of the group's members were convicted of sexual abuse (163). Even though Cohen has since left the group, the influence of inner healing and touch therapy remains on his ministry (Besen 163). An unstable figure for even the evangelical movement to rely on, in the mid-seventies Cohen would switch between Judaism, Christianity, and the Unification church in a period of three years (Besen 166). In the late 1980s Cohen volunteered as an HIV/AIDS educator for the American Red Cross, till the Red Cross objected to his efforts to proselytize sick AIDS patients (Besen 169).[11]

Cohen, who aims for "mainstream" respectability in the ex-gay movement, is a follower of Moberly and does borrow eclectically from Moberly's writings (Besen 170). But Moberly appears positively cautious compared to the work of Cohen. Besen, no friend of ex-gay therapy, sees Cohen's book as the "most well-written ex-gay book ever published" (Besen 171). Besen is actually too generous here. While Cohen's vocabulary and rhetorical skills may impress the average lay reader, his work resembles Ed Smith's theophostic prayer ministry (with which it shares fellow roots) in its appeal to a mind-numbingly large number of steps before true healing can commence (Cohen 63–101). Similarly, as Besen notes, Cohen's theory also relies on a wide variety of possible causes for homosexual behavior—many of which are conveniently clinically unverifiable—such as hypersensitivity, "divorce, a death in the family, and adoption" (Besen 173).

Cohen's work relies on inner child therapy as a "key part" of its curative process (Besen 184). Cohen, basing his work on Payne, promotes the bizarre idea that homosexuality can result from "painful intrauterine experiences" (Cohen 51; Besen 184). Cohen has also promulgated the idea that he can help bring men back to the womb during therapy and thus help them leave homosexuality (Besen 184). Elizabeth Loftus, perhaps the United States' most respected memory expert and a major critic of the recovered and repressed memory movement, bluntly told Besen that "few if any respected psychologists would believe these [memories brought up by Cohen] are authentic memories" (Besen 185). Another of Cohen's methods is called bioenergetics, which can help people recover lost feelings by beating a pillow with a tennis racquet. Cohen believes that "many people never learned how to express the feeling of anger in healthy ways, or the family of origin rejected the expression of this feeling. The person who thinks that anger is unacceptable needs to understand that this is a natural God-given emotion" (Cohen 176–177; Besen 186). Cohen has also argued that the spirits of dead ancestors can seek revenge for wounds inflicted upon them (Cohen 188).

Because Cohen's therapeutic regimen is so radical, his professional credentials so flimsy, and his public reputation among both nonevangelicals and evangelicals so notorious, his influence over the ex-gay movement has not been as great as it could have been. But Cohen's work shows just how flimsy the line between "professional" reparative therapist, inner healer, and exorcist is. Cohen's practice is clearly shaped more by the New Age–like teachings of the Inner Healing movement, with their flimsy (often nonexistent) grounding in mainstream science, than by any appeal to professional psychological research. But so desperate is the evangelical right for any talking head that will support conversion therapy that the movement is willing even to endorse a therapist like Cohen, despite the fact that his therapeutic system is built on a number of ideas (not just reparative therapy, but recovered memory work and inner healing prayer as well) that have come under heavy criticism from the professional scientific community for decades. That Cohen retains any relevance at all in the continued debate about counseling methods in the evangelical church shows just how shamefully all the major evangelical therapeutic and healing schools—deliverance ministries, biblical counseling, and reparative therapy— have treated the LGBT community. That this maltreatment continues even as the most prominent ex-gay ministries continue to lose members, even fold entirely (as in the case of Exodus International), speaks to the enduring power of homophobia to shape evangelical cultural policy. As this book has shown, the evangelical community has enough truly mentally ill individuals—people who could use real therapy and real psychological help—without performing unnecessary and harmful hate treatment on LGBT people. It is those mentally ill individuals who need to stick up for their fellow evangelical Christians in the gay community. For if they do not, who else will?

Conclusion

Reparative therapy was birthed in professional psychology and professional psychology does, as we will see in the next chapter, actually exist within evangelicalism. But while its methodology is somewhat better than that of the truly alternative forms of evangelical therapy, its track record does not imbue mental health treatment seekers with much confidence. Whether professional Christian psychology can save mentally ill, LGBT, and female evangelical sufferers from the oppression they have undergone over the last forty years continues to remain a very open question.

8

Integrationism and
the Popularizers

Up to this point, aside from those engaged in psychologically based reparative therapy, most of the people discussed in this book have not had professional degrees in psychiatry and psychology; even if they did, they were often (as in the case of many biblical counselors with such degrees) vigorously opposed to professional psychiatry and the concept of mental illness. In this chapter, we will discuss the area of professional evangelical psychology. To this point, there is no unified school of evangelical professional psychology. Rather, there are a number of smaller divisions within the field. Broadly speaking, there are three schools of thought. The most well-known school is integrationism. The term is so often used by biblical counselors and even many supporters of Christian psychology that many people have to come to believe it is the only known school of Christian psychology. The integrationist school is difficult to define, but roughly it seeks to combine the best of psychological and Christian approaches without sacrificing truth in either area (see Collins, "Moving Through the Jungle," 34). However, unlike more secularized forms of evangelical psychotherapy, integrationism tends to be more willing to criticize secular psychotherapy (Johnson and Jones, "A History," 39), especially if a secular therapeutic practice is seen as conflicting with scripture. Popular Christian integrationists over the last forty years include Frank Minirth, Paul Meir, and the immensely influential James Dobson (arguably the most powerful evangelical of the last two decades) (see Johnson and Jones, "A History," 39).

The second school of thought is the "levels of explanation" approach, also known as perspectivalism. This approach attempts to highlight the difference between "the domains (or 'levels') of psychology and theology" (Johnson and Jones 37). This group, arguing that there are different levels of reality, contends that it confuses things to try to combine theology and psychology because these two fields have "different objects of study and answer different questions. Confusing them would distort both" (Johnson and Jones 38).

Because of this viewpoint, perspectivalists tend to be less concerned about the effects of secularism on psychology (Johnson and Jones 38). Though it is by no means perfect, this school of thought also seems to be most concerned with maintaining academic and scientific integrity, even if this brings them into conflict with the mainstream of the evangelical psychotherapeutic establishment. Perhaps the most influential perspectivalist is David G. Myers.

The third and last school is the "Christian psychology" model. Unlike biblical counseling, purveyors of this model believe that it is permissible to have a Christian psychology, but that this psychology should be based on Christian and not secular principles. Therefore, it tends to distinguish itself against the more accommodationist integrationist and the more secular-influenced perspectivalist approaches. Philosopher C. Stephan Evans, therapist Dan Allender, and particularly some of the later writings of Larry Crabb, are identified with this movement (Johnson and Jones, "A History," 40–41). In practice, however, it is often hard to tell integrationists and "Christian psychology" supporters apart, so it is best to distinguish mainly between integrationists and perspectivalists, where the differences in ideology are more severe.

In addition to these distinctions, there is obviously a large output of evangelical pop psychology and a number of quite idiosyncratic counseling techniques. Charles R. Solomon's spirituotherapy combined Freudian ideas with a view of sin only imperceptibly more sympathetic to the mentally ill than that of Jay Adams. June Hunt's *Hope to the Heart* program reaches millions with a small dose of Christian pop psychology and a large dose of her own form of "biblical counseling" (which does not seem to be particularly related to the Jay Adams model). Then there is William Backus's popularization of the "Sin Scale," an idea that literally seems to argue that the mentally ill are more predisposed to certain forms of immorality than neuronormatives (Backus, *What Your Counselor Never Told You,* loc 243–245). Indeed, in many ways Backus's "Sin Scale," which attempts to provide scientific legitimacy to prejudice against the mentally ill, is far worse than Adams's biblical counseling model. While Adams very likely believes the same things about the mentally ill that Backus did, Adams at least never had the desire to try to scientifically legitimize those prejudices.

It is impossible in this one chapter to cover every model of Christian psychology. What I seek to do in the chapter is provide a historical overview of these movements, along with some background on some of the major players in "professional" (i.e., secularly certified) Christian counseling and Christian pop psychology. As we will see, the boundaries between pop expert and professional, Christian psychologist and Adams-loving biblical counselor, are often far more narrow than one might think.

History of Christian Counseling

Traditional Christian psychology emerged during the 1950s as a fusion of two distinct traditions: the neo-evangelical movement of Carl F. Henry and E.J. Carnell and the Dutch Reformed tradition, a form of Reformed Christianity which has tended to stand in a middle road between theological modernism and the more revivalist impulses of evangelical, Charismatic, and fundamentalist churches (Kinghorn 26). One of the earliest attempts at such integration occurred when Hildreth Cross in 1952 published *An Introduction to Psychology: An Evangelical Approach.* Relatively simplistic, this text included many citations from the Bible and criticisms of evolution, in addition to providing a somewhat superficial overview of mainstream science concerning the nervous system, perception, and learning (Johnson and Jones, "A History," 34–35). During the mid–1950s, groups of Christian psychologists got together for conferences "that explored the relation of psychology, psychiatry and religion" (Johnson and Jones 35). This led to the formation of the Christian Association for Psychological Studies (CAPS) in 1956. This organization continues to hold conferences about faith's relationship with counseling and has long since dropped a solely Reformed identity (Johnson and Jones 35).

Also, in the mid 1950s (1954), Clyde Narramore started a radio show called *Psychology for Living*, which eventually played on more than two hundred Christian radio stations nationally. In 1960, Narramore published *The Psychology of Counseling.* This work, one of the most influential texts in the history of Christian counseling, outlined an evangelical approach to therapy that incorporated Christian ideas and conservative hermeneutics with a modified form of Carl Rogers' person-centered therapy. Donald F. Tweedie, meanwhile, wrote the book *Logotherapy and the Christian Faith* (1961), which was—though not uncritically—supportive of the logotherapy methodology of Viktor Frankl (Johnson and Jones 35, 52).

By the mid-sixties many evangelicals began to think that there was a need for advanced training in psychology from a distinctively Christian viewpoint. In 1964, Fuller Theological Seminary became the first evangelical school to begin a doctoral program in clinical psychology. Rosemead School of Psychology followed soon after (1970), this time with prompting from Clyde Narramore and under the leadership and guidance of Bruce Narramore, Clyde's nephew. In 1973, Rosemead initiated the *Journal of Psychology and Theology*, giving evangelical academics and counselors an academic outlet for publishing. By the early 1970s an increasing number of evangelicals began writing works on counseling or modern psychology, ranging from Gary Collins to Robert Schuller (see Powlison, *The Biblical Counseling Movement*, 52).

In 1973, Narramore was joined by John Carter, whom David Powlison sees as one of the most significant critics of biblical counseling and certainly one of the best theoreticians of integrationism (Powlison 52). Carter would become famous for his typology of the relationship between psychology and Christian theology, derived from Richard Niebuhr's similar typology outlined in *Christ and Culture* (1951). Carter would relabel some of Niebuhr's models, eventually creating four secular models of psychology with four corresponding Christian models. Only the fourth model, psychology-integrates-religion and the scripture-integrates-psychology, remained viable for Carter (Stevenson, "Introduction," 4). To this day, Carter's typology represents one of the most sophisticated attempts to meaningfully define and map out the various schools of Christian counseling, as well as their relationship to the secular world.

In 1980, Gary Collins's "Big Yellow Book," *Christian Counseling,* was published (Clinton and Ohlschlager, "Competent Christian Counseling: Definitions and Dynamics," 41). The work would serve as the foundational text for the integrationist movement. Collins's text was followed by a flurry of activity in the Christian psychology and counseling scene. Christian institutions developed a number of new psychology programs, including one at the influential evangelical flagship school, Wheaton College (Johnson and Jones, "A History," 39). Self-help and recovery books became popular. In addition, there were soon Christian counseling and treatment centers flooding America. Due to the fact that CAPS was becoming more open to theologically liberal ideas, a breakaway group of Christian counselors decided to form the more conservative American Association of Christian Counselors (AACC). By the early 1990s Frank Minirth and Paul Meier's Minirth-Meier clinics had spread nationwide, with 25 treatment centers. Meanwhile, Rapha, founded by Southern Baptist psychotherapist Robert McGee, operated 32 programs in 17 hospitals. The Minirth-Meier model spread across the country and marketed itself for numerous problems (Powlison 203). In 1994, Minirth-Meier would merge with New Life Treatment Centers, further extending their reach (Powlison 204).

In recent years, two developments in professional Christian counseling have been particularly significant. The first is the new community model being offered by Larry Crabb. Crabb has long been one of the most conservative of Christian psychologists. His work attempts to bridge the gap between traditional biblical counseling and nouthetics and integrationism, combing the "best elements" of both (Clinton "Competent Christian Counseling: Definitions and Dynamics" 46). Crabb's counseling methodology, which will be discussed in much more detail later in the chapter, focuses on community as a center of healing (Clinton, "Competent Christian Counseling: Definitions and Dynamics," 46), much as Catholic programs of the past focused on spiritual instruction.[1] Crabb's widespread popularity should be cause for concern among those aiming for an ethical evangelical psychotherapy, as it is often difficult to discern precisely where his methodology differs from traditional biblical counseling.

Perhaps the most significant, original work of Christian counseling theory in recent years has been Eric L. Johnson's monumental *Foundations for Soul Care* (2007). His psychotherapeutic methodology combines traditional integrationist ideas with a highly idiosyncratic and original Christian take on the combination of evangelical theology, integrationist psychology, and semiotics. His work is intensely concerned with discourse—both our own internal discourse and how God's discourse affects us. Unlike many other, more sloppy, integrationist and "Christian psychology" writers, Johnson takes seriously not only the ideas of integrationism, but the criticisms of both secular and evangelical opponents of traditional evangelical psychotherapy (particularly the biblical counseling movement). Therefore he offers guidelines for what he sees as the "translation" tasks of integrationist psychology. Johnson encourages Christian psychologists to approach secular psychology as translators, not simply interpreters, realizing that the discursive practices of both fields essentially represent separate languages. As translators, these therapists and therapeutic writers will then be able to tell when secular psychological texts are corrupting the native dialect system of evangelical Christianity (Johnson 220–235).

Johnson's work is in many ways quite brilliant. Not since Jay Adams published *Competent to Counsel* (1970) has there been an evangelical counseling text that so distinctly bears the mark of its author's own internally derived ideas. But there is also danger in Johnson's work, because his system tends to much more closely integrate questionable ideas from the nouthetic and conservative end of the integrationist model to Christian counseling than does the much more scientifically-oriented, but systematically underdeveloped perspectivalist position. Nevertheless, Johnson's work perhaps should be more commended for its attempt to achieve true authorial originality than condemned for its admitted but also limited flaws.

Where does evangelical psychology stand on individual secular psychotherapeutic systems? And how, in their methodologies, do science and faith interact? In large part, what secular models are favored depends on which individual evangelical psychotherapist or school of psychotherapy one is talking about. This is largely due to the fact that most evangelical psychotherapists, with the noted exception of Eric Johnson, have not really tried to create a distinctively original psychotherapeutic system, instead relying on an eclectic mix of Christian and secular methods (Clinton and Ohlschlager, "Competent Christian Counseling: Definitions and Dynamics," 48).

Perhaps the most comprehensive overview of Christian psychology's concerns about secular psychotherapies occurs in Stanton Jones's and Richard Butman's *Modern Psychotherapies* (1991), an influential text used by both perspectivalists and integrationists. A crucial point for Butman and Jones, as for most integrationists, was the issue of revelation. According to Butman and Jones, the Bible is "an essential foundation for a Christian approach to psychotherapy" but is not "an all sufficient guide for the discipline of counseling" (Jones and Butman 27). The popular manifestation of this idea, often repeated (and quite often criticized) within the integrationist movement is "all truth is God's truth" (Tan 197). Thus the integrationist movement, and even more so perspectivalists, assumed a priori that psychological truth would ultimately line up with evangelicalism's interpretation of scripture.

Therefore, if there were discrepancies between the fields of Christian theology and psychology, they were caused either by an inadequate understanding of psychology or a hermeneutical misunderstanding of scripture (Jones and Butman 28). However, perspectivalists and integrationists would tend to differ on how to approach these discrepancies. Integrationists typically believe, in the words of Lawrence Crabb, that the most important duty of a Christian counselor is to "screen secular concepts through the filter of Scripture" (Eck 233). Integrationists are more likely therefore tend to pick and choose what elements of secular therapy they support, depending on whether or not these therapeutic methodologies line up with Christian theological truth. Often, this means rejecting research when it conflicts with scripture (Eck 232–233). The most widely used metaphor for this model of approaching scientific truth among integrationists is "Spoiling the Egyptians," a phrase we will return to in discussing the work of evangelical psychologist Larry Crabb.

The individual school of secular psychotherapy that Christians are most likely not to want to claim to "spoil from" is classic psychoanalysis. According to Butman and Jones, there are three main concerns about this therapy in conservative Christian circles: "(1) the emphasis on sex and aggression as motivational bases for behavior (2) the deterministic and naturalistic assumptions of the model; and (3) the direct attacks on religion Freud made in his later writings" (Jones and Butman 65). Like most evangelical psychologists, Butman and Jones tend to have a more complex view of Freud than the rather simplistic vision of him offered up by biblical counselors.[2] Whereas biblical counselors tend to see Freudianism as having a relatively lax view of human nature, Jones and Butman persuasively—and accurately—point out that Freudian psychology hardly sees human beings as intrinsically good. Instead, its dark reading of human nature "is much closer to biblical reality than romantic humanism [here meaning humanistic therapies]" (Jones and Butman 81). Jones and Butman are more concerned that traditional psychoanalysis can lead to a form of Gnosticism in which knowledge of self is the primary means of "self-salvation" (Jones and Butman 81). The *Baker Encyclopedia of Psychology and Counseling,* for a long time the alternative DSM of evangelical culture, expresses graver reservations about Freud, seeing his theory of neurosis as "inadequate" and his view of motivation as too concerned with human sexuality (S.B. Narramore, "Psychoanalytic," 936).

Behaviorism is critiqued by mainstream integrationism as well. Christian psychotherapists object to the behaviorist school primarily because of its naturalism, seeing it as "obviously" being "at odds with the Christian faith" (Jones and Butman 154–155). As with Freudian psychotherapies, Butman and Jones (and most integrationists, for that matter) are concerned with the deterministic nature of behaviorism (155). Like biblical counselors, Butman and Jones fear that accepting a deterministic model of human behavior will lead to a rejection of the notion of personal responsibility. Thus, to a Christian, regardless of whether they are Arminian or Calvinist, limited human freedom to make decisions is a necessity of belief (Butman and Jones 157). Butman and Jones express fear that behaviorism, in reducing human beings to a series of behaviors, essentially throws out the concept of morality entirely (162). Nevertheless they admit that behavioral therapy does have some psychotherapeutic uses, particularly for children and those for whom "verbal discussion is an ineffective impetus for change" (Butman 170). R.K. Bufford, in *The Baker Encyclopedia* raises many similar objections, charging as well that behavioral therapy too easily succumbs to an evolutionary worldview and is prone to "scientism" (Bufford 129).[3] In all likelihood, as with biblical counselors, part of the strident objections to behaviorism voiced by some members of the integrationist and Christian psychology communities likely result from the realization that many of the therapeutic and indoctrinatory principles used by Christian counselors of all stripes (professional or not, integrationist, perspectivalist, or biblical counselor) are implicitly behaviorist in practice, if not explicitly so in public orientation.

Space prevents me from describing the standard integrationist, Christian psychology, or perspectivalist viewpoint of every school of secular psychotherapy, but brief mention should at least be made of their approach to the person-centered therapy of Carl Rogers, often seen by evangelicals as the face of humanistic psychology. Although appreciative of certain elements of humanistic therapy, Butman and Jones are concerned with what they see as its emphasis on self and its emphasis on personal wholeness to the expense of other-centered ethics. This criticism, again, is one shared by biblical counselors, and it must be said it is not entirely inaccurate when applied to some of the popularizers of humanist psychology in the seventies and eighties (Butman and Jones 262–263). The *Baker Encyclopedia* sees humanistic psychology as particularly dangerous for Christians because of its superficially "seductive pull" to those with theistic beliefs. As H.A. Van Belle points out, humanistic therapy helped to reduce the "antispiritual, materialistic, and reductionistic grip of psychoanalysis and behaviorism on psychology." However, humanistic psychology also leads to a "subjectivistic, pantheistic, and world-denying spiritualism in which wholeness is the highest good to be attained" (Belle, "Humanistic Psychology," 590).

In the final analysis, from a theoretical standpoint, integrationist—and to a lesser extent perspectivalist—criticisms of traditional psychotherapy are not always all that dissimilar from objections lodged against it by biblical counselors. What distinguishes them from the biblical counseling model is not their criticisms of traditional psychotherapy but their words of (often cautious) support. Coming from a more diversified background than the largely Reformed biblical counseling movement, integrationists and perspectivalists cannot afford to offend anyone. Therefore, as a movement, integrationists and their allies tend to be cautious in their assessment of theological and secular foes alike. While this has proved to be a savvy move politically, it has also led to charges of theological eclecticism (from the biblical counseling movement) and of moral spinelessness. The latter charge, in particular, is hard to refute, particularly when one looks in depth at the therapeutic practices integrationists have been willing to countenance over the years. For instance, Tim Clinton's and George Ohlschlager's *Competent Christian Counseling* (2002), a major Christian psychology text, rather than simply telling therapists outright they should not practice deliverance, cult deprogramming, recovered memory therapy, or reparative therapy—practices all largely seen as unscientific or unethical or both by the scientific community—instead suggests that therapists "require a more detailed discussion with patient-clients or client representatives" outlining the "procedures, risks and treatment alternatives" concerned with these practices. After this, the therapist should secure a "detailed written agreement for the procedure" (Clinton and George Ohlschlager, "The Ethical Helping Relationship," 261).

In short, what Clinton and his fellow writers are concerned about is legal liability, not the safety of the patient. Nor is this some isolated event. Clinton, who was president of the influential American Association of Christian Counselors (AACC) (which claims to be the "largest and most diverse Christian counseling association in the world"), in many ways the Christian equivalent of the American Psychiatric Association (though admitting pastoral and lay counselors as well as psychiatrists and psychologists), endorses outright David Appleby's deliverance manual, *It's Only a Demon* (Appleby, Endorsements; Clinton and Ohlschlager, *Competent Christian Counseling*, back dustjacket).[4] This would be like the head of the APA endorsing an exorcism manual, to give one some idea of how truly weird Clinton's actions were.

The Baker Encyclopedia of Psychology and Counseling is even more explicit in its promotion of deliverance, speculating openly on the best means of distinguishing between demonic possession and actual mental illness, completely rejecting the idea that the demonism portrayed in the New Testament might simply refer to psychiatric or neurological conditions (or a form of acted out religious performance as we have seen Levack suggest) (such as schizophrenia or epilepsy) (Virkler 326). The manual even counsels evangelical therapists on how to minimize their risk of legal liability when performing deliverances (Virkler 332), itself a seemingly unethical behavior.

Integrationists and perspectivalists typically tend to have a more sympathetic attitude toward the mentally ill than do biblical counselors, but there are important and quite major exceptions to this. Larry Crabb, though not quite as extreme as Jay Adams, is hardly a progressive on mental health issues. William Backus, as mentioned previously, was even more critical of the mentally ill than were the most extreme elements of the biblical counseling movement. June Hunt's counseling methodology, though covered in this chapter, is in many ways much closer to the overtly biblicist approach of Jay Adams and his disciples than it is to traditional psychotherapy; her views on mental illness, though more compassionate than those of Adams and his allies, are nevertheless not primarily informed by secular standards of counseling practice. Frank Minirth's therapeutic practice, at least as conveyed in works like *Happiness Is a Choice* (1978), seems to be fairly harsh. Similarly, the advice manuals of evangelical author Tim LaHaye (who in his early life was a kind of pop psychology promoter), though they could broadly be considered integrationist, are, like William Backus's works, very negative in their orientation to the mentally ill, particularly the depressed.

To get a better idea of the breadth and scope of integrationism and Christian pop psychology, in the next section I will discuss a number of prominent integrationists, both popularizers and respected professionals. But it is best to start at the beginning. And the beginning of Christian psychotherapy is Clyde Narramore.

Major Christian Psychology Figures: From Skilled Specialists to Sin-Scale Promoters

Clyde Narramore almost single-handedly founded the modern Christian psychology movement. As Powlison points out, Narramore was the "first well-known author, speaker and counseling practitioner who was certifiably both a psychologist and a conservative Protestant" (Powlison, *The Biblical Counseling Movement,* 27). Even Powlison admits that Narramore's Narramore Christian Foundation "provided a vehicle for publicizing mental health needs" as well as "distributing self-help literature, training pastors and other Christian workers, and offering counseling services" (27). Narramore was the institutional guru behind the formation of the Christian integrationist movement. Because of that, his influence over the movement has been underestimated. As Gary Collins points out quite correctly, Narramore's "contribution has been lost in discussions of integration, perhaps because he was not a scholar writing for professional publications" (Collins, "An Integration View," 104). As the first important voice in the integrationist movement, Narramore's role was largely that of a popularizer, someone who would make psychology "respectable" for evangelical Christians (Collins 104).

Susan Myers-Shirk, in her otherwise excellent study of twentieth-century pastoral counseling,[5] tends to elide the theoretical differences between Narramore, Jay Adams, and evangelical popularizer Tim LaHaye over the issue of mental illness. While it is correct, as Myers-Shirk asserts, to point out the similarities between Narramore's assertion that the majority of Christians with problems were "not letting Christ control their actions" and Adams's association of mental illness with sin, there is a considerable difference in both the tone and the substance of Nararmore's critique of the mentally ill (Susan Myers-Shirk loc 4331). Narramore's *The Psychology of Counseling* (1960) is much more cautious in its approach to mental illness than Adams's work, and for every criticism of the mentally ill or other pathologized groups (notably homosexuals) Narramore offers words of encouragement to the mentally ill. Indeed, compared to many later integrationist works, *The Psychology of Counseling* is refreshingly unambiguous about mental illness, advising counselors to "accept his [the mentally ill person's] illness as a natural condition for him" (179). Significantly, as well, Narramore does not accept any Szaszian definition of psychiatric conditions, arguing that "the most important thing to do is realize that mental illness is truly an illness" (167).

What ultimately separated Narramore and later integrationists (and even more so perspectivalists, who were even less charitable to the biblical counseling model) from the biblical counseling/nouthetic model was not the idea that sin could cause mental illness. Integrationists readily conceded this could sometimes be the case (see Bixler 1124–1125). Rather, what separated the two movements was the fact that the nouthetic/biblical counseling movement made this assumption a priori in all cases of "non-biological" mental health conditions. Even more fundamentally, integrationists believed in an illness model in relation to psychiatric conditions, whereas the nouthetics movement believed the illness model was fundamentally in error.

There are many ironies implicit in this relationship. First, despite the fact that the integrationists' arguments were better grounded in the science of their day and would largely be seen as more palatable to contemporary members of the medical and scientific community, from a philosophical and theological standpoint Adams arguably was asking deeper and more penetrating questions about the nature of mental health pathologization. For just as the biblical counseling movement had its presuppositionalist a priori assumptions, so did the integrationist movement: And foremost of those assumptions was the unquestioned presupposition that mental illness was a pathology. Admittedly, it was a pathology for which they did not typically blame the mentally ill, but it was a pathology none the less. This assumption, shared by the secular psychiatric establishment, while probably necessary if patients were to receive effective mental health treatment, failed to note the stigma-inducing effects of psychiatric pathologization of mental health conditions. Nor did Narramore meaningfully confront the very real psychiatric abuses of the 1950s and 1960s such as aversion therapy, reparative therapy, and insulin coma therapy (ICT). Indeed, Narramore himself helps perpetuate the psychoanalytic explanation of homosexuality in *The Psychology of Counseling,* a model that would later be adapted, either wittingly or not, by the reparative therapists of the eighties and early nineties such as Elizabeth Moberly (Narramore, *Psychology of Counseling*, 210–211).

Narramore's effect on Christian counseling was an ambiguous one. While his efforts were crucial in providing a space for something approaching reputable clinical treatment for the mentally ill, by setting integration rather than scientific integrity as the goal of the then infant evangelical counseling scene Narramore compromised the ability of evangelical psychotherapy to provide effective mental health care. Simply put, because integration was the goal, most integrationists—ranging from the simplistic Narramore to the proficient and brilliant Eric Johnson—became risk averse when dialoguing with (or about) the biblical counseling movement. Few integrationists (with the significant exception of Dwight L. Carlson in *Why Do Christians Shoot Their Wounded?*) proved willing to critique biblical counseling outside of their own professional journals. Even fewer found traction within the Christian publishing field when they did. This led to an often dangerously thin line between psychotherapeutic science and biblical counseling or deliverance pseudoscience. The worst integrationist offenders in this regard, notably Larry Crabb, were often virtually impossible to distinguish from the mainstream biblical counseling movement. And Narramore's efforts, though clearly wellintentioned by the standards of his culture, paved the way for a horde of psychological popularizers who had neither his ethical integrity nor scientific background.

Foremost among these popularizers was Tim LaHaye. Long before Tim LaHaye became famous as America's "apocalyptic sage," he passed himself off as an expert on psychology even though he was totally untrained in either psychology or counseling (Stephens and Giberson, loc 1179). Born in Detroit in 1926, LaHaye grew up deeply religious. After serving in World War II as a tailgunner, he came back to America and attended Bob Jones University for his undergraduate degree (Guyatt 218–219). His move to southern California in the late 1950s positioned him to be one of the key members of the religious right. At the time, the area was a beehive of political activity. Two prominent California Republicans would capture the White House within a 12 year period (Ronald Reagan and Richard Nixon, between 1968 and 1980). In addition, southern California by the early 1980s would possess such major voices as Robert Schuller, John MacArthur, Chuck Smith, and LaHaye himself, giving the area an influence among evangelicals that until this day it has not entirely lost (Guyatt 219).

By the early 1960s, LaHaye was allying himself with the John Birch Society and giving speeches at their training seminars (Guyatt 220). Although his initial encounters with the John Birch Society (JBS) were not entirely pleasant (the JBS thought LaHaye was too prone to depoliticizing their members), these encounters, as well as a bruising struggle with the San Diego city council, spurred LaHaye into political activism (Guyatt 220–222). In the 1970s, LaHaye would successfully juggle his skills as a prophecy author, Christian pop psychology advocate, and political figure, producing over a dozen books on issues ranging from Noah's Ark to an "eye-wateringly explicit Christian sex manual called *The Act of Marriage*" (Guyatt 230).[6] In 1978, LaHaye would publish *The Unhappy Gays* (1978), one of the most influential pieces of antigay literature to emerge in the wake of Anita Bryant's successful discrimination campaign against LGBT individuals in Florida. LaHaye used the political and social capital he had gained among evangelical fans of pop psychology in his book *Transformed Temperaments* (1971) as a rationale for arguing for the inferiority of homosexuals, using rhetoric that (not surprisingly) came straight out of psychoanalytic descriptions of overbearing mothers and submissive fathers (Guyatt 231–233).

By the early 1980s, LaHaye's role as a founding member of the Moral Majority placed him in a vaunted position among evangelical Christians. But it was his book *The Battle for the Mind* (1980), in some ways superficially a less psychological work than his earlier *Spirit Controlled Temperament* (1966), that paved the way for the politicization of evangelical counseling so successfully undertaken in the eighties and nineties by the ex-gay movement and Focus on the Family. LaHaye's work, which will be discussed in detail in the following pages, popularized Francis Schaeffer's concept of Christian worldview theory (Martin 196). His work was vitally important. First, it was able to convey Schaeffer's complex prose into readable, accessible form. In particular, it took the figure of the "secular humanist," a dangerous but tragic figure in Schaeffer's worldview theory, and turned him into the bogeyman of the Christian right.

To LaHaye and those who followed in his footsteps, secular humanists were engaging in a conspiracy to gain "control of the nation's social institutions, the most important of which was the public schools" (LaHaye, *Battle for the Mind*, 55). What makes this work, indeed LaHaye's entire oeuvre, significant in the history of evangelical counseling practices is that LaHaye's writing specifically incorporated his particular reading of human psychology as a foundational element in understanding the secular humanist conspiracy. Though that model was simplistic, its very simplicity made it an effective tool in conveying complex psychological truths to the evangelical masses. However, LaHaye's efforts also encouraged other Christian counselors, both in the biblical counseling and mainstream psychological schools (integrationism, perspectivalism, etc.) to interpret their clients as political signifiers, even political weapons. At its most reprehensible, as in the campaigns to promote the ex-gay movement as an alternative to legalized same-sex marriage, the evangelical movement would use LGBT, mentally ill, and female evangelical clients as political tokens to prove the supremacy of evangelical values, with little regard to these clients' actual physical well-being.

LaHaye, perhaps, did not realize this when he wrote his first book on counseling, the *Spirit-Controlled Temperament* (1966). As Stephens and Giberson wryly and all too correctly note, in this work LaHaye "retreaded truly ancient ground" (Stephens and Giberson loc 1180). Essentially, LaHaye merely updated Hippocrates, arguing that there were four main human temperaments (Stephens and Giberson loc 1178–1182). LaHaye did not judge any one temperament as inherently superior or inferior (though in his later work *How to Win Over Depression,* it is hard to resist the interpretation that he has an implicit prejudice against melancholics). Each contained strengths and weaknesses (LaHaye, *Spirit-Controlled Temperament*, 22–23). LaHaye argued that a truly effective Christian, whatever the inherent natural temperament, could develop an effective, Christianized personality by replacing the inherent temperament with a "Holy Spirit-filled temperament" (LaHaye 45). This supernatural temperament did "not have weaknesses; instead it has nine all-encompassing strengths" (LaHaye 45). These traits were love, joy, peace, long-suffering, gentleness, goodness, faith, meekness, and self-control (LaHaye 45–55).

There are a number of major problems with *The Spirit Controlled Temperament* which would almost immediately classify the work as pseudoscientific, even if this were not obvious by the lack of attention paid to careful footnoting and research. The first is simply the idea of temperament scales serving as the sole basis of one's understanding of human personality. LaHaye goes so far as to talk about percentages of personality types (LaHaye 11), essentially dividing human beings into four-pronged entities of sanguine, choleric, phlegmic, and melancholic (five-pronged for the Christian who is spirit-filled). Essentially, LaHaye's personality theory turns every human being into not one individual but a composite of four individuals within one being, making his version of the human psyche even more confusing than the now discredited Freudian tripartite personality. Worse, how would one test what personalities are and are not spirit-filled? LaHaye does not provide direction in this regard. Nor is it clear why traits such as "love ... joy ... peace ... and self-control" (LaHaye, *Spirit Filled*, 45–56) should automatically prevail over more supposedly "negative" emotions. LaHaye's psychological system, like most of the therapeutic systems offered up by evangelical pop psychologists, deliverance ministers, inner healers, and positive psychologists, focuses largely on accenting the "positive" emotions, promoting a "joy-centric" view of human identity that privileges happiness and marginalizes those who either cannot be happy or those who see some value in human suffering and sadness.

Given this theoretical background, it is not surprising that LaHaye promotes the idea that depression is the result of "self-pity." According to LaHaye, "the truth of the matter is, a person becomes depressed only after a period of indulging in the sin of self-pity. I have questioned hundreds of individuals who were depressed and have yet to find an exception to this rule" (LaHaye, *Spirit Filled Temperament*, 106). Again, LaHaye provides no scientific backing for this assertion, instead relying on personal experience. Lacking the understanding of psychology possessed by the mainstream integrationist or biblical counseling movements, he relies on a canard that Jay Adams might have found simplistic. Even if self-pity is a causal factor in depression—and how would one ascertain that fact?—it is debatable of what use that information is to a true psychologist or even pastoral counselor, since the counselor still must determine the causal factors of that self-pity, *which may be biological in origin.*

Perhaps the most unscientific and reprehensible idea, however, that LaHaye promotes is the concept of national and racial temperaments:

> Since temperament traits are received genetically from our parents and hence are unpredictable, one should keep in mind some of the character factors that influence temperament. Nationality and race certainly play a part in one's inherited tempera-ment. We use such expressions as, "an excitable nationality," "an industrious nation-ality," "a cold nationality," to describe what seems to be apparent [LaHaye 6].

Again, even at that time, the concept of race as a scientific category was under-going increasing critical scrutiny, which any competent counselor—indeed, any college-educated individual—should have been aware of. While certain cultures may produce distinctive differences in temperament, there is no proof that such links are racial in origin. One can only speculate why LaHaye would argue for such a racialized psychology, but given his history as a Bob Jones graduate (a school long famous for its racial prejudice), the time at which *The Spirit Controlled Temperament* was written (the racially charged mid-sixties), his actions on behalf of a largely racist Christian right movement in the ensuing decades, the often implicitly if not explicitly racist character of the *Left Behind* series (which LaHaye co-wrote), and his connections with the historically para-noid and often anti–Semitic John Birch Society, it does not seem to be a stretch to speculate that some racial animus may have been involved in LaHaye's analy-sis of racial temperaments. Whatever the case, the concept has no place in psy-chological science, which makes it disturbing that LaHaye's influence over popular Christian perceptions of psychology was as wide as it was.

Another of LaHaye's major works of pop psychology, *How to Win Over Depression* (1974), initialized the process of LaHaye's politicization of psychol-ogy. Though the work is still largely a self-help manual, LaHaye also ventured into theorizing on how the "occult" and contemporary music might be causing depression (LaHaye, *How to Win Over Depression*, 180–191). These topics, though perhaps apolitical to a secular audience, were part of an evolving Chris-tian fear of secular culture and were particularly responsible for the virulent "worship wars" that began in the 1970s, which pitted rock-loving, primarily Charismatic and seeker-sensitive Christians against an older, more traditional, and largely fundamentalist Christian audience that fully rejected all forms of contemporary music. LaHaye's positioning of himself on the side of orthodoxy thus assured him of a respectful hearing from concerned Christian parents when he finally did decide to totally politicize his psychological system.

Aside from his comments on the occult and music, there was little truly new in *How to Win Over Depression,* as the book largely merely expanded on the theme of self-pity developed in the *Spirit-Controlled Temperament*. One important point LaHaye wants to make clear in *How to Win Over Depression* is his theory of volition:

> Your will can determine what new material you put into your mind, but it cannot govern your attitude toward the old material, nor can it fully regulate the mind. This is particularly true of the subconscious, which cannot be controlled by the will directly, but may be influenced through the imagination. The governor of your mind is the imagination. As the imagination goes, so goes the mind, both conscious and subconscious.... Only by projecting wholesome and positive images on the screen of your imagination will you rise above the inadequate view of yourself that ensnares most people [LaHaye, *How to Win Over Depression*, 126].

LaHaye's theory of will, while promoting a voluntaristic attitude towards happiness (happiness is one's personal responsibility), also warns against the danger of giving the will, in the form of the imagination, too-free rein. Because the imagination has such a powerful influence over human imaging processes, LaHaye fears that, when directed wrongly, it can lead to an inadequate, depression-inducing view of self. Given his view of the occult and contemporary Christian music, both fields that have often been associated with excessive imagination by members of the Christian right (particularly fundamentalists), it is also likely that LaHaye views the imagination as a potentially dangerous tool when not used properly, especially for the teenagers and young adults most likely (in his eyes) to get involved in "rebellious" and "occultic" activities. It is not an uncommon occurrence in the Christian right, even today, to hear parents and adults associating interest in creative ideas as a doorway to the occult. Indeed, so pervasive is the fear of imagination-induced mental illness that this phobia produced one of the great unsung cultural hysterias of the 1980s, the aforementioned role-playing game panic (Waldron). It should be noted here how different LaHaye's theory of the imagination is from Francis Schaeffer's. While Schaeffer was by evangelical standards a lover of high culture who encouraged imagination whenever he could, LaHaye represented a different strain of evangelical belief that was deeply fearful of imaginative people and the potential psychological and disciplinary problems they presented the church.

LaHaye's psychological theory receives its fullest expression, however, in *The Battle for the Mind* (1980), in which he uses popular concepts of emerging neuroscience and psychology to promote his vision of a new Christian social order. For LaHaye, the brain is "the most complex mechanism in the world and the most influential organ of your body. It accounts for your ability to think remember, love, hate, feel, reason, imagine and analyze" (LaHaye 13). He promotes an idea of the mind's functioning that has some similarities with faculty psychology. According to LaHaye, the mind's main function is housing "memory" as well as "intuition, conscience, sexuality and many other things" (LaHaye, *Battle for the Mind*, 15).

For LaHaye, a crucial area of concern for Christians is the brain's ability to learn. He sees the conscious mind, subconscious mind, and imagination as the most important elements of the brain (15). And it is here that he begins incorporating a distinctive vision of Christian right pedagogical and psychological ideology. LaHaye believes that "the eyes and ears" play a crucial role in communicating concepts to one's brain, and how one employs them "determines how you think (your philosophy of life)" (LaHaye 16). His psychology therefore focuses heavily on the dangers of putting faulty, primarily secular data into the Christian's mind. While LaHaye does acknowledge the existence of nonvoluntary mental and physical responses, he believes that the brain does have 3 voluntary responses: "WHAT WE SEE, WHAT WE HEAR, [and] HOW WE THINK" (LaHaye 17, capitalization in original). Prior to the modern generation (here dated probably from the 1960s), LaHaye believed that parents represented the most important force in shaping children's worldviews. However, he feared that with the advent of advanced means of "modern technology," with its "ingenious ways" of assaulting people's minds orally and visually, parents had "lost their children's minds to rock stars, atheistic-humanistic educators, sensual entertainers, and a host of other anti–God, amoral, anti-man influences" (LaHaye 17). Thus, for LaHaye, as for the reparative therapy movement and biblical counseling, interpretations of contemporary neuroscience were directly tied to evangelicalism's usually hostile relationship to the secular world.

LaHaye believed that feelings were a direct response to mental input:

> One of the great myths of our times is that feelings are spontaneous. Actually they are created by what you put into your mind. Computer people repeatedly warn, "You get out of a computer only what you program into it," or, more crudely stated, "Garbage in—garbage out." The same can be said for the mind. Whatever the eyes and ears communicate, the mind in turn dispenses. The other senses—smell, taste, and touch—influence our thinking but do not have as significant an impact on our mind [LaHaye 19].

LaHaye's brain theory here resembles somewhat the ideology of New Thought and New Age thinkers, who believe that positive (or in LaHaye's theory, Christian) mental input will produce positive thoughts and mental results. What becomes crucial for LaHaye and the rest of the Christian right is that people, particularly children, get the correct mental input from whomever is outputting information. For LaHaye, as Fritz Detwiler notes, secular humanism gained control of the nation through controlling the nation's social institutions, but the "most important" of these institutions were the public schools (Detwiler 55). Therefore, LaHaye's computer metaphor is not simply some innocent reference to the new and exciting field of computer science but represents a crucial attempt to use neuroscientific and computer analogies to further a Christian right pedagogical and political agenda.

The third and last area or characteristic of the brain, for LaHaye, is the will. He argues that "no one knows where it is located, but we suspect it resides in the brain, because it is so dependent on the mind and emotions" (LaHaye 20–21). LaHaye also promotes the idea that, because of inherited temperaments, people can have either strong or weak wills. All of this, of course, sounds perfectly reasonable, except that LaHaye never defines terms, or even bothers to question whether human beings have a will at all (a matter still of considerable debate). But the will, along with the other aspects of the brain, proves the foundation on which LaHaye constructs the rest of *The Battle for the Mind* (1980), which is essentially a political jeremiad decrying such "sins" as homosexuality (207–210), atheism (59), evolution (60–62), and the state of Swedish society (115). What any of these topics have to do either with a Christian theory of the mind or with Christian theology in general is not clear. What is clear, however, is that LaHaye builds his credentials for his audience based on a populist, largely propagandistic explanation of contemporary science, one that is often woefully simplistic.

Charles R. Solomon's spirituotherapy is another of the prominent alternatives to biblical counseling offered up by early Integrationists. The basic idea of Spirituotherapy is that the Holy Spirit becomes the Therapist of the individual and "renews the mind and transforms the life in accordance with Romans 12:2" (Solomon, *Handbook to Happiness,* loc 146–149). In 1969 Solomon founded Grace Fellowship International (GFI), a nondenominational organization devoted to promulgating Solomon's view of therapy. Solomon initially began counseling while working as an engineer. In 1972, he received a doctorate of education, which, according to the book *Handbook to Happiness* (1971), was based mainly on the "original research, counseling, writing, and teaching associated with the new discipline of Spirituotherapy" (Solomon, loc 146–157). Solomon's work is significant in that, in some ways, it resembles the model of Jay Adams, and yet it is difficult to tell whether Solomon was influenced by Adams or drew separately from the resources of O. Hobart Mowrer and Thomas Szasz (Solomon, loc 2085–2087).

Solomon has been accused by some evangelicals of following an essentially Freudian approach to therapy, despite his therapy's largely biblicist reputation and orientation.[7] This accusation, despite coming from some of the more radically anti-psychiatric elements of evangelicalism, does seem to be at least partially accurate. A large part of Solomon's therapeutic regimen concentrates on helping people overcome the pain of "traumatic events of their childhoods" (see Solomon, *Handbook to Happiness*, loc 249). The focus on childhood experiences is, of course, classically Freudian and was even more closely aligned with Freudian presuppositions in the 1970s than it is today, thanks to that period's now notorious overuse of childhood-trauma centered therapies as explanatory mechanisms for explaining everything from mild distress to legitimate mental health issues unrelated to such traumas. While Solomon does not go as far as do the inner healing and recovered memory movements in endorsing the kind of paranoid thinking promoted in the SRA scandals, his therapeutic regimen does seem to significantly overemphasize Freudian past-oriented therapeutic ideas over the presentist orientation of behaviorist and cognitive therapies.

This alone, of course, is not a fatal flaw for a therapeutic school. Significant good therapeutic work is still done by psychoanalytic and psychodynamic therapists, especially when they avoid the primitive therapeutic tools that were dangerously overused in the seventies and eighties (integrating DID "parts," recovered memory therapy, hypnosis, etc.). Such therapy is often still needed for sexual trauma victims who do not automatically always respond well to the sometimes over-devotion to presentist ideas found within behaviorist and cognitive-behaviorist thinking. Of more concern in Solomon's therapy is the troubling way he borrows from Freud on one hand, only to condemn Freud and significant elements of traditional psychotherapy on the other hand. For instance, despite the obvious Freudian elements of his therapy, Solomon complains: "Personally, I do not think it coincidental that Freud and Lenin were contemporaries, since both were guided by the god of this world, Satan" (Solomon, *Handbook to Happiness*, loc 2053–2054). The absurdity of this comparison, along with Solomon's general misunderstanding of Freudian thinking, is made even more painfully obvious by his statement that "few have made the connection between Freud's pronouncements about the centrality of sexuality and the 'free sex' of the sixties and seventies and 'safe sex' of the eighties and nineties" (Solomon, *Handbook to Happiness,* loc 2057–2058). This is, as pointed out before, a basic misreading of Freud. Freud did help bring sexuality and sensuality to the fore of our understanding of the world, and his theories were used to justify looser sexual mores. But Freud himself can hardly be blamed for this. He was an almost puritanical figure, with a very traditional and "modest" sex life (Schultz and Schultz 49; Rellahan 86–88). It was hardly his fault that American culture took his works—which, despite evangelical claims to the contrary, are not automatic endorsements of id impulses (Schultz and Schultz 49, Rellahan 86–88)—and ran with them. But Solomon chooses this kind of simplistic explanation of psychology instead of one that deals in more complexity with the legacy of Freudian thought.

Like Adams, Solomon warns, "It is important to use a model that accords with Scripture when we try to explain psychological and spiritual functions and that we use biblical terminology rather than a purely psychological model" (loc 364–365). To implement this implicitly biblicist therapy, Solomon adopts a tripartite view of human beings: spirit, body, and soul. He argues that human beings relate to other people through their soul, to God through their spirit, and to their environment through the use of their bodies. To further complicate these distinctions, Solomon argues that the soul is "composed of mind (or intellect), the emotions (or affections), and the will (or volition)" (Solomon loc 393–396). Solomon believed that difficulties in one area of this tripartate reality would affect other areas. So, for instance, physical problems could affect one's emotional state (i.e., the body affects the soul). Similarly, one could have psychological problems that affected the spirit, and those spiritual symptoms could in turn affect one's psychology (Solomon loc 397–400). All of this is somewhat convenient for Solomon, as it leaves his therapeutic system free from the burden of needing empirical proof. The soul and spirit, by Christian definitions, are not measurable phenomena, but supernaturally gifted parts of human personality.[8] Solomon therefore has a backdoor available should anyone accuse his therapy of not working: He can just claim that they are not spiritually working out their problems with the degree of spiritual responsibility they should be using.

Indeed, Solomon's whole therapeutic system, despite its attraction to Freudian ideas, is anything but me-oriented. Instead, Solomon's explanation for mental health conditions often resembles that of Tim LaHaye. After describing a number of mental health problems, Solomon writes as follows:

> To summarize, it is because self is at the center of the life that all of this conflict develops and continues to grow. The problems may have been there since childhood, but the fact that they continue means that self is running the life. It may be a good self; it may be a bad self; it may be in between; but it is still self, and self in control of the life is repugnant to God [Solomon, *Handbook,* loc 658–660].

For Solomon, as for LaHaye, the central problem involved in mental health is the self. While Solomon is clearly much gentler on those people who are self-oriented (with whom he clearly seems to lump most mentally ill people), he comes to the same basic conclusion about them as LaHaye does: If they were less self-oriented, they would have fewer mental health problems. Yet the connection between self-centeredness[9] and mental illness seems to be a pretty weak link. How does one judge who is and is not self-centered (or "flesh-centered," Solomon's other favorite term)? How does one account for the numerous individuals who do not fit into this conceptual pattern? Indeed, aside from a few people in the positive psychology movement, no one has seriously attempted to define this kind of personality pattern and mental health behavior in psychological terms. Yet, even if one accepts positive psychology presuppositions (which is a big if, given that movement's rather basic presuppositional flaws), one still has to ask why we should pathologize any particular personality orientation over any other. If self-centeredness or introspection proved evolutionarily or socially adaptive, why should we not preserve some parts of those behavior patterns? Yet, Solomon never even explains why people diagnosed with mental illness are simultaneously diagnosed as having these particular personality patterns in the first place, and his rhetoric in many ways sounds all too similar to the kind of simplistic rendering of mental illness offered up by LaHaye and Adams.

Solomon, like Adams, rejects the term mental illness, since "by definition it would suggest that the problem is in the mind" (Solomon loc 2077–2078). However, unlike Adams, Solomon seems more willing to accept biological explanations of mental health conditions, as long as we do not label them mental illnesses. He does, for instance, accept the theory of "chemical imbalance" as a viable one in "the brains of severely depressed patients" (Solomon loc 2083–2084). While Adams also theoretically accepts the possibility of chemical imbalance, in practice nouthetics supporters almost always reject it as an explanation for mental illness.[10] Yet Solomon argues that some of the miraculous changes he has seen in his therapy cannot be the result solely of medication, since they happened so quickly. He argues that in these miraculous cures, the "chemical imbalance—if it did exist in these cases—obviously gave way to the work of the Holy Spirit" (Solomon loc 2083–2084).

The idea that the Holy Spirit is behind one's cure is ultimately the most troubling aspect of Solomon's treatment method, because it affects profoundly how the therapist engages in diagnosis and symptom analysis. According to Solomon,

> Even though the symptoms are mental and emotional, and classifying such symptoms can aid our communication about them, to attempt therapy in the realm of the psyche or mind is folly since it is merely symptomatic treatment. Some symptoms respond in varying degrees to psychotherapy, although the source of the problem is seldom, if ever, touched on in the process. In Spirituotherapy, there is no benefit to offering different diagnoses from a psychological standpoint. This is merely a method of classifying symptoms. Since the source of the problem is ultimately spiritual in nature, it is infinitely more important to determine the spiritual state of the individual [Solomon, *Handbook to Happiness*, loc 2083–2084].

Solomon's therapeutic system assumes that psychological diagnosis, as opposed to spiritual diagnosis, is profoundly unhelpful. This is because if one uses solely the psychological approach, one is focusing only on symptom management instead of getting to the individual's root problems. The mind and the psyche therefore are the wrong area to treat. Indeed, Solomon believes that focusing on these areas ultimately leads to a focus on self. The prime problem he has with traditional psychotherapy is that its focus on self, if it cures symptoms, ends up leaving the person's core self—which is focused on self-centeredness—stronger. He expresses the concern then that, even though the symptoms may be alleviated, the "real problem, self-centeredness, always gets worse" in traditional psychotherapy (Solomon loc 661–665). By contrast, his own system believes only in finding root causes to problems and then solving those root causes. But this begs the question of how one can even find the root causes, let alone deal with them, without also engaging in symptom management. And that is assuming that one buys into his selfist explanation for mental health problems, one that is clearly not accepted by the mainstream scientific community.

Solomon's therapy therefore rather thinly straddles the line between integrationist and biblicist therapies and in many ways his work represents a non-biblical counseling form of biblicist therapy something along the line of the alternative biblical counseling offered by June Hunt. What mainly distinguishes Solomon from Adams is that while Adams drinks from the wells of classical Calvinism, Solomon is more influenced by the Keswick revivalists of the 1800s and their fusion of Calvinist and decidedly often (though not always) non–Calvinist Holiness teachings (Solomon loc 11, 157–159).[11] But the comparison seems an apt one. What ultimately makes Solomon's and Hunt's therapeutic ideas less dangerous than those of Adams is not that the ideas are any less intrinsically flawed or harmful, but that the people conveying those ideas are more modest and more principled than Adams. Solomon, for instance, shows good sense by not even attempting anymore to deal with schizophrenia, warning his readers that "we have not found chronic schizophrenics to be good candidates for spiritual counseling in an outpatient setting" (Solomon loc 2125–2131). Yet Solomon does claim to be able to treat disorders that are only marginally less severe than schizophrenia, including anorexia, bulimia, and "obsessive-compulsive behavior." And like many biblical counselors, he continues to treat homosexuality as a spiritual problem, despite all evidence to the contrary (Solomon loc 2125–2131). Given therefore, the very real problems this study has documented with traditional biblical counseling, there is significant reason to fear that Solomon's therapy may prove similarly problematic, even fatal, when misapplied.

By the late 1960s, however, another vein of truly professionally trained—though by no means always professional—Christian integrationists was coming into vogue as an oppositional force against popularizers like Bill Gothard, Charles Solomon, and Tim LaHaye. The leader of this wave of integrationists was Gary Collins. Born in 1934 in Ontario, Canada, Collins developed an interest in psychology while a freshman in college (Wade 1,14). He saw secular psychology dominating the psychological profession and felt that there needed to be a correction to what he felt was an "exclusion of any meaningful contribution by theology" (Wade 6). After attaining an undergraduate degree at McMaster in 1956, Collins ended up attending the London School of Economic and Political Science, followed by Purdue and the University of Oregon Medical Hospital, where he did his internship while completing his PhD for Purdue (Wade 17). Along with writing a succession of acclaimed works on the integration of Christianity and psychology, Collins served as president of the influential American Science Affiliation, an interdisciplinary organization of Christian scientists, and eventually became president of the American Association of Christian Counselors (AACC), the flagship institution for Christian integrationists that has largely surpassed the older Christian Association for Psychological Studies organization (Wade 91). Collins was influenced by a number of figures, notably Paul Tournier and the Narramores (Wade 26–27). He also engaged in a good deal of surprisingly friendly interaction with Jay Adams (Wade 29), with Adams in particular respecting "Collins as a Christian gentleman," according to Powlison's account (Powlison 49).

Collins's psychology, much like Clyde Narramore's, was built on the foundational assumption that the Bible was "the infallible, inerrant Word of God" (Wade 49). From this, Collins would eventually conclude in his influential *The Rebuilding of Psychology: An Integration of Psychology and Christianity* (1977) that God is also the "source of all truth." (Guy 38). Collins felt this was "true by definition" (38). From this standpoint, he deduced another premise: Human beings can know and understand truth (Guy 39). Again, he felt that this premise was a "self-evident" truth. He concluded from this "evidence" that Christians, at the very least, could know the truth (Guy 39). James D. Guy Jr., himself working out of Fuller Seminary's Graduate School of Psychology, pointed out some serious potential flaws in this logic. The most important one, from Guy's standpoint was that, just because the premise "God exists and is the source of all truth" is presuppositionally true, it does not mean that human beings must automatically be capable of knowing truth themselves (Guy 39). Indeed, reading much of Collins's oeuvre, it is tempting to assume that Collins may have been influenced by Francis Schaeffer's interpretation of presuppositional apologetics, as Schaeffer's name was much in vogue at the time. Considering his cordial relationship with Jay Adams, it is difficult to believe Collins would not have had a detailed knowledge of that field, since Adams drank at the same theological trough as did Schaeffer. But an even simpler flaw with Collins's logic, as with so much of presuppositional thinking, is that he offers no seriously defensible reason why God is the source of all truth or why, if that truth is self-evident, so many people reject Christian theology.

Regardless of the illogical foundations of his psychology, Collins moved from this starting point to suggest ways in which psychology could aid the evangelical church. There were several areas where he thought psychology could be of great use to evangelical churches. First, it could assist people in understanding "the nature of man relative to human development." Second, psychology offered the church a gateway into interpreting abnormal behavior. Third, psychology could aid the church in promoting psychological stability in its members. Fourth, it could help evangelicals understand the effectiveness of their various methods of ministry. Last, Collins believed that psychology played a critically important role in helping Christians "comprehend psychological critiques of Christianity" (Wade 54). What is significant for the mentally ill in Collins's critique of psychology's role in the church is how little it focused on addressing the issues of those damaged by the church, and how much it focused as its starting point on the church itself. It is the organization, not the individual members, he ultimately seems loyal to.

Collins, though not as short-sighted as many integrationists in this regard, also made several concessions to critics of mainstream psychology. He argued that psychology had a number of weaknesses and that its critics made important points. For instance, as Wade points out, in professional psychology's history, the field had developed relatively few laws of behavior (Wade 55). Collins argued that "much of what passes for psychology is simply personal pontificating on certain issues." He also felt that contemporary psychology was over-fragmented and over-specialized, a common complaint of contemporary psychology's critics (Wade 56). None of these complaints, of course, were completely without merit. However, they evaded significant issues about how science approaches human behavioral patterns in the first place. For instance, Collins's simplistic complaint about psychology being unable to deduce laws of human behavior plays into popular reductionistic ideas of human psychology, in which the human body and human psychology can be reduced to a few simple laws. Yet as anyone with any understanding of contemporary science knows, the human organism is incredibly complex—indeed, today's evangelical intelligent design proponents constantly point out that fact—so it would seem unlikely for psychological researchers to have yet developed a complete list of psychological laws in the first place, even if such a set of laws proves to be completely feasible, given the relative youth of scientific psychological and psychiatric practice. But, just as scientists do not throw out Einstein's theory of relativity or quantum mechanics because we can't find a Grand Unified Theory of Everything, similarly one should not readily concede to anti-psychiatry critiques of professional psychology unless those doing the critiquing have a better theory of human behavior to put in its place, which neither integrationists nor their biblical counseling critics have even come close to achieving.

Collins argued that integration was not only possible but also "necessary and of great importance. Integration is both possible and necessary because both psychology and theology study the same basic issues and because truth is unified" (Wade 76). Again, while Collins clearly aided many evangelicals in approaching psychology from a productive angle, his foundational assumptions here are even more faulty than those of the biblical counseling movement, which were at least philosophically consistent. While one could make a somewhat convincing case that psychology and theology study the same issues, this is a far cry from arguing that they use the same methods. Nor, for that matter, does that mean they use the same tools of inquiry, nor does it imply that those tools of inquiry are of equal value. One of the crucial areas of disagreement between secular psychology and both integrationists and biblical counselors is that the secular academy does not recognize the Bible as providing any foundational truth about human psychology, though many secular psychologists and psychiatrists would readily admit that the Bible often offers rich insights into human personality that should not be lightly dismissed. As James D. Guy Jr., himself a Christian, notes, Collins's view of psychology may simply have too optimistic an attitude about arriving at a unified theory of truth. Guy points out that "the Bible seems to indicate that we are incapable of discovering and systemizing total truth. We are a limited creation; though we were created in the image of God, we were not given the ability to know the mind of God.... Our created limitations hinder us from knowing truth as God knows it.... Experience provides evidence that we cannot know total truth with complete accuracy" (Guy Jr. 39). The problem with a unified theory of truth, for Guy, is that human beings simply are not able to know things absolutely in the sense that a god can know them. Indeed, one could add further that this is a fundamental difference between human beings and God with profound psychological implications, since it would imply that only humans, not God, can learn. Thus, learning is a capability consistent only with human psychology, while possessing true knowledge is a skill only God possesses.

One last area of Collins's psychological theory deserves special note. He promoted an idea called psychological apologetics. This field would include "clarifying models used by psychology and theology, articulating the place for the Bible in psychology and studying religious experience" (Wade 67). Though it took a significant amount of time for this idea to catch on within the wider evangelical community, it is arguably one of the more important concepts developed by the integrationist movement. Several fields of evangelical psychology and sociology—particularly such major research projects as the Templeton-funded Flame of Love project—have relied on this vision of biblical and psychological interaction to justify research that is at its best of questionable scientific validity. Research projects started in the 1990s, particularly those sponsored by the National Institute for Healthcare Research (NIHR), poured millions of dollars into validating the health benefits of prayer and other forms of religious experience (Sloan 62). Much of the justification for such projects, though not explicitly tied to Collins's method of psychological apologetics, used similar means of marketing their scientific agendas, arguing to the secular world that one's knowledge of the world could not be complete without a functional understanding of religious phenomena, while simultaneously arguing to the evangelical world that psychology played a valuable role in validating the truth of their faith experience. Thus, various psychological apologists—ranging from Larry Crabb to Gary Collins to the various major adherents of the reparative therapy movement—were able to build personal religious and psychological empires by promoting a radical fusion of science and theology that arguably would not have been possible before the foundation of this psychological apologetics agenda.

Along with Collins, a crucial early voice in integrationism was Dr. Larry Crabb, who was born in 1944 in Evanston, Illinois (Beavan 91). Even in the 1970s, while still a relatively young man, Crabb was one of the most conservative members of the integrationist movement. As Powlison points out, for Crabb, as for Adams, "the Bible addressed all nonorganic problems in living." Crabb, also like Adams, "wanted to create a counseling model that emerged distinctively from the Bible" (Powlison 74). Over time, Crabb's view of the Bible, in Powlison's estimation, "evolved to become virtually identical to Adams's" (Powlison 171). Where Crabb differed from Adams was on matters of emphasis. In particular, Crabb believed that clients' actions should not be viewed solely in terms of personal responsibility, something that Adams had often been faulted for doing (Powlison 175–176). Instead Crabb wanted to view counselees as both "hurting and demanding, both needy and sinful" (Adams 176). Therefore, while Crabb still emphasized the sinful aspects of human nature (Powlison 176), he also believed that Adams "had lost the suffering side of human nature" (Powlison 176).

Crabb advocated a populist model of identifying what was truly Christian counseling, in which he noted four primary means of true biblical counseling (Neil Anderson, Zuehlke and Zuehlke, *Christ Centered Therapy*, 65). While it is beyond the purview of this study to discuss all four elements of Crabb's model—which in any case, is rather markedly inferior to John Carter's masterful use of Niebuhrian theology in dissecting Christian counseling's internal divisions—two elements of Crabb's conceptualization of counseling are worthy of note. Crabb at this early point in his career condemned what he called "Nothing Butterists" counselors. These counselors were those elements of evangelicalism (by which Crabb clearly meant the biblical counseling movement) who aimed at "disregarding psychology altogether. Their basic tenet is Nothing But Grace, Nothing But Christ, Nothing But Faith, Nothing But the Word" (Crabb, *Effective Biblical Counseling*, 40; Anderson, Zuehlke, Zuehlke 66). For Crabb, this approach was faulty because it tended to reduce counseling interaction, which he has consistently seen as a complex human interaction, into a "simplistic, 'identify-confront-change' model" (Crabb, *Effective Bible Counseling*, 47; Anderson, Zuehlke and Zuehlke 66). Again, Crabb was less concerned with the ideological commitments of Adams's biblical counseling approach, such as its desire for a sin-based diagnosis of psychopathology, than he was with Adams's tendency to a kind of biblical reductionism that failed to note the spiritually complex nature of human beings.

Perhaps Crabb's most important contribution to the integrationist cause was his metaphor of "Spoiling the Egyptians" (Anderson 67). For Crabb, this approach was an "attempt to screen secular psychological concepts in order to determine their compatibility with Christian presuppositions," with the goal being to "select concepts and research data from the field of psychology that supports a biblical approach to understanding and relating to God and humans." The actual use of the term referred to how the Israelites left Egypt with the goods of Egyptians in tow. These goods, though from "idolaters," would later be used by the Israelites to sustain themselves. Similarly, according to followers of the Spoiling the Egyptians model, a psychologist can use effective secular ideas and principles so far as they align with the Bible (Anderson, Zuehlke and Zuehlke 67; Crabb, *Effective*, 47–49). The Spoiling the Egyptians model clearly puts psychology in a subservient place to scripture, but it allows for an integration of those psychological truths into professional practice that do not contradict what evangelicals believe constitutes authentic biblical truth. Eventually, Crabb's model would be restated (with admitted differences in emphasis and viewpoint) by Gary Collins (Eck, "Integrating the Integrators," 233); and arguably Eric Johnson's semiotic, translation-based approach to integration is merely an infinitely more sophisticated variation on Crabb's work.

By the late 1980s, Crabb was beginning to sound quite conservative in his approach to counseling. He repudiated integrationism and aimed to return counseling to the province of the church (Powlison, *The Biblical Counseling Movement: History*, 207). Crabb's programmatic work in this period was his *Understanding People* (1987). *Understanding People* lacked the intellectual vigor of Adams's or Johnson's works, mainly because it did not possess the kind of carefully worked out, internally self-consistent system of presuppositions offered up by those two authors. Instead, *Understanding People* represented more a series of individual observations about various facets of Christian counseling.

One issue that troubled Crabb during this phase of his career was that psychologists, as well as some theologians and preachers, tended to "redefine sin as lack of self-esteem or inability to love—anything other than morally evil, blameworthy rebellion" (Crabb, *Understanding People*, 18–19). He was concerned that such an approach to people's personal problems ultimately enfeebled the ability of Christ to work in their hearts and minimized the "atoning work of Christ on the cross" (Crabb, *Understanding People*, 19). Crabb believed that this "overemphasis" on self-esteem led to a corresponding lack of ability to deal with the "sinful roots of emotional disorder" (Crabb, *Understanding People*, 20). What made his model of counseling different from what he called the "Stiff Exegetes" (a term that roughly approximates the "Nothing Butterists" of the 1970s) was that the Stiff Exegetes ignored the "relational and life-changing vitality" of scripture in exchange for a "nonrelational, impersonal understanding of the Bible" (Crabb, *Understanding People*, 10). For Crabb, this was a crucial flaw of much of the conservative counseling movement at the time, because it pushed evangelical counseling into a rigid, hyper-scholastic direction that ignored the counselee's need for love and "chosen holiness" (Crabb 10).

Crabb's system in many ways, however, was more critically flawed than that of Adams, despite Crabb's greater degree of professional credentials. Unlike Adams, whose system was internally self-consistent, though clearly erroneous when looked at from outside an evangelical worldview, Crabb's counseling methodology was more a patchwork of eclectically arrived at and unsystemized "truths" that changed from era to era in his career. A frequent complaint made about Crabb in evangelical circles is that he is simply impossible to understand—not because he is too complex a thinker, but because he is ultimately too simplistic. Crabb complains about those who "excel more in scholarship and theological rigidity than in love"—a complaint clearly directed at the mainstream biblical counseling movement.[12] But the biblical counseling movement's greater willingness to put itself under scholarly scrutiny speaks to the greater intellectual vibrancy and mental (if not moral) integrity of many of the thinkers in the movement (notably Adams, Almy, and Powlison), who often proved more willing to engage foundational issues concerning psychiatry and psychology than were the more populist elements of the integrationist movement (such as the Narramores, Collins, Crabb, and James Dobson). While there were significant voices in integrationism, and even more so in perspectivalism, that were able to engage the arguments of the biblical counseling movement with a great deal of success (notably John D. Carter and David G. Myers), it was not typically these counselors that got "play" in evangelical circles, but the more self-help oriented popularizers like Crabb.

Crabb's system is inherently antirationalist. He complains that rationalists "own no authority beyond their reason. Rather than simply trying to reasonably understand what may be going on, they require all data to fit within their framework of logic or they summarily reject them. They rebel against the view that every model of understanding people must have some very ragged edges" (Crabb, *Understanding People*, 31). Crabb here takes one seemingly plausible idea—that human beings, as relational organisms, are almost indecipherably complex organisms—to come to the radically implausible solution that one should not try to come up with more scientifically grounded ways of understanding human consciousness and action (Crabb, *Understanding People*, 32). He instead prefers using the Bible as the final arbiter over natural revelation. While he admits that faulty human interpretation will sometimes lead to error entering into a biblical model of counseling, ultimately that model of counseling, being based on the Bible, will cause less error than one "developed according to scientific research" (Crabb, *Understanding People*, 42). Thus, Crabb becomes a radical kind of reverse-integrator in *Understanding People*. Instead of finding excuses for bringing psychology into the church, he looks for means of bringing biblical "truths" into psychology.

Crabb's 1980s model of psychotherapy focused mainly on the status of human beings as God's image-bearers. Writing at a time when image-based therapies, particularly the controversial visualization therapies offered by many secular and inner healing proponents of recovered memory, were becoming common, Crabb finds value in the association of aesthetic ideas of "mental pictures" with psychotherapy, but he also cautions against reducing such image-based therapies to simply "the necessary imprint of the parental treatment we received" (Crabb 139). For Crabb, human beings are more "agents" in their own fates than victims. Thus, while the inner healing movement's focus on "healing memories" dealt more with blaming parents for victimization, Crabb argued that "the struggles we experience have more to do with the defensive images and beliefs we hold *right now* than with the manner in which our parents victimized us" (Crabb, *Understanding People*, 139). As with traditional biblical counseling, Crabb's counseling methodology tended to focus itself too exclusively on the problems of faulting those claiming victimhood, thus inverting the inner healing movement's over-identification with purported victims and instead favoring the exclusion of the possibility that those claiming victimization were actually victims.

Over the last two decades, Crabb has moved from a solely bible-based counseling approach to a kind of Protestant adaptation of the traditionally Catholic practice of spiritual direction (Beavin 96–97). Though no longer as readily identifying with integrationism, Crabb has had a profound effect on both integrationist and biblical counseling practice. In the biblical counseling movement, his recent work can be seen as having furthered the agenda of prominent biblical counseling advocates like Bob Kelleman, who also advocate a more nouthetically based form of spiritual direction (Beaven 68). Though Crabb's works overall give the impression of a rather genial figure who seems unwilling to court controversy, his association with the biblical counseling movement points to the growing inability of integrationists and biblical counselors to maintain the significant borderlines between their disciplines that existed, at least for a brief time, in the 1970s. Though many supporters of biblical counseling, and even more the radically anti-psychological elements of the Christian right (notably the Bobgans, who have devoted a whole book to exposing the heresies of Larry Crabb), are unhappy with Crabb's ministry and the frequent (mistaken) association of his methodology with traditional biblical counseling, it cannot be denied that certain elements in the biblical counseling movement, particularly those in agreement with the Christian Counseling and Education Foundation (CCEF), are willing to ally themselves with Crabb in order to legitimize their work among more mainstream psychotherapists (see for instance, Powlison, *Biblical Counseling Movement: History*, 216).

Similarly, Crabb's early work among integrationist therapists is of crucial importance in that it gave many of the movement's less intellectually geared members simple-to-understand, spiritual-sounding metaphors to explain the professional boundary-line distinctions within the evangelical movement. Crabb's work furthermore paved the way for the slew of evangelical psychological popularizers to take their practice out of the professional market and into the lucrative world of pop Christian psychological advice. Whereas LaHaye was not professionally trained and Collins largely conformed to academic standards of intellectual respectability in his writing, Crabb proved to be all too willing to forego critical intellectual engagement with professional psychology (or its critics) in the pursuit of popular success. Although he was not the most successful of these Christian pop psychologists (that title clearly belongs to James Dobson), his efforts in the pop psychology arena are important for both the length of time Crabb has spent in the counseling field and for the way these efforts highlight the often thin line separating professional, presumably scientific, integrationist psychology from its nonscientific cousin practice, traditional biblical counseling.

If Crabb's practice highlights this difference succinctly, William Backus's practice of psychotherapy ultimately arrived at such radical conclusions about both the mentally ill and LGBT individuals that his career serves as a damning reminder of the moral and professional bankruptcy of Christian integrationism in the 1970s and 1980s. Backus was born in Elko, Nevada, on May 5, 1926. He obtained a BA as well as a masters of divinity degree at Concordia Seminary in St. Louis, Missouri. He then became pastor of St. Paul's Lutheran Church in St. Louis, Missouri. In the late 1950s, he began serving a Lutheran parish in Pleasant Hill, California. By 1969, he had received a PhD in clinical psychology from the University of Minnesota. Subsequently, he founded the Center for Christian Psychological Services (CCPS) and became an important promoter of Christian psychology, promoting many of his books to a national audience ("William Backus Obituary").

Backus's therapeutic system, developed alongside his colleague Marie Chapian, was known as "misbelief therapy." According to Backus and Chapian, "misbelief therapy ... involves putting the truth into our value systems, philosophies, demands, expectations, moralistic and emotional assumptions, as well as into the words we tell ourselves.... Jesus Christ is the living truth" (Backus and Chaplain, *Telling Yourself the Truth,* 10). Backus and Chapian's therapeutic system was built on a simple three-step process: "(1) Locate and identify the misbelief in your thinking and self-talk... (2) Argue against the misbelief... (3) Replace the misbelief with the truth" (Backus and Chapian 181). Backus's therapy is typically seen as cognitive in orientation, having similarities with Ellis's model of psychotherapy (Backus and Chapian 27). But because Backus incorporated the idea of sin into his model of psychopathology, his diagnosis of mental health conditions took on a stigmatizing identity almost entirely lacking in most traditional cognitive models. In addition, Backus's radical commitment to a totally cognitivist approach leads him to underestimate environmental and biological influences on psychopathology. Part of this theoretical alignment is quite understandable. Backus entered professional psychology in the late sixties, and the heyday of his career was in the 1970s and early 1980s. During this period, cognitive models were being held out as offering promising new avenues in treating mental health conditions (Hunt, *The Story of Psychology,* 680–681). While that promise has not entirely dissipated—many therapists still prefer cognitive therapies (especially cognitive behavioral therapy (CBT) or dialectical behavioral therapy (DBT) treatments that fuse cognitive therapy insights with behaviorism) for certain forms of psychopathology (notably anxiety disorders)—Backus clearly overestimated the cognitive model's ability to line up Christians' cognitive allegiances to Christianity with their cognitive abilities to maintain mental health. Instead, Backus and Chapian believed that if a therapist changed "a man's beliefs," the therapist would subsequently "change his [the man's] feelings and behavior" (Backus and Chapian, *Telling Yourself the Truth*, 27).

Despite his cognitivist commitments, Backus, like many Christian pyschotherapists and biblical counselors, aligned himself against contemporary psychological science. Backus felt that a "scientific view of human behavior, constrained by the dogmas of secularism, must be incomplete, even distorted, because science has limited itself to consideration of material cause and effect" (Backus, *What Your Counselor Never Told You*, 24). For Backus such a position contradicted people's inherent basic knowledge of themselves as beings with a "spiritual dimension" (Backus 24). This led him to conclude that mental health conditions, though not necessarily always caused by sin (Backus 18–20), often did contribute to the "spiritual disarray" seen in individuals suffering from various psychopathological conditions (Backus, *What Your Counselor Never Told You*, 24). Since Backus believed that "misbeliefs are the direct cause of emotional turmoil, maladaptive behavior and most so-called 'mental illness'" (Backus and Chapian, *Telling Yourself The Truth*, 17), there was an uneasy slippery line between psychopathology and sin in Backus's model.

Where this line became outrageously psychophobic was in Backus's 2000 work *What Your Counselor Never Told You: Seven Secrets Revealed; Conquer the Power of Sin in Your Life* (2000). In the work Backus claimed to have "developed an inventory for researching the relationships between sin and psychological disorders," which he gave the moniker of Sin Test (Backus 24). He literally argued that one could empirically measure sin and that there was a correlation between sinful behavior and psychopathology (Backus 24). Why one should use the evangelical model of sinfulness, let alone the highly specific model of sinfulness offered up by Backus (one that is likely not shared by most other integrationists, or even many biblical counselors), is a question Backus never addresses, nor does he address the question of how sin can be effectively measured (what kind of "units" of sin can truly be verifiably argued for in a Sin Scale?). Instead he claims to have found that there is empirically verifiable evidence for a "consistent trend toward higher total Sin Test scores for psychiatric patients than for nonpatients. Moreover, certain Sin Scales were significantly related to specific diagnoses" (Backus 244). Backus found that performing poorly on the Sin Scale was "positively related to psychopathology" (Backus 244–245). In other words, the mentally ill were worse sinners than the general populace, and certain diagnoses made one especially vulnerable to certain sins—which Backus relates to the seven deadly sins, an ancient church diagnostic criterion for sin that is not normally used in the modern diagnosis of psychopathology (see Backus 243–246).

The explicitly psychophobic views of Backus, which openly promote discriminatory attitudes towards those diagnosed with mental illness, are far worse than any other evangelical leader in *any* counseling movement. Even the leaders of the biblical counseling movement would hesitate to make such broad and sweeping statements about the mentally ill, especially considering the fact that the biblical counseling movement is built on questioning the whole functional system (psychiatry) on which the medical pathologization of mental illness is based. Backus's system, though clearly influenced by Jay Adams (Backus, *Telling the Truth to Troubled People,* 9), shows how frighteningly dangerous an integrationist model can be when it is divorced from any responsibility to maintaining scientific integrity or respectability. Adams's model has done untold damage to mentally ill evangelicals. But at least it has never claimed to be science. Backus's model takes the worst aspects of biblical counseling psychophobia and tries to legitimize them scientifically, making his work perhaps an even more dangerous threat to mentally ill evangelicals than biblical counseling is. That threat is compounded by Backus's involvement in aversion therapy for homosexuals and other populations that he considered "sexually deviant," a widely condemned practice seen as totally harmful to LGBT individuals but one Backus was supporting as late as 1985, when the practice's harm should have been readily apparent to any unbiased observer (Backus, *Telling the Truth to Troubled People,* 251).

Before discussing the most famous integrationist, James Dobson, brief mention should be made of popular radio biblical counselor June Hunt. Hunt's model of biblical counseling seems to be fully consistent in most respects with that promulgated by Jay Adams and David Powlison. What distinguishes her methodology is the much greater emphasis she places on the "grace" aspect of the gospel, as opposed to the law. The daughter of a Texas oilman (Tomaso), Hunt is not in the biblical counseling practice so much for the money as she is for the spiritual influence it gives her; arguably her concern for those who follow her model is quite sincere. Like biblical counselors, Hunt places the ultimate authority of her counseling system under the guidance of the Bible (June Hunt loc 338) and sees the Bible as the primary source for extracting counseling truths. However, though her methodology is dictated by the same biblicist message as Adams and Powlison, her much warmer public persona has allowed her to translate that exclusivist biblicism to a much wider audience than would accept the more rigid biblicism of Adams or Powlison. Listening to Hunt, it is easy to admire the clear compassion detectable in her "answers" to suffering individuals' problems, even as her answers to their problems are often little better than those offered by the mainstream biblical counseling movement. Hunt represents the ultimate fusion of the integrationist and the biblical counselor, where the line between popularizer, anti-psychologist, and mainstream integrationist become utterly indecipherable.

By contrast, James Dobson, despite his desire to be seen as the font of theological orthodoxy in the evangelical movement, would suffer considerable criticism from biblical counselors for his fusion of Christian pop psychology with an evangelical message. But it was this fusion that would allow Dobson to turn his integrationist ministry, Focus on the Family, into the most powerful political force within evangelical Christianity, one that to this day has a disproportionate influence on the evangelical movement. It is to Dobson and Focus on the Family that we now turn.

James Dobson and Focus on the Family

James Dobson is far and away the most influential psychologist in evangelicalism. Indeed, he is—or was, until recently—arguably the most influential evangelical in the entire movement, barring perhaps Billy Graham and C. Peter Wagner. Dobson was born in Shreveport, Louisiana, in 1936, at the height of the depression (Gilgoff 19). His family were devout members of the Nazarene church, a form of pietistic Christianity that is strongly Arminian and steeped in Wesleyan theology. Dobson has somewhat played down his Nazarene past, because some evangelicals "misconstrued its holiness doctrine—the command to continually renounce sin after being saved in order to emulate Christ—as a claim to perfection or sinlessness" (Gilgoff 20). The pietistic emphasis on personal holiness and accountability, however, marks Dobson in many ways. It also gives him an air of authority that other leading members of the Christian right tend to lack, because whatever the actual morality of Dobson's actions, he does appear to believe sincerely in their rightness, something that is not so easily said about the more smarmy evangelical leaders who built their reputations on the backs of televangelism.

In 1958, Dobson graduated from Pasadena College (Gilgoff 20). He subsequently earned a PhD from the University of Southern California and joined the staff of the Children's Hospital in Los Angeles. His research on mental retardation was recommended by the Menninger Clinic (Feinberg 384). Dobson's interest in psychology was in part influenced by a meeting with the famous Clyde Narramore (Stephens and Giberson loc 1214). Dobson was deeply alarmed by the social dishevel of the sixties. His response was to write the book *Dare to Discipline* (1970),[13] perhaps the most famous book ever written by an evangelical psychologist. Here he railed against what he perceived as the misapplication of the teachings of Dr. Benjamin Spock, the popular child advice guru of the time. Dobson, as Gilgoff relates, actually felt quite sympathetic to Spock but also believed people had fundamentally misunderstood Spock's message, leading them to embrace a form of permissive parenting that was ultimately detrimental to the stability of the American nuclear family (see Gilfgoff 22–23). Dobson's book supported the use of corporal punishment for children, advice that has since become controversial (Gilgoff 22–23). While he may now play down his association with behaviorist psychology, even his more recent version of *Dare to Discipline,* titled *The New Dare to Discipline* (1992), is free with references about the need for reinforcement to control people's behavior (Dobson, *New Dare to Discipline* 92, 94; Yu 88).

In 1977, Dobson, capitalizing on his huge success on the evangelical lecture circuit, founded Focus on the Family (Stephens and Giberson, loc 1268–1272). By 1979, he was having to hire staff, so great was the volume of mail Focus was receiving (Stephens and Giberson loc 1272). By 1981, Dobson had expanded his program to a 30-minute daily format. By 1987, the daily broadcast reached nearly 800 stations nationwide (Gilgoff 24). He had, in barely a decade, made himself a major player in evangelical culture.

As Gilgoff recounts, a large part of Dobson's success in the evangelical community was due to the amount of time and care he invested in making sure his listeners' emotional needs were met. He hired professionally trained staff to make sure every letter his organization received got the attention it deserved (Gilgoff 26). Dobson believed the success of his organization depended on how effectively and speedily each person who called into his program was helped. His staff answered phone calls in three rings, no answering machines or automated phone attendants being allowed. The turnaround time for letters Focus received was three days (Gilgoff 27–28). As Gilgoff relates, "Dobson reviewed constituent mail and built broadcasts around what was on his listeners' minds." In short, Dobson was concerned with Focus meeting its consumers' needs. In many ways, this made Focus on the Family a more principled organization in its approach to dealing with the mentally ill than some of the organizations founded by the biblical counseling movement. For instance, as letters to his ministry mounted in the late 1980s, Dobson's organization spent considerable time compiling his advice on a wide variety of different topics so that it would be instantly accessible to phone and letter correspondents (Gilgoff 28). Focus also has an impressive networking system to provide people mental health care or advice. Callers who need more help that a Focus correspondent can give them—over a thousand per week—are transferred from these correspondents to a licensed Focus counselor. These counselors then conduct brief phone sessions before referring the caller to one of the two thousand therapists in Focus's therapeutic network (Gilgoff 50). Focus, in other words, does take its counseling responsibility seriously.

But there is a very big downside to Focus on the Family. Focus is one of the leading Christian right organizations that puts its money and time behind the ex-gay movement. The most famous example of this is Focus's Love Won Out Ministry. As Gilgoff perceptively points out, Love Won Out is "vintage Focus because it puts a gentler face on a controversial social issue without compromising the orthodox position" (Gilgoff 55). Love Won Out promotes a kind of "compassionate condemnation" that has become the centerpiece of recent evangelical antigay efforts. Yet Focus on the Family still promotes the idea that homosexuality is dangerous to society as well as to individuals who feel same-sex attraction (Gilgoff 56). Focus also provided important moral and political support to Exodus International before that ministry's collapse in 2013 (see Erzen 44).

Focus on the Family is perhaps the most explicitly political therapeutic organization to come out of the evangelical movement. As Carol Feinberg points out, Focus arose at a time when right-wing psychologists "magnified the impact of their disciplinary knowledge by expanding the advocacy missions of their professional organizations.... [T]he opinion makers of the right built and expanded their own bases in think tanks, lobbying groups and policy organizations" (Feinberg 82). Dobson, in other words, traded on his power as an advice guru to achieve and maintain political capital. And that political capital was formidable.

The Family Research Council (FRC), for instance, which Dobson helped found and named by Focus staff as their "Washington embassy," has "long replaced" the Christian Coalition's D.C. office as the main center for evangelical and Christian right lobbying in the nation's capital (Gilgoff Location 180). Dobson played an important part in getting Republican senator John Thune elected in 2004 (Gilgoff 6). Dobson has shown his political muscle in a variety of ways, from helping successfully promote a 1992 Colorado ballot initiative that forbade the state to pass antidiscrimination laws for LGBT individuals to making a variety of endorsements of Republican candidates beginning in the 1990s (Gilgoff 10). In the 1990s, Focus played a vocal part in criticizing the "don't ask, don't tell policy" in the military (Focus wanted even sterner measures), while challenging Bill Clinton on abortion rights. When Clinton's extramarital affair was discovered, Focus "called for his impeachment" (Stephens and Giberson loc 1289–1290).

Much of this political power was built on evangelicals' perception of Dobson as being a psychological and political expert (Stephens and Giberson loc 1291). The problem here was that Dobson, though at least a professional, was at heart a psychological popularizer. Like Tim LaHaye, he focused "less on current research than on homey advice for families" (Stephens and Giberson loc 1297–1299). As Stephens and Giberson point out, professional psychologists paid little attention to Dobson's work and when they did, "their assessment was uniformly negative" (Stephens and Giberson loc 1297–1299). Indeed, according to Dobson, the professional class—behavioral scientists, psychologists, scientists of all stripes—had helped create some of our culture's societal problems by their lack of trust in the Judeo-Christian tradition (Stephens and Giberson loc 1302). Like LaHaye, Dobson was willing to take from psychology what he could gain out of it—to "spoil the Egyptians," as Crabb advised—but he was unwilling to listen to secular evidence that contradicted his personal views on human psychology, views based not on science (though occasionally on pseudoscience) but on scripture. He also had a tendency to pronounce himself qualified on technical matters far outside his professional field of expertise, such as the use of gender-inclusive language by Bible translators (Stephens and Giberson loc 1310).

Dobson has consistently promoted himself as a child-rearing expert, and it is this field, along with the related field of familial relations, that he has built his reputation on. However, mainstream child-rearing experts differ sharply from him on parent-child relations. The hierarchical parenting relationship promoted by the LaHayes and Dobson argues that children are essentially sinful, an idea rooted in basic evangelical beliefs about original sin (see Stephens and Giberson loc 1366–1367). Dobson believes that children are disposed to "rebellion, selfishness, dishonesty, aggression, exploitation, and greed" (Stephens and Giberson loc 1370), and this provides the basis of his counseling practice. Therefore, while mainstream psychology—which tries to take a middle ground between Dobson's vision of the *Lord of the Flies* (1954) and the New Age movement's Indigo Children pop psychology—promotes the idea of children gaining self-respect and self-confidence through the help of their parents' empathy and compassion, Dobson's system is almost entirely different, focusing on parental authority, albeit of a gentler variety than that practiced by many evangelicals (Stephens and Giberson loc 1375). Dobson encouraged parents, therefore, to control their child's will from an early age (Yu 108).

While Dobson did promote the idea of childhood self-esteem (to his credit, as he received considerable criticism for this idea from other evangelicals), he also saw childhood rebellion as a symptom of an inferiority complex. Because of this, Dobson's theory of childhood left itself open to the kind of suppressive parenting that one still sees among IFB churches and the Quiverfull movement. This kind of hostile environment is created by the confrontational role Dobson advises parents to take towards children, particularly young children (Yu 115).[14] While admittedly Dobson is a better person to turn to for familial advice than some of his fellow child-rearing authorities in the evangelical movement, his family advice still represents a departure from responsible professional conduct. As Stephens and Giberson point out, Dobson's parenting advice differs significantly from the current scholarly consensus on child-rearing practices (Stephens and Giberson loc 1366–1370).

Dobson's lack of professionalism is even more clearly evident in his deliberate distortion of other academics' research. American feminist and psychologist Carol Gilligan, for instance, as well as Kyle Pruett, alleged that Dobson distorted their research in furtherance of his attempt to promote the idea that same-sex couples could not effectively raise their children. Gilligan went even further, alleging that Dobson had distorted her research for purely political ends (Stephens and Giberson loc 1395–1398). Scholar Angela Phillips also objected to the use of her research by Dobson for the same goal and unsuccessfully tried to get Focus to let her publish a letter of clarification on their Web site explaining what her research actually stated (Stephens and Giberson loc 1402).

Professional research seemed to contradict almost every claim Focus made about LGBT people. The children of LGBT parents often rated higher in traditional markers of success than their straight peers (Stephens and Giberson loc 1402). Similarly the American Psychological Association argued that sexual orientation likely resulted from a complex interaction of "environmental, biological and cognitive influences, and was certainly not a choice" (Stephens and Giberson loc 1414–1416). Therapeutic attempts to fix "homosexuality"— therapies that Focus supported—foundered on their basic foundational presupposition: that there is something to fix (Stephens and Giberson loc 1414–1416). But for Focus, this represented a secular conspiracy on the part of the APA and its allies (Stephens and Giberson loc 1417). This was too much even for Warren Throckmorton, who complained that Dobson's vision of homosexuality, based on the same "poor dad, overbearing mom" psychoanalytic ideas promoted by the reparative therapy movement, was fundamentally in error: "'Most homosexuals had decent dads,' he [Throckmorton] remarked, but Dobson and his followers 'can't see that because it compromises their best political tools, that homosexuality is mutable'" (Stephens and Giberson loc 1427–1428).

In the final analysis, Dobson's therapeutic system is a bit of a wash for mentally ill evangelicals and their allies. While he does promote a greater awareness of mental illness among evangelicals, he is more than willing to sell them out when it proves inconvenient, as happened in the New Life shooting case, where the mentally ill shooter Matthew Murray was also shamelessly sold out by his parents, who blamed his actions on "Satan" rather than on the extremist Gothard-inspired parenting he had endured throughout his childhood (see Blumenthal). Worse, Dobson may be occasionally supportive of the mentally ill, but that support does not extend to LGBT people. His encouragement of strict gender hierarchicalism and parenting likely exacerbates already tense situations for evangelical women and children. But the Christian right does not care about this. Dobson had found the perfect vehicle for conveying hatred and ignorance in the form of pseudo-professionalism. Unfortunately, Christian professional psychology had proven all too ready to forgo scientific rigor when faced with the conflict between promoting the faith and promoting science. And mentally ill, LGBT, and female patients continue to pay the price for that ignorance.

Conclusion

When I started my research for this book, I thought that the integrationist and perspectivalist movements would prove far less problematic in their assumptions about psychology and the practice of counseling than would biblical counseling or deliverance ministries. And to a certain extent this is true. David G. Myers, a prominent perspectivalist psychologist, has expressed a greater willingness to reach out to the gay community than almost any other evangelical in the movement (Myers 79). Though there is cause for concern with some of the allies Dr. Myers has made in recent years, particularly his close association with the Templeton Foundation,[15] his willingness to recognize the validity of current clinical research on the causation of homosexuality is a welcome departure from the lockstep approach evangelicals have taken on this issue (Myers 77–78). And while Eric Johnson's therapeutic system may be flawed, the intelligence of the man who constructed it should be acknowledged.

But it is difficult to endorse an evangelical movement which increasingly uses professional psychology as a tool for propaganda and proselytization, ranging from the despicable political actions of Focus on the Family to Dr. Armand Nicholi's (Nicholi was a founding member of the FRC) skillful promotion of C.S. Lewis in his hatchet-job documentary on Freud's relationship to Lewis, titled *The Question of God,* which incredibly got PBS airtime (*The Question of God* DVD). For Nicholi, in both the documentary and his similarly titled book on Freud and Lewis, the incredible and tragic life of Sigmund Freud becomes a means of promoting a rather ridiculous Schaefferian rendering of the conflict between Lewis and Freud's "worldviews" (Nicholi, *The Question of God,* 6), with Lewis inexplicably seeming to come out the winner.[16] Only in the evangelical world could C.S. Lewis, an important but still second-line intellectual, be equated as an equal with Sigmund Freud, one of the most important—though often wrong-headed—intellectuals of the twentieth century. The comparison is absurd, and Nicholi's constant harping on Freud's pessimism reeks of the kind of thinly veiled "dirty old Jew" stereotype of Freud promoted by much of the evangelical movement. Nicholi's a Harvard professor, and he has to know the comparison is fundamentally dishonest. But what matters to him is not the small truth that human beings can truly comprehend, but the capital "T" truth that it is his duty to impart. The role of the proselytizer supersedes that of the psychologist and academic.

As long as the Christian psychology and integrationist movements prove themselves vulnerable to this kind of antirationalistic, ultimately dishonest discourse, the field will prove useful only insofar as it causes less harm to mentally ill and LGBT individuals than does biblical counseling or deliverance practices. But why not aim for something higher?—to actually help patients by maintaining academically respectable and responsible standards of research, professional accountability, and fundamental honesty about the limits of *both psychology and theology.* Johnson and Myers's work is a welcome start in this direction, but there needs to be much more if Christian psychology is to turn from being a harbinger of death and pain to its counselees to a truly welcome palliative measure for relieving the pain that we all, Christian and non–Christian alike, must ultimately face.

Conclusion
Evangelicals and Mental Illness

The alternate mental health-care system that evangelicalism has created has proven itself unable to deal with the evolving nature of mental health treatment and diagnosis in this country. Biblical counselors, for instance, seem fundamentally unaware of crucial theoretical weaknesses in their argument, particularly the fact that adopting a Szaszian approach to mental illness makes sense only if one depathologizes not just mental health but also mental illness (since either term is nonsense in a Szaszian system) (see Brassington 120–124). Deliverance and inner healing ministries are even further behind the biblical counseling movement in their understanding of, and relationship to, the mentally ill, even if they outwardly adopt psychotherapeutic rhetoric.

There needs to be a cultural shift in the way the evangelical movement relates to disadvantaged social groups, especially groups that sexually or mentally deviate from the white, mentally healthy, heterosexual male norm that has dominated evangelicalism for the last forty years. A large part of this culture shift needs to occur through a deliberate effort to move away from politicizing psychotherapeutic discourse. As this book has consistently pointed out, the evangelical movement has repeatedly used the anti-psychiatric methodology of biblical counseling, the quasi-psychiatric rhetoric of the deliverance and inner healing movements, and the ostensibly pro-psychiatric rhetoric of reparative therapy and integrationist and perspectivalist psychology as a means of social control of "deviant" populations.

But why have the mentally ill, women, the LGBT community, and sometimes children been the particular target of this social concern? A large part of that concern lies not so much in outward hatred of these groups—though that certainly exists to a depressingly large degree—as in the evangelical movement's commitment to an outdated literalist hermeneutic, one which is proving increasingly unable to adapt to our changing knowledge of neurology, evolutionary biology, and psychiatry. For evangelicals, if one accepts that biblical commandments do not apply equally to all peoples at all times and that they may in fact be subject to change and revision, the question becomes whether any scriptural commandments can still hold scriptural validity in a modern context. There is not an easy answer for evangelicals in this regard. Insofar as the wider evangelical movement has experimented with a more open hermeneutical strategy for reading scripture, these attempts have not always been successful. In Pentecostalism, such experimentation has led to the dangerous promotion of hierarchical, cultic leadership that presents major challenges not only to evangelicals but also to much of the Western World (through the influence of the NAR). In the Emergent church, by contrast, such adoption of nonliteralistic reading practices has largely divorced Emergent believers from more than a casual identification with their evangelical heritage.

Therefore, it is possible to understand and even sympathize with evangelicals who do not want the old interpretive traditions to die. I myself grew up in those traditions as a pietistic fundamentalist in a nondenominational, deeply unpolitical evangelical church. Many of the best people I have ever met adhered to those old interpretive traditions, and, contrary to what many people in the secular community might expect, they were often surprisingly loving, even to non-neuronormative people like myself. The problem is that such loving acceptance of others, which used to be normative in at least the Wesleyan branch of evangelicalism, is becoming increasingly rare, even in the pietistic churches that I so admired (and still do). Increasingly, the old depoliticized form of evangelicalism—an evangelicalism that might reject LGBT people, women and the mentally ill in theory but love them in practice and certainly would not make lobbying against them a political priority—is becoming an utter rarity. This means that oppressed evangelical communities, particularly sexual and non-neuronormative minorities, are going to have to start lobbying for their own well-being.

This will not be an easy process, and it requires the cooperation of groups who may distrust each other: the mentally ill, LGBT people, and many of the women in the anti-patriarchal movement. The evangelical church will likely never come to a consensus on the sinfulness or non-sinfulness of mental illness and same-sex attraction and behavior, and it is only marginally more likely that the church as a whole will support a non-patriarchal reading of scripture. That is the world of realpolitik that our three communities are forced to deal with. But if sexual and mental minorities are to have any success in fighting against the dominant oppressive therapeutic system that evangelicalism has set up, it can only be done through uniting peoples of disparate genders, sexual orientations, mental health statuses, and political allegiances. This can be done only if all these communities prove themselves willing to forgo the fear-based rhetoric directed at their potential allies, be they gay or straight, male or female, mentally ill or mentally healthy. For mentally ill evangelicals, in particular, it is cultural suicide to continue countenancing, or even listening to, antigay rhetoric. That rhetoric is *fundamentally predicated* on the exact kind of fear and intolerance that has traditionally been directed at the mentally ill. The LGBT community, likewise, needs to realize how linked the fates of the mentally ill and LGBT people have been over the last forty years. There is danger in being labeled allies of the mentally ill for the LGBT community, especially considering that it was only recently that same-sex attraction was depathologized by the psychiatric community itself. But the gay community has always been at its best when confronting those who attempted to enforce normalcy on its members. The same should be true of evangelical LGBT people as well—and there needs to be a space for that kind of religious identification within our culture. Being evangelical and gay, like being evangelical and mentally ill, should not be seen as an oxymoronic statement, but a quintessential unity of nonconflicting identities.

All these groups need to be willing to reach out beyond the evangelical community, to find allies among secular and nonevangelical individuals. One of the reasons the Mercy Survivors group was so phenomenally successful in combatting Mercy Ministries Australia was that it lobbied for and gained the support of many committed Australian secularists, most notably the courageous blogger Sean the Blogonaut. The Mercy Survivors' willingness to ally evangelicals with ex-evangelicals and nonevangelicals gave the organization a reach far beyond that achieved by many other survivor organizations, a reach that was further helped by the skepticism of a secular Australian nation towards any therapeutic system based solely on religious faith.

However, the kind of abuses that occurred at Mercy Ministries will likely continue for the foreseeable future in evangelicalism if there is not a concerted movement to oppose such ministries. Fortunately, there is some evidence to suggest that victims of religiously based abusive ministries are starting to more actively organize. The Community Alliance for the Ethical Treatment of Youth (CAFETY) has lobbied for more ethical treatment of people at youth residential facilities, which would at least help teenagers admitted into Mercy Ministries or other potentially abusive youth treatment facilities. The Independent Fundamentalist Baptist Cult Survivors (IFBCS) network has also done some surprisingly successful work in raising awareness about abuses of both youth and adults within IFB churches and "homes." There also has been a very successful campaign conducted by various ex-members of the evangelical group Battlecry (particularly by the blogger Recovering Alumni), which has drawn national attention to that organization's now notorious abuses of some of its teenage members ("Mind Over Mania").

What is perhaps needed at this critical juncture is a group that can work with victims of religious abuse specifically. Such a group could target ministries and groups like Mercy Ministries, Sovereign Grace Ministries and the Independent Fundamentalist Baptists, which have had a relatively long history of criticism directed at them, as well as other ministries that have flown under the radar. It could also, more positively, serve as an equivalent of the Evangelical Council for Financial Accountability (ECFA) by giving approval or disapproval ratings to religious treatment facilities. Though the majority of these treatment groups have often acted inappropriately over the years, one does not want to paint with too broad a brush. It would be foolish, for instance, to totally reject an organization like Catholic Charities, which, whatever its limitations, has done a phenomenal job in reaching out to mentally ill people over the years. A social justice organization for the mentally ill operating under an ECFA-like paradigm could praise organizations like Catholic Charities for their good work, while working internally to change the more negative aspects of their politics.

Such a group would, like Mercy Survivors, need to operate pragmatically. That means it would have to accept both religious and nonreligious members, survivors who still have some positive feelings about their experience and others who loathe the ministries that the group fights against. There can be problems with such an approach, of course. For instance, there's the possibility that with such a wide clientele some of the ministries targeted might try to infiltrate a survivor network. Also, the broader the clientele base, the more difficult it will be to construct a unified sociopolitical agenda to deal with abusive treatment regimes at facilities like Mercy. But the alternative is to be too selective in admitting members, thus denying the legitimacy of those narratives that do not fit into the mainstream survivor discourse surrounding Mercy and similar organizations.

Members of survivor groups—whether they were put through reparative, biblical, deliverance or patriarchal counseling practices—must also learn to react with grace to those members of "abusive" organizations who do not subscribe to the survivor narrative. There are both pragmatic and ethical reasons for approaching anti-survivor groups in this way. From a simple public relations standpoint, usually groups that appear compassionate and rational tend to win the day over groups that use inflammatory or demeaning language. Part of the reason that the Mercy Survivors organization was so successful in Australia was that ministry survivors there were unfailingly polite, even to those with radically differing opinions from their own. The often vitriolic attacks launched at the survivor network, particularly at early members of the network such as Naomi Johnson, often ended up hurting the attackers more than the survivors themselves, so obvious was the difference between the survivors' compassion for Mercy supporters and the supporters' well-intentioned but often rhetorically barbed attacks on survivors' moral character. The testimony of survivors took on a credibility which allowed them to advocate their position to the Australian media and Australian secular groups with a great deal of success.

In addition, survivor groups are far more likely to attract supporters away from abusive therapeutic movements if they are compassionate than if they fight fire with fire. In the case of Mercy Ministries, for instance, it is a testimony to the ethically grounded nature of the Mercy Survivor network that it is almost impossible to find any trace online or off-line of survivors attacking supporters' moral or ethical character. Whether one agrees with the survivor network or not about the inefficacy of Mercy, it would be difficult to deny that its primary motivation has been anything other than to help former Mercy clients, whether survivors or supporters, "recover" from their experiences. A similar degree of restraint has also usually characterized the survivors of reparative therapy, despite the considerable pain and anger that the reparative therapy and conversion therapy survivor community understandably feels at the actions of ministries like the former Love in Action or Desert Stream Ministries.

Mercy Ministries, Sovereign Grace Ministries, and the various abusive ex-gay organizations in this country might not change overnight. They might never close down. But survivors and survivor advocates can at the very least make young LGBT, mentally ill, and female clients aware of the potential risks associated with entering organizations like these. And we can do so without dehumanizing the people who support them. In so doing, groups like the Mercy Survivor Network or the phenomenal survivors group Ex-Gay Watch, at their best, offer more than just a paradigm for combatting abusive evangelical organizations. They offer a whole new way of looking at survivorship itself.

Rather than following the attack model offered by the anticult survivor movements or the depressive model of hopelessness and vindictiveness that characterizes the "victimhood" movement surrounding ritual abuse, this new form of survivorship refreshingly acknowledges that the experience of any abusive organization is different for each individual and may not even be quantified as abuse in all cases. Groups like Mercy Survivors, in short, allow narrative freedom for multiple types of religious and survivor experiences without falling into the trap of creating the same kind of hermeneutically sealed interpretive models used by cultic or fundamentalist organizations. As Anne Rothe points out, too many survivorship models are about victimization and then blazing recovery (Rothe 55–56). The model of survivorship promoted by groups like the Mercy Survivors network is simply about accepting life as it is and trying to change it for the better, whether or not there is a redemptive story at the end. That is why I, a skeptic when it comes to the recovery movement, feel groups like Mercy Survivors, CAFETY, and Ex-gay Watch serve as paragons of proper civic engagement by victimhood groups. And it is why I hope they continue to do so for years to come.

Appendix A

A Christological Vision of a Mad Christ

Mental Illness and Jesus

Disdain for the mentally ill helps justify the central argument of evangelical apologetics, C.S. Lewis's famous trilemma, commonly shortened to "lunatic, liar, or Lord." Lewis contended that "a man who was merely a man and said the sort of things Jesus said would not be a great moral teacher. He would either be a lunatic ... or else he would be the Devil of Hell. You must make your choice. Either this man was, and is the Son of God: or else a madman or something worse" (Lewis, *Mere Christianity*, 50–51). Nonbelievers typically respond to this argument by stating that Jesus could very well have been a lunatic, assuming that he existed at all. I want to take a different tack here and suggest that perhaps we should see Jesus as lunatic and Lord and thereby envision a liberatory theology of mental illness for "mentally ill" evangelicals.

The argumentative strategy of creating a trilemmic dilemma predicated upon Jesus not being mentally ill is a common one, used by many Christian apologists. For instance, Josh McDowell, one of the most prominent Christian apologists of the seventies, eighties, and nineties, writes as follows: "Someone who believes he is God sounds like someone today believing himself Napoleon. He would be deluded and self-deceived, and probably he would be locked up so he wouldn't hurt himself or anyone else. Yet in Jesus we don't observe the abnormalities and imbalance that usually go along with being deranged. His poise and composure would certainly be amazing if He were insane" (McDowell "Jesus: God or Just a Good Man?"). Peter Kreeft, a Catholic apologist very popular among some evangelicals, has similarly argued that "a measure of your insanity is the size of the gap between what you think you are and what you really are. If I think I am the greatest philosopher in America, I am only an arrogant fool.... But if I think I am God, I am even more insane because the gap between anything finite and the infinite God is even greater than the gap between any two finite things" (Kreeft).

Why is the sanity of Jesus Christ such a crucial issue to evangelicals? For McDowell, and apologists arguing along the same lines as McDowell, the issue seems to be that insanity ultimately and inevitably means self-delusion and God can by definition not be self-deluded. Kreeft's argument follows similar lines. Also at issue for many Christians, though it is not commonly admitted, is the biblical association of madness with demonic possession. Biblical passages such as John 10:20 associate demon possession directly with madness, while other verses seem to imply it.[1] There are, however, major problems with such an argument. Most formidable of these problems is that there is nothing in the character of God, even accepting the evangelical theological concepts of God's existence, omniscience and omnipotence, that negates the possibility of God, let alone Christ, being self-deluded. This is because delusion is a relative, and profoundly anthropocentric, concept. In Nazi Germany, for instance, believing that Jews were human beings and not bacilli could have been seen as delusional thinking. Going further back, in the 1800s there was a literal mental health diagnosis called *drapetomania,* whose delusional aspect was defined as slaves fleeing their masters (Bynum). Any undergraduate psychology student could point out the highly context-specific nature of mental illness— its dependence on certain specific physical environments, social stigmas, and actual biological processes. Not only is it not necessarily problematic to view God as mad, it is also an idea that has been at least hinted at in church tradition. For instance, Michel Foucault notes Nicholas of Cusa's description of the "abysmal madness of the wisdom of God":

> [U]nutterable in any language, unintelligible to every intellect, and immeasurable by every measure. It cannot be limited by any limit, nor bounded by any boundary. No proportion is proportionate to it. No comparison can be compared to it.... It cannot be formed by any formation, and it cannot be moved by any motion ... because it cannot be expressed in any speech, no limit to such modes of expression can be grasped. This is because that Wisdom by which, in which and from which all things exist is unthinkable in any thought [Nicholas of Cusa 24–25 qtd. in Foucault 31].

From a human vantage point, what is infinite sanity to God can only be madness to humanity and vice versa. This is not even necessarily because of any will on humanity's part, let alone God's. Our mutual apprehension of each other as mad is predicated on the very different spiritual and physical states in which we exist. God, as a morally perfect, timeless, immaterial being, is not apprehensible to morally flawed, temporal, material beings like humans. His mentality, his whole method of "life" and "being" is beyond humanity. Indeed this may be why some philosophers have talked about God as a "Being-beyond-

Being."[2] As such, a human psychiatrist, be he Freud or Erich Fromm, can quite naturally find God's psychological motivation to be neurotic, even pathological, nor are they wrong for believing so. It is doubtful that any human-centered psychology could realistically come to any other conclusion, even if it was predicated on Christian presuppositions. From this vantage point, the very effort of apologetics—to rationalize what to human beings must seem madness—is the height of human folly. Only by convincing our fellow human beings that we worship the maddest of mad Gods can Christians convince nonbelievers of the wonder of the Christian message.

Reformed, and to a lesser extent fundamentalist, apologists make a mistake when they predicate their apologetic arguments on rationalist presuppositions. As critic Fritz Detwiler has noted, the "epistemological foundations" of "biblical" Christianity are "rooted in the writings of seventeenth century philosopher Francis Bacon and eighteenth-century Scottish Common Sense philosophers" (Detwiler 90). Detwiler, in opposition to more naïve secular critics, points out that, far from being antirational, this methodology allows for a "highly rational intellectual tradition" (Detwiler 92). The problem, from a secular standpoint, with such rationalism is that it is based on faulty philosophical presuppositions, presuppositions that the Reformed movement, in particular, has persistently and rather disingenuously failed to correct. But for the purpose of this argument, the problem with Reformed presuppositionalism is far more fundamental. In accepting an Enlightenment narrative of rationality, it privileges reason over madness and thus constructs a narrative of Christian belief that fails to acknowledge the "insane" aspects of God's character. Foucault pointed out that from the standpoint of St. Vincent de Paul, "Christ had wanted not only to be surrounded by lunatics, he had also wanted to pass himself off as a madman, experiencing in his incarnation all the miseries to which the flesh was heir. Madness therefore became an ultimate limit, the last degree of God made man, before the deliverance and transfiguration on the cross" (Foucault 153). Even though Vincent de Paul lived at the beginning of the Enlightenment, he realized the fragility of human reason, and therefore the corresponding need to value the image of Christ even in the "mad." For Renaissance man, with his appreciation of the "scandal" of the "madness of God made man," this was an even more fundamental distinction.

And here there is a great point that the apologists, tied to reason-based systems, have overlooked: the problem with atheist arguments in favor of Christ's lunacy is not that they are incorrect. For Renaissance man, at least, the madness of God was plausible, and we can see such figures in literature as well, even as late as the 19th century, in Prince Myshkin of Dostoyevsky's *The Idiot,* who presents a memorable image of a mad Christ-figure (Foucault 152–

154). No, the problem with atheist arguments against a mad God is that they stigmatize the mentally ill without carefully thinking through the ethical implications of their argument. There are, in fact, a number of scenarios in which Jesus could still be God and be either viewed as mentally ill or, in fact, actually be mentally ill.

Perhaps the most obvious scenario that neither side in this debate wishes to bring up is that Christ, even if God, was not necessarily omniscient while on earth. This argument appears quite plausible, indeed probable (from a religious standpoint at least), considering the fact that Jesus appears to have made many questionable prophecies during his lifetime, few which appear to have come to pass, at least within the time frame he specified (see Wells 3). The assumption frequently if unconsciously made by many apologists is that an omniscient God could not have been mentally ill, as we understand it, because that would mean his knowledge base would be fallible. It might also imply that his brain is fallible, which would lead one to wonder if a "broken-brained" God could still be God. There are a number of objections to this position, some logical, some ethical. First and foremost, there is no reason to suppose God needed an infallible knowledge base while on Earth. Indeed, there is good reason to argue that he could not have been omniscient while living on Earth. As Foucault points out, even the people of the classical age assumed that "by coming into this world, Christ accepted to take on all the signs of the human condition, and even the stigmata of fallen nature. From misery to death, the path of the Passion was also the path of the passions, of wisdom forgotten and of madness. And because it was one of the forms of the Passion—the ultimate one, before death—madness was seen in those who suffered from it as an object commanding respect and compassion" (Foucault 154). If Jesus was to truly become God-made-flesh, he would have to suffer the flaws of human beings. That includes a limited knowledge base, including quite possibly mental illness. If Jesus had a limitless knowledge base while on earth, how in any sense could he be tempted? He would know, with absolute certainty, that his suffering was temporal, would know with certainty that he would be raised from the dead and would live forever in heaven. No human being can truly make such claims, not even God's elect. It is difficult to see how such a God could then claim the right to judge humanity, having not truly suffered the uncertainty human beings daily live with.

Could a God whose brain did not function "properly" still be God? Again, here we are applying an arbitrary standard of normalcy. If Jesus did not have a normal brain, if he had a brain that would be classified as bipolar or schizophrenic or obsessive-compulsive, what is it especially about those conditions that makes those brains abnormal? What makes human beings think that Jesus's brain had to function according to a standard of "normality" versus "abnormality"? Indeed, this would again be impossible, since there is no such thing as a "normal" brain and never could be. Normal is just a statistically devised average that can vary from time to time. Therefore, when Reformed groups and atheists argue for or against the existence of a "brain-diseased" Jesus, they are tilting at windmills. Of course Jesus had mental abnormalities; how could he not, when one is judging the world in the context of "normality" and "abnormality"? We are all abnormal to each other.

On the other hand, if we define Jesus's brain as normal and all other brains as abnormal, why do biblical counselors and deliverance ministers label those with "mental illnesses" as especially sinful or demonic? It will not do here for biblical counselors to argue that they do not believe in the concept of mental illness. The problem still remains that biblical counselors are arguing that somehow "normals" are less sinful than the abnormal "mentally ill," based on purely arbitrary definitions of what constitutes "more" sinful behavior. If Jesus's brain and behavior patterns are our neural ideal, then any deviation from them can be considered an abnormality or mental illness, regardless of whom is behaving in such a manner. All behaviors then become sins. The reason why those labeled with mental illness are especially singled out for criticism by these groups is a question left unanswered by organizations like CCEF and NANC. On the other hand, if we are not using any preset notion of normality, who gives these organizations the right to arbitrarily decide for the rest of evangelicalism what constitutes normalcy?

Opponents of the possibility of Jesus's having a mental illness also tend to make a false equation between "madness" and "mental illness." In fact, someone can be perfectly "sane" and be mentally ill. Nor is it clear how the behaviors associated with mental illnesses can be considered in themselves sinful. The ethical behaviors associated with religiously based OCD (scrupulosity), for instance, from an evangelical standpoint seem to be far more plausibly equated with a godly than an ungodly spirit. Similarly, it seems to make little sense for biblical counselors like Mary and Marshall Asher to claim that the schizophrenic has "unmitigated guilt and much to fear. For this reason a schizophrenic should be considered an unbeliever until proven otherwise (even if he has a history of effective Christian ministry)" (Asher and Asher 164). Yet, what makes the hallucinations or delusions of a schizophrenic ungodly? What disqualifies such people from being saints or even deities? The Ashers are transposing 21st-century psychiatric values to the first century, which is ironically the very thing the biblical counseling movement originally formed to prevent.

Indeed, if Foucault's *History of Madness* (2006, English translation) and the anti-psychiatric movement from which biblical counseling draws much of its ideology have taught us anything, it is that madness is an evolving concept that changes over time. It is not in a steady state. Consequently, if the experience of madness is not continuous, neither should the treatment be continuous. Therefore, Jesus could have been perfectly correct in using exorcism to treat mental illness in the first century A.D. At the time, it may have been the only method of healing that people would accept. It does not follow logically, however, that Jesus would then expect all successive generations of human beings to use the same medical treatment. Indeed, if one views Christ not as a faith healer but as a true healer working with the best medicine the Jewish people would accept at the time, then the position of both deliverance ministries and biblical counselors becomes extremely dubious. If Jesus was omniscient while on Earth, he would have surely known that human beings would progress technologically and that medical treatment would change. He would therefore have expected our treatment methodologies to change with it. On the other hand, if Jesus was not omniscient on Earth, then it seems foolish to base our medical practice on the best medical knowledge he had available to him at the time, since our knowledge base has obviously improved since AD 33.

The rejection of a mad God has nothing to do, therefore, with logic or creed. It is based, quite simply, on prejudice and nothing more, prejudice ironically exhibited equally by Christians and atheists alike. But the God mentally ill evangelicals should serve, indeed that all Christian dissidents have served throughout the centuries, is a God who committed suicide on the cross, a God who taught such "insane" doctrines as turning the other cheek, forgiving seventy times seven, and the meek inheriting the Earth. People during Jesus's time questioned whether he was mad (John 10: 19–21). John assumes that this was a wrong interpretation. But perhaps it was not John but Jesus's opponents who unwittingly realized the genius of Jesus's message: That in its love, in its endorsement of sacrificial, redemptive, self-destroying love, it could only be the gospel of an insane man—an insane man who believed in the ultimate form of madness: that there is something in human beings worthy of redemption.

Appendix B

Mercy Ministries' View of the Body

Mercy's theory of eating disorders is heavily predicated on the issue of "choice." Alcorn assumes that eating disorders represent willed behavior, and thus any attempt to starve oneself involves sinful behavior:

> [B]ehaviors associated with an eating disorder make you feel that you are in control. However, just the opposite is true. When you choose to give in to the harmful behaviors of anorexia, bulimia, or binge-eating, you are actually giving control of your life to your enemy, the devil. The enemy wants you to believe that because you can deny yourself food you have some sort of power over your body and over your life. But the Bible says that we are slaves to whatever controls us [Alcorn, Starved, 21].

A couple of things should be noted right away. First, Alcorn argues that women gain free will—choice—only by the denial of choice, agency only by the denial of agency. Obviously, it is a good thing when women do not starve themselves. But Alcorn's vision for why women should not engage in this behavior revolves more around Pauline and Petrine assumptions about the body being the temple of God than it does about women's control over their own bodies. In line with Alcorn's pro-life politics, she tends to associate anorexia with what women should not do with their bodies, rather than allowing women the freedom to do what they want with them. Even if one assumes the correctness of pro-life logic—and one could certainly make a case for it—a system like Alcorn's, by emphasizing the powerlessness of women over their own lives, just encourages the reproduction of anorexic and bulimic behavior patterns.

Alcorn's explanation for why people develop eating disorders relies heavily on her pronounced bias against secular media forms. Alcorn writes: "In today's culture, media—movies, TV, magazines, the Internet—and fashion are doors that Satan easily creeps through. Neither media nor fashion is necessarily a bad thing, but Satan often uses them to distort God's truth about who you are. Movie stars, television icons, and fashion models define beauty and promote the lie that anything less is unacceptable. The irony is that the perfect

261

image doesn't even exist" (Alcorn, *Starved*, 24). Alcorn thus places the primary blame for eating disorders on secular media forms, which to her mind gives young women an unnatural vision of what constitutes a healthy female body. Alcorn's rhetorical strategy here is broadly consistent with wider evangelical suspicion of secular media. Ron Luce, for instance, has deemed the secular media so toxic that he argues that MTV is engaged in "virtue terrorism" (Luce, *Battlecry for My Generation,* 9). Dr. Linda Mintle has confirmed Alcorn's media-based analysis, with chatty critical asides about the role Britney Spears, Lindsay Lohan and Pamela Anderson play in determining women's view of their breasts and general body image (see Mintle, *Making Peace with Your Thighs,* 49).

Of course, neither Alcorn nor Mintle are totally wrong in focusing on the power of media to construct our view of our bodies, but their analysis fails in several critical areas. Perhaps the most obvious is that, for Alcorn and Mintle, the male eating disorder victim is totally invisible. To read Alcorn's *Starved* (2007) or Mintle's *Making Peace with Your Thighs* (2006), one would think such individuals do not exist. Again, to a certain extent, this vision of eating disorders (ED) reflects the general societal perception that only women can develop ED symptoms. The problem, of course, is that while women are much more likely to develop eating disorders then are men (Barlow and Durand 235–236), there are male anorexics and bulimics.[1] The question then becomes why Alcorn does not appear to be cognizant of that fact. One could, of course, argue that since Alcorn's ministry is geared towards women, she simply genders her language in *Starved* to reflect that reality. But our reading of Alcorn's writing should not be so innocent. Alcorn has a vested interest in promoting a vision of victimized femininity, even if we assume that she is truly intent on helping Mercy's clients. The image of victimized, physically fragile women fits in well with our society's general misogynistic view of women's physical abilities. It fits in even more with evangelicalism's generally patriarchal attitudes towards women, which focus on female vulnerability and disempowerment. By promoting the image of weak women, Alcorn is not so subtly hinting to evangelical men that an investment in Mercy is an investment in the perpetuation of patriarchy. Protect an anorexic, and she may grow up to be your very own submissive bride

The existence of male anorexics, which throws into doubt the evangelical message of the domineering aggressive male, is not conducive to the evangelical narrative of gender. In that narrative, as Heather Hendershot points out about the 1994 True Love Waits conference, young women are "told a sentimental fairy tale about true, eternal love and the achievement of the feminine dream of romance through the preservation of virginity. Boys, conversely, were directed to loudly chant 'We are real men! We are real men!' ... Ironically, in order to control the male body, to save it from its own heterosexual aggression, that body must be constructed as aggressively heterosexual and masculine" (Hendershot 93). There is a reason why this gendered narrative of anorexia is necessary for Alcorn:she is a powerful woman in a branch of evangelicalism that has a very paradoxical vision of femininity. On one hand, Pentecostal theology has historically been more open to powerful women than other branches of evangelicalism. Along with Holiness churches, Pentecostal churches are the only evangelical churches in which one is likely to find any women preachers. Because of their powerful position in Pentecostalism, Pentecostal female leaders face a two-sided position. On the one hand, they can exercise enormous power in their sphere of influence; on the other hand, that influence is always predicated on their willingness to bend to existing evangelical gender norms, when necessary. Thus, while Alcorn is by no means a weak woman, she does evidently find it necessary to promote the ideal of female weakness in order to garner support for her ministry (a consequence of which is that she, perhaps unintentionally, aggrandizes more and more power to herself as she disempowers others).

It's not entirely clear, at times, that Alcorn is in fact even attempting to critique the media's admitted distorted view of women's bodies. For instance *Starved,* the very book that Alcorn uses to criticize secular media images of women, has an endorsement from "International Supermodel" Niki Taylor featured prominently inside the book (Alcorn, *Starved*, v). Thus, in the very act of trying to tear down stereotypes of women, Alcorn merely reinscribes them, reinforcing the idea that a woman's opinion is more valuable if she is beautiful or sexy. This position is even further reinforced by the association with Mercy Ministries of Barlow Girl, a Christian band known for its talented but also rather airbrushed female singers (Alcorn v). Though it is hard to quantify something as perceptually subjective as an organization's depiction of female appearance, most Mercy advertisements do seem to feature "classically" physically attractive, thin, vulnerable looking, and, usually, white young women. Healthier, more realistic images of female beauty, though not totally absent from Mercy's promotional material, tend to take second place.

But what is even more tragic about Mercy's explanation for eating disorders is that Alcorn's approach to the disorder is so one-dimensional. Alcorn's theory of eating disorders is solely predicated on the media imagery surrounding anorexia and bulimia.[2] Mintle, though a little better in that regard, is almost as narrowly focused. But eating disorders have many possible causal factors. For instance, sexual abuse often plays a role in the development of disordered eating patterns (Dubose, et al. 50), a point Alcorn seems perplexingly unaware of, even though this point should be obvious to anyone who has lived or worked in a group home environment like Mercy's, regardless of their level of training.[3] More significant, as Hendershot points out, "according to evangelical books, magazines, and videos, the cure for eating disorders is religious, but the causes are not. Evangelical youth media rarely portray girls' eating disorders as stemming from family pressures, an authoritarian home life, or the tremendous pressures that being a 'good Christian' can entail" (Hendershot 109). Alcorn sees religion as the solution to ED issues, when in fact it may in many cases be the primary problem causing these behaviors. Thus, the sicker an anorexic woman may get from treatment at Mercy, the more Mercy Ministries may think the young woman is in need of their therapy, which in turn just makes her sickness worse.

Insofar as Mercy has a theory of the body, that theory revolves around the idea of the "bodily temple." As Alcorn relates, "The Bible is very clear that your body is the temple of the Holy Spirit and that you should honor God with your body" (Alcorn, *Starved*, 33). For Alcorn, therefore, respect for the body is tied to respect for God. Respect for the self, while important, is of secondary importance in determining one's self-value. What takes primacy is what an external figure—one implicitly, if not explicitly, linked with the male gender (God)—thinks of the anorexic female. Again, Alcorn's treatment methodology, like much of evangelical mental health practice in general (even legitimate practice), assumes that the figure the faith reveres cannot be part of the problem the anorexic young woman is undergoing. Yet there is every likelihood that an anorexic or bulimic teenager or young adult will associate God, and even more so Jesus, with the underlying culture of male oppression that characterizes Christianity in general and evangelicalism in particular. This is even more the case if the anorexia is the by-product of sexual or physical abuse, especially if that abuse came at the hands of fellow Christians. Alcorn's theory of the body, therefore, is clearly inadequate as an explanatory model for any mental illness, let alone those as complex and multifaceted in their causal factors as anorexia and bulimia.

Mintle's theory of the body is even stranger. Alcorn has labeled Mintle a significant influence on her ministry, claiming that "Linda has played a key role in training our counselors and staff, and has provided resources that are used daily in our Mercy Ministries' homes" (Alcorn, "Beauty Is in the Eye of the Beholder"). Alcorn in particular highly recommends *Making Peace with Your Thighs* (2006), a book whose vision of anorexia likely influenced Alcorn's, considering the fact that Mintle trained Mercy counselors and staff, as well as the fact that Mintle herself lists Alcorn as a helpful eating disorders resource

(Mintle 233; Alcorn, "Don't Wait for Tomorrow"). What makes Mintle's theory of the body so odd is not her vision of anorexia per se, which though potentially destructive is at least more grounded in contemporary psychological practice than Alcorn's. No, it is her *theory of nudity* and its relationship to eating disorders that is truly original ... and deeply disturbing.

Mintle suggests that eating disorders literally began in the Garden of Eden. According to her theory, "body image distortion began in the beginning. In the third chapter of the book of Genesis in the Bible, an explanation of how we moved from originally accepting our created bodies to embracing feelings of shame and inadequacy is provided. In the short form, and to put it bluntly, the origins of our distorted body image developed when a man and a woman decided to share a treat [the apple in the garden]" (Mintle, *Make Peace with Your Thighs*, 15–16). Mintle argues that "Adam's and Eve's view of their nakedness changed based on their decisions to act independently from God. Eve believed the lie and sinned. Adam ignored God's voice of authority and sinned. Sin resulted in fear and hiding and a condemnation of their natural state.... On their [Adam and Eve] own, they tried to cover their nakedness and not feel shame, but they failed. And self-hatred began" (19).

One could not fault Mintle for a lack of theological creativity—her reading of Genesis is as brilliant as it is perverse. But Mintle, responsible for training an institution that claims an expertise in eating disorders, pushes the idea that body image problems are caused by the "sharing of a treat," a sharing that she paradoxically then later reads as not a condemnation of food but a condemnation of a focus on "appearances." Eve, she notes, "took her attention off of God and the truth of what He'd said and got all caught up in appearances [the apple specifically]" (Mintle 17). Eve's obsession with biting the poisonous fruit therefore is inexplicably not an act of consumption but an act of denial, a spiritualized anorexia that starves her from the love of God. By contrast, a physicalized anorexia in which she had not eaten the apple would be a form of spiritual consumption by which Eve would be sustained, not through the food of knowledge but the food of God's love. Spiritual anorexia, therefore, is not just cutting oneself off from the consumption of food, but the pursuit of knowledge. A little knowledge is a dangerous thing, particularly when one becomes obsessed with what Mintle calls "false wisdom" (16). The adoption of such knowledge leads the believer to "distorted" perceptions based on the fact that, "like Eve, we tend to listen to the voices all around us who don't have our best interests in mind" (19). Knowledge is to be distrusted because it may distort both one's body image and one's faith. For the anorexic believer at Mercy, listening to the outside world becomes impossible, as one is trapped in a solipsistic nightmare: If one listens to the media of the world, one is listening to the demons that cause both mental health problems and false body image distortions. It does not matter if that secular world is also sending more positive messages, because those messages do not reflect the diabolic reading of eating disorders promoted by Mercy Ministries.

This is not to say that Mintle's philosophy of the body is all bad. Her application of Christian theology to the problem of aging, which affirms the dignity of aging and weakening bodies, is commendable (103). But Mintle's application of that theory is predicated on an anti-intellectual interpretation of Freud, whom she condemns for making "science his god" (Mintle 103). Thus, even at their philosophically strongest and most sophisticated, Alcorn and Mintle tend to reject scientific readings of mental health problems for more spiritualized conceptions of those issues. And when that spiritual reading involves risking the lives of young women, it is definitely cause for concern.

List of Acronyms

AACC	American Association of Christian Counselors
BCF	Biblical Counseling Foundation
CAPS	Christian Association for Psychological Studies
CBMW	Council on Biblical Manhood and Womanhood
CBT	Cognitive Behavioral Therapy
CCEC	Christian Counseling and Educational Center
CCEF	Christian Counseling and Educational Foundation
CCHR	Citizen's Commission on Human Rights
CI	Christian International (also known as Christian International Ministries)
CLC	Covenant Life Church
CPC	Crisis Pregnancy Center
CPS	Child Protective Services
DBT	Dialectical Behavioral Therapy
DID	Dissociative Identity Disorder
DSM	Diagnostic and Statistical Manual of Mental Disorders
ECFA	Evangelical Council for Financial Accountability
ED	Eating disorders
FBCM	Faith Baptist Counseling Ministries
FRC	Family Research Council
GARBC	General Association of Regular Baptist Churches
IABC	International Association of Biblical Counselors
IFB	Independent Fundamentalist Baptist
IG	Integrity Group
IHP	Inner Healing Prayer
KJV	King James Version
LGBT	Lesbian, Gay, Bisexual, Transgender
MPD	Multiple Personality Disorder
NANC	National Association of Nouthetic Counselors
NAR	New Apostolic Reformation
NARTH	National Association for the Research and Treatment of Homosexuality

NIHR	National Institute for Healthcare Research
NRM	New Religious Movement
OCD	Obsessive Compulsive Disorder
PDI	People of Destiny International
PTSD	Post-Traumatic Stress Disorder
RMT	Recovered Memory Therapy
RPG	Role-playing game
RTF	Restoring the Foundations
SBC	Southern Baptist Convention
SBTS	Southern Baptist Theological Seminary
SGM	Sovereign Grace Ministries
SLSW	Strategic Level Spiritual Warfare
SRA	Satanic Ritual Abuse
TPM	Theophostic Prayer Ministry
VCF	Vineyard Christian Fellowship

Glossary

Adams, Jay—Founder of the biblical counseling movement.

Amillennialism—A theory of prophecy that holds "that the prophecies concerning both the struggles with anti–Christ and the reign of Christ are being partially fulfilled already in the present church age so that the 'millennium' does not represent a separate historical period" (Marsden 270).

Arminianism—This book largely uses Mark Noll's definition of Arminianism, which emphasizes that Arminian belief is the idea that "God gave prevenient grace (a grace coming before full salvation) to all people so that original sin could be overcome and all could make a free choice for God" (Noll 563). Noll's work covers a period when Arminian belief was largely confined to Methodism within the United States; today it is theologically dominant among most non–Reformed Protestants and is seen as the polar opposite of Calvinism. Originally, Arminians also believed that it was possible for Christians to be "liberated from all known sin" (563). While this belief persists in some more dogmatically Wesleyan churches, most Arminians today would not go that far.

Battlecry Campaign—A movement run by Ron Luce that has been extremely effective in mobilizing evangelical youth but has also garnered widespread criticism for practices deemed to be abusive by former members of its most exclusive and brutal training program, Honor Academy.

Biblical counseling—An explicitly anti-psychiatric evangelical movement predicated on the idea that most serious mental health conditions are actually not the result of "mental illness"—a concept the biblical counseling movement rejects— but are instead the result of sinful behavioral patterns. The movement was founded by Jay Adams and continues to be the dominant voice for anti-psychiatric thinking within the evangelical world.

CCEF—Christian Counseling and Educational Foundation. The dominant force behind "progressive" biblical counseling.

Charismatic renewal movement—The Charismatic renewal was a major revival movement which incorporated many traditional Pentecostal practices that occurred outside the established Pentecostal denominations, beginning in the 1960s. It was characterized by a pragmatic ability to unite across disparate denominational and ideological groups within Christianity at large (including mainline Protestantism and even Catholicism) and had a strong missionary focus (Holvast 35; see also Synan 177–231).

Charismatics—In typical evangelical parlance, Charismatics are usually seen as "Pentecostals-lite," that is, the less radical element of the wider Charismatic and Pentecostal movement. In reality, however, if one is defining Charismatics by the more technical sense of those who indulged in the Charismatic renewal, the exact opposite impression emerges. In general, Charismatic is used in the popular sense of the term (or alternately to refer to the entire Charismatic/Pentecostal movement), since it's so ubiquitous. But readers should remember that denominational Pentecostalism is in many ways less radical than its Charismatic descendants. Regardless of whether one is talking about the Charismatic movement, Charismatic Renewal, or Pentecostalism, all three groups are characterized by a strong belief in the gifts of the spirit, such as speaking in tongues, prophecy, the casting out of demons, and the like.

Complementarianism—An idea "of manhood and womanhood modeled on roles of female submission and male headship" (Joyce x). Particularly popular with the Council on Biblical Manhood and Womanhood (CBMW). Complementarianism has deeply affected the patriarchal arm of biblical counseling practice.

Deliverance—Casting out (or alternately casting away) of evil spirits (Collins 4). Cuneo specifically refers to deliverance as a "form of exorcism" (Cuneo 42). Collins tends to emphasize deliverance's differences from exorcism slightly more than Cuneo (Collins 4), but even he admits the terms are closely linked (4). It is crucial to understand that in most, though not all, Protestant deliverance practice, the sufferer is demonically oppressed or "demonized" rather than possessed (4). Most deliverance practitioners in evangelicalism today are Charismatic, or sometimes neo-evangelical.

Demonic oppression—Term roughly corresponding to demonization but focusing more on demons as external, rather than internal, forces. Demonic oppression also typically can occur from demons operating outside of the human body, something that is somewhat less common in definitions of demonization.

Demonic taxonomies—Systems set up by deliverance practitioners as classifying and diagnostic systems for labeling classes and subclasses of demons, as well as the various afflictions these demons inflict on people. A crucial area of debate within the deliverance community is how to tell between "authentic" cases of possession and mental illness. Despite the claims of deliverance proponents, no taxonomical system has come reasonably close to doing this, though some systems (notably Kurt Koch's) have made some valiant attempts.

Demonization—"To be oppressed, influenced or, even, controlled by demons in some way" (Collins 4). Significantly, Charismatics typically argue that Christians can be demonically oppressed but not possessed.

Emergent Church—A group that self-consciously seeks to elude definition. Nevertheless, it is characterized by a general postmodernist critique of evangelical culture, asserting that "America's youngest generations doubt the human ability to know absolute truth" (Bielo 8). The Emergent Church eclectically borrows from a number of theological traditions, though its origins are clearly evangelical in the main. It is widely seen by many evangelicals as the greatest heresy within the contemporary evangelical church. The present work does not support that position.

Fundamentalism—Fundamentalism was a conservative Protestant movement that, during its period of national prominence during the 1920s, opposed theological modernism and evolutionary theory (Marsden 3–4). Detwiler lists "insistence on the Virgin Birth, the miracles of the Bible, the bodily resurrection of Jesus, and the power of Jesus' sacrificial death to remove the stain of sin from us," along with personal conversion, as the main markers of fundamentalism (Detwiler 151). Fundamentalists are chiefly distinguishable today by their whole-hearted support for biblical inerrancy (in the original texts), creationism, and traditional as opposed to higher critical hermeneutical strategies.

Gay conversion therapy—Term sometimes used synonymously with reparative therapy. In this study, most usages are meant to imply the overall evangelical practice of trying to make LGBT people straight, which may or may not involve reparative therapy but also often incorporates even more pseudoscientific (or simply nonscientific) practices like deliverance ministries and biblical counseling.

Generational curses—A common term in current Charismatic parlance, in which demons are seen as being inherited from ancestors. In Cuneo's work it is variously referred to as "intergenerational evil" or "congenital demonism" (see Cuneo 149). The concept is the same. The idea of generational curses tends to hurt mentally ill evangelicals because many deliverance practitioners assume that genetically inherited mental health problems—indeed, all genetic-based health problems—are actually the result of inherited demons.

Ground-level deliverance and spiritual warfare—Delivering individual human beings and animals from their demons (see Holvast 189 on ground-level demons); Otis Jr. refers to it as "ministry activity that is associated with individual bondage and/or demonization" (Otis Jr. 253). This form of spiritual warfare is opposed to occult level deliverance and spiritual warfare and deliverance from "principalities and powers," (pretty much synonymous with strategic level spiritual warfare), the highest form of deliverance, which typically involves "intercessory confrontations with demonic power concentrated over given cities, cultures, and peoples" (Otis Jr. 257).

Guided imagery—A process in which clients are "encouraged to visualize episodes of violence or abuse during therapy." Oftentimes clients may have "difficulty separating these imaginary events from reality. Researchers have found that people who 'recover' pseudomemories of trauma are often more suggestible and more prone to dissociate—that is, to feel separated from their actual experiences—than most other people" ("false memory syndrome").

Higher Criticism—Term commonly used for the advanced methods of biblical criticism pioneered in the late 18th and 19th centuries, primarily by German theologians. These methods were widely seen as calling traditional interpretations of scripture into disrepute.

Holiness Tradition—Holiness Christians "emphasize religious behavior and the moral life as the marks of a true Christian" (Detwiler 152). Holiness Christians tends to emphasize pietism over political activism. By far the most influential holiness Christian, both in the mental health debate and in evangelicalism as a whole, is James Dobson. Charles Solomon's biblical counseling-like form of psychotherapy—spirituotherapy—also appears to be at least somewhat related to the Holiness tradition, through its connection to the Keswick movement.

Inner healing—A form of healing seen as a "new approach to recovery. It is a therapeutic process where two or more people are involved and wherein God's Spirit is allowed to touch the root cause of disturbances, hurts, and agonies and to restore health in the deepest core of the person's being" (N. Abi-Hashem and H.N. Malony, "Inner Healing"). Inner healing practice commonly intersects with deliverance models, as Chapter 2 points out in great detail. Indeed, the inner healing and deliverance paradigms are arguably somewhat merged at this point in time.

Integrationism—The integrationist school is difficult to define, but roughly it seeks to combine the best of psychological and Christian approaches without sacrificing truth in either area (see Collins, "Moving Through the Jungle," 34). However, unlike more secularized forms of evangelical psychotherapy, integrationism tends to be more willing to criticize secular psychotherapy (Johnson and Jones, "A History," 39), especially if a secular therapeutic practice is seen as conflicting with scripture. Popular Christian integrationists over the last 40 years include Frank Minirth, Paul Meir, and the immensely influential James Dobson (arguably the most powerful evangelical of the last two decades) (see Johnson and Jones, "A History," 39). Integrationism remains the dominant school of professional evangelical psychology and also has attracted a fair number of pop psychology popularizers to its ranks as well, notably Tim LaHaye.

Integrity group (IG)—In this model, the IG leader, as well as other members of the Integrity Group, help determine for the individual what his "norms" should be, often regardless of whether those norms were in the best interest of the client. Mowrer's integrity groups had some influence on Jay Adams.

Keswick Movement—A movement "dedicated to the notion of personal holiness." Its name comes "from a gathering place in Keswick, England." According to Randall Balmer, Keswick theology was marked by a rejection of "the traditional notion that justification was immediate but that the process of sanctification was long and arduous. Instead, Keswick promised deliverance from sin by claiming 'victory in

Christ.' Although neither sin nor the temptation to sin was eradicated, both were counteracted by 'victorious living' through the power of the Holy Spirit" (Balmer 318).

KJV–only churches—Churches that believe in using only the KJV translation of the Bible in church and which vigorously oppose other translations. At their most extreme, KJV–only churches do not even accept the salvation of readers of the NIV, NASB, or other modernized translations. Many KJV–only churches run in the Independent Fundamentalist Baptist (IFB) orbit.

Latter Rain Movement—"A Pentecostal movement of the mid 20th century that, along with the parallel healing movement of that era, became an important component of the post–World War II evangelical awakening" (Riss, "Latter Rain Movement," 830). William Branham and Franklin Hall (see Chapter 1; also Riss, "Latter Rain Movement," 830) were important influences on the movement, which explicitly promoted manifest sons theology (Riss, *Latter Rain* 95–97). Latter Rain teaching was immensely influential on the New Apostolic Reformation (see Holvast 164) and can therefore be seen as an influence on a number of modern deliverance and healing practices, most notably the sozo and RTF models outlined in Chapter 1 and Chapter 2, respectively.

Mainline Protestantism—Here used to refer to the major liberal denominations, such as the Congregationalists, Episcopalians, Lutherans, etc. Note that even in mainline denominations there are many evangelical believers, and some of the counseling practices in this book, particularly deliverance, have made their way into mainline congregations.

Manifest Sons of God—"A belief in a new kind of Christian elite who wield special spiritual power in order to subdue the earth and who will actually conquer the earth in the end times" (Holvast 164). Manifest sons theology was an important influence on both the 1948 Latter Rain Revival and the New Apostolic Reformation. Bill Hamon, who is deeply connected to Mercy Ministries, is an important proponent of Manifest Sons teachings (see Holvast 164).

Multiple Personality Disorder/Dissociative Identity Disorder (MPD/DID)— "A condition in which, proponents believe, one or more 'alter' personalities emerge from a traumatized child to manage the dissociated memories" (Nathan and Snedeker 48). As Nathan and Snedeker point out, there is considerable skepticism about MPD having any "medical validity" and some nay-sayers see the disorder largely as "a social identity, often constructed as a joint effort of patients and their therapists" (Nathan and Snedeker 48). In Nathan's blockbuster deconstruction of the infamous *Sybil* (1973) (a book which should rightly now be considered fiction), *Sybil Exposed* (2011), she points out that in a 1999 sample of American medical professionals on the issue of DID, a clear majority responded that there was "insufficient evidence to justify listing it in the DSM and many suggested that it be deleted" (Nathan, *Sybil Exposed*, 233). Despite this, many deliverance healers openly speak of DID-like symptoms they are encountering in their clients, most notably the sozo healers. With a lack of evidence to support these claims, one must wonder why deliverance supporters continue to stand by them. Note that the DID diagnosis reformed some of the worst abuses in the MPD diagnosis, though many of the basic problems inherent in diagnosing MPD remain (see Nathan, *Sybil Exposed*, 225, 233–237).

NANC—National Association of Nouthetic Counselors. A certifying body for biblical counselors, intended to be used as an accrediting agency, providing "quality control" for nouthetic practice (Powlison 64) and widely seen now as the more conservative of the two major biblical counseling organizations. Recently NANC has changed its name to the Association of Certified Biblical Counselors (ACBC), though the former appellation is used in this book.

Neo-Evangelical—The term is used here approximately as the term born-again evangelical is deployed in Fritz Detwiler's *Standing on the Premises of God:* Neo-evangelicals would be characterized by a "conversion experience" similar to other evangelicals but would not (necessarily) have the hard-line position on inerrancy and creationism that fundamentalists would have nor the emphasis on spiritual gifts that is a part of Charismatic and sometimes Holiness practice (Detwiler 153). The term is a nebulous one in many ways, and the rule of thumb that an evangelical "was [once defined as] anyone who identified with Billy Graham" (Marsden 234) still holds some validity even today. It is difficult to define neo-evangelicals, so it is hard to say if any of the figures covered in this book are explicitly neo-evangelical in orientation, though it is likely that at least some of the perspectivalist and integrationist counselors covered in Chapter 8 are.

New Apostolic Reformation (NAR)—A movement of evangelicals, primarily from the Charismatic tradition, who sought to restore the role of the apostles to contemporary church life. In practice, what this means is a different vision of church ecclesiology, focusing on relational networks over close denominational affiliations and controlled through the natural charisma and authority invested in the apostle (for the relational aspect, see Holvast 159). Holvast relates that in the NAR, one is not "led by a group but by an individual apostle. It was this divinely appointed apostle, as opposed to a board or presbytery, a democratic vote or institution who was seen bearing responsibility for making decisions and guiding adherents" (Holvast 159). As argued in Chapter 3, the NAR's leadership structure allows it to quickly react to changes in contemporary Christian culture; the movement is further aided by its rather pragmatic approach to church growth, an approach inherited by NAR leader C. Peter Wagner from his mentor Donald McGavran. Both the sozo and RTF deliverance models originate in NAR teachings.

New Thought—An ideology—really a system of closely related ideologies—that held that "physical illnesses were manifestations of mental pathologies" (Souders 29). New Thought ideology had close affinities with Pentecostalism (see Souders 29–30, 38, 57) and continues to influence it through interactions between the New Age and positive thinking movement's modern reinterpreters of New Thought ideology. New Thought ideas are particularly noticeable in Word of Faith ideology.

Nouthetic confrontation—The specific practice of nouthetic counseling. Nouthetic confrontation is predicated on the assumption that there is something inherently wrong with the counselee, whether a sin or some other moral or life obstruction. Nouthetic confrontation presupposes that there is something in the client to be confronted. Its main goal is "*to effect personality and behavioral change*" (italics in original) (Adams, *Competent*, 45). Although not necessarily inherently abusive, the practice has seen more than its fair share of evangelical critics since its inception in the late 1960s and early 1970s.

Nouthetics/nouthetic counseling—The old term used for what is today usually called biblical counseling. Many biblical counseling hard-liners—including, significantly, Jay Adams—still seem to prefer the old term. Generally those biblical counselors who use the term nouthetics tend to be more conservative than those using the more "refined" biblical counseling label. In keeping with common convention, I have used the plural term nouthetics on some occasions to define the entire movement, even though technically such pluralization does not fit in with standard Greek usage.

Occam's razor—"The principle that in explaining anything no more assumptions should be made than are necessary" ("Occam's Razor").

Pentecostalism—A major subset of modern Christianity characterized by a strong belief in the gifts of the spirit, such as speaking in tongues, prophecy, the casting out of demons, etc. Pentecostalism can most productively be contrasted with Charismatic belief by pointing out Pentecostalism's stronger allegiances to traditional denominational structures, something that's becoming less and less a characteristic of Charismatic practice. Charismatic practice and ecclesiology also tend to be more ecumenical than traditional Pentecostalism, so long as the groups the Charismatic church allies with reflect conservative moral values.

Perspectivalism—This counseling approach attempts to highlight the difference between "the domains (or 'levels') of psychology and theology" (Johnson and Jones 37). Perspectivalists argue that there are different levels of reality, contending that it confuses things to try to combine theology and psychology, because these two fields have "different objects of study and answer different questions. Confusing them would distort both" (Johnson and Jones 38). Because of this viewpoint, perspectivalists tend to be less concerned about the effects of secularism on psychology (Johnson and Jones 38).

Pietism—The tendency to emphasize individual devotion and ethical behavior rather than the authority and corporate life of a church (OED). The term is used here particularly to refer to Holiness and fundamentalist churches that forsake political activism for the inner spiritual life. This present work unabashedly argues that the pietist strain in evangelicalism, contrary to some of its critics' assertions, represents the best and not the worst of the evangelical tradition.

Post-Abortion Syndrome—A fabricated mental health diagnosis, used among evangelicals, that claims that abortion creates symptomology similar to that suffered by veterans recovering from post-traumatic stress disorder (PTSD).

Postmillennialism—"The idea that "the prophecies in the book of Revelation concerning the defeat of the anti–Christ ... were being fulfilled in the present era, and were clearing the way for a golden age... Christ would return after this millennial age (hence 'postmillennialism') and would bring history to an end.... Postmillennialists typically were optimistic about the spiritual progress of the culture" (Marsden 49). Postmillennialists tend to be more optimistic about social change than premillennialists and therefore are more willing to alter society to bring about positive social change.

Premillennialism—Premillennialists "believe in Jesus Christ's bodily return before His Thousand-year earthly reign" (Boyer 2). Please note that not all premillennialists are dispensational premillennialists. Dispensational premillennialists believe that the history of the world is divided into a number of divinely decreed historical eras (dispensations), and that we are currently in the Church Age, stuck between one crucial event—the Crucifixion—and another—the Rapture (where Christians will be taken bodily up in the air to be with God). The Rapture will be followed by the Tribulation, a 7-year period of great suffering. This will gave way to the Battle of Armageddon, in which Jesus and his saints will return to earth and defeat the Antichrist. Following this is the Millennium, in which Christ reigns a thousand years. A brief final revolt will then be conducted by Satan, the dead will be resurrected, and history's final event, the Last Judgment, will occur (Boyer 88). Please note, however, that this is merely the most popular narrative of the "End Times." "Post-Trib" premillennial dispensationalists believe that the Rapture will occur only after the Tribulation, even for Christians. "Mid-Tribbers" believe the Rapture will occur halfway through the Tribulation.

Presuppositionalism—In modern terms, as popularized by Frances Schaeffer, this philosophy aims to force "nonbelievers to a point of cognitive crisis by increasing their perception of incongruity between the world they believed existed and the world they experienced" (Detwiler 62). Schaeffer borrows largely from Cornelius Van Til in this area, as does Jay Adams (see Detwiler 110–112 on Van Til's influence on Schaeffer).

Preterist—"A person who believes that the prophecies of the book of Revelation have already been fulfilled" (OED).

Prosperity Gospel—"Name It and Claim It," or "Health and Wealth," gospel. Emphasizes the power of a motivated spiritual life to gain the adherent wealth and influence. Often this is done through donating to the ministry that promotes the prosperity gospel, leading to justifiable charges that prosperity ministries exploit their members.

Quiverfull movement—A patriarchal evangelical movement devoted to opposing birth control, including natural family planning, as well as feminism. Quiverfull ideology is typically predicated on a woman having as many children as possible (see Joyce, *Quiverfull*, 133–140).

Reality therapy—A behaviorist school of thought, often favored by schools and prisons. It was founded by William Glasser. The process of nouthetic confrontation bears uncanny similarities to Glasser's reality therapy, which, considering the fact that Glasser was a known influence on Jay Adams (Powlison 1), likely indicates some cross-pollinization going on, at least on the part of Adams.

Reconstructionism—"Broadly speaking, Reconstructionists believe that Christians have a mandate to rebuild, or reconstruct, all of human society, beginning with the United States and moving outward. They contend that the Bible, particularly Mosaic Law, offers the perfect blueprint for the shape a reconstructed world would take" (Martin 353). Reconstructionism is most well-known for its infamous desire to make homosexuality, adultery, blasphemy, and repeated disobedience on the part of children punishable by death (Martin 353).

Recovered memory therapy (RMT)—Any therapeutic process used to recover memories, usually of past abuse and/or torture. The idea behind the practice is to recover memories of events that one does not have current recall of. See, for instance, Priest and Cordill, 381–382. This book, as well as to a certain extent Priest and Cordill's article, makes a convincing case that RMT practices are depressingly widespread among evangelical Christians at this time.

Reformed Christianity—This tradition "draws its defining characteristics from the theological teachings of John Calvin" (Detwiler 154). It is noted mostly among other evangelicals (to a certain extent, too simplistically) for its emphasis on God's power to predestine individual salvation. Reformed Christianity, though the smallest part of the "Christian Right" (Detwiler 154), is also the most theologically influential on the movement as a whole (Detwiler 154). This work follows Detwiler in arguing that Reformed Christianity has disproportionate influence to its relative size. Although many Reformed evangelicals are quite sympathetic to psychiatry and psychology, the movement is also responsible for the largest explicitly anti-psychiatric movement within evangelicalism (and arguably within the United States, or even the world, as a whole): biblical counseling.

Reparative therapy—At its roots, reparative therapy is the idea that "therapy can repair early life traumas" (Erzen 137). This idea "became the basis of counseling" for NARTH and many other evangelical organizations. The basic theory behind modern reparative therapy usually is that male homosexuality is caused by an overbearing mother and a submissive or distant father (see Erzen 146–147, 157). This study contends that though deliverance practice and biblical counseling bear superficial similarities to traditional reparative therapies towards LGBT individuals, in many ways they actually pathologize gays through mechanisms even worse than any of those used by the mainstream reparative therapy movement. Therefore the alternate term "gay conversion therapy" has been used for all the differing types of therapy that have as their goal the "cure" of same-sex attraction.

Restorationism—A set of ideas prevalent within all of Protestantism, but particularly among Charismatics and Pentecostals, that something went dreadfully wrong with the early church, but that the church has been successively reviving itself since the Reformation to a better and better form of Christianity in preparation for Christ's return (Ware 1019). Restorationist thought within the NAR, even more than in most Charismatic movements, is distinguished by an intense hopefulness about the future, which distinguishes it from the pessimistic viewpoint of premillennial dispensationalists.

Satanic ritual abuse (SRA)—The pseudoscientific idea that there was a mass conspiracy of pedophiliac Satanists preying on children. This idea was quite popular in the eighties and nineties and still persists in some parts of evangelicalism. Fueled by an odd alliance of evangelicals (primarily Charismatic in orientation), feminists, and therapists, the SRA scandal would send countless individuals to prison on false charges (no one can estimate how many, but such charges were clearly rampant during this period) (see Nathan and Snedeker 5). Within the context of the evangelical movement's relationship to the mentally ill, the fear of SRA would lead to the persecution of a number of groups considered deviant by the evangelical mainstream, as well as open the door for the use of recovered memory therapy within clearly and totally nontherapeutic settings, such as deliverances. See Chapter 2 for two healing practices that seem to have benefited clearly from the SRA debacle: theophostic prayer ministry (TPM) and sozo healing.

Seeker-Sensitive Church—Evangelical churches devoted to gaining new followers and maintaining membership. There is no set denominational affiliation for such churches, though many do seem to straddle a middle ground between neo-evangelicalism and a "charismatic-lite" gospel. Seeker sensitive churches are often associated with the church growth movement and sometimes with the prosperity gospel. In recent years some of these churches have become more hard-line due to Charismatic, particularly NAR, influence.

Serpent seed doctrine—In the context of the Latter Rain movement, the idea that Eve had "sexual intercourse with the serpent in the Garden of Eden." The result of this sinful breeding was the division of the world between the descendants of Cain (the intellectuals and their allies, the serpent seed) and the godly seed carried through the bloodline of Abel. Branham taught a quite literal form of Christian genoism, where salvation was dependent upon one's bloodline (Douglas Weaver 123–125).

Shabar ministry—A practice in sozo healing circles that tries to heal people suffering from "dissociative" elements in their lives, which the method refers to as "parts." Shabar practice freely invokes DID/MPD terminology liberally, and seems to be quite near to deliberately inducing the symptoms of these "illnesses" so that it might treat them.

Shepherding movement—The shepherding movement, sometimes called the discipleship movement, put a particular emphasis on "accountability and submission to church leaders." Churches were centralized under a "pyramid-like authority structure," with progressively higher levels of shepherds submitting to progressively even higher levels of leadership above them. There were widespread complaints of abuse and cultic manipulation against the shepherding movement that continue to this day. Shepherding played an important part in the acceptance of deliverance ministries in the States. Two of its major leaders were also major leaders within the deliverance "movement," namely Derek Prince and Don Basham (Balmer 523–524). Shepherding practice has in some ways also been unintentionally adopted by some elements within Calvinist circles, particularly after the formerly mainstream Charismatic Sovereign Grace Ministries (SGM) entered the Calvinist fold.

Soul tie—"An ungodly covenant with another person, organization, or thing based on an unhealthy emotional and/or sexual relationship" (Kylstra and Kylstra 322). Soul ties are a particularly troubling concept for trauma victims because the idea of soul ties (particularly ungodly soul ties), in typical Charismatic parlance, means that a rape victim has a demonic tie to her rapist, usually caused by, as in Doris Wagner's deliverance system, the rape victim's unforgiveness (see Doris Wagner, "Forgiving the Unforgivable," 99).

Sozo healing—Influential form of healing that sprang out of the Revival Alliance apostolic network. Based on the deliverance practice of Pablo Bottari, sozo practice incorporates elements of traditional deliverance with inner healing practice and the bizarre idea of divine editing, in which a healer can literally edit memories out of the brain by touching a specific area at the back of the client's head.

Spiritual mapping—A movement, primarily among evangelicals and "neo–Pentecostals," "that specialized in the use of religious techniques to wage a territorial spiritual war against unseen non-human beings" (Holvast 1). Spiritual mapping was a popular practice of strategic level spiritual warfare (SLSW) in the 1990s, and it is partly due to its influence that the New Apostolic Reformation is so powerful today.

Spiritual warfare—"The concept of a dualistic war between good and evil" (Holvast 6). Arguably, some doctrine of spiritual warfare has always been present in the Christian church. However, Charismatics emphasize the idea to extents unheard of since at least the Dark Ages.

Spirituotherapy—Keswick-derived Biblicist therapy pioneered by Charles R. Solomon. It combines Freudian ideas with a Biblicist approach that differs mainly from Adams's nouthetics model in being modeled on a more pietistic form of Christian practice than Adams would prefer.

Spoiling the Egyptians—An idea developed by Larry Crabb that was an "attempt to screen secular psychological concepts in order to determine their compatibility with Christian presuppositions," the goal being to "select concepts and research data from the field of psychology that supports a biblical approach to understanding and relating to God and humans" (Anderson, Zuehlke and Zuehlke 67; Crabb, *Effective*, 47–49). Many later models of integrationism implicitly borrowed from Crabb's metaphor of Spoiling the Egyptians, even models as sophisticated as the semiotics-derived soul care model present in Eric Johnson's *Foundations for Soul Care*.

Strategic Level Spiritual Warfare (SLSW)—Practices that aim to "effect power encounters" that will essentially disempower territorial demonic spirits which hold possession over certain "social groups or geographical locations with which they are identified" (Collins 103).

Theophostic Prayer Ministry (TPM)—A process, according to inner healing prayer supporter Frecia Johnson, by which Jesus replaces false lies with the truth, thus allowing for healing (see Johnson 69). TPM ministry, which almost entirely derives from the teachings of Ed Smith, is one of the most controversial inner healing practices within evangelical circles. Though less dependent on demonism than many other IHP techniques, TPM relies on a number of questionable assumptions, particularly about the nature of memory and trauma.

Third-Wave Charismatic Movement—A term generally used to refer to evangelicals who "recognize the role of the Holy Spirit in divine healing, receiving prophecies, even casting out demons." Unlike traditional Pentecostals, however, they believe that believers "are baptized in the Holy Spirit at the moment of conversion," thus bypassing some of the more, to mainstream evangelicals, alienating elements of denominational Pentecostalism (Balmer 576). Contrary to Balmer and mainstream historians of the Charismatic movement, this work does not see denominational Pentecostalism as suffering from "schismatic tendencies" (576); quite to the contrary, this work asserts that it is precisely some of the Third Wave's later incarnations, particularly the New Apostolic Reformation (NAR), which are most responsible for the currently huge problem of factionalism within denominational Pentecostal churches.

Trilemma—The famous apologetic argument in Lewis's *Mere Christianity* that when simplified is commonly referred to as "Liar, Lunatic, or Lord." The current work argues that the trilemma is an argument mentally ill evangelicals must reject.

Word of Faith—A movement that "believes that the power of Christ is not limited to eternal life. Instead, God intends for all faithful believers to live healthy and wealthy lives in this world" (Souders 28). Basically akin to the prosperity gospel, or the gospel of health and wealth (Souders 28), there is oftentimes significant overlap between WOF teachings and NAR leaders, both of whom predicate their message on Charismatic presuppositions about the physical and spiritual world.

Worldview (or Christian Worldview) theory—Broad theory of culture developed primarily by Francis Schaeffer. Worldview theory was initially applied mainly to art (for this application, see my previous book, *Evangelicals and the Arts in Fiction*) but soon became an overarching philosophy for much of evangelical culture, particularly large sections of the Reformed movement. When extended to the realm of the mental health debate, worldview theory affected a wide range of scholars from various evangelical counseling movements. Elements of it are clearly seen in the thinking of Gary R. Collins. Jay Adams's biblical counseling, though certainly not modeled on Schaeffer's worldview theory, resembled it in many details. The most open combination of worldview thinking with ideas developed from evangelical counseling practice occurs in the mildly Integrationist *Battle for the Mind* by Tim LaHaye, a book that uses emerging scientific insights in psychology and neuroscience to further worldview theory. The effect of LaHaye's work in promoting evangelical acceptance of Schaeffer's ideas cannot be underestimated.

Chapter Notes

Preface

1. Except for the majority of integrationists dealt with in the last chapter.

Introduction

1. For biblical counseling's foundations in pastoral counseling, see Myers-Shirk, chapter 9, passim.

2. For this alignment, see Holvast, 40, 164–165.

3. For a typical biblical counseling view of self-esteem, see Asher and Asher, 175, in which they label self-esteem as "a manifestation of pride." See also, "Counseling and the Sinfulness of Humanity," 64–65, in *Counseling: How to Counsel Biblically* (2005), edited by John MacArthur and the Master's College Faculty.

4. For Powlison's arguments on this score, see Powlison along with his interlocutors, 89–123, in *Understanding Spiritual Warfare: 4 Views*, edited by James K. Beilby and Paul Rhodes Eddy.

Chapter 1

1. To understand territorial spiritual warfare, see Holvast et al., in particular 1, 2, 4.

2. See 397–401 in the RTF manual (but particularly 397), with its specific reference to ancestors as one possible mode of gaining demons.

3. See Pollard. Also see *Starved*, *Violated*, and *Trapped* for Alcorn's views on the mentally ill, trauma victims, and addicts respectively.

4. See Cuneo, 92, as well as Collins, 128–130, on Koch's and Dickason's fairly typical evangelical concerns about the capacity of Christians to be "demonized."

5. Similar diagnostic problems also occurred in the biblical counseling movement, which led to the creation of similar taxonomies that differed from the Pentecostal model mainly in labeling each mental illness as representing a specific type of sin-problem rather than a demonic problem. See in particular Asher and Asher but also Lisa and Ryan Bazler's *Psychology Debunked*. More sophisticated proponents of biblical counseling, however, have been moving away from such taxonomies in recent years.

6. For the popularity of films on MPD during the formative years of the deliverance movement, see Nathan and Snedeker's *Satan's Silence*, 48–49.

7. In general, neo-evangelical deliverance supporters were more cautious about diagnosing all mental health problems as demonic affliction.

8. Note that I quote from the 1993 edition.

9. See also Bass and Davis's whole chapter defending those who made accusations in the Satanic Panic, 475–534.

10. The most classic text in this regard is Phil Phillips's legendary *Turmoil in the Toybox* (1986). He has a whole chapter devoted to the evils of the *Masters of the Universe* (85–112), deals with the sins of *Star Wars* (139–42) and declaims the occult elements found in *The Smurfs* (76–77).

11. Benjamin Nolot, the leader of Exodus Cry, has stated at the 2012 Exodus Cry Summit, in his speech "Restoring the Ancient Path of Abolition," that "the sad reality as I look out ... there's people out there who have been restored [from prostitution] but they're not free. And the reality is many of them are nursing at the breasts of demons because they do not

know the comfort that comes from God.... Annie Lobert tells us she's been raped by demons hundreds of times, talking about the demonic forces that have raped them and it's truly, truly a deeply spiritual issue. I mean ... talking with Annie Dieselberg from Nightlight... She's had to buy into a whole method of deliverance just to do the ministry they are doing ... because these girls [sex workers] are so completely demonized" (demonization is a Charismatic term for being demon-inhabited) (Nolot).

12. Here, I am using the term evangelical in the broad sense since the term neo-evangelical is really inappropriate to the German theological context.

13. I have heard it sometimes asserted by popular sources, e.g., blogs, Wikipedia, that evangelicals in general and Warnke in particular are solely or primarily responsible for the Satanic Ritual Abuse Scandal. The truth is somewhat more complex. See Nathan and Snedeker's *Satan's Silence*, 5–7, in particular for a brief overview of the various forces involved. The rest of that book details the involvement of all the various groups in perpetuating the witch-hunting, including feminists, the justice system, and portions of the media.

14. See in particular Asher and Asher passim, Bazler and Bazler, 96–99, and to a much lesser extent Adams's foundational *Competent to Counsel*, 29–30, for biblical counseling conceptualizations of the mentally ill. Adams (and perhaps the Bazlers) would dispute this characterization of their work, yet it is hard for any objective reader to come to any other conclusion after fully sampling their writing.

15. I am unable to confirm, however, whether Basham bought into Prince's rather esoteric views of demonic origins.

16. This is not to say Prince's theory of demonology originated with him, as he himself admits. As mentioned before, it's derived from G.H. Pember's 1876 *Earth's Earliest Ages*.

Chapter 2

1. No relation, to my knowledge, despite the similar sounding name.

2. See Alcorn, *Violated*, 9, 20–22, and Doris Wagner, 92–93, in *How To Minister Freedom* for typical examples of this trend.

3. Spelling errors are in Smith's original statement, not in Fletcher's book.

4. Smith especially wants counselors for TPM clients to be "theophostic friendly." See Smith 260.

5. I italicize the term *sozo* only to refer to translation issues.

6. See the Britannica article on "natural selection" as an example of the nonrandomness of biological evolution.

7. See Brown's now infamous study on proximal intercessory prayer, "Study of the Therapeutic Effects of Proximal Intercessory Prayer [STEPP] on Auditory and Visual Impairments in Rural Mozambique," as well as her book *Testing Prayer* for examples of her scholarly practice.

8. Significantly, I could find no mention of the wall in Reese's work.

9. See all of chapter 9 in Reese, 153–175.

10. The man later sued one of the people who tried to use faith healing on him rather than go for medical aid. The case was decided against him, but the basic fact that his friends spent several hours trying to use Bethel-inspired faith healing practices on him rather than call for medical aid is not in dispute. See Sabalow, "Ex Bethel Student Not at Fault in '08 fall; Judge Says Woman Not Obligated to Act."

Chapter 3

1. A response to Mercy survivor advocate Lisa Kerr's article on Mercy Ministries, purporting to come from Mercy's director of marketing, claimed the following: "As Executive Director of Marketing at Mercy Ministries of America (MMOA), I wanted to respond to, clarify and correct some of the information contained in this commentary. Much of this commentary revolves around allegations leveled some years back against Mercy Ministries of Australia (MMAU). To clarify, MMAU was an autonomous entity distinct from MMOA, with separate funding, oversight, leadership, program design and organizational structure. Although it shared the 'Mercy' name, it was not founded by MMOA's Founder & President, Nancy Alcorn. Simply put, MMAU was an independent charity with no oversight from MMOA and was solely responsible for its operations and actions." See Kerr, "The Dark Side of Mercy Ministries." Nevertheless, the use of the "Wayback Machine" on Google shows that Mercy was advertising its Australian international homes as of 2006. See "Mercy Min-

istries: Locations." Mercy Australia also apparently considered itself linked to Mercy Ministries International, and thereby Mercy Ministries America. Again see the Wayback Machine, "Mercy Ministries International." Caleb Hannen's article "Jesus RX" also is clearly very skeptical about Alcorn's claims that Australia represented a rogue organization.

2. Mercy Survivors has, however, recently obtained a copy which they believe to be genuine. See Mercy Survivors, "Mercy Ministries Counseling Manual Exposed." The Survivors Network believes the changes in the manual to be largely superficial (as do I) and spin control, but it's hard to prove that without more extensive leaks from within the organization.

3. For Alcorn's statements on generational curses, see Alcorn, *Starved*, 46, on the curse of generational patterns being broken; see *Violated*, 50, which uses the terms pattern and curse. Talk of generational curses runs fairly rife through her writing.

4. See in particular this infamous clip from Nancy's speaking engagements that was put up on YouTube by survivor advocates: "Mercy Ministries and Exorcisms."

5. All quotations from *Echoes of Mercy* are from the first edition unless noted.

6. Alcorn is unclear when exactly she worked for the Tennessee government but internal textual evidence indicates it was likely sometime in the early to late seventies, possibly extending even longer than that.

7. For example, one should look at the discipline of reality therapy, a behaviorist school of thought often favored by prisons and high-crime schools, on which the repressive biblical counseling movement is based. The infamous behaviorist Stanford experiment, which Alcorn may very well have been aware of given her occupation, was also conducted during this period.

8. See Piercy's landmark *Women on the Edge of Time*, which remains to this day one of the best and most moving fictional treatments of mental illness ever written.

9. There's some overlap with Alcorn's work with the state and her volunteering for Teen Challenge.

10. Alcorn returned to Teen Challenge after going off volunteer status and before working with Mercy.

11. To be fair, such rhetoric characterizes many evangelical charities in general, particularly within the New Apostolic Reformation. For a particularly egregious example of such dualism, I suggest the reader check out the propaganda of the sex trafficking abolitionist group Exodus Cry.

12. See Alcorn 205, *Echoes of Mercy*, revised edition (2008), which clearly shows that the Australian homes were part of the wider Mercy Ministries movement and certainly not a "rogue" operation; also see Hannan, "Jesus RX," on Australian closings.

13. See *Starved*, *Cut*, *Trapped*, and *Violated* for Nancy's description of her ministry to each of these groups respectively.

14. The endorsement reads as follows: "God has granted Paula Kilpatrick insight and anointing in the area of deliverance and setting the captives free. Because of Paula's powerful experience of deliverance in her own life, she knows firsthand the tremendous need for this ministry today.... I have Paula come on a regular basis to minister to the girls at Mercy Ministries, and I highly recommend her as an anointed speaker and minister" (see Kilpatrick and Kilpatrick v).

15. The YouTube link to this video is also provided in the works cited for your convenience under the entry "Mercy Ministries and That Exorcism," is http://www.youtube.com/watch?v=soX-IOeO9jg.

16. See Appendix B for more material on Mintle and how her philosophy of eating disorders interacts with Alcorn's own.

17. The SPLC uses the older term for NAR, Joel's Army, which applies more to the most extreme elements of the movement today, which most groups in the NAR do still have some sympathy with. See Sanchez.

Chapter 4

1. See Hendrickson and Fitzpatrick, 28–30, for a particularly extreme example of Adams's disciples' writings in this regard.

2. Nouthetic counseling was the original term used for biblical counseling. Counselors who still prefer the term nouthetic over biblical tend to be slightly more conservative in their counseling approach.

3. The reader will recall that shepherding is a practice in which a higher member of a Charismatic church has almost complete control over a member of lower rank. It was popular in the seventies and eighties but has

since fallen out of favor. See Cuneo, 121–123, nineteen-seventies shepherding and Moore's more biased pro-shepherding account on the end of shepherding, 154–178.

4. Obviously, many (though not all) biblical counselors would be opposed to getting degrees in the former on foundational grounds. However, it is difficult to see how these counselors could realistically obtain knowledge about "organic vs. sin" problems without a degree in one of these two fields.

5. However, the coauthor of *The Christian's Guide to Psychological Terms*, Mary Asher, has a psychology degree. But it is unclear what school awarded this degree or what level of degree it was (see Asher and Asher, back cover).

6. This characteristic is somewhat less prevalent among some well-meaning third generation biblical counselors, such as Michael Emlet.

7. A deeply Calvinist friend of mine once commented to me that one of the fatal flaws of biblical counseling was its unintentionally Arminian theology of human volition, and I do not think she was wrong about this.

8. These ideas are in part suggested by Powlison in *The Biblical Counseling Movement: History and Context*, 185, in his analysis of anti-biblical counseling critiques, though he would understandably object to these critiques himself as he is a prominent biblical counseling advocate.

9. Mowrer, though often grouped with the anti-psychiatric movement, would probably reject the label.

Chapter 5

1. Powlison's characterization of Bettler is, of course, to a certain extent self-serving. As someone who ended up siding with Bettler's form of biblical counseling versus what was seen as the more extreme forms of biblical counseling/nouthetics promoted by Jay Adams and various extremist critics like Ryan and Lisa Bazler, Mary and Marshall Asher, and the infamous Martin and Deidre Bobgan, Powlison wants to cast Bettler in the best possible light. The current self-constructed narrative of the biblical counseling movement distinguishes between the "hard-line" position of Adams and the even more extreme critics to the right of him and the "moderates" that Powlison, as the ideological descendant of Bettler, now leads.

While this narrative is not totally false (Powlison is certainly less "anti-intellectual" than the Bobgans and less confrontational than Adams in his own self-presentation), it does tend to mask the fact that Powlison himself has at times supported dubious extremist causes (particularly Sovereign Grace Ministries). The link between Powlison and Sovereign Grace will be covered later in this chapter. In addition, though Powlison is a reasonably fair, if biased, historian considering his subject position, his writing lacks the kind of theological creativity that characterizes some of Adams more outlandish theological pronouncements.

2. Westminster is still well regarded today among conservative evangelicals.

3. For representative examples of Smith's work, see "Chronic Fatigue," "Lithium and the Biblical Counselor" and "Christian Doctors on Depression," the last coauthored with Addam Masri, Andy Smith, James Schaller and Ed Welch.

4. See Powlison, 213–214, on the professionalization of CCEF.

5. Note that a fairly well-known defunct blog, "Against Biblical Counseling," was run by the author of this text. Obviously, I was playing on the title of the Bobgan book.

6. The documentary is entitled "Psychology and the Church." (I have also cited it in the Works Cited section; see http://www.youtube.com/watch?v=K79ZhPUHFvQ.)

7. See "Return to The Word" citation at end of the book.

8. For instance, he's one of the only biblical counseling advocates to mention Wilhelm Fliess's crucial influence on Freud.

9. In fact, there were also reports in 2002 of "allegedly inappropriate behavior" between staff and children (see Swiech and also Guetersloh).

10. See Detwiler, 105–121, for an excellent overview of Christian worldview thinking.

11. See CCEF, "Hours, Fees, Directors," on lack of insurance reimbursement.

12. See Detwiler, 108, on Van Til's departure from Westminster.

13. Cited here as part of Powlison's *The Biblical Counseling Movement: History and Context*.

14. See http://www.sgmsurvivors.com/2009/05/18/what-sovereign-grace-teaches-pastors-about-counseling-part-3/ for a transcript of part three of the sermon, as well as

parts one and two. I have also independently verified the sermon existed and was recorded by the SGM Survivors blog with meticulous accuracy—and have an MP3 file of it.

15. For a list of Piper's articles in the JBC, see the next chapter.

16. Note that I found this document on Brent Detwiler's Web site. Detwiler is a well-known enemy of Sovereign Grace. However, more neutral sites, such as Wartburg Watch and SGM Survivors, do not dispute that this is an authentic court document.

17. For a good idea of Piper's view of gender, see the infamous video "Does a Woman Submit to Abuse?" to get an idea of where he's coming from. The video was still up on YouTube as of 8 August 2013 at http://www.youtube.com/watch?v=3OkUPc2NLrM. Piper's influence on evangelical patriarchal counseling will be covered in the next chapter.

18. Note that Taylor is not one of the critics I am referring to.

19. Mahaney's name has since been removed from the Web site, a sign, perhaps, of CCEF's growing unease with their attachment to him.

20. Charlton, T.F. "Sovereign Grace Sexual Abuse Lawsuit Just Got More Complicated." *Religion Dispatches.* 13 Jun 2013. Web. 8 Oct 2014. http//religiondispatches.org/sovereign-grace-sexual-abuse-lawsuit-just-got-more-complicated/

21. See Kris at http://www.sgmsurvivors.com/2009/05/18/what-sovereign-grace-teaches-pastors-about-counseling-part-3/ as well as parts one and two of that sermon, on this point.

Chapter 6

1. Please note that not all of these methods are an exact match with biblical counseling, however.

2. See "Treasuring Christ Together," *Journal of Biblical Counseling* 22, no. 2 (2004), 83–86, and "God's Glory Is the Goal of Biblical Counseling," *Journal of Biblical Counseling* 20, no. 2 (2002), 8–21, for representative examples of his articles in support of biblical counseling.

3. Moore was the chairman of the board for the Council of Biblical Manhood and Womanhood (see "Russell Moore: Chairman of the Board"). See Jeff Robinson on Moore's view of biblical counseling as well as Allen for

both Moore and his opponents' views of the shift to biblical counseling in the SBC.

4. Lambert was a peer reviewer on the Council of Biblical Manhood and Womanhood's journal as of 2013 (see *Journal for Biblical Manhood and Womanhood* [Spring 2013], 1). Lambert's *The Biblical Counseling Movement After Adams* (2012) is a well-known pro-biblical counseling text.

5. For Rekers's views on homosexuality, also to be detailed below, see Lochhead.

6. See acknowledgments in *The Excellent Wife* for her allegiance to and alignment with Jay Adams. See Scott, *Exemplary Husband*, loc 49, for Peace's relationship to his work.

7. For Mohler's effect on the Southern Baptist Convention, see Hansen's *Young, Restless, and Reformed* (2008), with its hagiographic rendering of Mohler's life. Mohler states to Hansen that he does not want to deliberately Calvinize the SBC, but he seems to contradict himself on pages 76 and 77 by pointing out why Calvinism and biblical inerrancy are two crucial issues that the modern SBC must deal with if it is not to forfeit "its theological heritage." If Mohler's intent is not to Calvinize the SBC, one must wonder why he sticks so ardently to Calvinist allies like C.J. Mahaney long after he has lost any strategic or moral reason for supporting them. For Mohler's connection to SGM, see SGM Survivors, "Al Mohler & John Bettler Honor C.J. Mahaney," for the now infamous video retrieved by the SGM Survivors group of Mohler and John Bettler praising C.J. Mahaney.

8. Titus 2 ministries refers to a diverse school of teaching and ministries related to biblical womanhood (see Joyce, *Quiverfull*, 61).

9. See Fitzpatrick, *Love to Eat, Hate to Eat,* 121, on idolatry in relation to weight; Fitzpatrick's "Helping Bulimics" is a particularly infamous use of the idolatry model in relationship to bulimia (see pages 16 and 18 specifically).

10. Some of Murray's pronouncements against ATI curriculum may have been fictional. See Megan on this.

11. See Case for information on Szasz's Jewish ancestry. Szasz was born to Jewish parents, but to my knowledge was a nonbeliever by the end of his life. For Szasz's atheism, see Stadlen.

12. Gothard's influence is particularly notable in regard to former Arkansas governor

and Republican presidential candidate Mike Huckabee. See Posner.

13. Readers should not take this statement on bias as a condemnation of Zichterman, who is a controversial but I believe ultimately valuable figure in evangelical survivor circles. It's simply meant as a statement of fact. In addition, I am in no way implying that Zichterman's account is wrong. Everything which I could independently verify from her account turned out to be accurate, which is why I have used her as a source, as getting information about IFB churches from outside of their environs is so difficult.

14. Many of Mercy's survivors have complained to me about Nancy Alcorn's position on this point.

15. Please note that the IFB does not keep membership lists and views each church or school as independent, though there are close alliances between the various members of this informal group. Therefore there is no formal list of IFB-affiliated colleges online, nor is there ever likely to be; many IFB colleges are also quite deceptive in noting their allegiances or even simply their recruiting practices (Pensacola Christian College is *famous* for this). The situation is further complicated by the fact that there are some independent Baptist groups that are definitely not IFB, simply independent. I therefore had to rely on a Wikipedia-derived list (pretty obviously put up by a critic) that I obtained through the almost always accurate Wartburg Watch discernment blog. The link to the Wartburg Watch site list of IFB colleges is under "The Independent Fundamentalist Baptist Church: Jesus Wore Pants, Not a Dress." I believe the list is unfortunately as accurate information as we are likely to get without IFB churches becoming more transparent in their internal operations. I carefully looked at all the school Web sites to get a feel for whether their ideology seemed to fit into IFB parameters, and as far as I could tell from the college descriptions the list was accurate.

16. I say this as an only recently former pro-lifer and as someone with a deep sympathy for the goal of ending the need for abortion, if not a deep desire to implement that policy legally.

Chapter 7

1. The basically antigay element of conversion therapy, however, remains consistent in all these "therapeutic" practices.

2. See Foster, 216, for a fairly typical (actually relatively enlightened by deliverance standards but not anyone else's) description of demonic afflictions resulting from homosexuality. Foster believes that demons can become part of a LGBT person's problems but denies that there is a "demon of homosexuality." The demon of homosexuality idea is still quite common in popular culture, however, as several recent high-profile exorcisms of LGBT individuals have shown us. For this depressing practice, see Netter.

3. This has been documented for a long time and was old news when *One Nation Under God* was filmed. See APA Task Force on Appropriate Therapeutic Responses to Sexual Orientation, *Report of the Task Force on Appropriate Therapeutic Responses to Sexual Orientation* (2009) for the APA's current stance on homosexuality, pages v, vii. Note that this is the American Psychological Association.

4. For Smith's influence on the Vineyard see Jackson, *Radical Middle*, 33–40. Note that the Vineyard movement eventually split from Smith (see Jackson, 85–87). See Poloma "The Toronto Blessing," 1149–1152, for Randy Clark's involvement in the Toronto Blessing. Clark is a prominent NAR apostle. See the advertisement "Randy Clark, C. Peter Wagner, Che Ahn," from a prominent New Apostolic Web site (Elijah List), which openly admits that Clark is a prominent leader in the NAR.

5. Recent media reports indicate that Anne is divorcing from John. See Brydum.

6. For Exodus's closing, see Do, Mather, Mozingo.

7. See, for instance, Pogue and Roberts.

8. The tragedy of Reimer's life opened some Americans' eyes to the existence of intersexuality, a term "used for a variety of conditions in which a person is born with a reproductive or sexual anatomy that doesn't seem to fit the typical definitions of female or male" ("What is Intersex?"). Intersexuality, as many evangelicals realize, poses major threats to the traditional antigay hermeneutic of the evangelical church, and even more so to evangelical attempts at outlawing gay marriage. If marriage is defined as between one man and one woman, some states may end up banning intersexuals from being married, if the law does not catch up with the modern scientific understanding of human sexuality. And here the fault will clearly be the state's, not that of the intersexual

community, who even the evangelical community cannot realistically blame for their sexual difference from those of "determinate" gender.

9. Also see also Payne, *Crisis of Masculinity*, loc 429, which embraces similar techniques.

10. Feminists rejected Freud's disavowal of the prevalence of familial incest, for quite understandable reasons, namely that it had been in Freud's self-interest to disavow his original research because of the controversy it generated. Nevertheless, the feminist movement in the seventies and eighties extrapolated insights from Freudian psychology and psychoanalysis that were clearly fallacious, especially relating to the reliability of memory (particularly children's memories) through "recovered memory" therapy.

11. The practice of proselytizing AIDS victims on their deathbeds for the supposed "sin" of homosexuality was a depressingly common one in the late 1980s and early 1990s. Several survivors of ex-gay therapy (as well as survivor advocates) in *One Nation Under God* tell absolutely horrifying stories of dying friends who faced similar proselytizing efforts as they were suffering from AIDS.

Chapter 8

1. See Beaven et al., but see particularly Beaven's concerns in chapters 3 and 4 of his work regarding Crabb's use of spiritual direction practices.

2. This is not as meant as a put-down of biblical counselors. Oftentimes they offer up more profound critiques of traditional psychotherapy than do integrationists. However, traditionally, biblical counselors have tended to have a very limited understanding of Freudian thinking, which they tend to dismiss too easily as sex-obsessed and navel-gazing, as opposed to humanistic therapy and behaviorism, which they often have quite interesting or at least accurate ideas about.

3. Scientism is, according to the *Baker Encyclopedia of Psychology and Counseling*, the idea "that science is the only legitimate way of knowing." See Bufford "Behavioral Psychology," 129.

4. Clinton's endorsement reads as follows: "David Appleby walks where angels fear to tread. And he does it well. He takes a hard look at spiritual warfare and engaging the enemy. Offering a fresh look at a practice [de-

liverance] that we otherwise tend to deny altogether or obsess about far too much, this book is a balanced, excellent resource that I highly recommend" (Appleby acknowledgments). Clinton's fellow academic and close collaborator George Ohlschlager also endorses the book and specifically commends its stance on deliverance, which makes it all but impossible for Clinton to claim he does not know what he is endorsing in Appleby's work. See Appleby acknowledgments. For information on the American Association of Christian Counselors, including their organizational framework, see Gary R. Collins, "American Association of Christian Counselors (AACC)," 72–73.

5. Myers-Shirk's work is to this date the only secular work, other than an essay in the *Journal of Religion and Popular Culture*, "Unpardonable Sins: The Mentally Ill and Evangelicalism in America," written by myself, to critically address the issues raised by the biblical counseling movement in anything approaching scholarly depth.

6. Guyatt is, if anything, too cautious in his description of this manual, which still makes for hilarious reading, including for culturally savvy evangelicals, in the more relaxed sexual atmosphere of 21st century America.

7. See Biblical Discernment Ministries' "Charles Solomon" for a typical anti–Solomon complaint.

8. This is also one of Solomon's most significant differences with Adams. Adams does not believe in a trichotomous view of the soul (see Adams, *A Theology of Christian Counseling*, 110–111). Adams's vision of the dichotomous nature of humanity argues that human beings are *duplex* beings, by which he means to stress "the unity of the elements (they are 'folded' together) rather than their separability (which, as we saw is unnatural for man)" (Adams 110). Though I appreciate Adams's rejection of the deeply unscientific elements of Solomon's theology, it is difficult to see how Adams's vision of humanity's duplex nature is anything more than monism subtly redefined, but here with the possibility of this monism being either all soul or all body. In this sense, Adams's vision of humanity's dichotomous nature, since it clearly is not biologically monist, verges on being a twisted version of the Docetist heresy, with Adams, despite his denials, being in a way a soul monist or perhaps an un-

intentional idealist on the Edwardsian line. Therefore, I would argue that, as flawed as less sophisticated biblical counseling proponents' theology usually is, the traditional concept of dichotomous thinking inherited from Cartesian elements of Christian practice is probably marginally more workable a theological idea than Adams's duplex vision. Both ideas, obviously, are highly problematic to secular thinkers in any case.

9. Solomon uses the term flesh as synonymous with self, so his words should more properly be seen as equaling flesh-centeredness. The rhetoric ends up meaning about the same thing (see loc 1539).

10. Indeed, almost all examples of purported mental illness in Adams's works turn out to be the result of patient malingering, which shows the rather obvious influence of Thomas Szasz on his work. Szasz's *Myth of Mental Illness* was practically predicated on this idea.

11. For information on the Keswick movement, the best source is probably D.W. Bebbington's *Evangelicalism in Modern Britain* (1989), 151–180.

12. Crabb has at various times in his career also called his treatment model biblical counseling.

13. Note that I use the revised edition of this work, the *New Dare to Discipline* (1992).

14. Dobson is more open to a slightly freer relationship between parents and teens.

15. See Myers's listing on "Supported Books"; but this is just one of his Templeton links. Myers was at one time also a trustee of Templeton. See Myers "Supported Books and Articles (Abstracts)."

16. See the epilogue to the book version for this point; Nicholi slightly more carefully shields his views in the documentary version of *The Question of God*.

Appendix A

1. An example is the famous casting of the demons into pigs (see Luke 8:26–39).

2. The apophatic tradition in Eastern Orthodoxy puts a particular emphasis on the idea of the unknowability of God (see Fairbain, 51–55). See Papinkalou, 359, on Orthodox ideas about God's ontological nature.

Appendix B

1. In fact, some historians believe that the current preponderance of female bulimics is a historical abnormality: "Historians of psychopathology note that for hundreds of years the vast majority of (unsystematically) recorded cases were male" (Barlow and Durand, 235).

2. Significantly, chronic obesity is not commonly dealt with by Alcorn, not because of legitimate debates about whether obesity is an eating disorder but probably because a picture of a 250-pound woman will not sell as many copies as a 100-pound starving fashionista.

3. Indeed *most patients know this*, even patients without eating disorders.

Works Cited

Abi-Hashem, N., and H.N. Malony. "Inner Healing." In *Baker Encyclopedia of Psychology and Counseling*. 2nd ed. Ed. David G. Benner and Peter C. Hill. Grand Rapids, MI: Baker Books, 1999.

Abildness, Abby H. *Healing Prayer and Medical Care*. Destiny Image, Kindle edition (2010–12–01).

Adams, Jay. *The Big Umbrella and Other Essays and Addresses on Christian Counseling*. Nutley, NJ: Presbyterian and Reformed, 1972.

_____. *The Christian Counselor's Manual*. Grand Rapids, MI: Zondervan, 1973.

_____. *Competent to Counsel*. Grand Rapids, MI: Zondervan, 1970.

_____. *A Theology of Christian Counseling: More Than Redemption*. Grand Rapids, MI: Zondervan, 1979.

Alcorn, Nancy. "Beauty Is in the Eye of the Beholder." nancyalcorn.com, 6 February 2009. http://www.nancyalcorn.com/2009/02/beauty-is-in-eye-of-beholder.html (accessed 8 August 2013).

_____. *Cut: Mercy for Self-Harm*. Enumclaw, WA: WinePress, 2007.

_____. "Don't Wait for Tomorrow." nancyalcorn.com, 23 February 2009. http://www.nancyalcorn.com/2009/02/dont-wait-for-tomorrow.html (accessed 9 August 2013).

_____. *Echoes of Mercy*. 1st ed. Nashville: Mercy Ministries of America, 1992.

_____. *Echoes of Mercy*. Revised ed. Mercy Ministries, 2008.

_____. *Keys to Walking and Living in Freedom*. 4-CD set. Disk 2. Sermon Mercy Ministries. Nashville, n.d.

_____. *Mission of Mercy: Allowing God to Use YOU to Make a Difference in Others*. Charisma House. Kindle edition (2013–05–07).

_____. "Nancy Alcorn Sets the Record Straight: An Open letter from Nancy Alcorn, Founder and President of Mercy Ministries." nancyalcorn.com, 25 February 2009. http://www.nancyalcorn.com/2009/02/nancy-alcorn-sets-record-straight.html (accessed 8 August 2013).

_____. "On the Road Again." nancyalcorn.com, 13 April 2009. http://www.nancyalcorn.com/2009/04/on-road-again.html (accessed 25 August 2013).

_____. *Starved*. Enumclaw, WA: Winepress, 2007.

_____. "Thousands Gathered to Pray for Our Nation: Update from the Call." Nacyalcorn.com, 8 September 2010. http://www.nancyalcorn.com/2010/09/thousands-gathered-to-pray-for-our.html (accessed 8 August 2013).

_____. *Trapped: Mercy for Addictions*. Enumclaw, WA: WinePress, 2008.

_____. *Violated: Mercy for Sexual Abuse*. Enumclaw, WA: WinePress, 2008.

Alden, Helena. "Identity Work and the New Christian Right: How Focus on the Family Rhetorically Constructs the 'Ex-gay' Self." PhD diss., University of Florida, 2008.

Allen, Bob. "Seminary Adopts 'Biblical' Counseling" *Ethicsdaily*.com, 16 March 2005. http://www.ethicsdaily.com/seminary-adopts-biblical-counseling-cms-5476 (accessed 18 August 2013).

Almy, Gary. *How Christian Is Christian*

Counseling?: The Dangerous Secular Influences That Keep Us from Caring for Souls. Wheaton, IL: Crossway, 2000.

Anderson, Allan. *An Introduction to Pentecostalism: Global Charismatic Christianity*. Cambridge: Cambridge University Press, 2004.

Anderson, Jack, and Joe Spear. "Communications Czar Uses Pentagon Post." *Nevada Daily Mail*, 13 January 1977 (listed online as 1/12/77), p. 4. http://news.google.com/newspapers?nid=1908&dat=19770112&id=mEYrAAAAIBAJ&sjid=ddQEAAAAIBAJ&pg=1707,727147.

Anderson, Jack, and Les Whitten. "Military Radio Mismanagement Cited." *Washington (D.C.) Post*, 13 January 1977, p. 13(?) (microfilm unclear).

Anderson, Neil. *The Bondage Breaker*. Eugene, OR: Harvest House, 2000.

_____. *Discipleship Counseling: The Complete Guide to Helping Others Walk in Freedom and Grow in Christ*. Ventura, CA: Regal, 2003.

Anderson, Neil, Terry Zuehlke and Julianne Zuehlke. *Christ Centered Therapy: The Practical Integration of Theology and Psychology*. Grand Rapids, MI: Zondervan, 2000.

Anonymous Organization. "Fact Checking CCHR's Board of Advisors," March 2008. http://forums.whyweprotest.net/threads/fact-checking-cchr-board-of-advisors.5761/ (accessed November 2011).

APA Task Force on Appropriate Therapeutic Responses to Sexual Orientation. *Report of the Task Force on Appropriate Therapeutic Responses to Sexual Orientation*. Washington, D.C.: American Psychological Association, 2009. http://www.apa.org/helpcenter/sexual-orientation.aspx.

APA Task Force on Mental Health and Abortion. *Report of the APA Task Force on Mental Health and Abortion*. Washington, D.C., 2008. http://www.apa.org/pi/women/programs/abortion/index.aspx.

Appleby, David W. *It's Only a Demon: A Model of Christian Deliverance*. Winona Lake, IN: BMH Books, 2009.

Asher, Marshall, and Mary Asher. *The Christian's Guide to Psychological Terms*. Bemidji, Minnesota: Focus Publishing, 2004.

"Autistic Boy Dies During Exorcism." *CBS News*, 11 February 2009. http://www.cbsnews.com/2100-201_162-570077.html (accessed 8 July 2013).

Backus, William. *Telling the Truth to Troubled People*. Minneapolis: Bethany House, 1985.

_____. *What Your Counselor Never Told You: Seven Secrets Revealed-Conquer the Power of Sin in Your Life*. Baker, Kindle ed., September 1, 2000.

Backus, William, and Marie Chapian. *Telling Yourself the Truth*. Baker, Kindle ed., February 1, 2000.

Bailey, Sarah Pulliam. "Psychologist Resigns from NARTH After Gay Prostitute's Claims." *Christianity Today*, 12 May 2010. http://www.christianitytoday.com/ct/2010/mayweb-only/29-32.0.html (accessed 18 August 2013).

Balmer, Randall. *Encyclopedia of Evangelicalism*. Louisville: Westminster John Knox, 2002.

Barlow, David H., and V. Mark Durand. *Abnormal Psychology: An Integrative Approach*. 2nd ed. Pacific Grove, CA: Brooks/Cole, 1999.

Basham, Don. *Deliver Us from Evil*. Grand Rapids: Chosen, 1972.

Bass, Ellen, and Laura Davis. *The Courage to Heal: A Guide for Women Survivors of Child Sexual Abuse*. 3rd ed. New York: HarperCollins, 1994.

"Battlecry." In *Battlecry and Acquire the Fire* promotion DVD, 2006.

Bazler, Lisa, and Ryan Bazler. "Adam Lanza 'on Medication' According to His Friends, Neighbors." *Psychology Debunked*, 2012 (?). 18 August 2013. http://psychologydebunked.com/adam-lanza-on-medication-according-to-friends-neighbors/.

_____. "Psychology Debunked: Exposing Psychology, Exalting Christ." *Psychology Debunked*. 2012. 18 August 2013. http://psychologydebunked.com/.

_____. *Psychology Debunked*. Lake Mary, Florida: Creation House, 2002.

Beach, Randall. "Expert in Religion Says Komisarjevsky's Family Were 'Religious Maximalists.'" *Register Citizen*, 15 November 2011. http://www.registercitizen. com/general-news/20111115/expert-in-religion-says-komisarjevskys-family-were-religious-maximalists-updated (accessed 8 August 2013).

Beaven, Neil. "Eschatology as Orienting Motif: A Practical Theological Approach to Transforming the Ministry of Evangelical Spiritual Direction at Urban Sanctuary, Edmonton, AB." Ph.D. diss., Boston University School of Theology, 2011.

Bebbington, D.W. *Evangelicalism in Modern Britain: A History from the 1730s to the 1980s*. London: Unwin Hyman, 1989.

Beck, J.R. "Pastoral Counseling." In *Baker Encyclopedia of Psychology and Counseling*. 2nd ed. Edited by David Benner and Peter C. Hill. Grand Rapids, MI: Baker, 1999.

Beilby, James K., and Paul Rhodes Eddy. *Understanding Spiritual Warfare: Four Views*. Baker, Kindle ed.

Belle, H.A. Van. "Humanistic Psychology." In *Baker Encyclopedia of Counseling*. 2nd ed. Edited by David Benner and Peter C. Hill. Grand Rapids MI: Baker, 1999.

Benner, David, and Peter C. Hill, eds. *Baker Encyclopedia of Counseling*. 2nd ed. Grand Rapids MI: Baker, 1999.

Berg, Jim. "Basics for Depressed Believers." Bob Jones University, 1995.

_____. "Biblical Counseling Series." Bob Jones University, 2013. http://www.bju. edu/bjuonline/personal-development/ ibe/courses/special-topics/biblical-counseling-series.php (accessed 8 August 2013).

_____. "Biblically Overcoming Anorexia and Bulimia." Greenville, SC: Bob Jones University, 1993. http://www.quieting anoisysoul.com/downloads/anorexia-bulimia-syllabus.pdf.

Besen, Wayne. *Anything but Straight: Unmasking the Scandals and Lies Behind the Ex-Gay Myth*. New York: Harrington Park, 2003.

Bethel Sozo. "About Bethel Sozo: Autism." http://bethelsozo.com/about#/4 (accessed 3 May 2013).

Bettler, John F. "CCEF: The Beginning." *Journal of Pastoral Practice* 9, no. 3 (1988): 45–51.

Bible (NIV). East Brunswick, NJ: International Bible Society, 1984.

Biblical Discernment Ministries. "Charles Solomon: General Teachings\Activities," December 2001. http://www.rapidnet. com/~jbeard/bdm/exposes/solomon/ general.htm (accessed 19 August 2013).

Bickle, Mike, and Dana Candler. *The Rewards of Fasting: Experiencing the Power and Affections of God*. Kansas City: Forerunner Books, 2005.

"Biochemistry." *Encyclopædia Britannica Online Academic Edition*. Encyclopædia Britannica, 2013. http://www.britannica. com/EBchecked/topic/65785/bio chemistry (accessed 31 August 2013).

Bixler, W.G. "Psychological Consequences of Sin." In *Baker Encyclopedia of Psychology and Counseling*. 2nd ed. Edited by David G. Benner and Peter G. Hill. Grand Rapids: Baker, 1999.

Blatter, Karen. "Accused Sex Abuser Treated Kids in Livingston." *Bloomington (IL) Pantagraph,* 4 March 2005, p. A3.

Blumenthal, Max. "The Nightmare of Christianity." *Nation*, 9 September 2009. http://www.thenation.com/article/ nightmare-christianity# (accessed 18 September 2013).

Bobgan, Martin, and Deidre Bobgan. *Against Biblical Counseling, for the Bible*. Santa Barbara: East Gate, 1994.

_____. *Psychoheresy: The Psychological Seduction of Christianity*. Santa Barbara: East Gate, 1987.

Bobick, Michael W. "A Biblical Alternative to Inner Healing." *Journal of Pastoral Practice* 6, no. 4 (1983): 25–45.

Boston Baptist College. "Our Faculty," 2011. http://boston.edu/academics/our-faculty (accessed 8 August 2013).

Brassington, I.M. "Actions, Causes, and Psychiatry: a Reply to Szasz (Debate)." *Journal of Medical Ethics* (April 2002): 120–124. Health Reference Center Academic, 1 September 2013.

Broger, John C. *Militant Liberty*. Washington, D.C: (Department of Defense) U.S. Government Printing Office, 1955.

_____. *Self-Confrontation: A Manual for In-depth Discipleship*. Nashville: Thomas Nelson, 1994 (original ed. 1978).

Brown, Candy Gunther, ed. *Global Pente-costal and Charismatic Healing*. Oxford: Oxford University Press, 2011.

Brown, Candy Gunther. "Introduction: Pentecostalism and the Globalization of Illness and Healing." In *Global Pentecostal and Charismatic Healing*. Edited by Candy Gunther Brown. Oxford: Oxford University Press, 2011.

_____. *Testing Prayer*. Cambridge, MA: Harvard University Press, 2012.

Brown, Candy Gunther, PhD; Stephen C. Mory, MD; Rebecca Williams, MB BChir, DTM&H; Michael J. McClymond, PhD. "Study of the Therapeutic Effects of Prox-imal Intercessory Prayer (STEPP) on Au-ditory and Visual Impairments in Rural Mozambique." *Southern Medical Journal* 103, no. 9 (September 2010): 864–869.

Brunero, Tim. "Mercy Ministries Exorcism Books Leaked." *Live News*, Australia, 26 November 2008. http://www.rickross. com/reference/hillsong/hillsong41.html (accessed 6 May 2013).

Brydum, Sunnvie. "John Paulk Formally Re-nounces, Apologizes for Harmful Ex-gay Movement." *Advocate*, 24 April 2013. http://www.advocate.com/politics/ religion/2013/04/24/john-paulk-formally-renounces-apologizes-harmful-ex-gay-movement (accessed 8 August 2013).

Bufford, R.K. "Behavioral Psychology" In *Baker Encyclopedia of Counseling*. 2nd ed. Edited by David Benner and Peter C. Hill. Grand Rapids, MI: Baker, 1999.

Bulkley, Ed. *Why Christians Can't Trust Psy-chology*? Eugene, OR: Harvest House, 1993.

Burroway, Jim. "Joe Dallas Splits from Exo-dus International." *Box Turtle Bulletin*, 6 May 2013. http://www.boxturtlebulletin. com/2013/05/06/55809 (accessed 18 August 2013).

_____. "Surviving an Exorcism to Cast Out the Gay." *Box Turtle Bulletin*, 6 June 2010. http://www.boxturtlebulletin.com/tag/ exorcism (accessed 8 August 2013).

Burton, Margaret. "*Nally vs. Grace Commu-nity Church*: Is There a Future for Clergy Malpractice Claims?" *Santa Clara Law Review* 37, no. 2 (1 January 1997): 467–

515. http://digitalcommons.law.scu.edu/ lawreview/vol37/iss2/5 19 (accessed Au-gust 2013).

Bynum, Bill. "Discarded Diagnoses: Drapeto-mania." *Lancet* 356 (November 4, 2000): 1615.

Calef, Scott. "Dualism and the Mind." In *In-ternet Encyclopedia of Philosophy,* 9 June 2005. http://www.iep.utm.edu/dualism/ (accessed 16 August 2013).

Campbell, Karen. "There Is Always a Why Behind the What: For Nancy Alcorn, Founder of Mercy Ministries, God Isn't About Treatment, He's About Transfor-mation," 23 April 2013. http://karen-campbellmedia.com/wp-content/ uploads/2013/05/MissionOfMercy-PressKit.pdf (accessed 8 August 2013).

Capone, Alesha. "Borders Passes the Hat for Anti-gay, Pro-life Charity." crikey.com, 14 November 2007. http://www.crikey.com. au/2007/11/14/borders-passes-the-hat-for-anti-gay-pro-life-charity/ (accessed 8 August 2013).

Carlson, Dwight L. *Why Do Christians Shoot Their Wounded?: Helping (Not Hurting) Those with Emotional Difficul-ties*. Downers Grove, IL: Intervarsity Press, 1994.

Case, Holly. "Mad, or Bad?: Even in the Decade of Dissent, Thomas Szasz Stood Alone When He Attacked the Idea of Madness from the Political Right." *Aeon Magazine*, 15 April 2013. http://www. aeonmagazine.com/world-views/holly-case-thomas-szasz-insanity-plea/ (accessed 8 August 2013).

Charisma Staff. "C.J. Mahaney Takes Leave Over 'Serious' Charges." *Charisma,* 12 July 2011. http://www.charismanews. com/us/31503-cj-mahaney-takes-leave-over-serious-charges%29 (accessed 19 Au-gust 2013).

Charlton, T.F. "Evangelical Church Accused of Ignoring Sexual Abuse, 'Pedophile Ring.'" salon.com, 12 March 2013. http:// www.salon.com/2013/03/12/evangelical_ church_accused_of_ignoring_sexual_ abuse_pedophilia_ring_partner/ (accessed 25 April 2013).

Christian Counseling and Educational Foundation (CCEF). "Board of Trustees."

N.d. http://www.ccef.org/board-trustees (accessed 22 August 2013).

_____. "Hours, Fees & Directions." N.d. http://www.ccef.org/hours-fees-directions (accessed 25 August 2013).

_____. "What Others Are Saying," 2 May 2013. http://www.ccef.org/what-others-are-saying (accessed 25 August 2013).

"Christian Counseling and Educational Foundation in Glenside, Pennsylvania." Faqs.org: tax exempt organizations, 2013. http://www.faqs.org/tax-exempt/PA/Christian-Counseling-And-Educational-Foundation.html (accessed 8 August 2013).

"Christian Healing Certification Program." In *Christian Healing Certification Program*. N.d. http://healingcertification. com/2-uncategorised?start=4 (accessed 8 August 2013).

Christian International Ministries. "Our Ministers: Mercy Ministries," 2011. http://www.christianinternational.org/index.php?option=com_content&view=article&id=1069:mercy-ministries530&catid=3:our-ministers (accessed 18 August 2013).

_____. "Suicide Bows Its Knee! Apostle Jane Hamon at Mercy Ministries, February 2011," 2011. https://www.christianinternational.com/index.php?option=com_content&view=article&id=470%3Asuicide-bows-its-knee-apostle-jane-hamon-mercy-ministries-february-2011&catid=26%3Amarketplace (accessed 25 August 2013).

Christianity Today. "After Judge Dismisses Sovereign Grace Lawsuit, Justin Taylor, Kevin DeYoung, and Don Carson Explain Their Silence," 24 May 2013. http://www.christianitytoday.com/gleanings/2013/may/after-judge-dismisses-sovereign-grace-lawsuit-justin.html (accessed 8 August 2013).

Churchill, Winston. "The Iron Curtain." In *The Penguin Book of Twentieth Century Speeches*. Edited by Brian MacArthur. London: Penguin, 1992.

Clark, Randy. *Global Awakening Ministry Team Training Manual*. Mechanicsburg, PA: Global Awakening, 2009.

Clarke, L. "Sacred Radical of Psychiatry."

Journal of Psychiatric and Mental Health Nursing 14 (2007): 446–453. Academic Search Premier. August 8, 2013.

Clinton, Tim, and George Ohlschlager. *Competent Christian Counseling*. Colorado Springs: Waterbrook, 2002.

_____. "Competent Christian Counseling: Definitions and Dynamics." In *Competent Christian Counseling*. Vol. 1. Edited by Timothy Clinton and George Ohlschlager. Colorado Springs: Waterbrook, 2002.

_____. "The Ethical Helping Relationship: Ethical Conformation and Spiritual Transformation—Accountability." In *Competent Christian Counseling*. Vol. 1. Edited by Timothy Clinton and George Ohlschlager. Colorado Springs: Waterbrook, 2002.

Cohen, Richard. *Coming Out Straight: Understanding and Healing Homosexuality*. Winchester, VA: Oakhill Press, 2006.

Collins, Gary R. "American Association of Christian Counselors (AACC)." In *Baker Encyclopedia of Psychology and Counseling*. 2nd ed. Edited by David G. Benner and Peter C. Hill. Grand Rapids, MI: 1999.

_____. *Christian Counseling: A Comprehensive Guide*. 3d ed. Nashville: Thomas Nelson, 2007.

_____. "An Integration View." In *Psychology and Christianity: 4 views*. Edited by Eric L. Johnson and Stanton Jones. Downers Grove, IL: 2000.

_____. "Moving Through the Jungle: A Decade of Integration." In *Psychology and Christianity: Integration*. Batavia, IL: Christian Association for Psychological Studies, 2007.

Collins, James. *Exorcism and Deliverance Ministry in the Twentieth Century: An Analysis of the Practice and Theology of Exorcism in Modern Western Christianity*. Eugene, OR: Wipf and Stock, 2009.

Colloff, Pamela. "Remember the Christian Alamo." *Texas Monthly*, December 2001. http://teenadvocatesusa.homestead.com/Roloff.html (accessed 8 August 2013).

Comiskey, Andrew. *Pursuing Sexual Wholeness*. Lake Mary, FL: Charisma House, 1989.

Compton, Bob. "Bible Conference Offers Answers to Marital and Emotional Issues." *Foundations in Genesis of Idaho/Oregon*, 12 September 2002. http://www.figionline.com/meetings/2002_meetings/meeting_2002-09-12.htm (accessed 18 August 2013).

Coscarelli, Joe. "More on George Rekers, the Latest Anti-Gay Crusader to Love Massages from Men." *Village Voice*, 8 May 2010. http://blogs.villagevoice.com/runninscared/2010/05/more_on_george.php (accessed 18 August 2013).

Cosgrove, Lisa, and Emily Wheeler. "Drug Firms, the Codification of Diagnostic Categories, and Bias in Clinical Guidelines." *Journal of Law, Medicine, and Ethics* 41, no. 3 (Fall 2013). Academic Search Premier.

Council of Biblical Manhood and Womanhood. "Russel Moore: Chairman of the Board," 2013. http://cbmw.org/russell-moore/ (accessed 8 August 2013).

Crabb, Jr., Lawrence. *Basic Principles of Biblical Counseling*. Grand Rapids, MI: Zondervan, 1975.

_____. *Effective Biblical Counseling*. Grand Rapids, MI: Zondervan, 1977.

_____. *Understanding People: Deep Longings for Relationship*. Grand Rapids, MI: Zondervan, 1987.

Cuneo, Michael W. *American Exorcism: Expelling Demons in the Land of Plenty*. New York: Doubleday, 2001.

Daily Mail Reporter. "'God Will Help Heal You': GP Told Patient to Stop Taking Medication and Took Her to Have an Exorcism Instead." *Daily Mail Reporter*, 15 April 2013. January 14, 2014.

Dalhouse, Mark Taylor. *An Island in the Lake of Fire: Bob Jones University, Fundamentalism and the Separatist Movement*. Athens: University of Georgia Press, 1996.

Derosa, Christopher. *Political Indoctrination in the U.S. Army from World War II to the Vietnam War*. Lincoln: University of Nebraska Press, 2006.

De Silva, Dawna, and Teresa Liebscher. "Sozo: Advanced, Healed, Delivered," Session 8 ("Shabar Wrap Up"). N.d., MP3.

_____. "Sozo: Advanced, Healed, Delivered," Session 9 ("Sozo Q + A"). N.d., MP3.

Detwiler, Fritz. *Standing on the Premises of God: The Christian Right's Fight to Redefine America's Public Schools*. New York: New York University Press, 1999.

Dever, Mark. *Nine Marks of a Healthy Church*. Good News, 2004, Kindle ed.

Diamond, Sara. *Not by Politics Alone: The Enduring Influence of the Christian Right*. New York: Guilford, 1998.

Dickason, C. Fred. *Demon Possession and the Christian: A New Perspective*. Wheaton, IL: Crossway Books, 1987.

Dickerman, Don. *When Pigs Move In*. Lake Mary, FL: Charisma House, 2009.

Do, Ahn, Kate Mather, and Joe Mozingo. "Shifting Tide Was Ministry's Doom: Exodus International in Anaheim Will Close After 37 years; Its Leader Apologizes for 'Gay Cure' Policies." *Los Angeles Times*, 21 June 2013. http://articles.latimes.com/2013/jun/21/local/la-me-0621-exodus-international-gays-20130621 (accessed 8 August 2013).

Dobson, James. *The New Dare to Discipline*. Wheaton, IL: Tyndale, 1992.

Donaldson James, Susan. "Biblical Reform School Discipline: Tough Love or Abuse?," 12 April 2011. http://abcnews.go.com/Health/independent-fundamental-baptist-discipline-call-tough-love-abuse/story?id=13310172#.UaByW9i1t8E (accessed 8 August 2013).

Drescher, Jack. "I'm Your Handyman: A History of Reparative Therapies." *Journal of Gay and Lesbian Psychotherapy* 5, no. 3/4 (2001): 5–24. Academic Search Premier.

Dubose, Auberi, et al. "Early Adult Sexual Assault and Disordered Eating: The Mediating Role of Posttraumatic Stress Symptoms." *Journal of Traumatic Stress* 25 (February 2012): 50–56.

Eck, Brian, "Integrating the Integrators: An Organizing Framework for a Multifaceted Process of Integration." In *Psychology and Christianity: Integration*. Edited by Daryl H. Stevenson, Brian E. Eck, and Peter C. Hill. Batavia, IL: Christian Association for Psychological Studies, 2007.

Elijah List. "Randy Clark, C. Peter Wagner, Che Ahn: 'Developing Structure for Apostolic Ministry.'" Advertisement, 11 July 2008. http://www.elijahlist.com/words/display_word/6637 (accessed 8 August 2013).

Ellis, Bill. *Raising the Devil: Satanism, New Religions and the Media*. Lexington: University Press of Kentucky, 2000.

Emerson, Michael, and Christian Smith. *Divided by Faith: Evangelical Religion and the Problem of Race in America*. New York: Oxford University Press, 2000.

Emlet, Michael. *OCD: Freedom for the Obsessive-Compulsive*. Phillipsburg, NJ: P & R, 2004.

Engle, Lou. *Digging the Wells of Revival: Reclaiming Your Historic Inheritance Through Prophetic Intercession*. Shippensburg, PA: Destiny Image, 1999.

Entwistle, David N. "Shedding Light on Theophostic Prayer Ministry 1: Practice Issues." *Journal of Psychology and Theology* 32, no. 1 (2004): 26–34. Proquest (accessed 10 August 2013).

_____. "Shedding Light on Theophostic Prayer Ministry 2: Ethical and Legal Issues." *Journal of Psychology and Theology* 32, no.1 (2004): 35–42. Proquest (accessed 8 August 2013).

Erzen, Tanya. *Straight to Jesus: Sexual and Christian Conversions in the Ex-gay Movement*. Berkley: University of California Press, 2006.

Eyrich, Howard A. "Hope for the Homosexual." *Journal of Pastoral Practice* 1, no. 2 (1977): 19–33.

Faculty, Detroit Baptist Theological Seminary. "Basic Library Booklist." *Detroit Baptist Theological Seminary,* 2011. http://www.dbts.edu/pdf/Booklist.pdf (accessed 8 August 2013).

Fairbairn, Donald. *Eastern Orthodoxy Through Western Eyes*. Louisville, KY: Westminster John Knox Press, 2002.

Faith Baptist College and Theological Seminary. "Minors/Biblical Counseling/Faculty," 2011. http://www.faith.edu/academics/degree-programs-and-courses/minors/biblical-counseling/faculty (accessed 8 August 2013).

"False Memory Syndrome." *Encyclopædia Britannica Online Academic Edition*. Encyclopædia Britannica, Inc., 2013. http://www.britannica.com/EBchecked/topic/1341171/false-memory-syndrome (accessed 17 May 2013).

Feinberg, Carol. "The Knowledge Traders: Psychological Experts, Political Intellectuals, and the Rise of the New Right." PhD diss., University of California, Santa Barbara, 2007.

Felshman, Jeffrey. "Shame of the VA: The Veterans Administration's Undeclared War on its Hospitals Has Turned Patients Back into Fighters." *Chicago Reader,* 22 June 2000. http://www.chicagoreader.com/chicago/shame-of-the-va/Content?oid=902627 (accessed 18 August 2013).

Fisher, G. Richard. "The Basic Life Principles of Bill Gothard: Benevolent Ministry or Bondage Making." *Personal Freedom Outreach,* 1998. http://webcache.googleusercontent.com/search?q=cache:-preJFIOGYwJ:www.pfo.org/bgothard.htm+cabbage,+%22Bill+Gothard%22&cd=1&hl=en&ct=clnk&gl=us (accessed 8 August 2007).

Fitzpatrick, Elyse. "Counseling Women Abused as Children." *Women Helping Women*. Edited by Elyse Fitzpatrick and Carol Cornish. Eugene, OR: Harvest House, 1997.

_____. "Helping Bulimics." *Journal of Biblical Counseling* 11, no. 2 (1993): 16–20.

_____. *Love to Eat, Hate to Eat: Breaking the Bondage of Destructive Eating Habits*. Eugene, OR: Harvest House, 1999.

Fitzpatrick, Elyse, and Carol Cornish, eds. *Women Helping Women*. Eugene, OR: Harvest House, 1997.

Fitzpatrick, Elyse, and Laura Hendrickson. *Will Medicine Stop the Pain?* Chicago: Moody, 2006.

Fletcher, Jan. *Lying Spirits: A Christian Journalist's Report on Theophostic Ministry*. Columbia, KY: Jan Fletcher, 2005.

Foster, David Kyle. "Freedom from Homosexual Confusion." In *How to Minister Freedom: Helping Others Break the Bonds of Sexual Brokenness, Emotional Woundedness, Demonic Oppression, and Occult Bondage*. Ventura, CA: Regal, 2005.

Foucault, Michel. *History of Madness*. London: Routledge, 2006.

Gaines, Adrienne. "Healing Rooms Movement Spreading Worldwide." *Charisma*, 21 October 2010. http://www.charisma mag.com/site-archives/570-news/featured-news/12034-healing-rooms-movement-spreading-worldwide (accessed 9 September 2013).

Gallagher, John, and Chris Bull. *Perfect Enemies: The Battle Between the Religious Right and the Gay Movement*. Lanham, MD: Madison Books, 2001.

Garzon, Fernado, and Margaret Poloma. "Theophostic Ministry: Preliminary Practitioner Survey." *Pastoral Psychology* 53, no. 5 (May 2005): 387–396. Academic Search Premier (accessed 8 August 2013).

Gilgoff, Dan. *The Jesus Machine: How James Dobson, Focus on the Family, and Evangelical America Are Winning the Culture War*. St. Martin's, Kindle ed. (2007-03-06).

Glasser, William. *Reality Therapy: A New Approach to Psychiatry*. New York: Harper Colophon, 1965.

"Global Awakening Online Bookstore." *Global Awakening*. N.d. http://global-awakeningstore.com/healing-books/?xsearch_e1=Candy+Gunther+Brown (accessed 8 August 2013).

Gofman, Mikhail. E-mail to the author, May 18, 2013.

Goodstein, Laurie. "Church Based Projects Lack Data on Results." *New York Times*, 24 April 2001. http://www.nytimes.com/2001/04/24/us/church-based-projects-lack-data-on-results.html?src=pm (accessed 25 August 2013).

Grace, Andre. "The Charisma and Deception of Reparative Therapy." *Journal of Homosexuality* 55, no. 4 (2008): 545–580. Academic Search Premier (accessed 8 August 2013).

Gruszecki, Debra. "Detroit Radio Station Probes Abuse, Church Link." *Times of North West Indiana*, 17 May 1993. http://www.nwitimes.com/uncategorized/detroit-station-probes-abuse-church-link/article_14a337d0-f46b-5ad5-95bf-0410dca96668.html (accessed 8 August 2013).

Guetersloh, M.K. "Home Ends Residential Program: Flanagan District Closes School on Salem Grounds." *Bloomington (IL) Pantagraph*, 15 February 2002, p. A1.

Guy, Jr., James. "The Search for Truth in the Task of Integration." In *Psychology and Christianity: Integration*. Edited by Daryl H. Stevenson, Brian Eck, and Peter C. Hill. Batavia, IL, 2007.

Guyatt, Nicholas. *Have a Nice Doomsday: Why Millions of Americans are Looking Forward to the End of the World*. New York: Harper, 2007.

Hall, Franklin. *Fasting: Atomic Power with God*. N.p., Wings of Healing, 1946. http://www.shiloahbooks.com/download/Atomic.pdf.

_____. *Glorified Fasting*. Revised ed. Franklin Hall, 1973.

_____. *Subdue the Earth*. Franklin Hall, 1966.

Hammond, Frank, and Ida Mae. *Pigs in the Parlor: The Practical Guide to Deliverance*. Kirkwood, MO: Impact, 1973.

Hamon, Bill. In *Restoring the Foundations*. By Chester and Betsy Kylstra. Foreword to 2nd ed. Hendersonville, NC: Proclaiming His Word Ministries, 2001.

_____. *Prophetic Scriptures Yet to Be Fulfilled: During the Third and Final Church Reformation*. Shippensburg, PA: Destiny Image, 2010.

Hannan, Caleb. "Jesus RX: The Untold Story Behind Mercy Ministries' One-Size-Fits-All Prescription for Recovery." *Nashville Scene*, 2 October 2008. http://www.nashvillescene.com/nashville/jesus-rx/Content?oid=1198270 (accessed 8 August 2013).

Hansen, Collin. *Young, Restless, Reformed: A Journalist's Journey with the New Calvinists*. Wheaton, IL: Crossway, 2008.

Hanson, B.A. "Satanic Ritual Abuse." In *Baker Encyclopedia of Psychology and Counseling*. 2nd ed. Edited by David G. Benner and Peter C. Hill. Grand Rapids, MI: Zondervan, 1999.

Harrell, Jr., David Edwin. *All Things Are Possible: The Healing and Charismatic Revivals in Modern America*. Bloomington: Indiana University Press, 1975.

"Healing Room Testimonies." Healingrooms. com, various dates. http://healingrooms. com/index.php?src=testimonies&page= 1&perpage=50&startingpage=1&ending page=10&orderby=dateDesc&category_ number=1272&l=&page_id=&testi monies=yes&view=global (accessed 8 August 2013).

Hendershot, Heather. *Shaking the World for Jesus: Media and Conservative Evangelical Culture.* Chicago: University of Chicago Press, 2004.

"Hephzibah House: Serving Christ Since 1971." Hephzibah House, 2013. http:// www.hephzibahhouse.org/page8/index. html (accessed 8 August 2013).

Hinman, Nelson E. "Healing of Memories? Inner Healing? Is There a Better Way?" *Journal of Pastoral Practice* 8, no. 4 (1987): 24–31.

Holifield, E. Brooks. *A History of Pastoral Care in America: From Salvation to Self-Realization.* Eugene, OR: Wipf & Stock, 1983.

Holvast, Renee. *Spiritual Mapping in the United States and Argentina, 1989–2005: A Geography of Fear.* Boston: Brill, 2009.

Horrobin, Peter J. *Healing Through Deliverance: The Foundation and Practice of Deliverance Ministry.* Grand Rapids: Chosen, 2008.

_____. "Sexual Sin: What It Is, What It Does and Finding the Way Out." In *How to Minister Freedom.* Edited by Doris Wagner. Ventura, CA: Regal, 2005.

Houreld, Katharine. "African Children Denounced as Witches by Christian Pastors." *Huffington Post,* 18 October 2009. http://www.huffingtonpost.com/2009/ 10/18/african-children-denounce_n_ 324943.html (accessed 6 May 2013).

Howard, Roland. *Charismania: When Christian Fundamentalism Goes Wrong.* London: Mowbray, 1997.

Huffington Post. "Prayer Alone Heals Mental Illness, Say One Third of Americans in LifeWay Research Poll," 21 September 2013. http://www.huffingtonpost.com/ 2013/09/21/prayer-heal-mental-illness_ n_3963949.html (accessed 8 February 2014).

Hunt, June. *Counseling Through Your Bible Handbook.* Harvest House. Kindle ed. (2008–03–15).

Hunt, Morton. *The Story of Psychology.* 2nd ed. New York: Anchor Books, 2007.

Hunter, Linda. "Ethical Issues in the Use of Prayer in Clinical Practice: An Examination of Theophostic Prayer Ministry." Ph.D. diss., Regent University, 2006 (Proquest).

ibethel.org. "Sozo overview," 2013. http:// www.ibethel.org/sozo-overview (accessed 6 May 2013).

"Idolatry of Christian Psychiatry." N.d. www. angelfire.com/psy/idolatry (accessed 5 November 2006).

"The Independent Fundamentalist Baptist Church: Jesus Wore Pants, Not a Dress." *Wartburg Watch,* 25 April 2011. http:// thewartburgwatch.com/2011/04/25/ the-independent-fundamental-baptist-church-jesus-wore-pants-not-a-dress/ (accessed 8 August 2013).

Jackson, Bill. *The Quest for the Radical Middle: A History of the Vineyard.* Cape Town, South Africa: Vineyard, 1999.

Johnson, Eric, and Stanton Jones. "A History of Christians in Psychology." In *Psychology and Christianity: 4 Views.* Edited by Eric L. Johnson and Stanton L. Jones. Downers Grove, IL: IVP Academic, 2000.

_____. *Psychology and Christianity: 4 Views.* Downers Grove, IL: IVP Academic, 2000.

Johnson, Eric L. *Foundations for Soul Care: A Christian Psychology Proposal.* Downers Grove, IL: IVP Academic, 2007.

Johnson, Frecia. "Experiencing Jesus: Inner Healing Prayer for Personal Transformation, Church and Mission." Ph.D. diss., Fuller Seminary, 2004 (Proquest).

Jones, Barbara, and Denna Allen. "Divorce for 'Healer' in Ritual Abuse Row: Preacher's Wife Reveals How Exorcism 'Obsessions' Wrecked Her Marriage." *Mail on Sunday,* 8 March 1992, p. 10. LexisNexus (accessed 2 January 2014).

Jones, Barbara, et al. "(1)Analysis 'Confession' Was Brought About by Horrific Vision of Born-Again Christian (2) 'Healers' Told Me I Killed My Baby, Says Woman in Ritual Abuse Film." *Mail on*

Sunday, 1 March 1992, pp. 8–9. Lexis-Nexus 28 (accessed December 2013).

Jones, Stanton L., and Richard Butman. *Modern Psychotherapies: A Comprehensive Christian Appraisal.* Downers Grove, IL: Intervarsity Press, 1991.

Journal for Biblical Manhood and Womanhood 17, no. 1 (Spring 2012):1–58. http://cbmw.wpengine.com/wp-content/uploads/2013/03/JBMW-Spring-12-Complete.pdf (accessed 2013).

Journal for Biblical Manhood and Womanhood 18, no. 1 (Spring 2013): 1–41.

Joyce, Kathryn. *The Child Catchers: Rescue, Trafficking, and the New Gospel of Adoption.* New York: Public Affairs, 2013.

_____. "Horror Stories from Tough-Love Teen Homes: Girls Locked Up Inside Fundamentalist Religious Compounds; Kandahar? No, Missouri." *Mother Jones,* July/August 2011. http://www.motherjones.com/politics/2011/08/new-bethany-ifb-teen-homes-abuse?page=1.

_____. *Quiverfull: Inside the Christian Patriarchy Movement.* Boston: Beacon Press, 2009.

Karwath, Rob. "3 Youth Home Counselors May Face Charges in Boy's Death." *Chicago Tribune*, 8 August 1986. http://articles.chicagotribune.com/1986-08-08/news/8602270123_1_counselors-home-s-license-youth-home (accessed 23 August 2013).

Kerr, Lisa. "The Dark Side of Mercy Ministries." *Reality Check,* 21 February 2012. http://www.rhrealitycheck.org/article/2012/16/dark-side-mercy-ministries (accessed 8 August 2013).

Kilpatrick, Paula, and Charlie Kilpatrick. *Deliverance: A Manual for Ministry to the Oppressed.* Shreveport, LA: Jubilee Ministries, 1995.

Kim, Gina. "Psychiatrist Accused of Boys' Sexual Abuse." *Chicago Tribune,* 18 February 2005. http://articles.chicagotribune.com/2005-02-18/news/0502180227_1_sexual-abuse-christian-counseling-boys (accessed 8 August 2013).

Kinghorn, Warren Anderson. "Mediating the Eschatological Body: Psychiatric Technology for Christian Wayfarers." Ph.D. diss., Duke University. 2011.

Koch, Kurt. *Christian Counseling and Occultism.* Grand Rapids, MI: Kregel, 1972.

Kraft, Charles. *Anthropology for Christian Witness.* Maryknoll, NY: Orbis Books, 1996.

_____. *Deep Wounds, Deep Healing: An Introduction to Deep-Level Healing.* 2nd ed. Ventura, CA: Regal, 2010.

Kreeft, Peter. "The Divinity of Christ." peterkreeft.com, n.d. http://www.peterkreeft.com/topics/christ-divinity.htm (accessed 1 September 2013).

Kris. "Noel's Story." *SGM Survivors*, 31 December 2008. http://www.sgmsurvivors.com/?p=276 (accessed 18 August 2013).

_____. "An Open Letter to Ken Sande at Peacemaker Ministries." *SGM Survivors,* 12 January 2009. http://www.sgmsurvivors.com/2009/01/12/an-open-letter-to-ken-sande-at-peacemaker-ministries/ (accessed 8 August 2013).

_____. "SGM Seeks Peace with Noel and Family" *SGM Survivors,* 9 January 2009. http://www.sgmsurvivors.com/2009/01/09/sgm-seeks-peace-with-noel-and-family/ (accessed 1 January 2014).

_____. "What Sovereign Grace Ministries Teaches Pastors About Counseling: Part 3." *SGM Survivors*. Transcript of a sermon given by Andy Farmer, 18 May 2009. http://www.sgmsurvivors.com/2009/05/18/what-sovereign-grace-teaches-pastors-about-counseling-part-3/ (accessed 13 September 2013).

Kron, Joshua. "In Uganda, Push to Curb Gays Draws U.S. Guest." *New York Times,* 2 May 2010. http://www.nytimes.com/2010/05/03/world/africa/03uganda.html?ref=africa&_r=0 (accessed 13 March 2013).

Kwon, Lillian. "New Paradigm Helps Gays with Conflicting Religious Values." *Christian Post,* 19 April 2007. http://www.christianpost.com/news/new-paradigm-helps-gays-with-conflicting-religious-values-26956/ (accessed 8 August 2013).

Kylstra, Chester, and Betsy Kylstra. *Biblical Healing and Deliverance: A Guide to Experiencing Freedom from Sins of the Past, Destructive Beliefs, Emotional and Spiritual Pain, Curses and Oppression.* Grand Rapids: Chosen, 2003.

_____. *Restoring the Foundations*. 2nd ed. Hendersonville, NC: Proclaiming His Word, 2001.

LaHaye, Tim. *The Battle for the Mind*. Old Tappan, NJ: Fleming H. Revell, 1980.

_____. *How to Win Over Depression*. Grand Rapids, MI: Zondervan, 1974.

_____. *Spirit-Controlled Temperament*. Wheaton, IL: Tyndale, 1966.

Leubsdorf, Ben. "20/20 to Feature Trinity Accusation: Former Parishioner Says She Was Raped." *Concord Monitor*, 8 April 2011. http://www.concordmonitor.com/article/250165/2020-to-feature-trinity-accusation (accessed 27 August 2013).

Levack, Brian. *The Devil Within*. Yale University Press, 2013, Kindle ed.

Levin, Tanya. "Why Mercy Ministries Was Godsent for Hillsong." *Sydney Morning Herald,* 18 March 2008. http://www.smh.com.au/news/opinion/why-mercy-ministries-was-godsent-for-hillsong/2008/03/17/1205602284113.html (accessed 8 August 2013).

Lewis, C.S. *Mere Christianity*. (In *The Complete C.S. Lewis Signature Classics*) New York: Harper, 2002.

Lifton, Robert Jay. *Thought Reform and the Psychology of Totalism: A Study of "Brainwashing" in China*. Chapel Hill: University of North Carolina Press, 1989.

"Locations." *Mercy Ministries*. N.d. http://www.mercyministries.org/who_we_are/about/locations.html (accessed 8 August 2013).

Lochhead, Carolyn. "Conservatives Brand Homosexuality a 'Tragic' Affliction." *San Francisco Chronicle*, 20 June 1997. http://www.sfgate.com/news/article/Conservatives-Brand-Homosexuality-a-Tragic-2834533.php (accessed 8 August 2013).

Loggins, Kirk. "Judge Won't Broaden Case on Abortion." *Nashville Tennessean,* 2 September 1992. Pagination unavailable in microfilm.

London, Perry. *The Modes and Morals of Psychotherapy*. New York: Holt, Rinehart and Winston, 1964.

Long, Ray, Christy Gutkowski and Stacy St. Clair. "State Targets More Health Workers Convicted of Sex Crimes or Violence."

Chicago Tribune, 24 August 2011. http://articles.chicagotribune.com/2011-08-24/news/ct-met-license-losers-20110824_1_health-care-workers-revocations-medical-licenses (accessed 18 August 2013).

Loue, Sana. "Faith Based Mental Health Treatment of Minors: A Call for Legislative Reform." *Journal of Legal Medicine* 31 (2010): 171–201. Academic Search Premier (accessed 19 August 2013).

Luce, Ron, and Mike Guzzardo. *Battlecry for My Generation: The Fight to Save Our Friends*. Colorado Springs: Nextgen, 2006.

MacArthur, John F. "The Psychology Epidemic and Its Cure." http://www.tms.edu/tmsj/tmsj2a.pdf (accessed 5 November 2006).

Macchia, F.D. "Theology, Pentecostal." In *The New International Dictionary of Pentecostal and Charismatic Movements*. Revised and expanded ed. Edited by Stanley M. Burgess and Eduard M. Van Der Maas. Grand Rapids, MI: Zondervan, 2002.

Mack, Wayne. Foreword. In *The Christian's Guide to Psychological Terms*. By Mary and Marshall Asher. Bemidji, MN: Focus, 2004.

Mack, Wayne A. "Preventing Homosexuality." *Journal of Pastoral Practice* 3, no. 3 (1979): 42–55.

"Man Guilty of Raping Teen Church Member." nbcnews.com, 27 May 2011. http://www.nbcnews.com/id/43198631/ns/us_news-crime_and_courts/#.UiRIk39Li3F (accessed 8 August 2013).

Marsden, George. *Fundamentalism and American Culture*. New York: Oxford University Press, 2006.

Martin, William. *With God on Our Side: The Rise of the Religious Right in America*. Revised ed. New York: Broadway, 2005.

Mason, Cynthia Palmer, and Jill D. Duba. "Using Reality Therapy in Schools: Its Potential Impact on the Effectiveness of the ACSA National Model." *International Journal of Reality Therapy* 29, no. 1 (2009): 5–12. http://digitalcommons.wku.edu/cgi/viewcontent.cgi?article=1036&context=csa_fac_pub (accessed 8 August 2013).

Mayes, Rick, and Allan V. Horowitz. "DSM-III and the Revolution in the Classification of Mental Illness." *Journal of the History of the Behavioral Sciences* 41, no. 3 (Summer 2005): 249–267 (Academic Search Premier).

McDowell, Josh. "Jesus: God or Just Good Man?" Excerpt from *Ready Defense*, 2013. https://www.cru.org/how-to-know-god/who-is-jesus-god-or-just-a-good-man/index.htm (accessed 8 August 2013).

McMichael Richard, and Marie. *Sozo Training Manual*. Spokane: Healing Room Ministries Sozo Team, n.d.

"Md. Church Member Accused of Molestation in 1980s." Washington.cbslocal.com, 4 February 2013. http://washington.cbslocal.com/2013/02/04/md-church-member-accused-of-molestation-in-1980s/ (accessed 18 August 2013).

"Meet Timothy Warner." Christianbook.com, May 2002. http://www.christianbook.com/html/authors/4802.html (accessed 9 September 2003).

Megan, Kathleen. "Komisarjevsky's Home-Schooling Called 'Soul-crushing.'" courant.com, 6 November 2011. http://articles.courant.com/2011–11–06/news/hc-komisarjevsky-home-schooling-20111106_1_home-schooling-komisarjevsky-web-postings (accessed 8 August 2013).

"Mercy Ministries and Exorcisms," 16 October 2008. http://www.youtube.com/watch?v=TLD6SHwC0iE (accessed 19 April 2013).

"Mercy Ministries Celebrates 22 Baptisms." *mercyministriesnews.com*. 2 September 2010. Web 24 August 2013. http://www.mercyministriesnews.com/2010/09/mercy-ministries-celebrates-22-baptisms.html.

Mercy Ministries. "Frequently Asked Questions." N.d http://www.mercyministries.org/who_we_are/about/faqs.html (accessed 8 August 2013).

_____. http://www.mercyministries.org/ (accessed 19 August 2013).

_____. "Mercy Ministries Surprised with Prestigious Award," 25 October 2011. http://www.mercyministries.org/news/35/2011/10–25/mercy-ministries-surprised-with-prestigious-award (accessed 26 August 2013).

_____. "Pastor Joel Osteen Invites Nancy Alcorn to Be the Guest Speaker at Lakewood Church," 14 August 2012. http://www.mercyministries.org/news/122/2012/08–14/pastor-joel-osteen-invites-nancy-alcorn-to-be-the-guest-speaker-at-lakewood-church (accessed 25 August 2013).

_____. "Results." 2008 Survey. http://www.mercyministries.org/what_we_do/results/ (accessed 8 August 2013).

_____. "Unforgettable Message of Hope from Marilyn Skinner," 19 October 2011. http://www.mercyministries.org/news/37/2011/10–19/unforgettable-message-of-hope-from-marilyn-skinner (accessed 8 August 2013).

"Mercy Ministries International." Wayback Machine, 2007. http://archive.org/web/20070212210348/http://www.mercyministries.com.au/pages/default.asp?pid=24 (accessed 8 August 2013).

"Mercy Ministries: Locations." Wayback Machine, 2006. http://archive.org/web/20061110142759/http://www.mercyministries.org/locations.html (accessed 8 August 2013).

Mercy Survivors. "Is Mercy Ministries a Cult?" *Mercy Survivors*, April 2012. http://mercysurvivors.com/2012/04/ (accessed 26 August 2013).

_____. "Mercy Ministries and Destructive Mind Control," May 1, 2008. http://mercysurvivors.com/tag/bite-model/ (accessed 25 August 2013).

_____. "Mercy Ministries Counseling Manual Exposed," 8 February 2013. http://mercysurvivors.com/2013/02/08/mercy-ministries-counselling-manual-exposed/ (accessed 18 August 2013).

Millenson, Michael. "North Chicago VA Hospital Under Fire: U.S. Bans Some Surgery after Deaths." *Chicago Tribune*, 27 March 1991. http://articles.chicagotribune.com/1991–03–27/news/9101270620_1_poor-care-hospital-surgery (accessed 18 August 2013).

Mintle, Linda. *Breaking Free from a Negative Self-Image*. Lake Mary, FL: Charisma House, 2002.

_____. *Breaking Free from Depression: A Balanced Biblical Strategy for Emotional Freedom.* Lake Mary, FL: Charisma House, 2002.

_____. *Making Peace with Your Thighs: Get Off the Scales and Get on with Your Life.* Franklin, TN: Integrity, 2006.

Mitchell, B.N. "Pastoral Care." In *Baker Encyclopedia of Psychology and Counseling.* 2nd ed. Edited by David G Benner and Peter Hill. Grand Rapids, MI: Baker Books, 1999.

Moore, S. David. *The Shepherding Movement: Controversy and Charismatic Ecclesiology.* London: T & T Clark International, 2003.

Morris, Linda. "Focus on Justice as Hillsong Changes Its Tune." *Sydney Morning Herald,* 3 July 2007. http://www.smh.com.au/articles/2007/07/02/1183351125260.html (accessed 13 August 2013).

Mowrer, O. Hobart. *The Crisis in Psychiatry and Religion.* Princeton, NJ: D. Van Nostrand, 1961.

_____. "My Philosophy of Psychotherapy." *Journal of Contemporary Psychotherapy* 6, no. 1 (1973): 35–42. Academic Search Premier (accessed 18 August 2013).

_____. *The New Group Therapy.* Princeton: D. Van Nostrand, 1964.

Mowrer, O. Hobart, and Anthony J. Vattano. "Integrity Groups: A Context for Growth in Honesty, Responsibility and Involvement." *Journal of Applied Behavioral Science* 12 (1976): 419–431. Academic Search Premier (accessed 8 January 2013).

Munson, Ziad. *The Making of Pro-life Activists: How Social Movement Mobilization Works.* Kindle ed.

Murphy, Ed. *The Handbook for Spiritual Warfare.* Nashville: Thomas Nelson, 1992.

Myers, David G. "A Levels of Explanation View." In *Psychology and Christianity: 4 Views.* Edited by Eric L. Johnson and Stanton L. Jones. Downers Grove, IL: IVP Academic, 2000.

Myers-Shirk, Susan E. *Helping the Good Shepherd: Pastoral Counselors in a Psychotherapeutic Culture, 1925–1975.* Medicine, Science, and Religion in Historical Context. Johns Hopkins University Press. Kindle ed. (2010–10–01).

Narramore, Clyde. *The Psychology of Counseling.* Grand Rapids, MI: Zondervan, 1960.

Narramore, S.B. "Psychoanalytic Psychology." In *Baker Encyclopedia of Counseling.* 2nd ed. Edited by David Benner and Peter C. Hill. Grand Rapids MI: Baker, 1999.

Nathan, Debbie. *Sybil Exposed: The Extraordinary Story Behind the Famous Multiple Personality Case.* New York: Free Press, 2011.

Nathan, Debbie, and Michael Snedeker. *Satan's Silence: Ritual Abuse and the Making of a Modern American Witch Hunt.* New York: Basic Books, 1995.

National Abortion Federation. "Post-Abortion Syndrome," 2010. http://www.prochoice.org/about_abortion/myths/post_abortion_syndrome.html (accessed 8 August 2013).

National Association for the Research and Treatment of Homosexuality (NARTH). "The Problem of Pedophilia," 1998. http://www.narth.com/docs/pedophNEW.html (accessed 11 September 2013).

National Association of Nouthetic Counselors (NANC). "History," 2011. http://www.nanc.org/About-NANC/History (accessed 18 August 2013).

"Natural Selection." *Encyclopædia Britannica Online Academic Edition.* Encyclopædia Britannica, Inc., 2013. http://www.britannica.com/EBchecked/topic/406351/natural-selection (accessed 31 August 2013).

Netter, Sarah. "Church Reported to State for Gay Exorcism." abcnews.go.com, 25 June 2009. http://abcnews.go.com/US/story?id=7928669&page=1 (accessed 8 August 2013).

New York Times. "VA Acts After 43 Die at Hospital," 28 March 1991. http://www.nytimes.com/1991/03/28/us/va-acts-after-43-die-at-a-hospital.html (accessed 1 September 2013).

Nicholas of Cusa. *The Layman on Wisdom and the Mind.* Trans. M.L. Fuhrer. Canada: Doverhouse, 1989.

Nicholi, Armand (2002–04–03). *The Ques-*

tion of God: C.S. Lewis and Sigmund Freud Debate God, Love, Sex, and the Meaning of Life. Free Press. (Kindle ed.)

Nolot, Benjamin. "Restoring the Ancient Path of Abolition." 2012 Exodus Cry Abolition Summit. Track 8, 2012 Exodus Cry Abolition Summit CD. Grandview, MO: Exodus Cry.

O'Hara, Debbie. "Christianity versus Psychology." *News with Views.* N.d . www. newswithviews.com/Ohara/debbbie16. htm (accessed 24 April 2007).

Olbermann, Keith. "George Rekers Resigns from NARTH." YouTube, 11 May 2010. https://www.youtube.com/watch?v=-fUU0evTWQI (accessed 8 August 2013).

Old English Dictionary Online. "Occam's razor." Oxford University Press. http://www.oed.com/view/Entry/234636? redirectedFrom=Ockham%27s+razor (accessed 13 September 2013).

Open Arms Internet Ministry. N.d. "What is Biblical Counseling?" www.oaim.org/bibcounsel.html (accessed 24 April 2007).

Osborne, Duncan. "A Ugandan Pastor with Global Reach" *Gay City News,* 15 December 2009. (accessed 1 January 2013) (Note: The article in its original format is no longer available online).

Otis, Jr., George. *Informed Intercession: Transforming Your Community Through Spiritual Mapping and Strategic Prayer.* Ventura, CA: Renew, 1999.

Papanikolaou, Aristotle. "Divine Energies or Divine Personhood: Vladimir Lossky and John Zizioulas on Conceiving the Transcendent and Immanent God." *Modern Theology* 19, no. 3 (July 2003): 357–385. Academic Search Premier (accessed 8 August 2013).

Payne, Franklin Edward, Jr. "God's Judgment and AIDS." *Journal of Pastoral Practice* 9, no. 4 (1989): 12–15.

Payne, Leanne. *The Broken Image: Restoring Personal Wholeness Through Healing Prayer.* Baker. Kindle ed. (1995–09–01).
_____. *Crisis in Masculinity.* Baker. Kindle ed. (1995–12–01, locations 432–432).

Peace, Martha. *The Excellent Wife: A Biblical Perspective.* Revised ed. Bemidji, MN: Focus, 1999.

Phillips, Phil. *Turmoil in the Toybox.* Lancaster, PA: Starburst, 1986.

Pierce, Cal. *Healing in the Kingdom: How the Power of God and Your Faith Can Heal the Sick.* Gospel Light. Kindle ed. (2011–08–26).

Pierre, Joseph. "Mental Illness and Mental Health: Is The Glass Half Empty or Half Full?" *Canadian Journal of Psychiatry* 57, no. 1 (2012): 651–658. Academic Search Premier.

Pilgrim, David. "The Survival of Psychiatric Diagnosis." *Social Science and Medicine* 65 (2007): 536–547. Academic Search Premier.

Piper, John. "Does a Woman Submit to Abuse?" YouTube, n.d. http://www.youtube.com/watch?v=3OkUPc2NLrM (accessed 18 August 2013).
_____. "God's Glory Is the Goal of Biblical Counseling." *Journal of Biblical Counseling* 20, no. 2 (2002): 8–21.
_____. "Treasuring Christ Together." *Journal of Biblical Counseling* 22, no. 2 (2004): 83–86.

Piper, John, and Wayne Grudem, eds. *Recovering Biblical Manhood and Womanhood: A Response to Evangelical Feminism.* Wheaton, IL: Crossway Books, 1991. http://dwynrhh6bluza.cloudfront.net/resources/documents/5153/Recovering_Biblical_Manhood_Womanhood.pdf?1343677387.

Pogue, Kara, and Renelle Roberts. "Monica Brown: 'Break the Soul Ties'" *700 Club,* 2013. http://www.cbn.com/700club/features/amazing/KLP17_monica_brown.aspx (accessed 8 August 2013).

Pollard, Ruth. "Ethics, Financial Probity for Review." *Sydney Morning Herald,* 18 March 2008. http://www.smh.com.au/news/national/ethics-financial-probity-for-review/2008/03/17/1205602293119.html (accessed 11 August 2013).
_____. "God's Cure for Gays Lost in Sin." *Sydney Morning Herald,* 19 March 2008. http://www.smh.com.au/news/national/gods-cure-for-gays-lost-in-sin/2008/03/18/1205602385236.html (accessed 8 August 2013).
_____. "Mercy Ministries Home to Close." *Sydney Morning Herald,* 28 October

2009. http://www.smh.com.au/national/mercy-ministries-home-to-close-200 91027-hj2k.html (accessed 11 August 2013).

———. "They Prayed to Cast Satan from My Body." *Sydney Morning Herald,* 17 March 2008. http://www.smh.com.au/news/national/they-prayed-to-cast-satan-from-my-body/2008/03/16/1205602195122.html (accessed 11 August 2013).

———. "They Sought Help but Got Exorcism and the Bible." *Sydney Morning Herald,* March 2008. http://www.smh.com.au/news/national/they-sought-help-but-got-exorcism-and-the-bible/2008/03/16/1205602195048.html (accessed 11 August 2013).

Poloma, Margaret. "Toronto Blessing." In *The New International Dictionary of Pentecostal and Charismatic Movements.* Revised and expanded ed. Edited by Stanley M. Burgess and Eduard M. Van Der Maas. Grand Rapids, MI: Zondervan, 2002.

Posner, Sarah. "'Taliban Dan's Teacher': Inside Bill Gothard's Authoritarian Subculture." *Religious Dispatches,* 6 February 2011. http://www.religiondispatches.org/archive/politics/4094/%E2%80%9Ctaliban_dan%E2%80%99s%E2%80%9D_teacher:_inside_bill_gothard%E2%80%99s_authoritarian_subculture/ (accessed 8 August 2013).

Powlison, David. *The Biblical Counseling Movement: History and Context.* Greensboro, NC: New Growth Press, 2010.

———. "The Classical Model." *Understanding Spiritual Warfare: Four Views.* Edited by James K. Beilby and Paul Rhodes Eddy. Baker, 2012. Kindle ed.

———. "Idols of the Heart and Vanity Fair." CCEF, 16 October 2009. http://www.ccef.org/idols-heart-and-vanity-fair (accessed 8 August 2013).

———. *Seeing with New Eyes: Counseling and the Human Condition Through the Lens of Scripture.* Phillipsburg, NJ: P &R, 2003.

Pride, Mary. *The Child Abuse Industry: Outrageous Facts about Child Abuse and Everyday Rebellions Against a System that Threatens Every North American Family.* Westchester, IL: Crossway Books, 1986.

———. *The Way Home: Beyond Feminism, Back to Reality.* 25th anniversary ed. Fenton, MO: Home Life Books, 1985.

Priest, Robert J., and Esther E. Cordill. "Christian Communities and 'Recovered Memories' of Abuse." *Christian Scholar's Review* 41, no. 4 (Summer 2012): 381–400.

Prince, Derek. *They Shall Expel Demons: What You Need to Know About Demons, Your Invisible Enemies.* Grand Rapids, MI: Chosen Books, 1998.

Purswell, Jeff. "Core Convictions Behind Theological Training." sovereigngrace ministries.org, 8 October 2009. http://www.sovereigngraceministries.org/blogs/cj-mahaney/post/about-sovereign-grace-ministries-pastors-college-jeff-purswell.aspx (accessed 18 August 2013).

Rattigan, Dave. "Reparative Therapy: Restored Hope Network v. Exodus International." Exgaywatch.com, 7 August 2012. http://www.exgaywatch.com/2012/08/andy-comiskey-on-exodus-restored-hope-network-and-reparative-therapy/ (accessed 8 October 2013).

Reese, Andy. *Freedom Tools for Overcoming Life's Tough Problems.* Grand Rapids, MI: Chosen, 2008.

Rekers, George. "Psychological Foundations for Rearing Masculine Boys and Feminine Girls." In *Recovering Biblical Manhood and Womanhood,* edited by John Piper and Wayne Grudem. Wheaton, IL: Crossway, 1991. http://dwynrhh6bluza.cloudfront.net/resources/documents/5153/Recovering_Biblical_Manhood_Womanhood.pdf?1343677387.

Rellahan, Jeanne Connelly. "At Home Among the Puritans: Sigmund Freud and the Calvinist Tradition in America." Ph.D. diss., University of Hawaii, 1988 (Proquest).

Return to the Word. 2009. http://www.returntotheword.org/ (accessed 18 August 2013).

Riddle, Lyn. "BJU Board Member Resigns: Alumni-circulated Petition Took Issue with How Phelps Handled Abuse Allegations." *Journal Watchdog* 1 (December 2011). http://www.journalwatchdog.com/schools/1303-bju-grads-seek-removal-of-board-member (accessed 8 August 2013).

Riss, Richard M. *Latter Rain: The Latter Rain Movement of 1948 and the Mid-Twentieth Century Evangelical Awakening*. Etobicoke, Ontario: Honeycomb Visual Productions, 1987.

Riss, R.M. "Latter Rain Movement." In *The New International Dictionary of Pentecostal and Charismatic Movements*. Revised and expanded ed. Edited by Stanley M. Burgess and Eduard M. Van Der Maas. Grand Rapids, MI: Zondervan, 2002.

Robertson, Josh. "Hundreds Attend Faith Healing Schools Linked to Fundamentalist Bethal [*sic*] Church." *Courier Mail,* 28 May 2011. http://www.couriermail.com.au/news/queensland/hundreds-attend-faith-healing-schools-linked-to-fundamentalist-bethal-church/story-e6freoof-1226064378133 (accessed 6 May 2013).

Robinson, Christine, and Sue E. Spivey. "The Politics of Masculinity and the Ex-gay Movement." *Gender and Society* 21 (2007): 650–676.

Robinson, Jeff. "Southern Seminary Launches New Vision for Biblical Counseling." *Baptist Press,* 15 February 2005. http://www.bpnews.net/bpnews.asp?id=20152 (accessed 8 August 2013).

Robinson, Howard, "Dualism." *The Stanford Encyclopedia of Philosophy*. Winter 2012 ed. Edited by Edward N. Zalta. http://plato.stanford.edu/archives/win2012/entries/dualism/ (accessed 8 August 2013).

Roth, Martin. "Schizophrenia and the Theories of Thomas Szasz." *British Journal of Psychiatry* 129 (1976): 317–326.

Rothe, Anne. *Popular Trauma Culture: Selling the Pain of Others in the Mass Media*. New Brunswick, NJ: Rutgers University Press, 2011.

Rubin, Julius H. *Religious Melancholy and Protestant Experience in America*. New York: Oxford University Press, 1994.

Sabalow, Ryan. "Ex Bethel Student Not at Fault in '08 Fall; Judge Says Woman Not Obligated to Act." *Redding Record Searchlight,* 13 December 2011. https://www.redding.com/news/2011/dec/13/

student-not-at-fault-in-08-fall/ (accessed 8 January 2014).

_____. "Faith Healing or Foul Play? 2008 Cliff Fall Victim Sues Bethel Students." *Redding Record Searchlight,* 21 October 2010. http://www.redding.com/news/2010/oct/21/faith-healing-or-foul-play-on-cliff/ (accessed 6 May 2013).

Salem 4youth. "Counseling" salem4youth.com, 2013. http://www.salem4youth.com/motivational/counseling/ (accessed 18 August 2013).

Salon Staff. "True Confessions: Men Who Have Been Through 'Ex-gay' Christian Ministries Share Their Stories; While Some Insist That They Have Overcome Homosexuality, Others Say They Were Driven to Attempt Suicide." *Salon,* 21 July 2005 (accessed 12 January 2014).

Sanchez, Casey. "Todd Bentley's Militant Joel's Army Gains Followers in Florida." *Intelligence Report* 131 (Fall 2008). http://www.splcenter.org/get-informed/intelligence-report/browse-all-issues/2008/fall/arming-for-armageddon (accessed 22 March 2013).

Sande, Ken. *The Peacemaker: A Biblical Guide to Resolving Personal Conflict*. Grand Rapids, MI: Baker Books, 2004.

Schaeffer, Robert. "Working the Emotional Roots of Homosexuality, Part 1." lifeministry.org, June 2006. http://www.lifeministry.org/working-emotional-roots-homosexuality-part-1 (accessed 8 August 2013).

Schowalter, John. "How to Manage Conflicts of Interest with Industry?" *International Review of Psychiatry* 20, no. 2 (April 2008): 127–133. Academic Search Premier.

Schultz, Duane P., and Sydney Ellen. *Theories of Personality*. 8th ed. Belmont, CA: Wadsworth, 2005.

Scott, Stuart. *The Exemplary Husband: A Biblical Perspective*. Focus. Kindle ed. (2013–01–07).

Scott, Stuart, and Heath Lambert, eds. *Counseling the Hard Cases*. B&H Academic, 2012. Kindle ed.

"Second Amended SGM Lawsuit." Brentdetwiler.com, N.d. http://abrentdetwiler.squarespace.com/storage/documents/

second%20amended%20sgm%20lawsuit. pdf (accessed 8 August 2013).

Shorter, Edward. *A History of Psychiatry.* New York: John Wiley & Sons, 1997.

Sloan, Richard. *Blind Faith: The Unholy Alliance of Religion and Medicine.* New York: St. Martin's, 2006.

Smith, Bryan. "The Five Most Revolting Details from the Evidence in the Jack Schaap Case." *Chicago Magazine,* 18 March 2013. http://www.chicagomag. com/Chicago-Magazine/The-312/ March-2013/The-top-five-revolting-x-from-the-latest-prosecutor-filing-in-the-Jack-Schaap-case/ (accessed 26 August 2013).

Smith, Ed M. *Theophostic Prayer Ministry: Basic Seminar Manual.* Campbellsville, KY: New Creation, 2005.

Smith, Robert. *The Christian Counselor's Medical Desk Reference.* Stanley, NC: Timeless Texts, 2000.

Smith, Robert, Addam Masri, Andy Smith, James Schaller, and Ed Welch. "Christian Doctors on Depression." *Journal of Biblical Counseling* 18, no. 3 (2000): 35–43.

Smith, Robert D. "Chronic Fatigue." *Journal of Pastoral Practice* 10, no. 3 (1991): 6–21.

———. "Lithium and the Biblical Counselor." *Journal of Pastoral Practice* 10, no. 1 (1989): 8–18.

Smith, Wes, and Tim Franklin. "Boys Death Puts Children's Home on the Defensive." *Chicago Tribune,* 17 August 1986. http:// articles.chicagotribune.com/1986-08-17/news/8603010425_1_pontiac-correctional-center-mechanical-asphyxiation-death (accessed 28 August 2013).

Smith, Winston. "Dichotomy or Trichotomy? How the Doctrine of Man Shapes the Treatment of Depression." *Journal of Biblical Counseling* 18, no. 3 (Spring 2000): 21–29.

Solano, Joy. "Tragic Misguidance: Gothard's View on Mental Health Treatment and the Petit Family Murders." Recoveringgrace.org, 17 November 2011. http:// www.recoveringgrace.org/2011/11/ tragic-misguidance-gothards-view-on-mental-health-treatment-and-the-petit-

family-murders/ (accessed 18 August 2013).

Solomon, Charles R. *Counseling with the Mind of Christ: The Dynamics of Spirituotherapy.* Old Tappan, NJ: Fleming H. Revell, 1977.

———. *Handbook to Happiness.* Tyndale House. Kindle ed. (2011–04–21).

Souders, Michael. "A God of Wealth: Religion, Modernity, and the Rhetoric of the Christian Prosperity Gospel." Ph.D. diss., University of Kansas, 2011.

Sovereign Grace Ministries Survivors. "Al Mohler and John Bettler Honor C.J. Mahaney." N.d. http://www.youtube.com/ watch?v=pNsy_tOPRps (accessed 8 August 2013).

Sozo. "Frequently Asked Questions." Sozo the Foundations. N.d. http://www.sozo thefoundations.com/faq/ (accessed 6 May 2013).

Spokane Spokesman Review and Spokane Chronicle. "Veterans Groups Alarmed by Report on Hospital Care," 28 March 1991, p. A8.

Stadlen, Anthony. "Thomas Szasz Obituary: Psychiatrist Who Fought Coercion and Denied the Existence of Mental Illness." *Guardian,* 4 October 2012. http://www. theguardian.com/society/2012/oct/04/ thomas-szasz (accessed 8 August 2013).

Stephens, Randall J., and Karl W. Giberson. *The Anointed: Evangelical Truth in a Secular Age.* Cambridge, MA: Harvard University Press, 2011. Kindle ed.

Stevenson, Daryl. "Introduction: The Nature of Integration and Its Historical Context." In *Psychology and Christianity: Integration.* Edited by Daryl H Stevenson, Brian E. Eck, and Peter C. Hill. Batavia, IL: Christian Association for Psychological Studies, 2007.

Stewart, Craig O. "Orders of Discourse in the Science-Based Controversy Over 'Reparative Therapy' for Homosexuality." Ph.D. diss., Carnegie Mellon, 2006.

Strudwick, Patrick. "Christian Counselors Ban Therapy Aimed at 'Converting' Gay Patients: Association of Christian Counselors Ban Therapy Aimed at 'Converting' Gay Patients." *Guardian,* 13 January 2014. http://www.theguardian.com/world/

2014/jan/13/christian-therapists-stop-conversion-therapy-turn-gay-patients-straight (accessed 2 February 2014).

Susnjara, Bob. "Counselor Accused of Sex Abuse: Psychiatrist Admits Molesting Two Boys, Prosecutors Say." *Arlington Heights (IL) Daily Herald,* 17 February 2005, p. 1.

Sweatte, Natahsa. "Mercy Ministries Offers Support to Sex Trafficking Victims." Kcbd.com, 26 August 2012. http://www.kcbd.com/story/19380533/mercy-ministries-offers-support-to-sex-trafficking-victims (accessed 8 September 2013).

Sweeney, Douglas. *The American Evangelical Story: A History of the Movement.* Grand Rapids, MI: Baker Academic, 2005.

Swiech, Paul. "Reins and Redemption: Area Children's Home Reborn to Help Rebuild Youths' Lives." *Pantagraph,* 8 April 2012. http://www.pantagraph.com/news/local/reins-redemption-area-children-s-home-reborn-to-help-rebuild/article_1debe648–810e-11e1-bfd7–001a4bcf887a.html (accessed 25 August 2013).

Synan, Vinson. *The Century of the Holy Spirit: 100 Years of Pentecostal and Charismatic Renewal.* Nashville: Thomas Nelson, 2001.

Szasz, Thomas S. *The Myth of Mental Illness: Foundations of a Theory of Personal Conduct.* HarperCollins. Kindle ed. (2011–07–12).

Tan, Siang-Yang. "Integration and Beyond: Principled, Professional and Personal." In *Psychology and Christianity: Integration.* Edited by Daryl H. Stevenson, Brian Eck, and Peter C. Hill. Batavia, IL: Christian Association for Psychological Studies, 2007.

Taylor, Justin. "C.J. Mahaney: 'Why I'm Taking a Leave of Absence.'" Gospel Coalition.org, 7 July 2011. http://thegospelcoalition.org/blogs/justintaylor/2011/07/07/c-j-mahaney-why-im-taking-a-leave-of-absence/ (accessed 8 August 2013).

Templeton Foundation. "Supported Books and Articles (Abstracts)." N.d. http://www.templeton.org/newsroom/newsletters_and_publications/books/sup ported_books/abstracts.html (accessed 8 August 2013).

_____. "Supported Books and Authors." N.d. http://www.templeton.org/newsroom/newsletters_and_publications/books/supported_books/ (accessed 8 August 2013).

Thayer and Smith. "Greek Lexicon Entry for Sozo." In *The NAS New Testament Greek Lexicon.* 1999. http://www.biblestudytools.com/lexicons/greek/nas/sozo.html (accessed 8 August 2013).

Tomaso, Bruce. "June Hunt Plans $46M Complex in Plano." *Dallas Morning News,* 20 May 2008. http://religionblog.dallasnews.com/2008/05/june-hunt-plans-46m-complex-in.html/ (accessed 9 July 2013).

Toscano, Peterson. "Muddy Waters in Montreal." In *Peterson Toscano's A Musing.* 28 September 2009. http://a_musing.blogspot.com/2007/09/muddy-waters-in-montreal.html (accessed 9 August 2013).

Trinity Baptist College. "Trinity Baptist College: Graduate Studies." N.d. http://www.tbc.edu/pages/page.asp?page_id=123941 (accessed 2013).

Tripp, Tedd. "Communicate with Teens." *Journal of Biblical Counseling* 23, no. 3 (2005): 28–37.

_____. "Dazzle Your Teen." *Journal of Biblical Counseling* 23, no. 3 (2005): 7–12.

Tuchman, Gary. "Hephzibah House: Ungodly Disciple." CNN, 1 September 2011. https://www.youtube.com/watch?v=-QB9ZWM-iq0 (accessed 8 August 2013).

Unger, Merrill F. *What Demons Can Do to Saints.* Chicago: Moody Press, 1991.

Veinot, Don. *A Matter of Basic Principles.* Midwest Christian Outreach. Kindle ed. (2003–08–25).

Virkler, H.A. "Demonic Influence, Sin and Psychopathology." In *Baker Encyclopedia of Counseling.* Edited by David G. Benner and Peter C. Hill. 2nd ed. Grand Rapids MI: Baker, 1999.

Wade, Stephen. "A Theological Analysis of the Functional Epistemology and Anthropology Underlying Gary R. Collins's Method of Integrating Psychology and

Theology." Ph.D. diss., Southern Baptist Theological Seminary, 2006.

Wagner, C. Peter. *Churchquake!: How the New Apostolic Reformation Is Shaking Up the Church as We Know It.* Ventura, CA: Regal, 1999.

_____. "How Deliverance Sustains Revival" In *How to Minister Freedom.* Edited by Doris Wagner. Ventura, CA: Regal, 2005.

_____. "Spiritual Warfare" In *Territorial Spirits.* Edited by C. Peter Wagner. Shippensburg, PA: Destiny Image, 2012.

_____, ed. *Territorial Spirits.* Shippensburg, PA: Destiny Image, 2012.

Wagner, Doris. "Forgiving the Unforgivable." In *How to Minister Freedom.* Edited by Doris Wagner. Ventura, CA: Regal, 2005.

_____, ed. *How to Minister Freedom.* Ventura, CA: Regal, 2005.

Waldron, David. "Role-Playing Games and the Christian Right: Community Formation in Response to a Moral Panic." *Journal of Religion and Popular Culture* 9 (2005). Academic OneFile (accessed 8 September 2013).

Ware, S.L. "Restorationism in Classical Pentecostalism." In *The New International Dictionary of Pentecostal and Charismatic Movements.* Revised and expanded ed. Edited by Stanley M. Burgess and Eduard M. Van Der Maas. Grand Rapids, MI: Zondervan, 2002.

Warner, Timothy. *Spiritual Warfare: Victory Over the Powers of This Dark World.* Wheaton, IL: Crossway, 1991.

Warnock, George H. *The Feast of the Tabernacles: The Hope of the Church.* Dallas: Bill Britton, 1951. http://ebookbrowse.com/feast-of-tabernacles-the-george-h-warnock-book-pdf-d255720380 (accessed 8 March 2013).

Washington Times. "Keeping Their Eyes on the Cross," 23 December 2002. http://www.washingtontimes.com/news/2002/dec/23/20021223-111002-4857r/ (accessed 13 July 2013).

Weaver, Douglas. *The Healer-Prophet: William Marion Branham.* Macon, GA: Mercer University Press, 2000.

Weaver, John. *Evangelicals and the Arts in Fiction: Portrayals of Tension in Non-Evangelical Works Since 1895.* Jefferson, NC: McFarland, 2013.

_____. "Unpardonable Sins: The Mentally Ill and Evangelicalism in America." *Journal of Religion and Popular Culture* 23, no. 1 (2011): 65–81.

Weiss, Elizabeth, et al. "A Qualitative Study of Ex-Gay and Ex-Ex Gay Experiences." *Journal of Gay and Lesbian Mental Health* 14 (2010): 291–319. Academic Search Premier.

Weitz, Mark A. *Clergy Malpractice: Nally v. Grace Community Church of the Valley.* Lawrence, Kansas: University Press of Kansas, 2001.

Welch, Edward T. *Blame It on the Brain: Distinguishing Chemical Imbalances.* Brain Disorders, and Disobedience. Phillipsburg, NJ: P & R g, 1998.

Wells, G.A. *Cutting Jesus Down to Size.* Chicago: Open Court, 2009.

West, Louis Jolyon. "Hallucination." *Encyclopædia Britannica Online Academic Edition.* Encyclopædia Britannica, Inc., 2013. http://www.britannica.com/EBchecked/topic/252916/hallucination (accessed 31 August 2013).

"What Is Intersex?" Intersex Society of North America. N.d. http://www.isna.org/faq/what_is_intersex (accessed September 13, 2013).

"William Backus Obituary." *Star Tribune,* 16 June 2005. http://www.legacy.com/obituaries/startribune/Obituary.aspx?pid=14267828#fbLoggedOut (accessed 8 August 2013).

Williams, Joseph. *Spirit Cure.* Oxford: Oxford University Press USA, 2011.

Winters, Amanda. "Bethel 'Signs and Wonders' Include Angel Feathers, Gold Dust, and Diamonds." *Redding Record Searchlight,* 19 January 2010. http://www.redding.com/news/2010/jan/19/bethels-signs-and-wonders-include-angel-feathers/ (accessed 2 September 2013).

_____. "Faith Healings, Dead Raising Teams Part of Bethel Experience." *Redding Record Searchlight,* 18 January 2010. http://www.redding.com/news/2010/jan/18/faith-healings-dead-raising-teams-part-of-bethel/ (accessed 6 May 2013).

Wiseman, Stephen. "Dr. Stephen Wiseman Investigates Thomas Szasz, Parts 1–6." YouTube, 22 July 2010. http://www.youtube.com/watch?v=hk691rHIrkE&list=PL7FE6526CD82DBBB4 (accessed 18 August 2013).

Yarhouse, Mark, Richard E. Butman and Barrett W. McRay. *Modern Psychopathologies*. Intervarsity Press: Downers Grove, 2005.

Yu, Mongens Chiu. "The Use of Theology and Psychology in Popular Christian Parenting Literature: An Analysis of Two Authors." Ph.D. diss., Fuller Seminary, 2000.

Zichterman, Jocelyn. *I Fired God: My Life Inside and Escape from the Secret World of the Independent Fundamental Baptist Cult*. St. Martin's. Kindle ed. (2013–05–14).

Zimmerman, Dean. "Dualism in the Philosophy of Mind." In *Encyclopedia of Philosophy*. Edited by Donald M. Borchert. 2nd ed., vol. 3. Detroit: Macmillan Reference USA, 2006. Gale Virtual Reference Library (accessed 1 September 2013).

Works Consulted

Gallagher, Sally. *Evangelical Identity and Gendered Family Life*. New Brunswick, NJ: Rutgers University Press, 2003.

Greene-McCreight, Kathryn. *Darkness Is My Only Companion*. Grand Rapids, MI: Brazos Press, 2006.

Hunt, Dave, and T.A. McMahon. *Psychology and the Church: Critical Questions and Crucial Answers*. Bend, OR: Berean Call, 2008.

Kelleman, Robert W. *Soul Physicians: A Theology of Soul Care and Spiritual Direction*. Winona Lake, IN: BMH Books, 2007.

Lambert, Heath. *The Biblical Counseling Movement After Adams*. Wheaton, IL: Crossway, 2012.

Lindsay, D. Michael. *Faith in the Halls of Power: How Evangelicals Joined the American Elite*. Oxford: Oxford University Press, 2007.

Mason, Carol. *Killing for Life: The Apocalyptic Narrative of Pro-Life Politics*. Ithaca, NY: Cornell University Press, 2002.

Minirith, Frank. *Christian Psychiatry*. Old Tappan, NJ: Fleming H. Revell, 1977.

Minirth, Frank B., and Paul D. Meier. *Happiness Is a Choice: A Manual on the Symptoms, Causes and Cures of Depression*. Grand Rapids, MI: Baker, 1978

Stanford, Matthew. *Grace for the Afflicted: A Clinical and Biblical Perspective on Mental Illness*. Colorado Springs: Paternoster, 2008.

Films

Fish Can't Fly. 2005. Dir. Tom Murray. Perf. Peterson Toscano. USA: T Joe Murray Videos, DVD.

Gattaca. 1997. Dir Andrew Niccol. Perf. Ethan Hawke, Jude Law, Uma Thurman. USA: Sony, DVD.

Jesus Camp. 2006. Dir Heidi Ewing, Rachel Grady. Perf Becky Fischer, Ted Haggard, Lou Engle. USA: Magnolia, DVD.

Mind Over Mania. 2011. MSNBC documentary. Perf. Raven, Ron Luce. http://www.youtube.com/watch?v=OAKGVF3EooA.

One Nation Under God. 1993. Dir Francine Reznik, Teodoro Maniaci. Perf Joe Dallas, Ralph Blair, Sy Rogers. USA: First Run Features, DVD.

Psychology and the Church. 2006. Dir T.A. McMahon. Writ. T.A. McMahon. Narr. Gary Carmichael. Perf. Deidre Bobgan, Martin Bobgan, T.A. McMahon. USA: Berean Call, DVD.

Question of God. 2004. Dir. Catherine Tatge. Perf. Armand Nicholi, Michael Shermer. USA: PBS, DVD.

This Is What Love in Action Looks Like. 2012. Dir. Fox, Morgan Jon. Perf. John Smid, Zach Stark, Peterson Toscano. USA: TLA Releasing, DVD.

Index